FIFTY EASTERN THINKERS

Close exposition and analysis of fifty major thinkers in eastern philosophy and religion form the core of this introduction to a fascinating area of study. The authors have drawn on the major eastern traditions, examining founder figures such as Zoroaster, Confucius and Muhammad, through to modern thinkers such as Mao Zedong, Nishitani and Gandhi. General introductions to the major traditions and a glossary of philosophical terms, as well as bibliographies and recommended further reading for each thinker, make this a comprehensive and accessible work of reference.

Diané Collinson is author of *Fifty Major Philosophers* and co-editor with Robert Wilkinson, of *One Hundred Twentieth-Century Philosophers* and *A Biographical Dictionary of Twentieth-Century Philosophers*.
Kathryn Plant is Associate Lecturer in Philosophy at the Open University. **Robert Wilkinson** is Senior Lecturer in Philosophy at the Open University. His latest book is *Minds and Bodies* (Open University Press, 1999).

ROUTLEDGE KEY GUIDES

Ancient History: Key Themes and Approaches
Neville Morley

Eastern Philosophy: Key Readings
Oliver Leaman

Fifty Contemporary Choreographers
edited by Martha Bremser

Fifty Eastern Thinkers
Diané Collinson, Kathryn Plant and Robert Wilkinson

Fifty Key Contemporary Thinkers
John Lechte

Fifty Key Thinkers in International Relations
Martin Griffiths

Fifty Major Economists
Steven Pressman

Fifty Major Philosophers
Diané Collinson

Key Concepts in Communication and Cultural Studies (second edition)
Tim O'Sullivan, John Hartley, Danny Saunders, Martin Montgomery and John Fiske

Key Concepts in Cultural Theory
edited by Andrew Edgar and Peter Sedgwick

Key Concepts in Eastern Philosophy
Oliver Leaman

Key Concepts in Language and Linguistics
R. L. Trask

Key Concepts in the Philosophy of Education
Christopher Winch and John Gingell

Key Concepts in Popular Music
Roy Shuker

Key Concepts in Post-Colonial Studies
Bill Ashcroft, Gareth Griffiths and Helen Tiffin

FIFTY EASTERN THINKERS

*Diané Collinson, Kathryn Plant
and Robert Wilkinson*

London and New York

First published 2000 by Routledge
11 New Fetter Lane, London EC4P 4EE

Simultaneously published in the USA and Canada
by Routledge
29 West 35th Street, New York, NY 10001

Routledge is an imprint of the Taylor & Francis Group

Typeset in Times by Keystroke, Jacaranda Lodge, Wolverhampton
Printed and bound in Great Britain by Clays Ltd, St Ives plc

British Library Cataloguing in Publication Data
A catalogue record for this book is available from the British Library

Library of Congress Cataloging in Publication Data
has been applied for

ISBN 0–415–20284–1

CONTENTS

INTRODUCTION

This book is designed to give the interested reader basic information about fifty major thinkers who belong with those several different traditions usually classed together by western culture as oriental or eastern.

One of the main points that will become clear is that this classification is over-simple, since it blurs distinctions between a number of schools of thought, some as different from each other as they are from the schools of the West. We have organized the material, with the exception of that on Islamic philosophy, under headings which are broadly geographical, and this arrangement coincides, by and large, with organization by philosophical tradition. Within each group of philosophers the material is set out chronologically. For the sake of simplicity, all dates are given in terms of the Christian calendar.

Differences between them notwithstanding, there is one feature common to these traditions – at least before the modern period – which they do have in common and in which they do differ from philosophical thought in the West since the Renaissance. This common characteristic is the non-separation of philosophical from religious endeavour. Most western philosophers of the present day would regard their subject as distinct from religion, though this would not have been the case, for example, in the Middle Ages. This distinction or outlook has appeared in eastern traditions, if at all, only very recently. The consequence is that in much of what follows the subject-matter is in many cases, of necessity, deeply informed by religious ideas. Whilst the emphasis in what we have written is on what in western terms is the philosophical aspect of the work of the figures concerned, those within these traditions would generally regard this as a distinction marking no difference of importance.

This book does not pretend to be a history of the schools of thought concerned; several libraries would be needed for that, even were all

the primary source materials available. Rather, our chief aim has been
to indicate the most influential and important lines of thought of each
philosopher by close reference to major works, though we hope in
addition that an indication of broad changes and constant features
within each tradition will emerge from a consideration of each group
of philosophers taken together.

Each essay follows a common plan: a short statement describing
the main thrust of the thought of the philosopher concerned; information about his life, and concise expositions of some central aspects
of his thought, with cross-reference, where appropriate, to other
philosophers. These cross-references are not only to other eastern
thinkers but also to philosophers in the western tradition: the same
philosophical problems have often generated similar lines of response
wherever they have occurred, and we have indicated the most
important of these in the text. Since, as we have indicated, the thinkers
concerned belong to a number of traditions, we have included brief
sub-introductions at appropriate points. These include basic historical
and philosophical information needed to set the scene for the group
of thinkers concerned. No living philosopher has been included in
this book.

At the end of each essay we have provided information that
can launch the interested reader into further, more detailed study.
First, there are notes to which the numbers in the text refer; second,
details of the philosopher's principal writings; third, a list of other
philosophers considered in this book whose thought relates in one
way or another to that of the philosopher in hand; and fourth, a list of
books in English suitable for further reading.

At the end of the book there is a short glossary of philosophical
terms. It contains brief explanations of technical or semi-technical
terms that occur a number of times in the book, where necessary in
more than one language. For the most part it has been possible to give
a brief explanation of such a term with its first use in the text, but it
was not feasible to repeat the explanation with each subsequent use.
These terms therefore appear in **bold** type on the first occasion of
their use in an essay, and this indicates that they are explained in the
glossary at the end of the book. The glossary entries should not be
taken to be either final definitions or complete explanations of the
terms they describe. They are meant to provide only a first foothold
for a reader not familiar with the philosophical terrain.

One of the difficulties facing anyone trying to come to grips with
the philosophical traditions dealt with in this book concerns the way
in which the key terms from the relevant languages have been

romanized, and our choices about which version to adopt have involved balancing a number of considerations: scholarly authority; relative familiarity and pronounceability for the English reader. We have in the main followed current scholarly usage, though where competing systems of romanization produce versions so different as not to be obviously versions of the same word, we have pointed this out in text, note or Glossary, as appropriate. This problem is especially acute with regard to Chinese. There are two complete, alternative systems for the romanization of Chinese into English: *pinyin* devised by the Chinese themselves, and the Wade–Giles system, of western origination. *Pinyin* is now standard in English scholarly works and we give all Chinese terms in this version. However, since most the English translations of Chinese works from (roughly) the first half of the twentieth century use the Wade–Giles system or some slight variant on it, and since many of these translations are still widely used, we have given the Wade–Giles equivalent in brackets at the point in the text where the term is used for the first time. For example, in the case of the great Daoist thinker, his name is given as Zhuangzi [Chuang Tzu]. In about one third of cases, the two systems give the same romanization, and so of course in these cases the term in question occurs without an alternative version. Additionally, to facilitate further study, we have included a list showing the *pinyin* and Wade–Giles romanizations for those cases where the systems produce different versions of the same terms.

Words from foreign languages are printed in italics, except where they are now standardly used in English, e.g. Vedanta, Zen. Quite often, as a result of the spread of ideas and especially the diffusion of Buddhism, key terms have been translated into a number of the languages native to the philosophers concerned, and these equivalences are explained as necessary. In the text and Glossary we have used the following shorthand to indicate the language from which a given term comes:

A = Arabic   P = Pali
C = Chinese   S = Sanskrit
J = Japanese   T = Tibetan
K = Korean

In one or two cases, where one version of such a term has become standard in modern English usage and where it would be confusing not to use it, we have used this one term throughout; thus Zen is always referred to by means of this its Japanese name, even though its roots lie in Chinese and Indian thought. These cases are noted in detail at appropriate points in the text. The linguistic origin of terms from other languages is indicated by giving the name of the language in full, e.g. Pahlavi, the language in which the Zoroastrian scriptures were recorded when given a written form.

Even though this book does not pretend to be in any way exhaustive, we hope that the figures we have been able to include give a sense of the richness, subtlety and formidable acumen to be found in these great philosophical traditions.

Diané Collinson
Kathryn Plant
Robert Wilkinson

NOTE ON THE ROMANIZATION OF CHINESE

As indicated in the foregoing Introduction, we here include a table showing the *pinyin* and Wade–Giles romanizations of Chinese sounds. This list does not include those cases – about one third of the sounds – where the romanization is the same in both systems.

pinyin	Wade–Giles	pinyin	Wade–Giles
ba	pa	cao	ts'ao
bai	pai	ce	ts'e
ban	pan	cen	ts'en
bang	pang	ceng	ts'eng
bao	pao	cha	ch'a
bei	pei	chai	ch'ai
ben	pen	chan	ch'an
beng	peng	chang	ch'ang
bi	pi	chao	ch'ao
bian	pien	che	ch'e
biao	piao	chen	ch'en
bie	pieh	cheng	ch'eng
bin	pin	chi	ch'ih
bing	ping	chong	ch'ung
bo	po	chou	ch'ou
bou	pou	chu	ch'u
bu	pu	chua	ch'ua
		chuai	ch'uai
ca	ts'a	chuan	ch'uan
cai	ts'ai	chuang	ch'uang
can	ts'an	chui	ch'ui
cang	ts'ang	chun	ch'un

pinyin	Wade–Giles	pinyin	Wade–Giles
chuo	ch'o	gei	kei
ci	tz'u	gen	ken
cong	ts'ung	geng	keng
cou	ts'ou	gong	kung
cu	ts'u	gou	kou
cuan	ts'uan	gu	ku
cui	ts'ui	gua	kua
cun	ts'un	guai	kuai
cuo	ts'o	guan	kuan
		guang	kuang
da	ta	gui	kuei
dai	tai	gun	kun
dan	tan	guo	kuo
dang	tang		
dao	tao	he	ho
de	te	hong	hung
deng	teng		
di	ti	ji	chi
dian	tien	jia	chia
diao	tiao	jian	chien
die	tieh	jiang	chiang
ding	ting	jiao	chiao
diu	tiu	jie	chieh
dong	tung	jin	chin
dou	tou	jing	ching
du	tu	jiong	chiung
duan	tuan	jiu	chiu
dui	tui	ju	chü
dun	tun	juan	chüan
duo	to	jue	chüeh
		jun	chün
e	o		
er	erh	ka	k'a
		kai	k'ai
ga	ka	kan	k'an
gai	kai	kang	k'ang
gan	kan	kao	k'ao
gang	kang	ke	k'o
gao	kao	kei	k'ei
ge	ko	ken	k'en

pinyin	Wade–Giles	pinyin	Wade–Giles
keng	k'eng	po	p'o
kong	k'ung	pou	p'ou
kou	k'ou	pu	p'u
ku	k'u		
kua	k'ua	qi	ch'i
kuai	k'uai	qia	ch'ia
kuan	k'uan	qian	ch'ien
kuang	k'uang	qiang	ch'iang
kui	k'uei	qiao	ch'iao
kun	k'un	qie	ch'ieh
kuo	k'uo	qin	ch'in
		qing	ch'ing
lian	lien	qiong	ch'iung
lie	lieh	qiu	ch'iu
long	lung	qu	ch'ü
lue	lüeh	quan	ch'üan
luo	lo	que	ch'üeh
		qun	ch'ün
mian	mien		
mie	mieh	ran	jan
		rang	jang
nian	nien	rao	jao
nie	nieh	re	je
nong	nung	ren	jen
nue	nüeh	reng	jeng
		ri	jih
pa	p'a	rong	jung
pai	p'ai	rou	jou
pan	p'an	ru	ju
pang	p'ang	ruan	juan
pao	p'ao	rui	jui
pei	p'ei	run	jun
pen	p'en	ruo	jo
peng	p'eng		
pi	p'i	shi	shih
pian	p'ien	si	ssu
piao	p'iao	song	sung
pie	p'ieh	suo	so
pin	p'in		
ping	p'ing	ta	t'a

pinyin	Wade–Giles	pinyin	Wade–Giles
tai	t'ai	yuan	yüan
tan	t'an	yue	yüeh
tang	t'ang	yun	yün
tao	t'ao		
te	t'e	za	tsa
teng	t'eng	zai	tsai
ti	t'i	zan	tsan
tian	t'ien	zang	tsang
tiao	t'iao	zao	tsao
tie	t'ieh	ze	tse
ting	t'ing	zei	tsei
tong	t'ung	zen	tsen
tou	t'ou	zeng	tseng
tu	t'u	zha	cha
tuan	t'uan	zhai	chai
tui	t'ui	zhan	chan
tun	t'un	zhang	chang
tuo	t'o	zhao	chao
		zhe	che
xi	hsi	zhen	chen
xia	hsia	zheng	cheng
xian	hsien	zhi	chih
xiang	hsiang	zhong	chung
xiao	hsiao	zhou	chou
xie	hsieh	zhu	chu
xin	hsin	zhua	chua
xing	hsing	zhuai	chuai
xiong	hsiung	zhuan	chuan
xiu	hsiu	zhuang	chuang
xu	hsü	zhui	chui
xuan	hsüan	zhun	chun
xue	hsüeh	zhuo	cho
xun	hsün	zi	tzu
		zong	tsung
yan	yen	zou	tsou
ye	yeh	zu	tsu
yi	i	zuan	tsuan
yong	yung	zui	tsui
you	yu	zun	tsun
yu	yü	zuo	tso

Acknowledgement

This table is adapted from Raymond Dawson's edition of the *Analects* of Confucius in the World's Classics edition published by Oxford University Press.

Part 1

ZOROASTRIANISM

ZOROASTER (ZARATHUSTRA) *probably some time between 1500 and 1000 BCE*

The Zoroastrian conception of human existence is essentially a joyful and life-affirming one that has been adhered to with courage by its believers through times of severe persecution and rejection.

Zoroaster was a prophet of ancient Iran (Persia) who claimed to speak directly with his God.[1] His teaching proclaimed a state of eternal struggle between good and evil and he held that human beings are free to choose between right and wrong. It has been maintained that he was the first prophet of monotheism in that he rejected the polytheism of the early Iranian religion and elevated just one of its *ahuras*, or 'lords', to the position of a supreme deity. The claim that Zoroastrianism is monotheistic is a debatable one. It has been the subject of prolonged scholarly controversy and is still a live issue.[2] Zoroaster's doctrine is embodied in seventeen psalms, the *gathas*, which are thought to have been his own work and which, along with liturgical writings, are part of the *Avesta*, the Zoroastrian holy book of which only a portion is extant.

Although there is little that can be unequivocally established about Zoroastrianism it is evident that it was an important and influential doctrine. It was the national religion of the Persian empire from the third to the seventh century CE, yielding dominion then to the devastating attack of Muslim invaders, but thereafter staunchly surviving a millennium of persecution, its faithful adherents living in small enclaves in remote or desert settlements. In the tenth century CE many Zoroastrians grouped themselves in India, chiefly around Bombay and became known as the Parsis (Persians). Zoroastrianism's basic tenets concerning good and evil, heaven and hell, judgement, resurrection and free will have informed the teachings of Judaism, Christianity and Islam.

There is considerable uncertainty about the dating of Zoroaster's lifetime, but evidence increasingly suggests that he was alive some time between 1500 and 1000 BCE and that he experienced massive migrations of Iranians and Indians, and also the attendant conflicts between those who were peaceful herdsmen and those who were members of roving bands of plunderers. The system of religious belief in which he grew up was based on a creation myth that saw the world as having been generated by gods from inchoate matter passing through seven stages of development. This cosmogony maintained that once order had been achieved and human life established in the centre of the created world, physical and spiritual equilibrium could be maintained by making appropriate sacrifices to the gods. Zoroaster inherited a priesthood in this religion and possessed the genius to reform it in a way that allowed it to develop in a vital and consistent manner.

It is a traditional view that Zoroaster spent most of his adult life in north-eastern Persia, having been forced to travel after the failure of his early missionary efforts in search of a powerful ruler who would accept his faith and protect him. The story relates that he eventually settled in the north-east after converting the ruler, Vishtaspa, by healing his favourite horse when it was deemed to be mortally ill. Some doubt is cast on this placing of Zoroaster in the north-east by the fact that the *gathas*, the hymns or psalms attributed to his authorship, are written in a language that is thought to have belonged to the north-western region of Iran.

It is, again, tradition that informs us that Zoroaster's birth was signalled by miracles and that a divine protection kept evil forces from harming him. His childhood, it seems, was solitary and in his youth and early manhood he was trained for the priesthood. He received his first vision and prophetic calling at the age of 30 and thereafter began his teaching mission. To prepare himself he spent time alone on a mountain and it is reported that for two weeks, while his spirit communed with God, his body was completely motionless on the mountainside. His first missionary teachings were rejected outright and he was subjected to ridicule and violence. Then his remarkable healing of Vishtaspa's horse brought about not only the conversion of the ruler but also the official adoption of his beliefs by the whole realm. Legend recounts that he was murdered in old age while praying at the altar and that the event fulfilled forecasts that the prophet would live for exactly seventy-seven years.

As already mentioned, it has been argued that the description of Zoroaster as a prophet of monotheism is not correct and that the error came about largely as the result of the work of Martin Haug, a philologist who translated the *gathas* in the 1850s and established them as Zoroaster's own declaration of his faith and doctrine.[3] Haug interpreted the *gathas* as embodying a strict monotheism and also a rejection of ritual sacrifice, a view that ran completely counter to the tradition and practice of the early nineteenth-century Parsis of India who attended Haug's lectures in order to learn about the history of their religion. According to Mary Boyce, Haug based his understanding entirely on one or two philological points concerning the translation of the *gathas* without weighing the evidence of the living tradition and the available secondary writings. When, in the

1880s, a quantity of secondary Zoroastrian literature was translated by E.H. West in consultation with Parsi priests and with reference to current practices, a somewhat different conception of Zoroastrianism emerged, one more consistent with its known tradition of a belief in dualism, and which yielded a different understanding of the *gathas* from that propounded by Haug.[4]

The central issue in the debate which has ensued arose from the tension between Zoroaster's assertion of the fundamental dualism of the cosmos and later interpretations of his theology as monotheistic. It brought into prominence a number of difficulties that from time to time had exercised the minds of Zoroastrian theologians. For example, if Zoroastrianism is understood to posit that there are two principles, good and evil, questions then arise as to whether they are entirely distinct from one another, and what the status and source of each is. If it is claimed that both principles are gods and that they are separate, then either monotheism does not obtain or it has to be reinstated by invoking and describing an ultimate deity that somehow overarches both good and evil. If it is claimed that good is supreme, then the presence and power of evil and its relationship with the good have to be satisfactorily elucidated and any outstanding uncertainties about monotheism resolved.

Very few absolutely firm conclusions can be drawn about the exact character of Zoroaster's own thought, but this is not surprising in view of the incompleteness of sources and the difficulties of translation. The extant portions of his own writing, the *gathas*, as well as the rest of the *Avesta*, are capable of being translated in a variety of ways. What remnants we have of the *Avesta* consist of writings drawn from several centuries, embodying modifications and developments imposed by the priests and believers of many generations. The result is a body of doctrinal and liturgical matter that is largely unsystematic, that sometimes appears to be ambiguous or inconsistent within itself and that always needs to be seen in relation to the history of actual Zoroastrian practice. Any attempt to give an account of Zoroaster's ideas has to be made in awareness of this complex background.

Zoroaster's God of goodness, the One True God whom he claimed to have seen in visions, is Ahura Mazda. Opposing Mazda is Angra Mainyu, the personification of evil. Mazda epitomizes everything that is life-affirming and creative, and all activities that foster truth, the benign ordering of life and a pastoral care of the earth and its creatures. In contrast, Angra Mainyu represents destruction, untruth and bloodshed, and the aggressive life-pattern of the pillaging nomad rather than the settled pastoralist. These two beings are derived from the two kinds of gods, the *ahuras* and the **daevas**, who were affirmed by the Indo-Iranian polytheism that was largely rejected by Zoroaster. He repudiated the *daevas* as followers of evil and the Lie, and from among the *ahuras* took Ahura Mazda as the One True God.

It is at this point in the account that the interpreters of Zoroastrianism begin to diverge in their interpretations. There are passages in the **Yasna**, the Zoroastrian liturgy, that describe two Spirits, one of which chooses Good and the other Evil. We read that

> at the beginning of existence, the Holier spoke to him who is Evil: 'Neither our thoughts nor our teachings, nor our wills nor our choices, nor our words, nor our deeds, nor our convictions, nor yet our souls agree.'[5]

What is not clear in this is the relationship in which the two Spirits stand to Mazda. The Good Spirit is sometimes referred to as the son of Mazda and the two Spirits are on one occasion described as twins. But this means that the Spirit of Evil is as much the offspring of Mazda as the Spirit of Good, a conclusion that is not entirely acceptable since it seems to attribute the creation of evil to a God who is entirely good. A resolution of the difficulty, and one that is readily derived from parts of the *Yasna*, is that Mazda created two Spirits who freely chose their paths. This permits the understanding that the Spirit that chose evil was not created as an Evil Spirit but as one with the freedom to choose. Commentators have pointed out that Zoroaster nowhere attributes evil to God.[6]

Those who favour a strictly monotheistic understanding of Zoroaster's teaching cite passages from the *Yasna* in which Ahura Mazda is described as, for example, 'the creator of all things by the Holy Spirit'.[7] Those who regard the dualism of his thought as central emphasize, without denying the attribution of supremacy to Mazda, the opposition of Good and Evil, of Mazda and Angra Mainyu, that pervades all the Prophet's teaching. They are mindful of an early catechism of Zoroastrianism which says: 'I must have no doubt that there are two first principles, one the Creator and the other the Destroyer', and point out that it was in terms of this opposition that the religious life and practices of Zoroastrianism were conceived. Thus, in an essay published in 1978, Mary Boyce has said that

> in one sense, that of believing in only one eternal, uncreated Being who is worthy of worship, Zoroaster was indeed a monotheist, with a concept of God as exalted as that of any

Hebrew or Arabian prophet. But he was also a dualist, in that he saw coexisting with Ahura Mazda, another uncreated Being, who was maleficent, not to be worshipped.[8]

Boyce also points out that Zoroaster's doctrine does not entirely dethrone the other *ahuras* who, in Indo-Iranian polytheism, had ranked with Ahura Mazda.

In creating the world Mazda also created the 'Bounteous Immortals', six lesser divinities, to assist in the destruction of evil and the perfecting of the world. These beings, although beneath Ahura Mazda, were to be accorded worship and prayer. They personified attributes possessed by Mazda: qualities such as Wisdom, Right, Purpose, Truth, Wholeness and Loyalty. They were also linked with aspects of the physical creation so that the nurture and tending of the world were connected with the virtues and powers they represented. Zoroaster held to the ancient belief in a sevenfold creation in which there was first the enclosing shell of the sky, made of stone, then the world within it, then water in the shell, followed by the earth flat upon it; then a plant, an animal and a man in the centre of the earth. The gods were believed to have crushed and sacrificed these last, thereby causing their multiplication and beginning the cycle of life and death.

In summary, traditional Zoroastrianism teaches that Ahura Mazda is supreme and wholly good, but not omnipotent. Angra Mainyu is an active force of evil that is pitted against the good and that must be opposed with courage and resolution. It has been remarked that this is 'perhaps the most rational solution of the problem of evil ever devised'.[9]

There is little doubt that until the mid-nineteenth century, when Haug's research appeared and the Parsis of India were experiencing the reforming pressures exerted by monotheistic religions, Zoroastrianism flourished as a sturdily dualistic religion that provided a comprehensive framework for human and humane living. Although many of the details of its original doctrines are now lost, it is clear that the broad philosophical conceptions it embodied are of the kind that spring from and foster some of the noblest aspects of human nature: a love of freedom, the enjoyment of work, a sense of community, valour in the face of evil and an awareness of the mystery of creation and goodness that expresses itself in a sensuous care of the world and its creatures.

By the end of the twentieth century few Parsis remained to uphold Zoroastrianism. There are small groups of two or three thousand in London, Los Angeles and Toronto. The two largest communities, each of around 17,000, are in India (Bombay) and Iran. These communities observe rituals established by Zoroaster: a brief time of prayer five times each day and seven joyous feasts in each year dedicated to Ahura Mazda, the Six Bounteous Immortals and the Seven Creations. The most important of these feasts is No Ruz, or New Year's Day, held at the vernal equinox. It celebrates the new spring life and the idea of resurrection with flowers, new clothes and painted eggs.

Zoroastrianism's powerful influence is especially apparent in the Jewish sect of the Dead Sea Scrolls where there is a dualist doctrine concerning the creation of Two Spirits that is almost exactly the same as the Zoroastrian doctrine. The Zoroastrian practice of praying five times each day was adopted by Muslims and the Zoroastrian ethic has been compared with that of the Christian Bible's Book of Proverbs.

Notes

1 Modern practice decrees that the religion derived from Zoroaster's teaching is called 'Mazdaism' since that is how it is referred to by the worshippers of Ahura Mazda, the 'Wise Lord' of Zoroaster's doctrine. Since this essay focuses on theoretical foundations rather than religious practices, 'Zoroastrianism' has been used consistently as a generally descriptive term.
2 For a glimpse of the wide-ranging controversy concerning early Zoroastrianism see Julian Baldick, 'Mazdaism ("Zoroastrianism")', in Stewart Sutherland, Leslie Houlden, Peter Clarke and Friedheim Hardy (eds) *The World's Religions*, London: Routledge, 1988, pp. 552–68.
3 See M. Haug, *Essays on the Sacred Language, Writings and Religion of the Parsis*, 3rd edn, London: Trubner, 1884, repr. Amsterdam: Philo Press, 1971.
4 See the essay 'Zoroastrianism' by Mary Boyce in John R. Hinnells (ed.), *A Handbook of Living Religions*, Harmondsworth: Penguin Books, 1984, repr. 1991, pp. 171–90.
5 *Yasna* 45.2.
6 See, for example, R.F. Zaehner (ed.), *Encyclopaedia of Living Faiths*, 4th edn, London: Hutchinson, 1988, p. 204.
7 *Yasna* 44.7.
8 See Mary Boyce, 'Spanning east and west: Zoroastrianism', in Whitfield Foy (ed.), *Man's Religious Quest*, London: Croom Helm and the Open University Press, 1978, p. 608.
9 Ibid., p. 607.

Zoroastrian writing

Darmesteter, J. (trans.), *Zend-Avesta*, Oxford: Clarendon Press, Sacred Books of the East series, 1880–1887, repr. Delhi: Motilal Banarsidass, 1965

Duchesne-Guillemin, J., *The Hymns of Zarathustra*, trans. M. Henning, London: Murray, 1932

Sources and further reading

Boyce, Mary, *Zoroastrianism: Its Antiquity and Constant Vigil*, Columbia Lectures on Ancient Studies no. 7, Costa Mesa, Calif.: Mazda Publications in association with Bibliotecha Persica, 1992

Boyce, Mary, *A History of Zoroastrianism*, vol I, Leiden: Bull, 1975, 1996

Dabu, K.S., *A Handbook of Information on Zoroastrianism*, Bombay: P.H. Mehta Educational Trust, 1969

Duchesne-Guillemin, J., *Religion of Ancient Iran*, trans. K.M. Jamasp Asa, Bombay: Tati Press, 1973

Hinnells, J.R., *Zoroastrianism and the Parsis*, London: Ward Lock Educational, 1981

Mehr, F. *The Doctrine of Zoroaster*, Cambridge, Mass.: Harvard University Press, 1991

Moulton, J.H., *Early Zoroastrianism*, Amsterdam: Philo Press, 1972

Zaehner, R.C., *The Dawn and Twilight of Zoroastrianism*, London: Weidenfeld & Nicolson, 1975

Part 2

ISLAMIC PHILOSOPHY

INTRODUCTION

Islamic philosophy was given impetus and direction in the eighth century CE by the surge of translations of Greek writings into Arabic that began to be made at that time. Numerous Greek works, many of them on medical subjects, had been translated by Christian Syrians into Syriac in the fourth and fifth centuries and it was a group of Syrian scholars who were invited to the Baghdad court in 750 CE to undertake the translations into Arabic. In the ninth century a school of translators and scholars, known as the House of Wisdom, was founded at Baghdad. It was largely through the work of these men that the writings of Plato, Aristotle and the Neoplatonists became familiar to Arab thinkers and, subsequently, to the western world.

Two important factors, each of which has its own internal complexity, contributed influentially to the character of early Islamic philosophy. The first of these was the theology of the Islamic scriptures, the **Qur'an** [Koran], which informed every aspect of Muslim culture, including its political, legal and social institutions. This theology was first delivered by Muhammad the Prophet (*c.* 570–632 CE) who saw himself as the messenger of God and the transmitter of God's exact words, the words of the Qur'an. The Qur'an declares that its message is universal and that Muhammad is the ultimate Prophet. It sets out the Five Pillars, a practical doctrine that requires the Muslim to undertake the following: to testify publicly, on at least one occasion in a lifetime, that 'There is no god but God, and Muhammad is his prophet'; to pray five times each day; to pay *zakat*, a poll tax for the benefit of the needy; to fast during Ramadan, the ninth month of the lunar year; and to perform pilgrimage to Makkah [Mecca] at least once in a lifetime. Further rules and customs for daily living, known as the *sunnah* (literally, 'the well-trodden path'), were based on the

11

Prophet's example and enshrined in **hadith**, reports of advice and injunctions held to be traceable back to the Prophet's actual words and deeds. The *sunnah* and *hadith* were closely interactive with Islamic jurisprudence.

By the eighth century CE two main schools of Islamic theology had been established: a rationalist school, the Mutazila, whose adherents held that reason can discover truths which are confirmed by revelation and that God does not act unreasonably, and the Sunni, who opposed the rationalism of the Mutazila, claiming that God obeys no norms, that actions become good or bad by God's declaration, and that rational reflection cannot discover God's will. It was, broadly, upon this complex cultural structure, grounded on faith and dogma but capable of internal debate, that the translations of Greek philosophical thought impacted.

The second element that gave Islamic philosophy its distinctive character was formed largely by an accident of intellectual history. Through an error of attribution, part of a work, the *Enneads*, by the Neoplatonist Plotinus, was attributed to Aristotle and became known as *The Theology of Aristotle*. In consequence, certain Platonic and Neoplatonic ideas became assimilated to those of Aristotle so that Greek philosophy came to be seen and treated by its translators as more unified than it actually was. This meant that the early Arab philosophers tended to assume that in studying the Greek writings they were dealing with a coherent body of thought containing a strong element of mysticism that derived from all the Greek philosophers. In fact, the mysticism that attracted them was a characteristic peculiar to Neoplatonism rather than ubiquitous among the Greek authors. But it was with Neoplatonic mysticism that Islamic theology found its closest affinity and, in consequence, a vision for its own secure development in relation to Greek philosophy.

The task undertaken by the early philosophers of Islam was that of demonstrating how the unchallengeable revelations of the Qur'an, adhered to by faith, might be shown to be consonant with and re-inforced by the conclusions of Hellenic reasoning. The carrying out of the task between the ninth and twelfth centuries not only established an Islamic philosophical tradition of the highest excellence but also, in due course, brought about the burgeoning of fresh philosophical thought in the West. Translations of the Greek writings began to reach the West in the first part of the twelfth century; but it was not just an Aristotelian or generally Greek influence that made itself felt, for the writings and thought that were transmitted were presented in the context of the Islamic philosophers' intellectual struggle to reconcile reason and faith, a struggle that western theologians and philosophers, fired by the example of Muslims such as al-Kindi, al-Farabi, Ibn Sina, al-Ghazali and Ibn Rushd, were to make their own in succeeding centuries.

In the latter part of the eleventh century the philosopher and theologian al-Ghazali challenged the reasoning of the philosophers who preceded him, not by reasserting the primacy of faith but with arguments that undermined those claims of his predecessors that had put strain on Qur'anic dogma. He espoused the teachings of Sufism, that Islamic sect which practised an austere asceticism in its search for a mystical communion with God. But even as his scholarly advocacy of Sufism worked to effect a reconciliation of its stance with the mainstream of Islamic doctrine, an extremely rigid and highly organized system of Islamic education was being established throughout western Asia in the *madrasa*, or colleges, that were rapidly springing up. Standard textbooks on theology, ethics, law and the Qur'an guaranteed a uniformity of education, an uncritical acceptance of authority and, as time passed, a stultification of intellectual enquiry and enterprise. A century after al-Ghazali, Sufism received further impetus from the teaching of Ibn Arabi whose profound mysticism evoked a widespread response within and beyond the Islamic community. Sufism survived and developed in various ways but underwent, in some of its manifestations, corruption by charlatans who exploited the natural piety of simple people with tricks and pseudo-miracles. It was not until the eighteenth century that a revival of the fundamental doctrines of early Islam began to take place and a fresh concern to maintain a balance between reason and revelation became apparent in the work of theologians and philosophers.

In the twentieth century, Islamic philosophy and Islamic culture as a whole have had to confront the challenge presented to them by ideas and forms of life from which they had previously been more or less insulated. In particular, Islam has had to work out an attitude to rapid technological change and a political strategy for survival. Its philosophers have sought to cultivate a dynamism in Islamic thought, a movement clearly exemplified in the philosophy of Muhammad Iqbal (1876–1938), who saw both the rationalism of the Greeks and the mysticism of the Sufi as having exerted an adverse influence on Islam. Iqbal drew on the ideas of Henri Bergson, the French philosopher of process, and on Hegelian dialectic to help him generate a more dynamic sensibility for Islamic philosophy.

In the late twentieth century Islamic philosophers worked on a broad front encompassing politics, ethics, metaphysics, methodology and theology as well as the scholarly and critical study of their magnificent medieval tradition. Their fundamental task remains unchanged: to show that Islam, as a comprehensive form of life, is compatible with other forms of life in the contemporary world.

MUHAMMAD THE PROPHET c.570–632 CE

Muhammad founded the Islamic movement that has spread from his native Arabia to almost every part of the world. His central aim was to establish monotheism in place of the prevailing polytheism of his time and to teach a total allegiance to the commands of the one God. The Muslim profession of faith announces that 'There is no god but God, and Muhammad is the messenger of God'. The word '**Islam**' means 'submission' and **Muslims** are 'those who submit'. The Islamic scriptures, the Qur'an [Koran] are held by Muslims to be the infallible word of God.

What is known of Muhammad's circumstances is largely derived from a life of the Prophet written by Ibn Ishaq in the eighth century CE.[1] He was born into the Quraysh tribe around 570 CE near Makkah [Mecca], a town long established as a sanctuary and place of pilgrimage. Makkah had been founded by monotheists but by the time of Muhammad's birth it had become predominantly pagan and polytheist. The Prophet's early life was not a settled one. As an infant he was cared for by foster parents who were poorly off. He was then returned to his mother who died when he was 6. After two years in his grandfather's charge he was sent to an uncle, Abu Talib, with whom he stayed for the rest of his formative years. While still a young man he became the commercial agent for a rich widow, Khadija, who in due course married him. He did not emerge as the Prophet until his middle years but accounts of his life relate that all the signs were there from his birth: a heavenly light seen by his mother around her infant son's head, the blessing of a Christian monk, his own tendency towards solitude and long hours of reflection.

Muhammad's calling came to him at around the age of 40 while he was engaged in an annual religious practice. It was the custom to spend one month of each year on Mount Hira, often with one's family, in order to bestow goods and food on the visiting poor. One night while on the mountain Muhammad dreamed that he was visited by the angel Gabriel who taught him the words that are now part of the ninety-sixth chapter of the **Qur'an**: 'Recite, in the name of your Lord, the Creator, who created man from clots of blood . . . '. Over the next decade or so, further revelations of the scriptures were transmitted from God to Muhammad by means of the dream figure of Gabriel. Muhammad also dreamed of a visit to Jerusalem to meet Abraham, Moses and Jesus. These incidents determined him to begin his mission to preach monotheism, first within his family and tribal group and then to the people and pilgrims at Makkah. It seems he was at first deeply puzzled by his dreams but his confidence in his mission gradually increased; in particular when it was confirmed that the description of Jerusalem he derived from his dream – for it seems he had never actually been to that city – was an accurate one. Emboldened by this and by the steady sequence of revelatory dreams, he began to teach to a wider circle. Thus from tentative beginnings there developed Islam, a movement and form of life of immense influence and power.

The remarkable success that eventually attended Muhammad's mission is appreciated only through an understanding of conditions prevailing in Arabia and its environs at the time. That vast country is largely desert and in the sixth century its peoples were mostly nomadic, tribal and in frequent conflict with each other. The absence of a central controlling power that might have mobilized and united a formidable fighting force meant that Arabia presented little threat, other than that of an occasional marauding frontier raid, to adjacent territories. Even its traditional polytheism was beginning to feel the effects of the monotheistic influences of Jews and Christians. It has been pointed out that this picture of a large but disorganized country is one that might well have led a shrewd observer at the time to predict that Arabia would probably soon fall prey to external or invading powers and that if monotheism came to dominate there then it would do so in a Christian or Jewish form. The events which actually ensued were utterly different from any such well-reasoned conjecture.[2]

The ground for Muhammad's work was probably prepared by his great-grandfather, Hashim, who, using Makkah as a base, established the Quraysh community as influential merchants by organizing two caravan journeys a year and by gaining protection for his merchants in the territories of the Roman empire and, in due course, in Persia, the Yemen and Ethiopia. Hashim maintained the family tradition of caring for the pilgrims who visited Makkah and did not attempt to interfere with its pagan rites. Muhammad was therefore heir to an extensive and secure trading system and a tradition of liberal toleration within his own community. When his mission developed and he began to speak out against polytheism, tensions began to manifest themselves. Schisms and regroupings occurred in the tribes as some members aligned themselves with the new monotheism and others clung to polytheism. Those who dissented from their tribal leadership were vulnerable to attack from their own group and were also insecure in their relationships with other groups. Muhammad himself was protected by the Quraysh but he arranged to send a group of his supporters, for their safety, to Ethiopia, where he was already held in considerable esteem. He then sought to strengthen his following by means of itinerant preaching, but with little success until he met six members of the Khazraj tribe in the oasis city of Yathrib. The agreement he reached with these men was a momentous one: they would protect him completely, even in the face of aggression from his own Quraysh people. Muhammad's Makkah disciples then emigrated to Yathrib while he remained to await God's command to follow them. His own emigration, known as the *hijrah*, took place in 622 CE, about twelve or fifteen years after his first dream encounter with the angel Gabriel. The *hijrah* marks the first year of the Muslim era and the starting point of the Muslim calendar.

The Prophet lived at Yathrib for the remaining ten years of his life. During that time he completed his compilation of the Qur'an. The angel Gabriel continued to appear in dreams revealing details of rituals of prayer and fasting, cleansing, alms-giving, worship and pilgrimage. One year after the *hijrah* had taken place it was ordained that Muslims, when praying, should turn towards Makkah instead of towards Jerusalem. Seven years later Makkah was regained. It was then purged of its polytheism and made wholly Islamic.

After the *hijrah*, Yathrib became known as Medina. Muhammad's followers there were called the *ansar*, the helpers, and those who went with him from Makkah were called the *muhajirun*, the emigrants. Muhammad's mission now took an overtly militant and political turn. A document was drawn up to establish his followers as a community. It commanded them to refer any disputes between them to Muhammad and thereby to God. Rules of conduct and especially those for the conduct of warfare were laid down and so began the conquest of southern Arabia. By the time of Muhammad's death, in 632 CE, the eleventh year of the *hijrah*, Muslim domination was reaching out towards the Roman empire in the north. Its spread was resisted by Arabian Jews and to some extent by Christians, but with little effect on what had become an engulfing tide.

In the eighth century Islam spread into Central Asia, Sind and Spain. In the eleventh century it began to be transmitted by Turks into southern Russia, India and Asia Minor. It was taken to the Niger basin and in the fourteenth century became dominant in the Balkans and spread into China. It largely disappeared from Spain in the fifteenth century and in the nineteenth and twentieth centuries its influence in the Balkans dwindled. It now flourishes in many parts of Africa and in certain regions of North and South America and, in the 1990s, began to reaffirm itself in Albania.

Muhammad saw himself simply as the recipient and channel for the transmission of the Islamic scriptures, but he occupies a special place in the series of monotheistic prophets recognized by Islam for he was taken to be the last in a succession of 'warners' among whom were Noah, Abraham, Moses and Jesus. It is in the context of the belief that the world had a life of only six or seven thousand years that this position was accorded him. By his lifetime the world was thought to have already endured for five or six thousand of its allotted years. The revelation of the Qur'an to Muhammad was therefore seen as the culmination of a sequence of such revelations, following on from the imparting of the Pentateuch to Moses and the Gospel to Jesus. The Muslim belief is that Muhammad was the last messenger of God before the end of the world.

The writings that constitute the Qur'an were put together in an authoritative version, shortly after Muhammad's death, during the reign of the third caliph, Uthman (644–56 CE). A few very minor changes were subsequently made in the tenth century. The Qur'an has 114 chapters, or **suras**, that were arranged so that the *suras* with many verses precede those with fewer verses.[3] All the *suras* were assigned in their headings either to Makkah or Medina. Quotations and recitings of the Qur'an are always introduced by the phrase 'God has said', thus emphasizing Muhammad's role as the transmitter rather than author of the scriptures. The structure of the content of the Qur'an reflects the genesis and development of Islam. Broadly speaking, its earlier sections are concerned with God's majesty and power, its later ones with juridical matters and directives for conduct within the community. Its dominant theme is the uniting of believers in a total obedience to a God whose word is unchallengeable. The absolute acceptance of its doctrine is reinforced by the Islamic practice of committing the Qur'an to memory. Learning and reciting it means that its precepts inhabit the believer's mind and heart, shaping and predisposing every thought and action.

Some time after Muhammad began to preach publicly, but before the *hijrah*, there occurred the incident of the 'satanic verses'. This refers to *sura* 53, known as 'The Star', which is reported to have originally stated that three pagan goddesses, al-Lat, al-'Uzza and Manat, with shrines not too far from Makkah, were empowered to make intercessions to Allah. Commentators have pointed out that Muhammad delivered this revelation at a time when he was seeking to convert influential merchants to Islam and that the message did bring about their conversion. But a later revelation from the angel Gabriel to Muhammad made it clear that the message had been 'put upon his tongue' by Satan. The correct *sura* was then imparted to him. It stated that the three goddesses 'are but names which you and your fathers have invented: Allah has vested no authority in them'.[4]

The cosmogony of the Qur'an describes creation as consisting of seven earths stacked on one another beneath seven heavens, similarly stacked. The undermost earth houses the devil. Humankind inhabits the highest earth and the lowest heaven is the sky above the highest earth. The seventh and topmost heaven is Paradise. God is omnipotent, omnipresent, omniscient and indivisible. Any suggestion that his divinity might embrace a trinity or multiplicity of any kind is always rejected. In the second *sura* of the Qur'an we read: 'They say: "Allah has begotten a son." Allah forbid! His is what the heavens and earth contain; things are obedient to Him. Creator of the heavens and the earth! When He decrees a thing, He need only say "Be" and it is.' The Qur'anic Allah is remote, mysterious and entirely other, having 'no need of the worlds' yet knowing and influencing every detail of creation.[5]

Muhammad was a prophet rather than a philosopher. But any influential declaration of the kind that he made concerning God, the universe and the relationship of both with humankind is always the object of critical scrutiny by sceptics and of justification by its upholders. From such activity there emerges a refining of concepts and ideas along with methods of analysis and discussion. And so philosophy develops. Early Islamic thought was largely theological in character and was dominated by the debate between progressive Muslim thinkers who were prepared to subject revelation to rational scrutiny, and a conservative or orthodox element that regarded any such scrutiny as impious. Both positions were rooted in theology and both had to confront difficulties about the interpretation of scriptural commands and legislation for issues and conduct not covered by the scriptures. Discussion tended to focus on the concepts of God's supreme majesty and power and on the relationship of total obedience in which human beings stood to God. In such a context questions about free will soon surfaced, since the notion of the absolute authority of God suggests the absence of freedom of choice on the part of his obedient subject. Within Islam, the presupposition of all such debates was the view that saw politics, philosophy, law and every aspect of societal life as emanating from and dependent on the one God.

Internal debate was not the only critical stimulus to the development of Islamic philosophy. The Arab conquest of Alexandria in 641 CE meant that Muslim thought became open to investigation from many quarters. In the seventh century, Alexandria was the pre-eminent centre for the study of Greek philosophy and was in touch with smaller centres of learning such as Syria and Iraq. Thus the dogmatic theology of Islam was required to respond to comment from Greeks, Christians, Jews and others and to construct a rational justification for the Qur'anic scriptures as delivered by Muhammad.[6] The free exchange of all kinds of ideas and doctrines was greatly facilitated by the enthusiastic translation, in, the two centuries after Muhammad's death, of Greek works on medicine, science and, in due course, philosophy, into Arabic. This did much to enrich the vocabulary of Arabic as well as to inform Muslim thought with the ideas of Greek philosophy, especially those of Plato, Aristotle and the Neoplatonists. By the beginning of the ninth century CE the scene was set for the emergence of Islam's first important philosopher, the Arab prince Ya'qub ibn-Ishaq al-Kindi.

Notes

1 This work is called the *Sira* or *Sirat*. It has been translated into English as *The Life of Muhammad* (see sources and further reading).
2 See, for example, remarks in Michael Cook, *Muhammad*, Oxford: Oxford University Press, 1983, p. 11.
3 Numerous attempts have been made to reorder the *suras* but there seems to be no standard critical edition of the Qur'an.
4 See pp. 112, 113 (*sura* 53) in the Penguin edition of the Qur'an, trans. N.J. Dawood, Harmondsworth, 1959.
5 *Sura* 3.
6 See the introduction to Islamic philosophy in this book, pp. 11–14.

Muhammad's writing

Muhammad's claim was that he was the transmitter, not the author, of the words of the Qur'an. There are numerous translations. The edition named below gives the traditional numbering of the *suras*.

The Qur'an, trans. N.J. Dawood, Harmondsworth: Penguin Books, 1959

See also in this book

Al-Kindi, al-Farabi, Ibn Sina, al-Ghazali, Ibn Rushd, Ibn Arabi, Muhammad Iqbal

Sources and further reading

Cook, Michael, *Muhammad*, Oxford: Oxford University Press, Past Masters series, 1983

Fakhry, Majid, *A History of Islamic Philosophy*, London: Longman, 1983

Forward, M., *Muhammad: a short biography*, Oxford: Oneworld 1997

Goldziher, I., *Introduction to Islamic Theology and Law*, Princeton: Princeton University Press, 1981

Guillaume, Alfred, *Islam*, Harmondsworth: Penguin Books, 1956

Guillaume, Alfred (trans.), *The Life of Muhammad: A Translation of Ibn Ishaq's Sirat Rasul Allah*, Oxford: Oxford University Press, 1955

Nasr, S.H. and Leaman, O. (eds), *History of Islamic Philosophy*, London: Routledge, 1996

Watt, W.M. *Muhammad at Makkah*, Oxford: Oxford University Press, 1953

—— *Muhammad at Medina*, Oxford: Oxford University Press, 1956

—— *Muhammad, Prophet and Statesman*, Oxford: Oxford University Press, 1961

—— *Islamic Philosophy and Theology*, Edinburgh: Edinburgh University Press, 1987; 1st edn, 1962

AL-KINDI *c.*812–*c.*873 CE

Al-Kindi was the first important Arab philosopher. He was a poly-math whose written output was prodigious: 242 written works are attributed to him, although few are extant. His works dealt with logic, arithmetic, metaphysics, music, geometry, astronomy, medicine, theology, politics, alchemy and meteorology. He vigorously encouraged and participated in the burgeoning movement of the eighth and ninth centuries to translate the writings of Greek and Indian thinkers into Arabic and he sought at all times, by means of his thorough assimilation of Greek rationalism, to provide philosophical justification for Islamic theological dogma.

Information about al-Kindi's early life is scant. He was a prince born in the Mesopotamian city of Basra, into the eminent southern Arabian tribe of Kindah, during the time when his father was governor of the city of al-Kufa. As a young man he moved to Baghdad, the centre of Islamic culture, where he worked under the patronage of successive caliphs. A story is told of an unhappy incident in his life when two courtiers at Baghdad, hostile to his ideas, entered into an intrigue against him with the result that he was deprived of his huge library of books for a time. All that is known of his character is that he seems to have been regarded as a somewhat mean man. In a book written shortly before his death, the *Book of Misers*, he is described as avaricious.[1]

Al-Kindi's philosophy, although distinctively Islamic in character, owes much to the Aristotelian and Neoplatonic ideas that were impacting vigorously on Islamic thinkers in the ninth century, and he brought the methods and concepts of Greek philosophy to bear on

Muslim ideas. He defined philosophy in general as 'the knowledge of the realities of things, according to human capacity', and metaphysics as 'the knowledge of the First Reality which is the cause of every reality'.[2] Within the tradition of Islamic theology he adhered to Mutazilite doctrine. The Mutazila were Muslims who in about 720 CE formed their own group by separating themselves from the issue of whether a sinful Muslim was to be described as a believer or an unbeliever. They wanted any such sinner to be described as 'a reprobate'. From this position of separation the group developed a rational and scholastic theology known as Kalam. This theology asserted the absolute unity of God and held that God had created the world rather than that it was eternal. The Mutazila also affirmed the doctrine of the freedom of the will, arguing that the concept of divine justice required the condition of freedom in humankind. They maintained, too, that good and evil may be known through the exercise of reason and independently of any knowledge of them imparted by revelation. These views shocked the orthodox of Islam who believed that God left nothing to the human will but ordained every detail and event of the universe; that he 'guides whom he wills and turns astray whom he wills' and that he re-creates the universe according to his own will at every successive instant. As well as adopting the Mutazilite belief that God created the world out of nothing, al-Kindi seems to have espoused the neo-Platonist view that reality is a perpetual outflow or emanation from God rather than the product of an act of creation. What he does not tell us is how it is possible to accept those two contradictory accounts of the universe.[3]

Al-Kindi's thought, like early Muslim philosophy as a whole, was much influenced by the translation of a philosophical work that was wrongly attributed to Aristotle. The work was known as the *Theologica Aristotelis* (The Theology of Aristotle) and it was translated into Arabic at al-Kindi's request at about the same time as Aristotle's *Metaphysics* was translated. The *Theologica* has since been shown to be a paraphrasing of books IV, V and VI of the *Enneads* of Plotinus. It sets forth the neo-Platonic doctrine of Emanation in considerable detail, expounding a cosmology in which the One, the Cause of all causes, generates the entire universe through a process of emanation which is the flowing forth of the divine Essence. Plotinus' philosophy derives from Plato's and he is chief among a group of philosophers who flourished in the first four centuries CE and who were known as the neo-Platonists. He produced a close-knit metaphysical system the dominant themes of which are the One, the Intellectual Principle, and Soul. Soul is central in his philosophy and is the concept which enables us to understand his account of reality and the place of the human being within it. In his system the ultimate reality is the One, the ineffable unknowable that is beyond existence, but is at the same time its source. Below the One in the hierarchy of reality, Plotinus places the Intellectual Principle, which pertains to knowledge and thought. The Intellectual Principle stands above Soul, but Soul has the capacity to come to the knowledge embraced by the Intellectual Principle.

Plotinus used the word 'soul' to refer both to the world-Soul and to individual souls. He held that the body that obeys its soul achieves a harmony with the higher elements of reality and is able to approach a state of union with the world-Soul, or reality as whole. But a soul dominated by its body loses its unity with the world-Soul and becomes dispersed among the individual physical things that command its attention. The ultimate mystical state is a complete union with the One, a union in which the soul is eventually separated from all matter. The emanation of all things from the One occurs in a gradation from the shining lightness of the One to the disintegrated heaviness of matter. Taken in its totality, this graded reality is the best and fullest expression of the One. Thus, reality as a whole is the best possible world, even though some individual parts of it are less than perfect. But it is always possible, Plotinus maintains, for the less perfect to achieve an excellence peculiar to itself within the total unity. Matter, for instance, although of low status, is the necessary stuff for the embodying of Forms from a higher level and a felicitous embodying of a Form is efficacious in raising a soul to a higher level.[4]

Both the direction and the detail of Plotinus' ideas were extremely appealing to al-Kindi, intent as the latter was on developing a philosophical rationale for Islamic theology. In particular, Plotinus' account of the interdependence of the things of the world and of their forming together the best of all possible worlds was of considerable significance for him, for it showed a way to treat an important problem arising from Islamic monism, namely, that of accounting for evil in a reality that is conceived of as entirely the product of the one God who is also good. Plotinus maintains, in Aristotelian vein, that the soul is the principle of life and the 'rational form' of the species in which it inheres, conferring essence and definition on the species. In affirming this he seems to be in agreement with Aristotle's claim that body and soul are a single substance. At the same time, he adopts the Platonic understanding of the soul as separate, whose union with an organic body is contingent and temporary and whose true affiliation is with the incorruptible, heavenly spheres. On this Platonic view, soul substance is analogous to the substance of the Creator, much as the light of the sun is analogous to the sun.

Al-Kindi set forth a view concerning the attributes of God which was adopted by many subsequent Muslim philosophers. He maintained that God's chief attribute is unity and that anything possessing unity has derived that unity from God. God's unity is a simple unity, without matter or form and not to be differentiated in any way. God is able to bring forth things from nothing and this is what action is in its primary sense. The seeming actions of humankind are merely derivative and, properly understood, are in fact the passively received effects of primary action. In his account of secondary action it is clear that al-Kindi is seeking to reconcile the Islamic belief in Allah's unqualified control of every detail of the universe with accounts of the universe characteristic of Greek philosophical enquiry in which is posited a causal network of changes and events. The tensions within al-Kindi's concept of an immanent and all-pervasive God who is nevertheless transcendent and indescribable guaranteed the prosecution of a virtually inexhaustible philosophical debate within the ensuing tradition of Muslim philosophy.

Al-Kindi was succeeded by philosophers such as al-Farabi, Ibn Sina and al-Ghazali who eventually became better known than he. But his founding work for Arab philosophy and, in particular, his understanding of the need to establish rational as well as revelatory grounds for Islamic doctrine inspired and significantly informed the thought of those who inherited his ideas. In one of his earliest works he wrote some words that epitomize the character of the high centuries of Islamic philosophy:

> It is fitting to acknowledge the utmost gratitude to those who have contributed even a little to truth, not to speak of those who have contributed so much . . . We should not be ashamed to acknowledge truth and to assimilate it from whatever source it comes to us, even if it is brought to us by former generations and foreign peoples. For him who seeks the truth there is nothing of higher value than truth itself; it never cheapens or abases him who searches for it, but ennobles and honours him.[5]

Notes

1 The author of the *Book of Misers* was al-Jahiz, who was alive during the middle years of the ninth century.

2 In his *First Philosophy*, quoted in Majid Fakhry, *A History of Islamic Philosophy*, London: Longman, 1983, p. 70.
3 There is a fuller account of Mutazilite doctrine in W. Montgomery Watt, *Islamic Philosophy and Theology*, Edinburgh: Edinburgh University Press, 1962, Pt Two, p. 7.
4 For a fuller account of Plotinus' views see Diané Collinson, *Fifty Major Philosophers*, London: Routledge, 1991, pp. 26, 27.
5 Quoted in Richard Walzer, *Greek Into Arabic*, Oxford: Bruno Cassirer, 1962.

Al-Kindi's writings

Al-Kindi was author of the earliest metaphysical work in Arabic. It is translated by Alfred A. Ivry as *Al-Kindi's Metaphysics*, New York: Albany State University Press, 1963 and 1974.

There is an Arabic text of twenty-four scientific and philosophical texts:

Rasa'il al-Kindi al-falasafiyyah, ed. and int. Abd al-Hadi Abu Ridah, 2 vols, Cairo, 1950–3
See also

'Al-Kindi's treatise on intellect', trans. R.J. McCarthy in *Islamic Studies*, vol. 3, no. 4, 1964, pp. 119–49.

See also in this book

Muhammad, al-Farabi, Ibn Sina, al-Ghazali, Ibn Rushd, Ibn Arabi, Muhammad Iqbal

Sources and further reading

Leaman, Oliver, *An Introduction to Medieval Islamic Philosophy*, Cambridge: Cambridge University Press, 1985
Netton, Ian R., *Allah Transcendent: Studies in the Structure and Semiotics of Islamic Philosophy, Theology and Cosmology*, London: Routledge, 1989
Walzer, Richard, *Greek Into Arabic*, Oxford: Bruno Cassirer, 1962, ch. 11
Watt, W.M. *Islamic Philosophy and Theology*, Edinburgh: Edinburgh University Press, 1987; 1st edn, 1962
—— *Muhammad at Mecca*, Edinburgh: Edinburgh University Press, 1953

AL-FARABI *c.*870–950 CE

Al-Farabi was widely known as 'the second master', Aristotle being the first. He achieved high eminence as a logician and was also a physicist, metaphysician, astronomer and musician. He expounded Aristotelian logic for the Arab-speaking world and wrote detailed and comprehensive commentaries on both Plato and Aristotle. He worked to create a reconciliation of their two philosophies and a synthesis of philosophy and religion. The main thrust of his own thought takes its impetus largely from Aristotelian ideas and methods but also shows, like the work of other Arab philosophers of the time, the influence of neo-Platonic ideas. Al-Farabi is regarded as the founder of the Arab neo-Platonism that culminated in the philosophy of Ibn Sina, known later in western philosophy as Avicenna. His work is significant for its emphasis on reason rather than revelation.

Al-Farabi is thought to be of Turkish origin. His family name suggests that he came from the vicinity of Farab in Transoxiana. He is reported to have grown up in Damascus, working as a garden overseer by day and reading philosophy at night by the light of the watchman's torch. He was taught logic by a noted Christian logician, a Nestorian called Yuhanna ibn-Haylan, and then received more general philosophical instruction in Baghdad from Abu-Bishr Matta ibn Yunus, a renowned Aristotelian scholar who was also a Christian. Al-Farabi eventually became closely concerned with the theoretical and practical aspects of political life and spent his latter years in Aleppo at the court of the ruler, Sayf-ad-Dawla, though it is not known in what capacity. Some reports of his life suggest that he was a reclusive person with rather boorish manners, a picture that does not easily fit with other accounts describing his skill as a musical performer and his interest in government and politics. His death occurred when he was about 80 and is thought to have been the result of an accident or an attack by robbers when he was travelling near Damascus.

After the Islamic conquests of Syria, Egypt, Mesopotamia and Persia that took place in the years after the death of the prophet Muhammad (570–632 CE), numerous texts of Greek philosophy began to be translated into Arabic along with the writings of Indian thinkers, Christians, Jews and many others. The neo-Platonic element, already mentioned, in al-Farabi's thought came in the main from a book which at the time was attributed to Aristotle. The book was known as the *Theologica Aristotelis* (The Theology of Aristotle) but in fact was a translation of three volumes of Plotinus' *Enneads*, a major work of neo-Platonism.[1] As a result, al-Farabi's exposition of what he thought was a fundamentally Aristotelian metaphysics is imbued with neo-Platonic ideas, the most significant of which is the doctrine that maintains that the universe is an emanation from the One.

It is in his political work, the *Opinions of the Inhabitants of the Virtuous City*, that the scope of al-Farabi's own thought is most clearly revealed and his synthesis of Islamic theology with Aristotelian, Platonic and neo-Platonic philosophy is most successfully expounded. The work was inspired by Plato's analysis of the ideal state in the

Republic and has three parts. The first sets out al-Farabi's predominantly Aristotelian metaphysics, the second his psychology, and the
third his theory of the structure of the political state. The whole is
bound together by a fundamentally unitary conception of reality
that is grounded in the unqualified monotheism of Islamic theology.
In this conception of things al-Farabi's account is well served by the
doctrine of Emanation contained in the Neoplatonic *Theologica
Aristotelis*. A consequence of al-Farabi's monism was that he regarded
political structures as extrapolations from the metaphysical scheme
that saw God as a unity, as the First Cause of all things and as in essence
intellectual. To this conception of God was added al-Farabi's version
of the Neoplatonic doctrine of Emanation, which held that the
universe is generated by God's nature as it overflows in a super-
abundance of being.

According to al-Farabi's account of the cosmos, the emanation, or
bodying forth, of God's nature produces a series of ten Intelligences
which generate the heavenly bodies, all the planets, the stars and
the moon. He maintained that God is a necessary being and an
absolutely single and simple entity from which only one thing can
emanate. This one thing is the First Intelligence, which flows
from God in virtue of his self-knowledge; for with God, to conceive
of something is to create it. Once God has actualized the First
Intelligence a dualism has come into being: the First Intelligence is
not, like God, a necessary being, but a possible one that has been
actualized by God. This primary dualism begins a process of further
generation. The First Intelligence gives rise to a Second Intelligence,
which is its acutality, and also to the first and highest sphere, its
possibility. The process continues, each Intelligence producing a
further Intelligence and a sphere or planetary body until there are nine
such bodies and ten Intelligences. Within the heavenly regions the
emanatory development takes place from the highest downwards; in
the terrestrial region from the lowest elements upwards. At the top of
the heavenly hierarchy is God, the ruler who is ruled by no one; at the
bottom of the earthly hierarchy is that which is ruled but does not
itself rule anyone. This account is broadly consistent with Ptolemaic
theories of astronomy in which the cosmos consists of nine encircling
spheres which move eternally around the earth. Al-Farabi writes:

> From the First emanates the existence of the Second. This
> Second is, again, an utterly incorporeal substance, and is not
> in matter. It thinks of (intelligizes) its own essence and thinks
> the First. What it thinks of its own essence is no more than

its essence. As a result of its thinking of the First, a third existent follows necessarily from it; and as a result of its substantification in its specific essence, the existence of the First Heaven follows necessarily.[2]

In al-Farabi's hierarchical system, the terrestrial planet, the earth, is developed and governed by the sphere of the moon and the Tenth Intelligence. From this Tenth Intelligence, called Active or Agent Intelligence, flows prime matter, giving rise to the four elements of air, fire, earth and water and all their variations, with humankind at their pinnacle. In Islamic philosophy, Active Intelligence is often spoken of as the angel Gabriel, the angel believed to have imparted the words of the **Qur'an** to Muhammad. The sublunar planet, the earth, aspires to a higher knowledge and perfection and is moved to seek them. The other planets and spheres, and the Intelligences, similarly desire what is higher than themselves and all desire, and so are moved to seek, the One Prime Mover who is immovable.

Al-Farabi's emanationist account of the nature of things effects a synthesis of certain important philosophical and theological issues concerning the nature of reality. It provides a reasoned explanation of how the absolute unity of God was able to generate the multiplicity of the cosmos, and in this we see al-Farabi working to reconcile the requirement of Islamic theology for an absolutely pure monotheism with the philosophical requirement to account rationally for multiplicity and motion in the universe. It also posits the sphere of the moon and Active Intelligence as mediatory between the terrestrial and the heavenly regions, thereby providing a link between God and his peoples that was absent from Aristotle's account of God as entirely detached and impersonal, but which was required, again, by the theology of Islam.

Al-Farabi's psychology derives from Aristotle's *De Anima* and from Plato's account in *The Republic* of the ascent from the shadowy perceptions of the cave to the certain knowledge achieved in the light of the sun. It is closely related to his cosmological theory of the ten Intelligences. He separates the intellect into two parts: the practical, which reasons about what is to be done, and the theoretical, which rationally directs the soul towards its perfection. The theoretical intellect is subdivided into the material, the habitual and the acquired. Al-Farabi describes the material intellect as the ability to abstract the essence of a thing and to receive forms, much as wax receives impressions, so that they can exist in actuality in the mind rather than as potentialities in the objects of sense. From this level of apprehending abstractions it is possible to progress to the level of the acquired intellect, a level at which the intellect becomes apt to receive abstractions which have no connection at all with matter and objects of sense. Al-Farabi regards this as the highest form of understanding. It is comparable with Aristotle's active intellect which was 'separable, impassable and mixed' and with the Platonic *noesis*, that direct, intuitive knowledge achieved by the person who is able to contemplate the source of all knowledge.

Al-Farabi transposes his pattern of the structure of the universe into the political realm, producing a theory of the state that is both hierarchical and authoritarian and that sees the state's proper governance as consisting of the rule of reason, on an analogy with the rulings of the Intelligences in the cosmic structure already described. It is reason, he maintains, that is the means to the highest happiness and its exercise is required in every aspect of community and individual life. Its rule in the individual is analogous to its rule in the state and in the cosmos; it controls and regulates physical impulses and appetites and determines the will and judgement. Al-Farabi's conception of the ruler resembles Plato's picture of the philosopher-king: he must have wisdom, knowledge, magnanimity and courage, and an understanding of how justice is to be secured in relation to possessions, safety and dignity and to all one's transactions and relationships with others. But in addition, al-Farabi's ruler must possess a power of prophecy granted by God. He must be capable of the kind of contemplation and communion that will yield a direct knowledge of Active Intelligence which can then be imparted by the prophet-ruler to the citizens.

Al-Farabi's theory of prophecy is a complex one that is integrated with and supported by the broader structure of his philosophy. He takes the tenets of the theory from Islamic theology and justifies them by reference to his philosophical account of the human mind and its place within his broad metaphysical scheme. The concept of imagination is central to his account of prophecy. He regards revelatory truth as the imaginative expression of philosophic truth, philosophic truth being imparted by Active Intelligence to the passive intellect of the philosopher, and revelatory truth to the imagination. Imagination, he maintains, is the faculty that creates the kind of mental images that are not copies of sensible objects and that are the material of dreams and visionary insights. When the imagination is rid of conscious activities, as it is in sleep, it is able to create images of a spiritual nature, thereby experiencing celestial pleasures and receiving enlightenment by Active Intelligence. Such experiences are the source of prophetic messages. Al-Farabi writes:

> If the faculty of imagination is so powerful and perfected in a certain person, and is not completely overwhelmed by external sensations . . . it gets into communion with the agent [Active] intelligence from which images of the utmost beauty and perfection are reflected . . . Once the imaginative faculty in man is completely perfected, he may receive, when awake, from the agent [Active] intelligence the pre-vision of the present and future events . . . and thus . . . prophesy divine matters. This is the highest level to which imagination may be raised, and which man can attain through this faculty.[3]

Al-Farabi distinguishes between the virtuous state, or city, and four other types which are, in varying ways, corrupt. In the city of ignorance the people are attracted to false pleasures and so do not seek what is genuinely good. In the wayward city they have seen the good but have not followed it. In the renegade city they have lapsed from the right path that they once trod. And in the erring city the people are ruled by a false prophet who deceives them, so that they have never been aware of the good. The virtuous city is governed through reason and its citizens aspire to the happiness that comes from an intellectual development which, at its highest and best, culminates in the serene contemplation of the truths of Active Intelligence. Al-Farabi maintains that if a person's rational faculties are not developed, spiritual happiness cannot be attained after death, since the soul has not achieved the necessary immateriality. Such a person is in bondage to the body and will undergo reincarnation in human and animal forms, degenerating eventually to extinction.

Al-Farabi represents a high peak in early Muslim philosophy. He is rated by some as greater than Ibn Sina (Avicenna) who adopted and strengthened many of his ideas. His greatness springs not so much from an originality of thought as from his capacity for synthesis and from the powerful unity it imparted to his system. He held that philosophy is essentially one, that Plato and Aristotle had formulated its scope and methods and that the so-called 'schools' of philosophy were merely different aspects of the one edifice erected by those two great thinkers. In addition to effecting a remarkable cohesion of philosophy within itself, he brought about a reconciliation between it and the dogma of Islamic theology so that the two could be seen to support and reinforce each other. The issues generated through the interaction of reason with revelation in his thought influenced and informed the medieval scholastic philosophy of the West.

Notes

1 The *Theologica Aristotelis* was translated into Arabic by a Syrian Christian, Abd al-Masih. For a fuller account of Plotinus' Neoplatonism see Diané Collinson, *Fifty Major Philosophers*, London: Routledge, 1991, pp. 26–8. See also pp. 22, 23 in this volume.
2 See Richard Walzer, *Al-Farabi on the Ideal State*, Oxford: Clarendon Press, 1985, p. 101.
3 Quoted in M.M. Sharif (ed.), *A History of Muslim Philosophy*, 2 vols, Wiesbaden: Harrassowitz, 1963–6, p. 464.

Al-Farabi's writing

Al-Farabi's Philosophy of Plato and Aristotle, trans. Muhsin Mahdi, New York: Glencoe, 1962
Al-Farabi's Commentary and Short Treatise on Aristotle's De Interpretatione, trans. F.W. Zimmermann, Oxford: Oxford University Press for the British Academy, 1981
Tahsil. Kitab Tahsil al-Sa'ada (The Attainment of Happiness) ed. Ja'far Al Yasin, Beirut: Dar al-Andalus, 1981

See also in this book

Muhammad, al-Kindi, Ibn Sina, al-Ghazali, Ibn Rushd, Muhammad Iqbal, Ibn Arabi

Sources and further reading

Galston, M., *Politics and Excellence: The Political Philosophy of Alfarabi*, Princeton: Princeton University Press, 1990
Leaman, Oliver, *An Introduction to Medieval Islamic Philosophy*, Cambridge: Cambridge University Press, 1985
Netton, I.R., *Al Farabi and His School*, London: Routledge, 1992
Sharif, M.M. (ed.), *A History of Muslim Philosophy*, 2 vols, Wiesbaden: Harrassowitz, 1963–6
Walzer, Richard, *Greek Into Arabic*, Oxford: Bruno Cassirer, 1962

IBN SINA (AVICENNA) 980–1037 CE

Among the early Islamic philosophers, Ibn Sina stands out as a thinker of exceptional power and versatility. The whole of his philosophy stems from his conception of God as a necessary being whose essence is to exist and from whom the universe necessarily flows. His thought is not highly original but it is marvellously systematic, fluent and lucid. It exhibits a blend of Platonism, Aristotelianism and neo-Platonism that is characteristic of Muslim philosophy of the time. He adopted and developed many of the ideas of his predecessor al-Farabi, imparting to them a spirituality that reflected an aspect of his own personality. When his work was translated into Latin it came to exert a powerful influence on the thirteenth-century scholastic philosophy of the western world. The hundred or so of his works that survive include books on science, logic, psychology, astronomy, language, literature and religion as well as his famous treatise *The Canons of Medicine* (al-Qanun fi al-Tibb). His major philosophical work is *Kitab al Shifa* (the Book of Healing), which he abridged as *Kitab al Najat* (the Book of Salvation). Ibn Sina's intellectual capability was remarkable. When he was only 16 he qualified as a practising physician. He was a brilliant logician and his writings include detailed commentaries on Aristotle. He became vizier to several sultans, travelled extensively in Persia and was frequently close to or involved in fighting with the Turks. At the age of 57, shortly before his death, he freed his slaves.

There is considerable knowledge of Ibn Sina's life because, unusually for a Muslim, he left an autobiography, which he had dictated to a pupil. He was born in northern Persia in the village of Afshanah, near Bukhara. His family then moved to Bukhara where he was given a private education and became acquainted with the Ismaili[1] doctrine of Islam. In his autobiography he is outspoken about his educational achievements and leaves the reader in no doubt that he excelled in his studies. By the age of 10 he had made a complete study of the **Qur'an** and a major part of Arab letters and was able to display a detailed understanding of numerous areas of knowledge. 'So much so', he recounts, 'that people wondered at my attainments.'[2] He outstripped his logic teacher when he was in his early teens and then turned of his own accord to physics, medicine, mathematics and, eventually, metaphysics. He relates that he read Aristotle's *Metaphysics* forty times without any real comprehension but then came across a copy of al-Farabi's *Intentions of Aristotle's Metaphysics* which succeeded in making Aristotle's ideas clear to him. Ibn Sina's life was a restless one. He rarely settled for long in one place but moved between the courts of the sultans to whom he was medical adviser. His health became much impaired by his over-indulgences and when he died at the age of 58 it was because he had been unable to cure himself of a severe and prolonged attack of colic.

The foundations of Ibn Sina's thought are firmly Aristotelian but its development and superstructure are imbued with neo-Platonism. He held that God is a necessary being and that he is the eternal, unmoved First Mover. His argument for the existence of God derives from the notion of causality. He says, first, that anything that exists must do so in virtue of being caused to exist; second, that causes cannot be linked either in an infinite series or in a circle; and third, as the conclusion of those premisses, that the series of causes must have their source in a necessary being that is not dependent on anything else for existence and who is God. God's essence is to exist and he cannot not exist. Since he exists eternally, the creation which he necessarily causes is also eternal.

Like al-Farabi, Ibn Sina expounds an emanationist theory of the cosmos that derives from the Neoplatonist philosophy of Plotinus.[3] But, as already mentioned, whereas al-Farabi held that the cosmos comes into being by God's acts, Ibn Sina argued that it is a necessary consequence of God's nature. He holds that although necessarily caused by God, each created entity is contingent in that, unlike God, it does not exist in virtue of its own essence: it is not Cause of Itself as God is. Thus Ibn Sina does not regard creation as a temporal event or as occurring 'out of nothing'; for him it is co-eternal with God. In this he is in agreement with Aristotle but not with Islamic theology which asserted a temporal act of creation and a limited existence for the cosmos.

Ibn Sina describes God as wholly good and without multiplicity. He therefore has to account for the evident multiplicity of the cosmos and it is here that the theory of emanation serves him well. The theory states that the world emanates from God as the consequence of God's knowledge of himself. Emanation begins because God's self-knowledge logically entails the existence of a pure Intellect. This Intellect, or Intelligence, is necessarily brought into existence by God but is in itself not a necessary but a contingent being, since its essence is not identical with its existence. It is known as the First Intelligence, and is aware of three things: of God as Necessary Being; of its own existence as necessarily produced by God; and of its own status as a possible being, dependent on God, rather than as a necessary being able to exist in itself. When the First Intelligence reflects on God it generates a Second Intelligence; when it reflects on itself as a possible or contingent being it generates the body of the first celestial sphere; and when it reflects on the necessity of its emanation from God it generates the soul of that first sphere. This triadic process continues. The Second Intelligence generates a Third Intelligence and a second celestial sphere, and so on until, with the Tenth Intelligence and the ninth celestial sphere, the sublunar world is produced. The Tenth Intelligence is known as Agent or Active Intelligence. It provides the forms that are received by matter, producing thereby the earthly realm of which humanity is a part. Ibn Sina's cosmology broadly follows the Ptolemaic system of the universe,[4] much as al-Farabi's does, but he does not lay down that there must be ten Intelligences for he was aware that new astronomical discoveries might be made. What he does stipulate is that there could not be fewer Intelligences than celestial spheres.

The Aristotelian notions of potentiality and actuality feature prominently in almost every aspect of Ibn Sina's thought. They are especially important in his theory of knowledge and his account of the soul. His teaching concerning the soul is very close to Aristotle's. He regards soul as an emanation from Active Intelligence and says that it may be vegetative, animal, or rational. The soul is the animation of the body that comes into being with the body; it is not something that exists prior to the body. Only the human soul is capable of rationality and it should, accordingly, be able to control the body and its passions. At death the soul separates from the body. If it has triumphed by realizing its rational potential it is able eternally to contemplate higher principles in a state of rapture. If it has failed it endures eternal torment as it searches to regain the body through which it might once have perfected itself.

According to Ibn Sina the soul is a potential being that is able to come to actuality by being moved by the senses and by receiving direct emanation from a higher realm. Knowledge begins with sense-experience which imparts a degree of actuality to the soul. This actuality increases and a higher understanding is achieved when the soul generalizes by reflecting on sense-experience; but it is only when Active Intelligence illuminates the sensible images to reveal their intellectual reality that the individual soul is able to participate in a universal kind of knowledge. Thought at this level is described as the Actual or Acquired Intellect. It operates by abstracting form from the images of particular objects so that the individuating particularities fall away leaving the purity of the object's form or essence. It is in this activity that the human soul reaches up to the divine. Its success in so doing represents a peak of human attainment and is surpassed only by a direct insight into the divine, an achievement which is within the capacity of only a few holy mortals. All souls aspire to what is above them, and so to God, and in the successive triads of Intelligence, sphere and soul, already described, it is a soul's desire for intellectual enlightenment that moves its sphere. Unlike God and the Intelligences, whose knowledge is of universals, souls have aspects which can connect materially with and so influence particular entities in the sublunar world. Souls are the mode of communication between the divine and the earthly.

The concept of prophecy is a vitally significant one in Muslim philosophy and Ibn Sina considers it in some detail. His treatment of it is consistent with his general emphasis on the intellect as the supreme form of spirituality. Both he and al-Farabi regard prophecy as the highest of human abilities but whereas al-Farabi sees it as essentially an imaginative capacity, Ibn Sina analyses it as the rare intellectual ability to achieve a swift, intuitive kind of apprehension, an insight inspired by a direct communion with Active Intelligence. But prophethood, he maintains, is not simply a matter of experiencing an occasional intuitive understanding of something piecemeal or partial. It requires a comprehensive and sustained vision. Moreover, its visionary insights must translate into a conception of things that not only appeals to the mass of people but also satisfies more critical demands for an intelligible world-view and a coherent future prospect. The prophet is a messenger from and a link with a higher reality, a person whose conviction concerning his prophecies must be unshakeable so that his delivery of his message compels and inspires. It is characteristic of prophetic vision that its insights are so vivid that the prophet has to speak of 'seeing' divine beings, of 'hearing' their voices; and his understanding of bliss and agony becomes objectified as heaven and hell.

Ibn Sina's conception of the cosmos as existing eternally rather than as the result of an act of creation was not palatable to orthodox Islamic thought. Nevertheless his view of the cosmos as a contingent being, unable to exist without the Necessary Being who is God, served as a strong argument both against an atheistic doctrine which maintained that the physical universe had existed eternally without need of God, and against a religious pantheism, equally repugnant to Muslim tenets, that identified God with the cosmos.

Ibn Sina's works were translated into Latin in Spain in the mid-twelfth century CE. They exerted a profound influence not only on the thought of St Thomas Aquinas, who came to know them through his teacher, Albert the Great, but on medieval philosophy in general. Half a century after his death, Ibn Sina's carefully reasoned synthesis of the dogmatic theology of Islam with traditional Greek thought was confronted by the remarkable challenge embodied in the views of his successor, al-Ghazali.

Notes

1 The Ismaili constitute a sub-sect of the Islamic Shi'ite sect. The Shi'a are distinguished from mainstream **Sunni** Islam by their devotion to the family

of Muhammad the Prophet, and by a special doctrinal emphasis on individual decision-making. The Ismaili sub-sect maintains a belief in a line of Islamic leaders, descended from Muhammad's family, and continuing to the present day.

2   See Soheil M. Afnan, *Avicenna: His Life and Works*, London: Allen & Unwin, 1958, pp. 57–75.

3   See the essay on al-Farabi in this book, pp. 25–31. There is an account of Plotinus' philosophy in Diané Collinson, *Fifty Major Philosophers*, London: Routledge, 1991, pp. 26–8.

4   Ptolemy's planetary system (second century CE) is an earth-centred one in which each planet moves in a small circular orbit which in turn travels around a larger circle. The Ptolemaic system was superseded by the Copernican system (sixteenth century CE) in which the sun is central, with the planets, including the earth, moving round it.

Ibn Sina's writings

Over one hundred of Ibn Sina's works have survived, most of which are in Arabic but some are in Persian. There is no collected edition of his works. In 1951 the University of Tehran published a series of his works to celebrate his millenary. Some translations are as follows:

Arberry, A.J. (trans.), *Avicenna on Theology*, London: Murray, 1951
Gruner, O.C. (trans.), *A Treatise on the Canons of Medicine*, London: Luzac, 1930
Rahman, Fazlur, *Avicenna's Psychology*, London: Oxford University Press, 1952

See also in this book

Muhammad, al-Kindi, al-Farabi, al-Ghazali, Ibn Arabi, Ibn Rushd, Muhammad Iqbal

Sources and further reading

Afnan, S.M., *Avicenna: His Life and Works*, London: Allen & Unwin, 1958
Corbin, H., *Avicenna and the Visionary Recital*, trans. W. Trask, Princeton: Princeton University Press, 1990
Fakhry, M., *A History of Islamic Philosophy*, New York: Columbia University Press, 1970
Gutas, D., *Avicenna and the Aristotelian Tradition*, Dordrecht, 1967
Goodman, L.E. *Avicenna*, London: Routledge, 1992
Sharif, M.M. (ed.), *A History of Muslim Philosophy*, 2 vols, Wiesbaden: Harrassowitz, 1963–6
Walzer, R., *Greek Into Arabic*, Oxford: Bruno Cassirer, 1962
Wickens, G.M. (ed.), *Avicenna: Scientist and Philosopher: A Millenary Symposium*, London: Luzak, 1952

AL-GHAZALI 1058/9–1111 CE

Al-Ghazali was a philosopher of great originality and critical acumen. He was deeply religious, a mystic as well as a penetratingly analytical thinker; a sceptic as well as a man of faith. His great desire was for a certainty that was unshakeable, a knowledge in which 'the object is known in a manner which is not open to doubt at all'.[1] He propounded a radical scepticism concerning the theory of knowledge embodied in the philosophical thought of his Arab predecessors and advanced a theory of his own that saw knowledge as direct and intuitive rather than as the product of demonstrative reasoning. In mid-life he abandoned his career as a professor of theology in order to adopt the way of life of **Sufism**.[2] Subsequently he made it his aim to establish a form of Sufism that could be a bastion to orthodox Islamic doctrine but would at the same time correct the excessively legalistic tendencies of that orthodoxy by cultivating an inward spirituality in believers. His sceptism has been likened to that of the eighteenth-century Scottish philosopher David Hume, and of the logical positivists of twentieth-century European philosophy.

The development of al-Ghazali's philosophy is closely bound in with the events of his life. He was born near Tus in Khurasan, in north-eastern Iran. His parents died when he was young and he was brought up by a devout Sufi who had been a friend of his father. He learned much of Sufism and studied theology and canon law. When he was about 20 years old he went to the Nizamiyyah Academy of Nishapur where he became known for his skills in debating and for the original quality of his thought. He questioned and tested everything, rejected all authoritative pronouncements and sought inspiration and enlightenment (though, he reports, without much success) in the practice of Sufist exercises. By the time he was 28 he was known and respected by the whole of the Muslim world of learning. He joined the court of Nizam al-Mulk, a vizier renowned for his generous patronage of scholarship, and at the early age of 34 was appointed to the much-prized chair of theology at the Nizamiyyah Academy of Baghdad.

As al-Ghazali's outward triumphs in the world of learning multiplied and grew, so did a whole host of inner uncertainties. An important aspect of his work at the academy was the elucidation and defence of **Sunni**[3] legal doctrine, along with all its corollaries and implications. As a consequence of this he became closely involved with matters of state. This meant that he was witness to and participant in a bitter conflict compounded of theological, legal, political and philosophical differences that was taking place between the Shi'ite caliphate at Cairo and the Sunnite sultan Malikshah.[4] Soon after al-Ghazali acceded to the chair at Baghdad this conflict became acute and extremely violent. He became deeply disillusioned with his work: sceptical of the dogma and authoritarianism of the theologians and contemptuous of the casuistic triviality that characterized many of the debates in the academy. He decided that reason alone was inadequate for the construction of a coherent theology and that all the sceptical conclusions now forming in his mind were entirely contrary to the doctrines he publicly espoused and taught. More radically still, he began to doubt the testimony both of the senses and of reason itself, arguing that there might exist, beyond reason, 'a higher authority, which would, upon its manifestation, show the judgement of reason to be invalid'.[5] This intense travail of heart and mind began in July 1095 and lasted for about six months. Al-Ghazali then relinquished his professorship, saying he wished to make a pilgrimage to Makkah. He in fact turned again to Sufism in order to seek the truth, certainty and peace of mind for which he yearned. There followed eleven years of ascetic practice, meditation, wandering and pilgrimage interspersed with periods of teaching and writing, during which he came to a resolution of his doubts and formulated a theory of knowledge that enabled him to accept the pronouncements of the **Qur'an**. When he returned to Tus, meaning to live there in seclusion, he was urged back into the world of the academy for a time. In 1106 he established his own seminary at Tus and it was there that he died in 1111. Five years before his death he wrote an autobiography, *Al-Munqidh min al-Dalal* (The Deliverer from Error). It includes a critical study of the philosophical methods of the time and advocates a fearless scrutiny of every form of knowledge. It describes how al-Ghazali had 'poked into every dark recess [and] made an assault on every problem' in his endeavour to separate the true from the false. In a vein of thought which, five hundred years later, through the writings of Descartes, was to become familiar in western philosophy, al-Ghazali declared that he wanted to construct all knowledge from a simple foundation of certitude.

His attack on the philosophers was mounted in two stages. The first stage, contained in his *Makasid al-Falasifah* (Intentions of the Philosophers), consists of a masterly exposition of their doctrines that is so thorough and careful a study that when its translated version reached Europe towards the end of the twelfth century it was taken to be the work of an Aristotelian peripatetic. In fact it was simply al-Ghazali's propaedeutic to a detailed critical examination of the Arab philosophers who had worked so assiduously to blend Hellenic with Muslim thought. His critique proper is *Tahafut al-Falasifah* (The Incoherence of the Philosophers). In the *Tahafut* he makes a threefold classification of the philosophers into materialists, naturalists (or deists) and theists. The materialists are those who deny the existence of God and assert the eternal existence of the material universe. The deists are those who reason from the orderliness of the universe to the existence of God, but deny the immortality of the human soul. The theists, among whom al-Ghazali numbers Plato, Aristotle, al-Farabi and Ibn Sina, are the main target of his attack; not because they are the most vulnerable to criticism but because in their own work they had successfully revealed the weaknesses of the materialists and deists (thought without, in al-Ghazali's opinion, providing any satisfactory replacement for their theories) and were therefore his most formidable opposition. In particular, al-Ghazali addresses himself to the work of Ibn Sina who, he felt, had subjugated the facts of religion to the speculative reasoning of metaphysics.[6] At first sight al-Ghazali's position may seem to be no more than a dogmatic assertion of faith, but he argues his claims with great philosophical acuity, maintaining that religious tenets are not of the kind that can be either proved or disproved and that they must be recognized as such.

One of al-Ghazali's main objections to Ibn Sina's philosophy is the latter's espousal of the view that the world has existed eternally. Ibn Sina had deployed Aristotle's notions of potentiality and actuality to argue that God, in the bestowal of forms on matter, is eternally bringing potential existence into actual existence. This is entirely contrary to the teaching of the Qur'an, which states that the world was created out of nothing by an act of God at a definite time in the past and that it was accordingly not infinite but finite. As already mentioned, al-Ghazali maintained that neither the Qur'anic nor the philosophic position could be established by reason. Accordingly he sees no need to make a reasoned defence of the religious account and concentrates instead on the task of systematically undermining Ibn Sina's arguments.

Another substantial target of al-Ghazali's critical onslaught is the concept of causality. He points out that the Muslim philosophers had accepted without question the assumptions, derived from Greek philosophy, that every event has a cause and that causes necessitate their effects. But all that can be claimed from the evidence of experiments, he says, is, for example, that cotton burns at the time of its contact with fire; not *because* of the contact with fire. Thus the relationship that can be asserted between the cotton and the fire is one of concomitance rather than causality. The wider context of this issue of causality is a debate concerning the will of God in which the orthodox Islamic view was that the uniformity of nature was the consequence of God's will rather than a causal necessity flowing from his essential nature. Here, as in everything, al-Ghazali's interest is theological: his concern is to contest any philosophical theory that contradicts or undermines the dicta of the Qur'an.

A third major object of al-Ghazali's critical scrutiny is Ibn Sina's doctrine that God knows the terrestrial world only in a universal way and has no knowledge of its particularities and individuals. This doctrine is a component of Ibn Sina's broader conception, again derived from Aristotle, of the cosmos as emanating necessarily from God. It stands in direct opposition to the Qur'anic view that God knows every detail of the cosmos and that he directs its every change by means of acts of his will. Al-Ghazali regards the doctrines of the eternity of the cosmos, the limitation of God's knowledge to knowledge of universals, and his denial of the resurrection of the body as wholly irreligious. He regards a further seventeen of Ibn Sina's conclusions as heretical and innovatory and charges him with, among other things, failing to prove the existence, unity, simplicity and incorporeality of God.

No exact dates can be given for al-Ghazali's polemical writings against the philosophers. It is thought that he composed them during the eleven years of his wanderings. Subsequently he wrote a lengthy synthesis of his views, the *Ihya Ulum al-Din* (Revival of the Religious Sciences), a work which has exerted an enduring influence on the thought of Sunnite Islam. His return to Sufism should not be seen as an escape from intellectuality into irrationality. His path to mysticism was carved out with the tools of reason and philosophy, a procedure that produced a paradox that has been much noted by commentators: al-Ghazali first declares that philosophical reasoning is unable to procure certitude, and then proceeds to use reason as a compelling means to demolish the reasoning of philosophy.

Al-Ghazali's mysticism is never of the pantheistic and frenzied kind for which some Sufis were condemned. He manages to remain within the bounds of traditional Islam while at the same time infusing it with a fresh spiritual vitality. He tried, it has been remarked, 'to make mysticism orthodox and . . . orthodoxy mystical'.[7] His success in this is largely due to his well-conceived accounts of God and of the knowledge that is possible for believers. He affirms the absolute unity and power of God and says: 'The First Principle is an omnipotent and willing agent. He does what He wills and ordains as He likes, and He creates in whatever manner He wills.'[8] Al-Ghazali's God is both transcendent and immanent. His presence is manifest in the beauty of his creation and his creatures may commune with him in virtue of the possession of soul. The human soul, al-Ghazali maintains, is an attribute through which humankind resembles God in that 'both God and soul are invisible, indivisible, unconfined by space and time and outside the categories of quantity and quality'.[9] The soul animates and wills the life of the body, and is the means of communion with God.

A danger of this doctrine is that it makes the human soul too much like God, so that the whole picture becomes open to the charge of being pantheistic, even though al-Ghazali is at pains to point out a fundamental difference between the human and the divine, namely, that God is entirely self-subsistent while humanity is wholly dependent on his will. The issue is a difficult one, since the total dependence of the world on God, from moment to moment and in all its aspects, may also be construed as a form of pantheism. What seems to be the case is that al-Ghazali's own religious experiences were characterized by a sense of mystical union with God and with his creation, but that he was also aware of the doctrinal hazards of translating such experience into a philosophical account of the nature of the cosmos. The tension between the need to insist on the transcendence of God and the need to declare God's intimate involvement with the minutiae of the lives of every believer has its counterpart in al-Ghazali's theory of knowledge. He writes of the gradual and laborious ascent by means of the study of the particular sciences, to a knowledge which is veiled and obscure in its otherness but which, once it begins to be revealed, has the directness and wholeness of Platonic *noesis*[10] as well as the incontrovertible certainty that al-Ghazali sought.

Al-Ghazali's refutations of the arguments of his predecessors did not go unchallenged. In the latter part of the twelfth century CE, the rationalist approach of the philosophers he had opposed was cogently defended by the Spanish Muslim philosopher Ibn Rushd (Averroes). Ibn Rushd was a dedicated Aristotelian. His answer to al-Ghazali's *Tahafut* is contained in a substantial work, the *Tahafut al-Tahafut* (The Incoherence of 'The Incoherence'), in which he comments systematically on al-Ghazali's criticisms and reasserts and argues for a broadly Aristotelian account of God and the cosmos. Numerous other philosophers and theologians joined the debate, engaging in it with remarkable energy and passion. Some regarded al-Ghazali's Sufism as thoroughly misguided. At one time in Spain all his books were burned and possession of them was forbidden. In North Africa, in the twelfth century, it was ordered that all his writings be destroyed. As is ever the way in human affairs, the liveliness of the debate and the zeal with which it was conducted guaranteed a widespread interest in its every aspect. The interest has continued unabated into the twenty-first century.

Notes

1 In Majid Fakhry, *A History of Islamic Philosophy*, London: Longman, 1983, p. 18.
2 A Sufi is a Muslim mystic for whom the inward, devotional life is of great importance. The name is derived from the word for the white woollen clothing worn by these mystics (*suf* = coarse wool).
3 Sunni is the majority sect of Islam. Its teaching places reliance on the Qur'an, tradition and community ruling. In contrast, the Shi'a sect emphasizes the importance of a line of rulers descended from Muhammad the Prophet.
4 In spite of al-Ghazali's disillusion with this kind of conflict and his subsequent abdication from involvement in it, he remained and still remains a thinker who is fully accepted within the Sunni tradition.
5 Fakhry, op. cit., p. 210.
6 See the essay on Ibn Sina in this book, pp. 31–6.
7 In M.M. Sharif, *A History of Muslim Philosophy*, 2 vols, vol. I, Wiesbaden: Harrassowitz, 1963–6, p. 617.
8 In Sahib Ahmab Kamali (trans.), *Tahafut al-Falasifah* (The Incoherence of the Philosophers), Lahore: Pakistan Philosophical Congress, 1958, p. 88.
9 Claud Field (trans.), *The Alchemy of Happiness* (al-Ghazali's Kimiya-i Sa'adat), London: Murray, 1910.
10 *Noesis* is Plato's term for the highest kind of knowledge. It is a direct, intuitive comprehension of universals, unsullied by the particularities of sense experience.

Al-Ghazali's writings

(Over seventy works attributed to al-Ghazali are extant in manuscript. Some of these attributions are thought to be incorrect.)

Kimiya-i Sa'adat (The Alchemy of Happiness), trans. Claud Field, London: Murray, 1910
Tahafut al-Falasifah (The Incoherence of the Philosophers), trans. S.A. Kamali, Lahore: Pakistan Philosophical Congress, 1958, 1963
Ihya Ulum al-Din: Selections (Revival of the Religious Sciences: Selections), trans. Muhtar Holland, London: Latimer New Dimensions, 1975
The Rembrance of Death and the Afterlife, trans. T. Winter, Cambridge: Islamic Texts Society, 1989
Al-munqidh min al-dalal (The Deliverer From Error) trans. R. McCarthy, *Freedom and Fulfillment*, Boston, Mass.: Twayne, 1980

For a commentary on al-Ghazali see:

Watt, W.M., *Islamic Philosophy and Theology*, Edinburgh: Edinburgh University Press, 1987; 1st edn 1962

See also in this book

Muhammad, al-Kindi, al-Farabi, Ibn Sina, Ibn Rushd, Ibn Arabi, Muhammad Iqbal

Sources and further reading

Fakhry, Majid, *A History of Islamic Philosophy*, London: Longman, 1983
Nasr, S.H. and Leaman, O. (eds), *History of Islamic Philosophy*, London: Routledge, 1996
Sharif, M.M., *A History of Muslim Philosophy*, 2 vols, vol. I, Wiesbaden: Harrassowitz, 1963–6
Ward, Keith, *Images of Eternity*, London: Darton, Longman & Todd, 1987
Watt, W.M., *Muslim Intellectual, a Study of al-Ghazali*, Edinburgh: Edinburgh University Press, 1963

IBN RUSHD (AVERROES) 1126–1198 CE

Ibn Rushd's life and thought represent the culmination of the remarkable development of Islamic philosophy that took place between 700 and 1200 CE. Through his dedication to the task of interpreting the philosophy of Aristotle he became known to the scholastic thinkers of the western world as the Commentator, much as Aristotle was known as the Philosopher. He opposed many of the views of his two great predecessors, Ibn Sina and al-Ghazali, who had asserted and argued powerfully for the supremacy of faith over reason. In response to al-Ghazali's famous work, *Tahafut al-Falasifah* (The Incoherence of the Philosophers), Ibn Rushd wrote an equally famous reply, *Tahafut al-Tahafut* (The Incoherence of 'The Incoherence'),[1] in which he set out to defend philosophy and reason without weakening any of the tenets of the Islamic faith. His fundamental aim was to demonstrate the compatibility of philosophy with religion.

Little of detail is known about Ibn Rushd's life. He was born in Cordoba in southern Spain, into a family known and respected for its eminent lawyers.[2] He received a broad education in philosophy, science, medicine, jurisprudence and theology. Much of his life subsequently seems to have been spent between Cordoba, Marrakesh and Seville. It is reported that on a visit to Marrakesh, probably in 1169, the caliph Abu Ya'qub Yusuf discussed with him the question: 'What is the opinion of the philosophers on the composition of the skies? Are they made of eternal substance or did they have a beginning?'[3] Subsequently, Ibn Rushd was encouraged by the caliph, who became his patron and friend, to write the commentaries on the works of Aristotle.

In spite of the interest of rulers such as Abu Ya'qub Yusuf, philosophy was not generally held in high esteem in the Muslim world of the twelfth century and few scholars were in a position to dedicate their lives to it. Much of Ibn Rushd's daily work was in the judiciary as a *qadi*, or judge. As such he performed duties which were not only civil but religious as well, since the Islamic legal system is founded on religion.[4] He was appointed *qadi* at Seville in 1169 and at Cordoba in 1171. In 1169 he published a major medical treatise, *Kitab al-Kulliyat*, and in 1182 became physician to Abu Ya'qub Yusuf at the court of Marrakesh. Abu Ya'qub died two years later but Ibn Rushd's position at court remained unchanged for a further ten years. Then, for complex political and doctrinal reasons, he and other philosophers fell from favour and were banished from the Marrakesh court to a small town near Cordoba. In 1195/6 Ibn Rushd moved to Seville and soon after was restored to favour at the Marrakesh court where he stayed until his death there in 1198. His remains were later transported to Cordoba on a mule, 'their weight being balanced by his works of philosophy'.[5]

Ibn Rushd became widely known and admired during his lifetime. He was held in high regard by the Jewish philosopher Moses Maimonides, and his works were translated into Hebrew shortly after his death. By then the world of scholarship was teeming with commentaries on his commentaries on Aristotle, many of which were being translated into Latin for the benefit of western scholars.

Ibn Rushd developed the art of commentary writing to a high level of excellence, providing commentaries for almost all the works of Aristotle, for Plato's *Republic* and for the *Isagoge* of the Neoplatonist Porphyry. But it is for his commentaries on Aristotle that he became famous. They consist of the Greater Commentaries, in which portions of Aristotelian text are given interspersed with Ibn Rushd's comments; the Middle Commentaries, in which he expounds and explains the main elements of Aristotle's thought; and the Little Commentaries, which are summaries or compendia of Aristotelian doctrine. These works became extremely influential among western scholars from the thirteenth to the mid-seventeenth century, but made little impact on Arabic thought.

Like other Arabic philosophers, Ibn Rushd relied heavily on a source widely known as the *Theologica Aristotelis*, a treatise believed at the time to be by Aristotle but shown subsequently to be the work of Plotinus, a Neoplatonist of the third century CE who expounded an emanationist cosmology and a metaphysical doctrine of aspiration to mystical union with the one.[6] The *Theologica* embodied ideas that appealed strongly to the temperament of Islamic theology. It described a system in which rational knowledge develops to a stage at which it is superseded by a mystical intuition of reality, and in which individualism is lost through fusion with the divine Whole. This was not Aristotelianism as it is now known, but a mode of thought in which the ideas of Plato, Aristotle and numerous other Greek thinkers were blended into a unity they did not actually possess. Ibn Rushd's own philosophical position has been described as 'Aristotle warped onto a Platonic frame'.[7] He managed to place the wide-ranging empirical data of Aristotle within the framework of a Platonic hierarchical system and endow it with an integrated organicism not conferred on it by Aristotle. So firm was his conviction that Greek philosophy comprised a unified system of thought, that when he was unable to obtain a copy of Aristotle's *Politics* he wrote a commentary on Plato's *Republic* to fill that place in the series of commentaries.

Ibn Rushd's *Tahafut al-Tahafut* (The Incoherence of 'The Incoherence') is a sustained rebuttal of al-Ghazali's objections to the rationalism of al-Farabi and Ibn Sina.[8] Ibn Rushd does not go about this rebuttal by constructing a systematic defence of the two philosophers attacked by al-Ghazali. Instead, he picks out what he sees as misinterpretations of Aristotelian texts irrespective of who has made them, with the result that he diverges as much from the views of Ibn Sina and al-Farabi as from those of al-Ghazali. All the time he works to show a compatibility, rather than an opposition, between reason and faith. He rejects the Neoplatonic theory of emanation espoused by Ibn Sina, in which the universe is held to flow necessarily from and to exist co-eternally with God, the unmoved First Mover. In its place he argues for a scale of being ranging from God to Prime Matter. He maintains that God draws the forms of all created things from Prime Matter and also creates the ten Intelligences that relate to the heavenly spheres. He also modifies another of Ibn Sina's claims, namely, that of the immortality of the individual soul, maintaining that when the passive intellect belonging to human beings becomes, under the influence of active intellect, the 'acquired intellect', it does indeed achieve immortality, although not as an individual immortal soul; it endures only as an element within the collective intelligence of humanity as a whole.[9]

Against al-Ghazali's view that the world was created by God at a certain point in time, and against the teaching of Islam that God created the world out of nothing, Ibn Rushd argues that if God had created the world at a particular time, this would mean that God underwent some change. But this, he says, is not possible, since God is perfect and changeless. He claims, for the same reasons, that the universe is eternal, since its coming to an end would also imply a change in God. Change is possible within the world, but not to its totality.

Many of Ibn Rushd's claims in *The Incoherence of 'The Incoherence'* turn out to be contrary to the tenets of Islamic faith. How then does he work to resolve the tensions between faith and philosophy? A full answer to that question is not possible here but an outline of his strategy and of its consequences can be given.

The disfavour with which philosophy was regarded in the Muslim world of the twelfth century led Ibn Rushd to write *Fasl al-Maqal* (The Decisive Treatise), a book which defends philosophy in the face of its condemnation as a pagan science. *Fasl* was written from a legal point of view and its stated purpose was 'to examine, from the standpoint of the study of the law, whether the study of philosophy and logic is allowed by the law, or prohibited, or commanded – either by way of recommendation or as obligatory'.[10] In it, Ibn Rushd writes as the learned judge he undoubtedly was. He invokes the Qur'an and the Traditions (**hadith**) derived from it to justify his conclusion that philosophic reasoning is an entirely legitimate enterprise. He cites the Qur'an exhortations to study the natural universe and interprets them as instructions to reason about the universe in order to secure knowledge of it. From such foundations he draws the inference that philosophical activity is obligatory for those who have the ability to engage in it, and that logic is its essential tool, the use of which is learned only through a study of ancient Greek philosophy. In this first part of the *Fasl* he proposes that there are three ways of attaining to religious knowledge and that the three ways correspond to three types of human mentality. These three types are, first, simple and unlearned persons for whom faith and authority are sufficient; second, persons able to engage in debate and who therefore require reasons to substantiate their beliefs; and third, those who demand secure arguments and absolute demonstrations of their tenets of belief.

Ibn Rushd next propounds a view that is clearly meant to rebut objections which point out that since philosophy is often at variance with scripture, it cannot be a study that scripture either condones or requires. He boldly claims that

> since this religion is true and summons to the study which leads to the knowledge of the Truth, we, the Muslim community, know definitely that demonstrative study does

not lead to [conclusions] conflicting with what scripture has given us; for truth does not oppose truth but accords with it and bears witness to it.[11]

What Ibn Rushd seems to be declaring here is that any apparent contradictions are not actual contradictions and can, by proper study, be reconciled in such a way as to be understood as a single truth; that the inner meaning of scripture, correctly interpreted, will be seen as consonant with the reasoned truths of philosophy.

Ibn Rushd then deals with the kind of reconciliation that should take place between scripture and philosophy. The reconciliation requires metaphorical or allegorical interpretations of scripture that are able to provide several levels of meaning for a passage or sentence. Of course, not any interpretation will do. An allegorical understanding must not contradict what is affirmed in any other part of the Qur'an, so there is a limitation on the scope of possible interpretations. Once again, it is philosophers who are seen to possess the ability and so the right to produce allegorical interpretations of scripture, for it is they who have conducted a reasoned enquiry into the real nature of the universe and who can therefore recognize the hidden unity of scripture and philosophy. Philosophy, he holds, is essentially plain and unmysterious, even though it is also a deep and difficult discipline. Scripture is imaginative, rich in meanings and implications; but both philosophy and scripture are founded on the same truths.

Over the centuries Ibn Rushd has been somewhat glibly accused of promulgating a 'double-truth' theory of the reconciliation of scripture with philosophy. This is the view that there is one truth for the masses and another for those of intellectual sophistication. Recent careful study of Ibn Rushd's writings shows that this is a distortion of his view; that he repeatedly affirms that both revelation and reason are true and are in fundamental agreement, and that the same truth is embodied in both kinds of exposition although their modes of presentation differ. He has recently been succinctly described by Ian Netton as 'a proponent of a multivocal expression of truth' and in commenting on the status of such multivocal expressions of truth, Netton has argued that we may

validly conceive of a universe of intellectual discourse in which contradictions flourish . . . and examine the articulation and inter-relatedness of those units of contradiction as they contribute towards the global structure of the discourse itself: the actual truth or otherwise of the individual units of such discourse may be left as a matter of faith rather than proof or reason.[12]

At the end of the twelfth century, the dynamic development of five centuries of Arabic philosophy waned rapidly in its own part of the world, but its influence then became potent in the West. The controversial doctrine of 'double-truth' became linked to the movement known as Averroism that began to emerge in the scholastic communities of thirteenth-century Europe with the arrival of eagerly awaited translations of Ibn Rushd's commentaries on Aristotle. Averroism flourished from the fourteenth to the eighteenth centuries and became the focus of numerous confrontations between scholarly Aristotelians and Christian theologians intent on resolving the crisis between the reasoned demonstrations of philosophy and the pronouncements of religion. It provoked severe criticism from church leaders and was condemned in 1209, 1215, 1240, 1270 and 1277 for its assertion of the eternity of matter and its denial of personal immortality as well as for the presumed doctrine of 'double-truth'. St Thomas Aquinas produced sedulously detailed attacks on Averroism, the best-known of which is *De Unitate Intellectus* (On the Unity of the Intellect). Aquinas was convinced that it was possible to make a coherent intellectual whole from Aristotelian philosophy and Christian theology and although he recognized the cogency of Ibn Rushd's expositions of Aristotle he was entirely opposed to the kind of reconciliation advanced by Averroist thought.

It is sometimes remarked that just as Aristotelianism was different from Aristotle's philosophy, so was Averroism different from the philosophy of Ibn Rushd. Ibn Rushd, the Commentator, achieved considerable success in realizing his ambition to purify corruptions of Aristotle, the Philosopher, even though his understanding of the Philosopher was marred by the elision of Aristotelian with Platonic thought. His seriousness and dedication show themselves in all he wrote, and especially in the following words:

> I believe that this man [Aristotle] is a rule in nature and an example which nature has devised to demonstrate supreme human perfection . . . It is therefore well said that he was created and given to us by divine providence that we might know whatever can be known.[13]

Notes

1 For further details of al-Ghazali's views in *The Incoherence of the Philosophers* see the essay on al-Ghazali in this book, especially pp. 37–43.

2 Since Ibn Rushd was born in Spain, it is questionable whether he should feature in a book about Eastern philosophers. He is included because of the importance of his thought in the mainstream of Islamic philosophy.

3 This story is related in most accounts of Ibn Rushd's life, but opinions vary concerning exactly when the event took place. See, for example, G. Hourani (trans. and int.), *Averroes on the Harmony of Religion and Philosophy*, London: Luzac, 1961, pp. 12, 13 and M. Fakhry, *A History of Islamic Philosophy*, London: Longman, 1983, pp. 270–1.

4 Any injunction of the **Sunnah**, the established law of Islam, was declared in **hadith**, statements of traditions authenticated by tracing their origins to the words or deeds of Muhammad the Prophet.

5 Dominique Urvoy, *Ibn Rushd* (Averroes), trans. Olivia Stewart, London: Routledge, 1991, p. 26.

6 For more on the *Theologica*, see the essay on al-Kindi in this book, pp. 21–5.

7 In Paul Edwards (ed.), 'Averroes', *Encyclopaedia of Philosophy*, New York: Macmillan, 1967, p. 21.

8 See the essays on al-Ghazali and Ibn Sina in this book, pp. 37–43 and 31–6.

9 For a fuller account of this see the essay on Ibn Sina in this book, especially pp. 34–5.

10 Hourani, op. cit., repr. 1976, p. 19.

11 Ibid., p. 22.

12 Ian Richard Netton, *Allah Transcendent: Studies in the Structure and Semiotics of Islamic Philosophy, Theology and Cosmology*, London and New York: Routledge, 1989, p. 328.

13 Quoted in G. Leff, *Mediaeval Thought: St Augustine to Ockham*, Harmondsworth: Penguin Books, 1958.

Ibn Rushd's major writings

Commentaries on:

Aristotle's *Categories, Posterior Analytics, Physics, On the Heavens, On Generation and Corruption, On the Soul, The Short Physical Treatises, Metaphysics, Rhetoric*
Plato's *Republic*
Porphyry's *Isagoge*

Medical works:

Kitab al-Kulliyat fi-l-Tibb (*Compendium on Medicine*)
A commentary on Ibn Sina's *The Canons of Medicine*

Other works:

Tahafut al-Tahafut (The Incoherence of 'The Incoherence')
Fasl al-Maqal (The Decisive Treatise)

Some translations:

Butterworth, C.E. (ed., trans. and int.), *Averroes' Middle Commentaries on Aristotle's Categories and De Interpretatione*, Princeton: Princeton University Press, 1983

Hourani, G. (trans. and int.), *Averroes on the Harmony of Religion and Philosophy*, London: Luzac, 1961; repr. 1967 and 1976

Lerner, R. (trans. and int.), *Averroes on Plato's 'Republic'*, Ithaca, NY: Cornell University Press, 1974

Van den Bergh, S. (trans. and int.), *Averroes' Tahafut al-Tahafut* (The Incoherence of 'The Incoherence'), 2 vols, London: Luzac, 1954, repr. 1969 and 1978

A fuller list of Ibn Rushd's works, and details of translations of them are in Leaman, *Averroes and His Philosophy*, pp. 197–201. There is also a very useful bibliographical guide in Urvoy (listed below), pp. 134–148.

See also in this book

Muhammad, al-Kindi, al-Farabi, Ibn Sina, al-Ghazali, Ibn Rushd, Muhammad Iqbal

Sources and further reading

Copleston, F., *A History of Philosophy*, vol. 2, pt II, New York: Image Books, 1962

Davidson, Herbert A., *Alfarabi, Avicenna and Averroes*, Oxford: Oxford University Press, 1992

Fakhry, Majid, *A History of Islamic Philosophy*, London: Longman, 1983

Genequand, C., *Ibn Rushd's Metaphysics*, Leiden: Brill, 1984

Hourani, Albert, *Islam in European Thought*, Cambridge: Cambridge University Press, 1991

Leaman, Oliver, 'Ibn Rushd on happiness and philosophy', *Studia Islamica*, vol. LII, 1980, pp. 167–81

Leaman, Oliver, *Averroes and His Philosophy*, Oxford: Clarendon Press, 1988

Leff, G., *Mediaeval Thought: St Augustine to Ockham*, Harmondsworth: Penguin Books, 1958

Mohammed, O.N., *Averroes' Doctrine of Immortality: A Matter of Controversy*, Waterloo, Ontario, 1984

Urvoy, D., *Ibn Rushd (Averroes)*, trans. Olivia Stewart, London and New York: Routledge, 1991

IBN ARABI (MUYIDDIN AL-ARABI) 1165–1240 CE

Ibn Arabi was an Islamic mystic, a Sufi, whose ideas occupy a significant position in the development of Islamic theology and practice. His thought is sometimes excluded from philosophical surveys on the grounds that he was a religious visionary rather than a philosopher, yet the intensity and penetration of his mystical thinking and its grounding in a conceptually rich account of the relationship between God and humankind have always invited and received philosophical comment and consideration. In particular, his doctrine of the Unity of Being, espousing the notion of a single Reality that both transcends and is manifest in the universe, has stimulated lively debate amongst Islamic intellectuals over many centuries.

Ibn Arabi's written output was prodigious and many of his works survive, some of them still in manuscript form.[1] Much of his writing possesses a poetic and visionary quality that has given inspiration and spiritual impetus to his readers. His works range from large treatises to letters, poems and fragments of wisdom, and they deal with a wide range of subjects that include cosmology, theology, metaphysics, mysticism and love. His largest book, *Al-Futuhat al-makkiyya* (The Meccan Revelations) has 560 chapters and treats chiefly with metaphysics. It has been remarked that this work is 'a veritable compendium of the esoteric sciences in Islam which surpasses in scope and depth anything that has been composed before or since'.[2] In the course of this work Ibn Arabi declared more than once that it was divinely inspired: 'God dictated to me everything that I have written through the angel of inspiration'.[3]

Ibn Arabi was born into a prosperous Arab family in Murcia, in Southern Spain, and received his early education in Seville. He was fortunate in being able to lead the kind of life suited to his natural propensities for reflection, spiritual experience and intellectual enquiry, and he enjoyed numerous encounters with religious and philosophical thinkers of his time. While still a young man he was for two years guided and instructed by Fatimah of Cordoba, a woman saint of great age and wisdom. At some time during a tour of the cities of Andalusia and Tunis he met and talked with Ibn Rushd (Averroes) at Cordoba.[4] Later he travelled extensively in the Muslim East and lived for a while in Makkah [Mecca] where he wrote his two major works, *Al-Futuhat al-makkiyya* (The Meccan Revelations), already mentioned, and *Fusus al hikam* (The Bezels of Wisdom). This latter is his best-known work and was probably written in 1229. Each of its twenty-seven 'bezels' (a bezel is a container in which a stone or jewel rests) is an exposition and examination of the life of a prophet regarded as a 'jewel', or 'bezel', of Islam. In 1223 Ibn Arabi settled in Damascus and it was there that he died, twelve years later, at the age of 75.

Sufism is a movement within Islam and is not, in itself, a philosophy. It describes a type of experience arising from reflection on the **Qur'an** [Koran] and the **hadith**, or Tradition. The name 'Sufi' is generally described as deriving from *suf*, meaning 'coarse wool', and as referring to the woollen garments worn by the early Sufis, but not all commentators agree about this derivation. The Sufi aim is mystical experience and communion with God, achieved mainly by a rigorous asceticism and ritual devotion.[5] The movement began in the eighth century as a predominantly ascetic one, perhaps as a reaction to the indulgences and high living resulting from riches acquired through the conquests of the Arab armies in the seventh century. The extreme austerity of early Sufism developed into practices that cultivated trance states, ecstasies and 'intoxication': feelings of being absorbed into a union with the divine reality. Such experiences were often life-changing and, like the Platonic seeker who struggled upwards from the darkness of the cave to find illumination but then returned to the cave to urge others towards the light, there were Sufis who wanted to share their joy and love with others. These men promulgated Sufi views and practices and the movement became popular. By the eleventh century it had attracted participants and disciples from all sections of Islam in Persia, Central Asia and India. Wherever Sufism flourished its exponents formed centres for education and evangel-izing among unbelievers and converts. Their practices included special breathing exercises, meditations of remembrance, chanting the name of God and dancing. They were sometimes known as 'dervishes' and, in North Africa, 'marabouts'. The 'whirling dervishes' of Konya in ancient Turkey were well known for their frenzied rotatory dancing. Sufist spiritual progress was delineated by a series of 'stages' through which the worshipper moved from repentance and renunciation to endurance of hardship, states of trance and vision, and mystical experience of the love of God. The Sufi orders were rarely segregated or austerely remote from ordinary people. The main element in their worship was remembrance of God (*dhikr*) and there was emphasis on a friendliness to everyone and an ethic of service to those in need.[6]

It is not difficult to see that Sufist claims to exalted states and to the achievement of mystical union with God were bound to have, at the very least, a disturbing effect on an Islamic orthodoxy that relied for its strength on the strict ordering of outward conduct rather than on the cultivation of ecstatic personal and inner experience as espoused by Sufism. The implications of Sufi doctrine for theology were radical and serious. It impacted also on philosophy, politics and education and in particular on jurisprudence which, in Islam, dominates and ordains conduct in every aspect of both personal and public life. At the heart of the concern of the jurists of orthodoxy was the thought that an unqualified and personal union with God was something wholly contrary to, perhaps even blasphemous in respect of, the established teachings of Islam.

It was against this background of, on the one hand, an increasingly organized and articulated culture of orthodoxy and, on the other, the burgeoning dissemination of Sufi practices and the growth of its communities and Orders that al-Ghazali, in the late eleventh century, sought to reconcile the exoteric and the esoteric of Islam.[7] He defended the Sufism to which he was a convert by arguing for the legitimacy of its practices and beliefs, seeking to show that they were grounded in the verses of the Qur'an and the Tradition, and pointing out their concordance with juridically established doctrine. A century later, Ibn Arabi set himself the task of making Sufist thought even more explicit and acceptable to those who were suspicious and disapproving of it.

Ibn Arabi's central doctrine of the Unity of Being, already mentioned, is probably best approached by first making clear what it is not. In asserting a unity of being he was not espousing a pantheism in which God and the universe are taken to be identical. Nor has his doctrine anything to do with philosophical **monism**, nor even, it is maintained, with panentheism, the latter being the belief that God includes but is not exhausted by all that is known in sense experience. Such beliefs would certainly have been unacceptable to orthodoxy and would have been regarded as opening a way to polytheism by implying a ubiquitous divinity. In Ibn Arabi's doctrine, God is always transcendent and is never contained by the universe. He declares God to be eternal, infinite, the cause of all things and manifest in every thing: there is nothing before God and nothing after God; he is his creation but he is also more than his creation; he is Pure Essence, or Pure Being. The unity of being Ibn Arabi affirms is 'the integration of paradoxes and ontological contrasts . . . the union of all the diverse qualities which characterize the order of multiplicity'.[8]

Ibn Arabi further holds that God as Essence cannot be known but that knowledge of him may be attained through knowledge of his attributes, and knowledge of his attributes is gained through certain forms of human thought. However, what is thus known is not knowledge of the attributes as they are in Reality, but only of them as they appear to the human mind: manifestations and revelations of God are shaped by or conform to the natures of their recipients. This somewhat Kantian notion means that there is no possibility of asserting an identity of the human mind with the mind of God, but in a larger dimension that embraces the whole nature of things as well as the nature of the recipients and their revelations and the manifestations, everything is encompassed by Divine Reality and this encompassing is what brings about the unity that ultimately reconciles all opposites and differences without abolishing ontological distinctions.

Ibn Arabi's account, outlined above, has been likened to the neo-Platonism of Plotinus (205–270 CE).[9] In Plotinus' system there is a hierarchy in which the ultimate reality is the One, the ineffable and unknowable source of everything. Below the One are levels of being, each related to or emanating from the level above it, but gradually descending from the perfect to the less perfect, from the light of the celestial to the dark heaviness of matter, though always with the possibility of each level achieving an excellence appropriate to it. Both Plotinus and Ibn Arabi believed that some kind of mystical union with God was the highest achievement for humanity.

Ibn Arabi's comparable hierarchical system has five levels. At its peak is the absolutely transcendent and unknowable Divine Essence (al-dhat). God's connexion with his universe is mediated through qualities manifest in the first level of self-determinination deriving from the Divine Essence. This means it is possible for Ibn Arabi to say that God is above all qualities and also that he is not without qualities. These qualities are without number and signify the possibilities immanent in the universe. In the Qur'an they are referred to by a group of Names and through contemplation of their manifestations in the world the devout Sufi may seek spiritual understanding and realization.

When Ibn Arabi discusses the creation of the universe he likens it to the production of a mirror in which God is reflected. This mirror is unpolished except in respect of the creation of the human essence, or soul, which is the realization of divine qualities: a microcosm of the macrocosm. In most human manifestations the divine qualities are not completely expressed, but in Muhammad they are; he is the Perfect Person, the prototype of the Universe and the highest realization of the qualities. The Perfect Person is the Word or Logos of God. He manifests all possibilities and is the model of all a human being might be, containing within himself all the qualities that the divine Names signify. The meaning of this Logos is succinctly enshrined in the *hadith* that states: 'I was a hidden treasure and I wanted to be known, so I created the world'.[10]

Ibn Arabi's conception of the human pilgrimage is entirely consonant with his hierarchical metaphysic. Humankind, having come into being by descending through the five levels must endeavour to make its journey back to God and return to a union with him. This return, if it is achieved, does not find its ultimate fulfilment in a loss of self through a mystical identification with God, but in an awareness of the unity and harmony of the self with the Divine Qualities. Just as the universe is a mirror in which God contemplates himself, so is God a mirror in which the mystic sees his own reality.

There are critical examinations of Ibn Arabi's ideas that judge his claims concerning the compatibility of the transcendence of God with God's manifestation in the universe as incoherent. This means that he is still judged by some commentators to be a pantheistic monist whose teaching is contrary to Islamic orthodoxy. Nevertheless, the testimony of mystical experience, not just in Islam but from within many religions, is remarkable and impressive in its unanimity in affirming sublime experiences consonant with the kind of claims Ibn Arabi articulates.

Notes

1 The Ibn Arabi Society estimates that Ibn Arabi wrote over 350 works. The Society is based in Oxford (PO Box 892, Oxford OX2 7XL) and has a web site that publishes papers and articles on Ibn Arabi.
2 In Seyyed Hossein Nasr, *Three Muslim Sages*, Cambridge, Mass.: Harvard University Press, 1964, p. 98.
3 Ibid.
4 See the essay on Ibn Rushd, pp. 43–50 in this book.
5 In Islamic languages a *Sufi* is one who has already achieved the condition of union with God, and the follower of Sufism is called a *fakir*, meaning 'poor in spirit'. See Nasr, op. cit., p. 156, note 3, and the essay on Vardhamana in this book, pp. 69–74.
6 Like many religious movements that come to have a popular appeal, Sufism has from time to time through the centuries been exploited and misused by charlatans. In the first half of the twentieth century some Sufist ideas were adopted by the movement propagating 'the perennial philosophy'. The late twentieth century saw something of a revivial of genuine piety and uncorrupt practice.
7 See the essay on al-Ghazali in this book, pp. 37–43.
8 Discussed in Nasr, op. cit., p. 105.
9 Plotinus is also discussed in the essays on al-Kindi and al-Farabi in this book.
10 Nasr, op.cit. p. 166, note 67.

Ibn Arabi's writings

The Meccan Revelations (*Al-Futuhat al-makkiyya*) There are no English editions of this work. There is a 4-volume Arabic edition published by Dar-Al-Sadr, Beirut (no date). Extended extracts are in W. Chittick, *Self-revelation of God*, New York: SUNY, 1998
The Treatise on Unity (*Risalat al-ahadiyah*), trans. A. Weir as 'Translation of

an Arab Manuscript in the Hunterian Collection, Glasgow University',
Journal of the Royal Asiatic Society (Malayan Branch), October 1901, pp.
809–25

The Wisdom of the Prophets (Fusus al-Hikam) trans. Fr. to Eng. by Angela Culme-
Seymour, Gloucestershire: Beshara Publications, 1998

Bezels of Wisdom, (Fusus al-Hikam) trans. Ralph Austin, London: SPCK, 1980

See also in this book

Introduction to Islamic Philosophy, al-Ghazali, Ibn Rushd

Sources and further reading

Arberry, A.J., *Sufism: An Account of the Mystics of Islam*, London: Allen & Unwin,
1950

Carr, Brian and Mahalingam, Indira, *Companion Encyclopedia of Asian Philosophy*,
London: Routledge, 1997

Chittick, William, *The Sufi Path of Knowledge: Ibn al Arabi's Metaphysic of
Imagination*, New York: Albany State University Press, 1989

—— *The Self-discourse of God: Principles of Ibn Arabi's Cosmology*, New York:
SUNY Press, 1998

Corbin, Henry, *Creative Imagination in the Sufism of Ibn 'Arabi*, Princeton:
Princeton University Press, 1969; now called *Alone with the Alone: Creative
Imagination in the Sufism of Ibn Arabi*, 1998

Fahkry, Majid, *A History of Islamic Philosophy*, New York: Columbia University
Press, 1970

Nasr, Seyyed Hossein, *Three Muslim Sages*, Cambridge, Mass.: Harvard
University Press, 1964

Shah, Idries, *The Way of the Sufi*, Harmondsworth: Penguin Books, 1974

Sharif, M.M., *A History of Muslim Philosophy*, 2 vols, Wiesbaden: Harrassowitz,
1963–6

MUHAMMAD IQBAL 1876–1938 CE

Iqbal was a poet as well as a philosopher. His philosophical ideas were
at first rejected but later revered in the Muslim world. His education
at European universities revealed to him the gulf that lay between
the developing scientific culture of the West and the entrenched
traditionalism of the Islamic world. At the same time it showed him
that there were relationships and affinities between Muslim and
western philosophies. He saw the possibility of a fruitful interaction of
Islamic and western ideas and sought to bring about the compatibility
of religious faith with philosophical reasoning, drawing on the
work of Hegel, Bergson and Whitehead to provide a philosophical
grounding for his synthesis. There is a strong vein of **Sufist** mysticism

in Iqbal's philosophy as well as in his poetry.[1] It is especially apparent in his analysis of the concept of God and in his poem 'Secret of the Self' (1915), which illustrates his concept of 'selfhood' (*khudi*) and which did much to revitalize the intellectual life of Muslims in India. In 1930 he became president of the Muslim League and proposed that there should be a Muslim India within India. In 1947, nine years after his death, the founding of Pakistan turned his proposal into a fact.

Iqbal's career was a distinguished one and he became known worldwide. He lived life intensely. His parents were deeply religious and he seems to have shared their dispositions to mysticism. He was educated first at the Scotch Mission College in Sialkut and then at the Government College at Lahore. At Lahore he was taught by Sir Thomas Arnold and began to make his name as a poet. In 1905 he travelled to Europe to study law at Lincoln's Inn and then at Trinity College, Cambridge. While in Cambridge he attended lectures given by two British philosophers, John McTaggart and James Ward. It was there, too, that he established a relationship with the Muslim League. He returned to Lahore in 1908 to pursue the professions of lawyer and college lecturer. In the years that followed he achieved fame as a poet, wrote numerous articles for journals and the press, and prepared the drafts of the lectures that constitute his *Reconstruction of Religious Thought in Islam*. Six of these seven lectures were delivered in Madras in 1928 and the seventh in England. In 1932 Iqbal visited France and there met Henri Bergson and also Louis Massignon, an orientalist with a profound knowledge of Sufism. He became more and more convinced that there were the very closest affinities between Bergson's account of Time and the views of Muslim mystics. In 1933, after he returned again to Lahore, his health began to fail. In 1935 he was unable to accept an invitation to give the Rhodes lecture in Oxford because of frequent attacks of asthma. He died in 1938 and was buried with great honour near the steps of Badshahi mosque in Lahore.

Iqbal saw his main purpose as that of transforming Islam by infusing its spirituality with the dynamism and vitality of the West, but without depriving Islam of its own moral values and cohesion. He regarded European intellectual culture as a development, albeit in some respects a wayward one, of the Islamic culture of the Middle Ages. 'Our only fear', he wrote, 'is that the dazzling exterior of European culture may arrest our movement and we may fail to reach the true inwardness of that culture.'[2]

In the *Reconstruction* he examines traditional arguments for the existence of God and concludes that none of them constitutes a proof. He then argues that materialist doctrines fail to provide a satisfactory account of the true nature of things and that we have to recognize that reality is ultimately vitalistic in character: that it is matter and mind together, in an ever-changing and active process, that constitute the totality of a universe in which Allah is perpetually creative. In this vitalist account of reality Iqbal draws freely on Bergson's conception of pure Time as a flowing sequence of continuous events which we are sometimes able to experience with an immediacy that connects us with the creative energy of the cosmos. But he rejects Bergson's view of the place of thought in the cosmic scheme. Bergson had maintained that thought worked with static concepts that reduced the burgeoning flux of reality to a series of stationary points, thereby yielding our notions of space and time.[3] But for Iqbal, thought is much more than an intellectual capacity for organizing and classifying the items of experience. It is, he says, 'as much organic as life . . . In conscious experience life and thought permeate each other. They form a unity. Thought, therefore, in its true nature is identical with life.'[4] From this fundamental notion of the identity of thought and life Iqbal endeavours to develop an account of reality that contains no hard distinctions between reason and other modes of experience, and that emphasizes its dynamic and fluctuating nature as well as its total encompassment by a creative God who is 'the First and the Last, the Visible and the Invisible'.[5] What he wishes to reject is the notion that thought is 'an agency working on things from without'. He writes:

> our present situation necessitates the dualism of thought and being. Every act of human knowledge bifurcates what might on proper enquiry turn out to be a unity into a self that knows and a confronting 'other' that is known . . . The true significance . . . will appeal only if we are able to show that the human situation is not final and that thought and being are ultimately one.[6]

To support this account he cites a wide range of theories and concepts derived from a range of philosophers of widely differing views.

The concept of self, or ego (khudi), is central to Iqbal's thought. He describes the self as being formed in the encountering and overcoming of obstructions in the physical universe. He writes of both a metaphysical and an ethical self. The metaphysical self is 'that indescribable feeling of "I" which forms the basis of the uniqueness of each individual'.[7] The ethical self is 'self-reliance, self-confidence, even self-assertion . . . in the interest of life and the power to stick to the cause of truth even in the face of death'.[8] The self, according to Iqbal, is partly determined, partly free, and is able to increase its freedom by drawing closer to God. It is capable of a personal immortality, achieved through the consolidation of its singularity by means of allegiance to a virtuous way of life. The self, he says, is distinct, though not apart, from God, who is the Ultimate Ego.

Iqbal's concept of God is a complex one. It has been described as panentheistic rather than pantheistic, that is, as conceiving of God as both including and transcending the world rather than as wholly identical with it. In this his thought is markedly Sufistic in character in that it permits the possibility and desirability of a mystical union of human beings with God and of the aspiration to a bliss that is attainable during a person's life on earth rather than in the life to come. This is entirely contrary to the orthodox Qur'anic doctrines of the absolute transcendence or otherness of God and of the divine ordering and knowledge of every detail of the universe and its life.

Iqbal endeavours to resolve the tensions between his own ideas and those of traditional Islamic thought by means of a radical inter-pretation of sections of the Qur'an. For example, he connects parts of *suras* 25 and 54 with Bergson's account of Time, declaring that the Qur'an, with characteristic simplicity, is alluding to the serial and non-serial aspects of duration. But it is extremely difficult to detect any such allusion in the verses, which are as follows:

> Put your trust in the Ever-living who never dies. Celebrate His praise . . . In six days He created the heavens and the earth and all that lies between them, and then ascended His throne . . . We have made all things according to a fixed decree. We command but once. Our will is done in the twinkling of an eye.[9]

Iqbal's broad grasp of western philosophy is impressive but he does not use it well in the service of his endeavour. In his employment of major concepts and ideas he tends to transmogrify their primary meanings by imposing unjustified interpretations on them or by reckless extrapolations from them. Many of his references to well-known philosophers amount to little more than name-dropping. Majid Fakhry, in his *History of Islamic Philosophy*, has remarked of him that

> Very often the multiplication of authorities, ancient or modern, Western or Islamic, is done at such a pace that the reader is left breathless. In the scope of six pages, for instance, the following names are cited: Berkeley, Whitehead, Einstein,

Russell, Zeno, Newton, al-Ashari, Ibn Hazm, Bergson, Cantor and Ouspensky – to mention only the principal figures or authorities.[10]

In spite of such failings there is something of a visionary quality in Iqbal's perception and appreciation of issues that were of profound practical significance for Muslim cultures and peoples. He wanted to reawaken the Islamic intellect to a fresh engagement with the kind of thought and discussion that had characterized the heyday of Islamic philosophy in the eleventh and twelfth centuries CE. His high hope was that he would resolve the tensions he found between eastern and western cultures; and that he would effect that resolution in depth, by means of philosophy.

Notes

1 A Sufi is a Muslim mystic for whom the inward devotional life is of great importance. The name is probably derived from the word for the white woollen clothing worn by Sufis (*sufi* = coarse wool. See the essay on Ibn Arabi in this book.)
2 In Muhammad Iqbal, *The Reconstruction of Religious Thought in Islam*, Lahore, Pakistan: 1968, p. 7.
3 For a fuller account of Bergson's views see Diané Collinson, *Fifty Major Philosophers*, London: Routledge, 1991, pp. 130–4.
4 Iqbal, op. cit., p. 52.
5 Ibid., p. 31.
6 Ibid.
7 In Syed Abdul Vahid, *Thoughts and Reflections of Iqbal*, Lahore, Pakistan: 1964, p. 236.
8 Ibid.
9 In *The Koran*, trans. N.J. Dawood, Harmondsworth: Penguin Books, 1959, p. 207 and p. 112.
10 In Majid Fakhry, *A History of Islamic Philosophy*, London: Longman, 1983, p. 354.

Iqbal's major writing

The Development of Metaphysics in Iran, Cambridge: Cambridge University Press, 1908 (Iqbal's PhD thesis, submitted to Munich University)
The Reconstruction of Religious Thought in Islam, Lahore: 1968
'McTaggart's philsophy', in *Proceedings of the Aristotelian Society*, vol. IV, 1932
Mysteries of Selflessness (Rumuz-i-Bikhundi), trans. A. Arberry, London: Murray, 1953

See also in this book

Muhammad, al-Kindi, al-Farabi, Ibn Sina, al-Ghazali, Ibn Rushd, Ibn Arabi

Sources and further reading

Gilani, Kamran, *Cultural Images in the post-Iqbal World*, Lahore: Bazm-i-Iqbal, 1988

Malik, Hafeez (ed.), *Iqbal: Poet-Philosopher of Pakistan*, New York and London: Columbia University Press, 1971

Qadir, C.A., *Philosophy and Science in the Islamic World*, London: Croom Helm, 1988

Raschid, M.S., *Iqbal's Concept of God*, London and Boston: Kegan Paul International, 1981

Schimmel, Annemarie, *Gabriel's Wing: A Study into the Religious Ideas of Sir Muhammad Iqbal*, Leiden: Brill, 1963

Part 3

INDIAN PHILOSOPHY

INTRODUCTION

The tradition of recorded philosophical thought of the Indian subcontinent is as ancient, rich and subtle as any in the world. With roots in the insights of *rishis*, or seers, in the second millennium BCE, the tradition has developed continuously since that time, diversifying into the many schools of Hindu thought, together with Buddhism, Sikhism and Jainism. All the great philosophical questions are investigated by the thinkers in this tradition: in all the branches of philosophy, the great options have been explored with rigour and thoroughness, and this central philosophical business goes on to this day.

The first evidence of philosophical thought occurs in the great collections of hymns we know as the Vedas.[1] As Radhakrishnan puts it, in the *Rig Veda* one finds generally 'the earliest phase of religious consciousness where we have not so much the commandments of priests as the outpourings of poetic minds who were struck by the immensity of the universe and the inexhaustible mystery of life'.[2] Most of the hymns are addressed to individual deities, but there are places in which a polytheistic account of reality is found wanting, and there is an intuition that there must be a single first principle behind all phenomena. Thus, in the important 'Creation Hymn' (S: *Nasadiya*) it is stated that 'The gods came afterwards, with the creation of this universe'.[3] Before the gods and this universe:

> There was neither death nor immortality then. There was no distinguishing sign of night nor of day. That one [S: *tad ekam*] breathed, windless, by its own impulse. Other than that there was nothing beyond.[4]

Prior to the universe there was *tad ekam*, something self-sufficient, to which no distinctions apply.

Hints such as these are taken up and developed philosophically in the *Upanisads*, constituting collectively one of the world's greatest and most seminal philosophical works.[5] The thought of the *Upanisads* stands to Indian thought much as does that of Plato and Aristotle to the West or that of Lao Tzu and Confucius to China: their leading ideas set the philosophical agenda for their tradition, and they have remained a living source of inexhaustible significance ever since they were composed. Though the work of many hands and many years, the *Upanisads* set out a coherent philosophical outlook. The world of ordinary human experience, of individuals standing in mutual causal relations in space and time (in S the **samsara**) is not reality. Reality is a oneness or absolute, changeless, perfect and eternal, **Brahman**. Again, human nature is not exhausted by its *samsaric* elements of body and individual consciousness or mind (S: **jiva**): there is further present in each one of us an immortal element, our true self, the **atman**. The *atman* has no form, and whatever is without form is without limit; whatever is without limit is omnipresent, and whatever is omnipresent and immortal is God. This is the basis for one of the most striking and central of *Upanisadic* doctrines, the assertion that Brahman and *atman* are in some sense the same:

> Containing all works, containing all desires, containing all tastes, encompassing this whole world, without speech, without concern, this is the self [*atman*] of mine within the heart; this is Brahman. Into him, I shall enter, on departing hence.[6]

It is this doctrine which is summed up in the phrase 'that art thou' (S: **tat tvam asi**), 'that' referring to Brahman.

If reality is Brahman, eternal, immutable, perfect, then an account must be given of the origin and status of the ordinary world of change, the *samsara*. The view given in the *Upanisads* to explain the existence of the *samsara* is that it is **lila**, or sport, an expression of Brahman's constitutive delight (S: **ananda**). The *samsara* is not reality but **maya** (S: illusion), and to take the phenomenal world to be the ultimate reality is to be in the condition of **avidya** or spiritual blindness. By means of suitable disciplines, we can overcome the condition of *avidya* and pierce the veil of *maya*: if this is done, our true self is revealed, and this true self is Brahman. To achieve this rare state is **moksa** or release from the cycle of birth and death which is the *samsara*, and *moksa* is the goal of life in the *Upanisadic* philosophy. Only by attaining release can we be liberated from the law of **karma**, the otherwise inescapable visiting on us of the consequences of our actions which rules the cycle of repeated births and deaths in the *samsara*.

This set of ideas is the philosophical core of the *Upanisads*, and it involves many intractable philosophical problems. These are explored in some detail in many of the essays in this section, which deal with the ways in which some leading Indian thinkers have tried to articulate precise answers to questions such as that of the exact relation of Brahman to the *samsara*; the nature of *atman* and its relation to Brahman; the status of the material world and its framework of space and time; why the *samsara* should involve pain and evil, and the means and nature of release. The earliest attempt to systematize the *Upanisadic* doctrines is the *Brahma Sutra* of Badarayana, which then itself becomes one of the foundations of the future of the tradition.

Post-*Upanisadic* thought in the Indian tradition is conventionally divided into the two broad classes of orthodox (S: *astika*) and unorthodox (S: *nastika*). To be orthodox in this sense is to accept the Vedas as infallible, and the orthodox schools are six in number: Samkhya; Yoga; Mimamsa; Nyaya; Vaisesika; and Vedanta. Of these, we have chosen to concentrate principally on thinkers from the Vedanta school,[7] partly because of its great importance, and partly so as to be able to give an example of how a philosophical school can develop. Sankara, Ramanuja and Madhva set out three classic sets of responses to the problems posed by *Upanisadic* ideas, and the modern thinkers included here – Vivekananda, Aurobindo, Radhakrishnan and to some extent also Gandhi – show clearly that this tradition is still a living presence.[8] The other orthodox school represented in this section is the Yoga school, introduced via its fundamental text, the *Yoga Sutras* of Patanjali. Knowledge of some of the basic *asanas* or exercises of yoga is now very widespread in the west; less so the complete philosophy which underlies them, set out in Patanjali's text.

The Indian philosophical tradition would be formidable enough were it composed of the orthodox Hindu schools alone. Yet it also includes unorthodox schools of equal philosophical sophistication and in some cases of global historical significance. Of these we have included Jainism and Buddhism. Certain practices of the Jains, like the yogic *asanas*, are relatively well known in the west, notably their scrupulous regard for all forms of life, extending to the wearing of face masks and sweeping the road before one's feet to prevent the unwitting destruction of insects. Once again less well known is the elaborate metaphysics and epistemology on which ethical practices of this kind rest, and this underlying world-view is set out below in the essay on the greatest of the founders of Jainism, Vardhamana.

In this section, Buddhism is represented by the Buddha himself, there is much more on the variety and development of Buddhist philosophy in the succeeding sections on Tibet, China, Korea and Japan, since the spread of this religion changed the philosophical and cultural histories of all these countries indelibly. The central concern of the Buddha himself was an ethical one: how to free humankind from all forms of suffering, and to this huge problem the Buddha proposes an answer. Suffering comes about through the non-satisfaction of desire, and the only way to be free of suffering is to be free of the desires which cause it. Desires are properties of the ego, and therefore the only way to be free of desires is to dissolve the ego. When the ego dissolves, what follows is enlightenment, and the condition of being free of self and desires is *nirvana*.[9]

The Buddha himself refused to speculate about the ultimate nature of reality, being concerned with the more urgent matter of the relief of suffering. Those of his followers who, broadly speaking, adopt this approach are members of the **Theravada** (S: Teaching of the Elders) school of Buddhism. Even if disinclined to speculation in certain areas, this tradition nevertheless involves a complex philosophy of its own, exemplified here in the work of Buddhaghosa. However, the urge to philosophize, to speculate, to construct a system to fill in the gaps deliberately left by the Buddha, proved irresistible, and over time there emerged a second major school of Buddhism, the **Mahayana** (S: Greater Vehicle), destined to have a major impact in Tibet, China and Japan.[10] If enlightenment is direct awareness of reality, then it is difficult to resist the urge to say something about what this reality might be. Two leading points of view developed on this question, each associated with a great philosopher in the Indian Buddhist tradition. They are the **Madhyamika** tradition of Nagarjuna and the Yogacara tradition associated with Vasubandhu. For Nagarjuna, ultimate reality can be described only as a Void (S: *sunyata*, i.e. is not properly characterizable in conceptual terms), while for Vasubandhu it can be said to be mental in nature, and Vasubandhu gives a detailed account of different types of consciousness. The influence of each of these philosophies on the development of Tibetan and East Asian Buddhism has been immense, as will become clear in the later sections of this book.

Notes

1 There are four Vedas: *Rig; Yajur; Sama;* and *Atharva.* The composition of the 1,017 hymns of the *Rig Veda* probably began around 1200 BCE and went on for some time, perhaps centuries. The word 'Veda' comes from S: *vid* = knowledge: the Vedas are 'sacred knowledge'.

2 Sarvepalli Radhakrishnan, *The Principal Upanisads*, London: Allen & Unwin, 1969, p. 30.

3 *Rig Veda*, X, 129, vs 6; trans. Wendy Doniger O'Flaherty, Harmondsworth: Penguin Books, 1981, p. 25.

4 *Rig Veda*, X, 129, vs 2; Doniger O'Flaherty, p. 25.

5 Canonically, there are said to be 108 *Upanisads*, but some scholars include over 200 works in the list. The earliest of them were probably composed in the eighth or seventh century BCE; the last ones are generally regarded as post-buddhistic. Between ten and twenty are regarded as philosophically of the first importance. The etymology of the word '*Upanisad*' is disputed. Radhakrishnan derives it from Sanskrit terms meaning 'sit down next to', a reference to the gatherings of aspirants seated at the feet of *rishis* to hear their insights. cf. Radhakrishnan, op. cit., pp. 19–20, for a survey of other etymologies.

6 *Chandogya Upanisad*, III.14.4. Radhakrishnan, op cit., p. 392.

7 **Vedanta** (S: end or completion of the Vedas) is a term used in two senses in Indian thought, and only the context makes it clear which is being employed. These senses are:
(a) the name of the orthodox Hindu school whose principal members are the subject of essays in this section;
(b) the name for the fourth and final section of a Veda. Each Veda has four sections: (i) *samhitas*: hymns to the various deities; (ii) *Brahmanas*: specifications of sacrifices and their value; (iii) *aranyakas*: 'forest treatises' which specify methods of meditation on symbols; and (iv) *Upanisads*: which deal with the path to release via knowledge (S: *jnana*).
Thus in sense (b) of 'Vedanta', the *Upanisads* are Vedanta. In this book, the term is always used in sense (a).

8 We have not space to discuss in this book the ideas and influence of one of the greatest of Hindu classics, the *Bhagavad Gita* (S: Song of the Lord), a section of the great epic *Mahabharata* which has the status of a separate work, and is the most popular spiritual classic in its tradition. Composed (probably) in the fifth century BCE, the *Gita* applies the ideas of the *Upanisads* (with which it has some verses in common) to the situation current at the time when it was written. It draws out from the austere philosophy of the *Upanisads* a path of religious devotion which gives solace to all and which all can follow. Though Brahman is still regarded as ultimate reality, the emphasis in the *Gita* is on Brahman's manifestation as *Isvara*, a personal Lord of creation, much more readily a source of devotion and consolation than an absolute. Without the *Gita*, the history of Hinduism would be unimaginably different.

9 The concepts of *moksa* and *nirvana* are very similar, and there continues to be much debate on the extent to which the Buddha was influenced by *Upanisadic* ideas (in which he would have been educated). This very large issue in the history of Indian thought we have not had space to deal with

directly. However, the similarities and differences between the ideas of the two philosophies will speak for themselves.

10 Mahayana Buddhism is conventionally said to have emerged as a distinct movement at the Second Buddhist Council, c.383 BCE.

VARDHAMANA (MAHAVIRA) 599–527 BCE[1]

Vardhamana is the central figure in the doctrine and history of Jainism. He was the last of the twenty-four teachers, the *Tirthankaras* (literally the 'ford-finders'), often called *Jinas*, who were revered for their formulation and transmission of **Jain** doctrine.

Jainism has been a major influence in Indian culture. Its fundamental tenet is that human beings can overcome the bondage and corruptions of mortal life through a stringent asceticism. In classical Jain doctrine this asceticism is practised in a rigorously ordered and detailed way that passes through fourteen *gunasthanas*, or stages, along the path to liberation from the **karma** that restricts the true reality of the soul. A significant element in Jain teaching is **ahimsa**, the scrupulous avoidance of actions that might damage or cause harm to other living creatures.

Vardhamana was an elder contemporary of the Buddha. He was born in Vessali, now Bihar, and was the second son of a Katriya chieftain. Traditional accounts relate that he lived in his parents' house until they died and his elder brother succeeded to the chieftaincy. Then, at the age of 28, he decided to embark on a spiritual training. After twelve years of an austere, nomadic life in which he practised self-mortification he was deemed to have attained **nirvana** and he began his kevaliship, a stage of life in which he was recognized as omniscient. He was accorded the title of *Jina*[2] ('the conqueror') and named the Mahavira ('great hero'). The rest of his life was spent in teaching and guiding his followers and in perfecting the Jainist doctrine inherited from his twenty-three predecessors. He died at Pava, in Bihar, of self-starvation and in accordance with monastic practice, at the age of 72. There are numerous legends about his life: that he was born of two virgins by transference of embryo; that he lived in great luxury as a young man but renounced the world at the age of 30; that he tore out five handfuls of his hair before wandering naked through India seeking release from **samsara**, the wheel of life.

Within Jainism there are some regional, linguistic and doctrinal differences, but in general its extremely ancient tradition has remained cohesive in many respects. A significant difference came about in the third century BCE at the time when the Jain community emigrated to Gujarat and Rajasthan. Its members became divided over the matter of their austere lifestyle, one group taking the view that no clothing should be worn, since Vardhamana was said to have gone naked, another preferring to adopt plain white robes. Those who advocated nakedness became known as *digambaras* ('the sky-clad') and those who wore robes as *shvetambaras* ('the white-clad'). The distinction persists to the present day, although the *digambaras* now wear clothes when they are in public. Another difference that arose between these two groups concerns the status of women. The *digambaras* do not admit women to the monastic orders because they hold that women cannot achieve liberation until they become reborn as males. *Shvetambaras* reject this idea and admit women to their monastic orders.

There is a broadly shared doctrinal basis for the variations within the tradition. The Jaina divide existing things into two categories: **jiva**, or sentient things, and **ajiva**, or non-sentient things. Every living thing is both *jiva* and *ajiva* and the belief is that through association with *ajiva* the *jiva* is prevented from realizing its immortal and true nature. Each *jiva* is entire and separate from all others. There is no doctrine of a 'fall' from grace that brings about the adhesion of the *ajiva* to *jiva*: their connection is said to be 'beginningless', although it may be altered and ultimately severed by means of the ascetic discipline.

Jains share in the Hindu belief that *karma* impedes the *jiva* in its quest for purification and immortality. They describe *karma* as a particular type or form of matter that adheres to the *jiva* in such a way as to cloud or obscure, though not radically to alter, its inherent properties. The effect of *karma* is that the *jiva* has to undergo a series of physical incarnations and the aim of the ascetic discipline taught by the *tirthankaras* is to rid the *jiva* of the physical accretions of *karma* so that its original nature may be liberated. Since *karma* is a subtle form of matter it is materially real and must be dealt with as matter. There must be a severing of all bonds that connect the *jiva* with the *ajiva* and a development of a person's reliance on spiritual qualities. Total release from physical dependency is arduous in the extreme, perhaps even impossible for most people, and there is only a very low expectation of final liberation.

An important component of the Jain discipline is the well-known practice of *ahimsa*, or non-injury, already mentioned. The aim of *ahimsa* is to separate oneself entirely from all actions and processes involving anything approaching aggression, injury, harm or possessiveness towards other living beings. Accordingly, the practice has arisen of carrying a small broom with which to brush lightly away any small living creatures that might be destroyed if a person sat or lay on them. Some Jains employ a person of another faith to wield the broom before them, in case the very act of brushing the path inadvertently destroys a small insect. With similar intent, many Jains wear masks to prevent the accidental ingestion of minute airborne creatures. For the same reason they also filter water before drinking it, and a vegetarian diet is the rule. Many Jains adopt professions that avoid activities that might lead to destructive acts.[3]

Jains do not posit a supreme or divine *jiva* or creator. According to their teaching, consciousness, or soul, is the essence of a *jiva*. The *jiva* is that which knows, and the belief is that every *jiva* is capable of complete knowledge and release, and therefore of realizing its own salvation. The *Jinas*, although profoundly revered as exemplars and for their teaching gifts, are never thought of as other than human. The rendering of *tirthankara* as 'ford-finder' exactly describes the role of the Jina: someone who has the gift of 'showing the way' to cross over to the other side and reach the eternal peace of *nirvana*.

The severity of Jain asceticism is apparent in the life of its lay people as well as in the monastic orders. There is continuity and sharing of practice between the lay and monastic groups, although the monastic life is, of course, the more regulated and single-minded, requiring complete dedication and self-vigilance. The Jain who reaches the fourth of the fourteen *gunasthanas* is deemed sufficiently free of *karma* to count as a pious layperson, but it is only at the sixth *gunasthana* that a person reaches the level at which monastic vows may be embraced. At this stage, given good health and moral fitness, and having already undergone considerable training, a person may be initiated and take vows. Thereafter the new monk must live a fully disciplined life, owning only the few possessions bequeathed at the initiation ceremony, begging for all nourishment, studying, wandering, instructing, helping others and making pilgrimages. Such a life, if there is no falling away, may result in the partial loosening of the bonds of *karma*, but it is accepted that many rebirths may be required before a person reaches the advanced *gunasthanas* and the threshold of liberation. In old age a monk may choose to die as Vardhamana did, by self-imposed fasting, and so renounce all possibility of clinging to material existence.

From the ancient traditions and from foundations established from the time of Vardhamana the Jains developed an extremely complex epistemology that can be described here only in briefest outline. Two main categories of knowledge, direct and indirect, each of which has five varieties or subdivisions, are posited. Direct cognition of whatever variety is believed always to be preceded by an awareness of the object of its perception. It includes knowledge through the five senses (*mati*), clairvoyant cognition (*avadhi*), knowledge acquired through the understanding of verbal messages and signs (*sruti*), direct knowledge of others' thoughts (*manaparyaya*), and omniscient or perfect knowledge (*kevala*). This last is the knowledge attained by Vardhamana when he became a Jina. It is knowledge that is independent of the senses, free from doubt of any kind, and it is unlimited by space or time. It cannot be described and is the prerogative of only the liberated *jiva*. Indirect cognition includes recollection (*smrti*), recognition (*pratnabhijna*), inductive reasoning (*tarka*), inference (*anumana*) and trustworthy testimony (*agama*). This last kind of knowledge is of scripture or of the words of a fully-liberated Jina. It is important as a means to truth for those who are still struggling towards release.

Since omniscient knowledge, *kevala*, cannot be described, there is a logical and conceptual problem about its transmission from a Jina to a layperson. The resolution of this difficulty gave rise to an important feature in Jain logic: the doctrine of standpoints, often spoken of as 'non-one-sidedness'. The basis of the doctrine is a distinction drawn between knowledge of a thing as it is in itself (*pramama*), and knowledge of it in relation to other things (*naya*). A *naya* is simply a standpoint from which we may make a statement about something in its relation to some other thing or things. What a particular standpoint and its resulting statement may be will depend on a person's particular purpose, but the adoption of one standpoint does not preclude or deny others. What is concluded from this is that knowledge is generally partial and relative to the standpoints taken, and that a partial truth is nevertheless a truth insofar as it is an aspect of the total reality. Jainism accepts and respects all such standpoints. Like the broader epistemological doctrine, *naya* is a doctrine with many elaborations and subdivisions. It analyses and defines the properties and implications of a whole range of standpoints and it also posits the notion of *nayaniscaya*, the 'complete point of view'. Even *nayaniscaya* may be of more than one kind: it may refer to a 'complete point of view' of pure unconditioned reality, or of a conditioned one. The *nirvana* sought by Jains does not bring about the extinction of the *jiva*. It admits the *jiva* released from all desires and physicality to eternal blessedness. Once freed it is pure consciousness and will remain so eternally. In *nirvana* the *jiva* is said to enjoy four infinite accomplishments: infinite knowledge, infinite vision, infinite strength and infinite bliss.

At the end of the twentieth century the Jain population worldwide was approximately 6 million, of which over 3 million are in India where the community grows steadily. Although not numerous, Jains have become an influential and important element in Indian society. They translate and publish their literature in their own publishing houses and promulgate scholarly research and study of their traditions and history. The ethical emphasis of their doctrine means that they have a lively social concern for others and, because they are predominantly members of the professional classes, the resources and capabilities to give practical help. But they also have to contend with widespread and rapid social change, with strong westernizing influences and with the threat of being engulfed by a homogeneous culture. Their modern task is to sustain the vitality of their severe and sublime vision of the recovery of original being in the face of all that assails them.

Notes

1 The dates given here are the traditional ones. Modern scholarship has suggested that 540–468 BCE are more accurate.
2 'Jina' is an honorific title, not a proper name, given to each of the great tirthankaras.
3 It is often pointed out how deeply Mahatma Gandhi was influenced by Jain doctrine, and in particular by ahimsa. See the essay on Gandhi in this book.

Jain writings

Jaina Sutras, ed. H. Jacobi, vol. 1, Oxford: Clarendon Press, 1884 (Sacred Books of the East, vol. 22) repr. Delhi: Motilal Banarsidass, 1968; New York: Dover Publications, 1968

Jains, and in particular, Vardhamana, did not accept the Vedas, and this means there is a distinct body of Jain literature. The oldest Jain texts were written in the early vernacular Indian languages. By the fifth century CE these texts were organized by the Shvetambara Jains into a canon of forty-four books known as the Siddharta. Of these books the *angas* is regarded as the most important because it contains sermons and dialogues of Vardhamana. The Digambara Jains were never entirely satisfied with this canon and held to two ancient Prakrit texts which, together with related commentaries, form their particular canonical texts. Later writings, dating from 700 CE onwards, are concerned with the development of lay disciplines and practices, and in the sixteenth century CE further revisions took place. The *Tattvarthadigamasutra* comprises doctrines acceptable to both *digambaras* and *shvetambaras*. In recent years there has been a considerable output of writing in English, presenting Jain thought to the western world.

See also in this book

Indian Philosophy Introduction, the Buddha, Gandhi

Sources and further reading

Dundas, Paul, *The Jainas*, London: Routledge, 1992
Jaini, Padmenabh S., 'Karma and the problem of rebirth in Jainism', in W.D. O'Flaherty (ed.), *Karma and Rebirth in Classical Indian Tradition*, Berkeley, Calif.: University of California Press, 1980

—— *Jaina Debates on the Spiritual Liberation of Women*, California: University of California Press, 1991

McGreal, Ian P., *Great Thinkers of the Western World*, New York: Harper Collins, 1995

Radhakrishnan, Sarvepalli, *Indian Philosophy*, 2 vols, vol. 1, London: Allen & Unwin

Tatia, Nathmal, *Studies in Jaina Philosophy*, Benares, India: Jaina Cultural Research Society, 1951

SIDHARTHA GAUTAMA: THE BUDDHA
c.563–483 BCE

A person now known as the Buddha, 'the Enlightened One', is believed to have lived in India in the latter part of the sixth and the early part of the fifth centuries BCE. The example of his life and teaching generated Buddhism, a tradition of beliefs and practices which, during two and a half thousand years, has spread peaceably through many parts of Asia. Buddhism has developed or been interpreted from the central tenets of the Buddha's teaching in a variety of ways. Although it has no god it is widely regarded as a religion. Any person may endeavour to achieve the buddhic condition of enlightenment: by eschewing extremes and following the Middle Way; by transcending the self of everyday life.

Buddhism is essentially a practical doctrine, dedicated primarily to the negation of suffering and only secondarily to the elucidation of philosophical issues. But of course, the two realms, the practical and the philosophical, are not unconnected and the Buddha's metaphysical conception of the impermanence and interdependence of all things profoundly influences his teaching about the conduct of daily life and the nature of human salvation.

There are no entirely reliable sources either for the facts of the Buddha's life or for his teaching (*dharma*), but there are numerous accounts compiled by his followers. Written records began to be put together about four centuries after his death and were taken largely from the recitings of monks and from the oral pronouncements passed down from the Buddha's original disciples. Although unverifiable and often conflicting, these accounts, taken as a whole, provide a rich and detailed picture of the Buddha's world and of the ideas that informed his thought.

Sidhartha Gautama, later to be called the Buddha, was probably born near Nepal in north-eastern India. Early Buddhist scriptures relate that his birth took place beneath a tree in the lowland country-side near Lambini and that his mother died seven days later. His family was undoubtedly a prosperous one, occupying a position of power within a Hindu community structured by a well-defined hierarchy of estates. This hierarchy separated people into those who prayed, those who fought and those who laboured. The **Brahmins**, who were the priests and scholars, constituted the highest estate. Next came the warriors who ruled and defended society, and among these were the Sakyas of whom Sidhartha was one. The third and fourth estates consisted of commoners and servants respectively. Mobility between the ranks of the estates was not easy. It has been remarked that 'It was as if the estates were different species. In this conception there were no human beings, only Brahmins, Warriors, Husbandmen and servants.'[1]

Sidhartha was brought up in the Hindu tradition, living in princely style and marrying at 16. When he was 29 his life changed as the result of four experiences that brought him to a realization of mortality and the pain of human existence. It is related that he encountered, first, an old man, then a mortally sick man, then a corpse and then a man with a shaven head and a threadbare yellow robe – a monk in search of spiritual truth. Sidhartha brooded deeply on the significance of these encounters and when night came he quietly left his sleeping wife and child and began a new life as a beggar. His aims were spiritual and practical ones: to discover the cause of suffering (*duhkha*) and to effect its cure. He wandered the Ganges plains, seeking out the *yogis* (see *yoga*) and subjecting himself to a regime of extreme frugality and discipline.

After six years of such practices Sidhartha seems to have achieved nothing of what he sought, but he resolved to persist in his endeavour. He bathed, ate a light meal and then began a prolonged meditation on suffering and rebirth, progressing through four stages of meditation and at last achieving the awakening he sought: first, by means of the realization that all desire is productive of pain, and then by experiencing release from every craving. In this way, at the age of 35, he achieved buddhahood. Buddhist scriptures relate that he described his joy in these words:

> I have overcome all foes; I am all-wise; I am free from stains in every way; I have left everything; and have obtained emancipation by the destruction of desire . . . I have gained coolness . . . and have obtained *Nirvana*.[2]

Nirvana is primarily a Hindu concept. It is sometimes spoken of as a state of bliss and peace that is secure because it is irreversible. It is also described as a state of 'unbecoming', or non-being, a condition thought to precede individual existence and which takes on the character of a far place to which the existing individual might return. Perhaps it is best thought of as something that is beyond ordinary comprehension, as experienceable rather than describable. Since it involves the disappearance of the desirous and suffering individual it is difficult, except in moments of imaginative insight, to conceive of such a state. It is the falling away of all the pains and uncertainties that characterize carnal existence, leaving a peace that is unassailable and without sensation. It is sometimes referred to in wholly negative terms as

> a condition where there is neither 'earth', nor 'water', nor 'fire', nor 'air', nor the sphere of infinite space, nor the sphere of infinite consciousness, nor the sphere of the void ... neither a coming nor a going nor a standing still, nor a falling away nor a rising up; but it is without fixity, without mobility, without basis. It is the end of woe.[3]

Commentators have sometimes objected that there is a contradiction in speaking of *nirvana* as, on the one hand, a kind of negation and, on the other, a state of bliss. The reply to that objection must surely be that if the descriptive account borders on contradiction then the resulting incoherence has to be understood as an indication of the inexpressibility and otherness of *nirvana*.

Nirvana is not something attainable only at death. A released person may continue, as the Buddha did, in physical existence, undergoing all the processes of ageing and bodily decay although invulnerable to spiritual regression. When he achieved enlightenment Sidhartha was ready to enter fully into *nirvana*, but he paused to reflect on whether he should do so at once or should embark instead on a teaching mission. He chose to teach. When he had prepared himself he delivered his first discourse, now known as the Benares Sermon, to the five men who had accompanied him on many of his wanderings. These followers were at first sceptical and disapproving. In their eyes, when he washed and ate before his long meditation, Sidhartha had lapsed from the extreme asceticism they deemed necessary for true enlightenment. But what he had found through that new approach was a path between the two extremes of worldly indulgence and punishing self-denial. His sermon marked the beginning of a teaching ministry dedicated to the exposition and exemplification of the undogmatic thinking of the Middle Way. That ministry continued until he died, forty-five years later. Most historians place his death in 483 BCE, recounting that it occurred as the result of eating food that contained a tainted ingredient. His body was cremated and its ashes distributed among eight groups of his followers.

The Buddha's teaching is largely about human conduct and salvation and its central concern is with the abolition of suffering. However, it has to be understood in relation to the Hindu doctrine of reincarnation, or transmigration of souls. In Hinduism this doctrine rests on the general belief that all living things are besouled and that souls become incarnate in a succession of different types of bodies. Which body a particular soul migrates into depends on the kind of life lived through its previous body and this conditioning or determining of its next incarnation is *karma*, the universal law that governs the distinctions between embodied souls and also their particular deeds. Reincarnation is thought of as a more or less perpetual bondage to *samsara*, the wheel of life, a bondage maintained by the individual's passions and cravings. But release is possible and may be achieved by a gradual bettering of one's *karma* so that migration to bodies capable of more ascetic and spiritual living and, eventually, entry into *nirvana* can take place.

In Hinduism the bliss of *nirvana* is broadly conceived of as a state of total union with **Brahman**, the ultimate and absolute Reality of the universe, in which individuality is completely abolished. Buddhist doctrine differs from this in some important respects. For one thing, it does not assert the existence of *Brahman* as the unifying and ultimate power of the universe. It also rejects the concept of the individual immortal soul. It maintains that the empirical personality consists of five kinds of entity, or **skandha** – body, feelings, desires, mental conceptions and pure consciousness – but that none of these is permanent and so cannot constitute anything that could be understood as soul. Accordingly, Buddhism concludes that there is an empirical personality that has a psychic or mental aspect, but it finds no reason to affirm the existence of an enduring soul capable of finding eternal salvation through absorption into a Brahmanic absolute.

This view has implications for the doctrine of reincarnation, since its argument, if accepted, renders incoherent the idea of a persisting soul that migrates through a series of incarnations. Thus the buddhistic view is not that there is an eternal soul that migrates, but that the cumulative disposition, or *karma*, of a life that is ending leaps forward into a fresh incarnation and conditions its development. Buddhist scriptures describe the *karma* of a dying person as finding a new embodiment, one that is appropriate to its past, in the embryo of a pregnant woman's womb. In this way, the whole disposition of a former life takes up habitation in and begins to influence a new one. A new consciousness arises, but with a disposition shaped by a previous one. Confronted with the question whether a released being continues to exist in some way after death, the answer given by Buddhism is that there is no appropriate answer.

Sidhartha did not hold that the development of a life is rigidly and wholly determined by the physical events that are the consequences of *karma*. Instead he taught that it is intentions, motives and volitions that are decisive for the *karma* of a future life. The painful consequences of the bad intentions of a previous life are inevitable and unavoidable, but good intentions or volitions, even those relating to a deed that fails to turn out well, can lead only towards *nirvana*, the condition of release. Accordingly, it is not pointless, in Buddhism, to seek a virtuous way of life.

In the Benares Sermon the Buddha's teaching begins with the listing of the Four Noble Truths: the fact of suffering, its cause, the requirement that it shall cease, and the method of its cessation. These truths clearly coincide with the insights that came to him in the four encounters that set him on the path to buddhahood. Their discussion is followed by an exposition of what it is to tread the Noble Eightfold Path, the course of conduct that can end suffering. The path requires one to live a life based on a right view, right thought, right speech, right conduct, right vocation, right effort, right attention and right concentration. The details of Buddhist practice are to be derived from this framework and worked out by reference to the principle of seeking the Middle Way in all things. In following the Middle Way, extremes are repudiated since they constitute the kind of ties and attachments that impede progress towards release. A person on the Middle Way

> neither constructs in his mind, nor wills in order to produce, any state of mind or body, or the destruction of any such state. By not so willing anything in the world, he grasps after nothing; by not grasping, he is not anxious; he is therefore fully calmed within.[4]

The literature of Buddhism is abundant and various. It falls into two main parts that correspond with the division of Buddhist doctrine into its two main schools, the **Theravada** (or **Hinayana**) and the **Mahayana**. The Theravada scriptures are written in Pali and are generally known either as the Pali Canon or the *Tripitaka*, usually translated as 'The Three Baskets'. The 'baskets' respectively contain a collection of the Buddha's reported sayings and sermons, the rules of conduct, and discussions of philosophical issues in Buddhism. These central works of the Pali Canon generated numerous commentaries and disquisitions. Mahayana literature is even more copious and has a somewhat different character that was imposed on it during the wider dissemination it received over several centuries in the early development of Buddhism. It was originally written in Sanskrit but many of those originals were lost after their transmission to China and Tibet. This has meant that, in more recent times, Chinese and Tibetan versions have had to be translated back into Sanskrit.[5]

It is not surprising that the central beliefs and doctrines attributed to the Buddha have endured, developed and flourished. They have a practical aspect that is readily absorbed into daily life. At the same time they deal with certain large questions that have always fascinated humankind: questions concerning the soul, the self, free will, death, God, reality and the meaning of life. Buddhism is sensitively agnostic concerning these ultimate questions and so allows for the human sense of mystery and transcendence and the propensity to speculate and reason that are part of human consciousness in general. But it is also down-to-earth and forthright in its conclusions derived from empirical fact and it offers clear guidance on how to realize spiritual aspirations. The Buddha taught an attitude of non-violence and an awareness of community and relatedness among all things. He condemned the rigid hierarchy of the Hindu estates, maintaining that inner virtue rather than birth or rank is to be valued, and he welcomed followers, both men and women, from all walks of life. He did not think of himself either as an innovator or as the maker of a philosophy, for he saw his teaching as deriving largely from the distillations of perennial human wisdom and practices. Nevertheless, his thinking is analytical and systematic and it has an independence and vigour that impart originality to it. It possesses, too, a broad coherence that knits it into a system of ideas embracing important philosophical issues.

After the Buddha's death his doctrine survived and spread in various forms. The monks who survived him did their best to preserve his ideas exactly as he had expressed them, reciting and promulgating the wisdom contained in the Three Baskets of the Pali Canon. In the first four or five centuries after Sidhartha's death Buddhism remained almost exclusively Indian. It then began to move eastwards through Asia and then to China as well, influencing and being influenced by all it encountered. Today, the Doctrine of the Elders (Theravada) prevails in the southern part of the Buddhist world and is the national religion of Sri Lanka, Burma and Thailand. In the northern parts of the Buddhist world, the Mahayana doctrines that developed at the time of the rise of Christianity are dominant in Nepal, Korea, China, Japan and Tibet. In the late twentieth century it was only in Sri Lanka that Buddhism was largely unfettered and worked in conjunction with the state.

The Buddha's teaching has not escaped criticism. Many have pointed out that it advocates a withdrawal from life and is suitable only for those who are willing to live in cloistered retirement, evading the abrasions and difficulties encountered in the wider world. But such a charge is no more relevant or damaging to Buddhism than it is to most other religions. Just as Judaism and Christianity, for example, are capable of sustaining a wide variety of lifestyles, ranging from those of monastic seclusion to those of full engagement with the political and economic business of the world, so is Buddhism able to do so. Its scope and temper are aptly summarized by Michael Carrithers in his remark that 'Buddhism is quintessentially tolerant, cosmopolitan and portable'.[6]

Notes

1   In Michael Carrithers, *The Buddha*, Oxford: Oxford University Press, Past Masters series, 1983, p. 15.
2   See M. Muller (ed.), *Mahavaga*, vol. XIII, Oxford: Oxford University Press, 1881, p. 90.
3   Quoted in Christmas Humphreys, *Buddhism*, Harmondsworth: Penguin Books, 1952, p. 127.
4   *Majjhima Nikaya*, vol. III, Pali Text Society edition, Oxford: Oxford University Press, p. 244.
5   The most renowned commentator on early Theravada doctrine is Buddhaghosa. See pp. 114–20 in this book for his work on the translation and interpretation of its literature in the fifth century CE.
6   Carrithers, op. cit., p. 80.

Writings of early Buddhism

After the Buddha's death his words and doctrines were regularly recited by monks in an attempt to preserve them accurately. Versions of these recitings were discussed at meetings held at intervals in the ensuing century and it was as the result of disagreements in these discussions that the two main schools of Buddhism, the Theravada and the Mahayana, developed. Numerous texts of Theravada Buddhism are published in scholarly editions by the Pali Text Society through Oxford University Press.

See also in this book

Nagarjuna, Buddhaghosa, Padmasambhava, Milarepa, Tsong kha pa, Huineng, Fazang, Dogen, Nichiren, Bankei, Hakuin, Nishida, Suzuki, Nishitani Keiji.

Sources and further reading

Carrithers, Michael, *The Buddha*, Oxford: Oxford University Press, Past Masters series, 1983

Conze, Edward, *A Short History of Buddhism*, London: Unwin Paperbacks, 1986

Humphreys, Christmas, *Buddhism*, Harmondsworth, Penguin Books, 1952

Ling, Trevor, *The Buddha*, London: Temple Smith, 1973

Ling, Trevor (ed.), *The Buddha's Philosophy of Man*, London: Everyman Library, Dent, 1993

Murti, T.R.V., *The Central Philosophy of Buddhism*, London: Allen & Unwin, 1955

Smart, Ninian, *Doctrine and Argument in Indian Philosophy*, Leiden and New York: Brill, 1992

Thomas, Edward J., *The History of Buddhist Thought*, 3rd edn, London: Routledge & Kegan Paul, 1949

PATANJALI Second century BCE

Patanjali is the compiler and systematizer of a set of aphorisms, the longest consisting of only a few lines, known as the *Yoga Sutras*. Scattered references are made to *yoga* in the **Vedas**, and the yogic tradition in Hinduism predates Patanjali. To many people in the West the term 'yoga' is associated with exercises, popular since the 1960s, in breathing and physical posture. The *Yoga Sutras* certainly incorporate such exercises: several of the sutras contain information such as, 'The mind may also be calmed by expulsion and retention of the breath', and 'posture is . . . firm but relaxed through control of the natural tendencies of the body, and through meditation'.[1] An improvement in posture and breathing is not the sole nor even the primary aim of yoga. Instead, it is either a therapeutic method of freeing the mind from false beliefs, or the insight into ultimate reality, the *dharmas*, achievable by this method. Yoga is an intricate and integrated system consisting of metaphysics, the philosophy of mind, the theory of knowledge, ethics and the philosophy of language. It aims at the union of *atman*, or that within the self which is ultimately real, with **Brahman**, or ultimate reality in its universal aspect.[2] Patanjali's work has been of enormous influence in all schools of Buddhism that follow the meditative method, particularly that of **Yogacara**.

Apart from his editorship of the *Yoga Sutras*, very little is known about Patanjali. Even his dates are uncertain. He is estimated by some scholars to have lived during the second century BCE, but by others during the fifth century CE. One of the reasons for this wide discrepancy is the scholarly issue of whether the whole of the text of the *Yoga Sutras* was compiled by Patanjali. The compilation is divided into four books or chapters on, respectively, meditation (or *samadhi*), yogic practice, psychic powers, and liberation from *samsara*, or the cycle of rebirth and suffering. It is generally agreed that the first three chapters are attributable to Patanjali. The fourth chapter contains arguments against Buddhist doctrines which cannot be found in written form before the fifth century CE. If the last part of the *Yoga Sutras* is Patanjali's work, it cannot have been compiled before this date either. Against this view there are several considerations. One is that the Buddhist teachings to which the *Yoga Sutras* are opposed may have been disseminated earlier in oral form, by being passed down from teacher to disciple. Another is that the Buddhist doctrines were recorded in earlier documents which are not now extant. A third is that the fourth chapter may be a later interpolation. Surendranath Dasgupta is inclined, on internal grounds of style, to favour the view that the *Yoga Sutras* is not one work, but two.[3] Whatever the merits of the various hypotheses which have been put forward, it is unlikely that the debate will ever be definitively settled.

The *Yoga Sutras* take over the metaphysical doctrines and concepts to be found in earlier Hinduism, particularly those of **prakrti** and **purusha**. The universe consists of elemental, undifferentiated stuff known as *prakrti*. This stuff is eternal, uncreated and indestructible. It has three *gunas*, a term variously rendered as qualities, forces or energies. There is *sattwa*, or intelligence, which contains unrealized or potential essences, forms or structures: in other words, the blueprint for whatever may become actual. *Tamas* is inertia or immobility, the force or obstacle which prevents *prakrti* from emerging from its potential to resolve itself into particular structured objects or phenomena. *Rajas* is motion, activity or dynamism, which can overcome *tamas* to allow the production of the particular things, or differentiated phenomena, of the universe. *Sattwa* is a disciplining force on *rajas* which if acting alone would be undirected, chaotic energy. *Sattwa*, *tamas* and *rajas* are in unstable combination. If they are in equilibrium, there is *prakrti* without the phenomena of the universe. When *rajas* predominates, there is the creation and evolution of particular things. When *tamas* predominates, everything is destroyed and falls back into the undifferentiated *prakrti*. The universe is thus subject to an endless cycle of cosmic evolution and dissolution. *Prakrti* is both caused by and incorporated into *Brahman*. All phenomena or modifications, and *prakrti* itself, are neither mental nor physical. An object in its individuality appears as matter and is a 'gross phenomenon' whereas when we consider the essence of an object, or what makes it the sort of object it is, it has the appearance of mental stuff and is a 'subtle phenomenon'. The aim of *yoga* is to liberate the *atman*, or true self, often referred to in the *Yoga Sutras* as *purusha*, from *prakrti*, and to allow its union with *Brahman*. *Atman*, according to Patanjali, is pure consciousness and transcends *prakrti*, and *Brahman* is ultimate reality, all-encompassing and without qualities.

Patanjali maintains that the empirical mind, which is a pheno-menon of *prakrti*, has three aspects or functions. It can receive sense impressions from phenomena; it can classify, identify and react to them; and it is self-conscious. The awareness of the ego leads us to the mistaken belief that sense impressions and reactions belong to it, and thus are private and subjective. All impressions and reactions are known as 'mental fluctuations' or 'thought-waves', and 'yoga is the control of thought-waves in the mind'.[4] When we reach the stage of perfect contemplation, we enter into our real nature, the *purusha*, which is different from the empirical mind. In particular, we rid ourselves of the false notion that we are separate, unique individuals. Instead, our true selves are not differentiated from each other, but are *atman*, which is to be identified with *Brahman*. Through yoga, the phenomenal mind rids itself of itself to allow the union of *atman* and *Brahman*.

Patanjali's teachings about the union of *atman* and *Brahman* leave us with certain difficulties. The transcendence of the ego which can be achieved by the empirical mind entails the annihilation of individuality. There is thus no individuated subject of experience. *We* cannot be such a subject, because there is no 'we', just undifferentiated ultimate reality. Our true selves are not distinct from that which is not our selves, as all differentiations are resolved into *Brahman*. Thus, even to talk of *our* true selves is a mistake; there is only undifferentiated, impersonal, qualityless Self. This position has implications for language, which operates on the assumption that the attribution of subjecthood differentiates the subject of experiences from its object, or that which is experienced. The *atman* which is *Brahman* does not have the attribute of pure consciousness; it is consciousness, without a subject. There is no object of which *atman* or *Brahman* is conscious, as there is nothing from which ultimate reality is to be distinguished.

Our character and predispositions are built up from the accumulation of thought-waves. A person who, for example, has often felt angry in the past becomes ill-tempered and is predisposed to react angrily in the future. Our tendencies and character need not, according to Hindu philosophy, develop over just one lifetime; we also retain dispositions from our previous lives. They can, however, be altered through the technique of *yoga*. Characteristics such as anger are detrimental to us, and lead to our continuing to be trapped in *samsara*. We can eliminate negative characteristics by developing beneficial ones: in the words of the *Yoga Sutras*, 'Undisturbed calmness of mind is attained by cultivating friendliness toward the happy, compassion for the unhappy, delight in the virtuous, and indifference toward the wicked.'[5]

There are certain obstacles to progress in *yoga*, the first of which is what Patanjali calls 'wrong knowledge'. A favourite example from yogic literature is that of a rope being wrongly identified as a snake. Wrong knowledge is thus due to a failure of the classificatory faculty of the mind. The second is referred to as 'verbal delusion', which 'arises when words do not correspond to [phenomena]'.[6] Patanjali does not give any examples of mismatches between language and phenomena, but they could range over calling things by the wrong name, as in the case of the rope and the snake; the mistaken belief that we are unique, separate selves; the assumption that reality consists only of the phenomenal realm; and ambiguity in the concepts which we use. Thus if we talk of yoga as merely a set of exercises, whilst being ignorant of its considerable philosophical ramifications, we are guilty of verbal delusion. Patanjali's concerns over language mismatch are similar to those of certain Chinese philosophers on the 'rectification of names', the confusion and lack of clarity in language which results in the misdescription of things and events, and lack of clarity in thought.[7]

There are two types of knowledge, the first being 'ordinary' or **smrti**, and consisting of 'direct perception, inference and scriptural testimony'.[8] Our perception of dark clouds, and our inference that it is going to rain, are two items of ordinary knowledge. They require no special techniques and are open to almost everyone. Scriptural testimony would include reports of, rather than participation in, yogic experience. The attitude of concentration in ordinary knowledge, whilst not itself yoga, is a useful preparation for it. The second type of knowledge, termed **sruti**, is a non-inferential, direct, immediate, mystical awareness of, and identity with, its object. We can attain such knowledge, or *samadhi*, through concentration or meditation on just one object, thus allowing us to suppress our thought-waves. There are several hierarchical degrees of *samadhi*, ranging from concentration on a 'gross phenomenon' to contemplation of *prakrti*. The most advanced form is meditation without content, known in Vedic literature as **nirvikalpa**. In the words of the *Yoga Sutras*, 'The other kind of concentration is that in which the consciousness contains no object . . . it is attained by constantly checking the thought-waves'.[9] We are then on the threshhold of achieving the union of *atman* with *Brahman*.

The teachings of the *Yoga Sutras* are similar in certain ways to various theories in western philosophy. Contemplation theory in aesthetics, whilst it is not always considered to lead to an insight into ultimate reality, maintains that a true appreciation of a work of art can only be achieved when all distractions and considerations other than of the work itself are left behind, and the spectator or listener is engaged in single-minded absorption in its object. Schopenhauer (1788–1860) believed that such contemplation leads to the transformation of the self from a subject of blind desire and will trapped in the phenomenal world of particular things, to an eternal, will-less subject of knowing freed from all desires. This theory stops short of union with ultimate reality, but it marks considerable progress away from the phenomenal world and the empirical self. Plato (427–347 BCE) maintained that ultimate reality, the unchanging Forms, essences or independent standards, of beauty and goodness which lie behind the particular, changing, temporal things of this world can only be known by a direct, non-inferential insight achievable after years of training to rid oneself of desires and emotions which cloud the understanding.[10]

All levels of *samadhi* except *nirvikalpa* are 'with seeds' or, in other words, they have not brought about the total elimination of all desires and attachments to phenomena. Instead, we are still subject to the cosmic law of **karma**, whereby all our actions inevitably have their repercussions, whether in this life or in some future one. Only when we attain *nirvikalpa samadhi*, or the purest level of contemplation, are we released from *karma* and reincarnation. *Nirvikalpa samadhi*, as Patanjali vividly expresses it, either has 'burnt seeds' or is 'seedless'. Either we still have desires but they are sterile and thus carry no karmic consequences, or we are completely free from desire, thereby being in a condition of perfect non-attachment and poised for union with *Brahman*.[11]

In the path towards self-dissolution, Patanjali gives special prominence to *Isvara*, often rendered as 'God' or 'personal deity'. He says, 'Concentration may also be attained through devotion to *Isvara*', and 'Isvara is a special kind of Being, untouched by ignorance and the products of ignorance, not subject to karmas or samsaras or the results of action'.[12] It is possible, as Patanjali makes clear, that the union with Brahman can be achieved without devotion to Isvara, but such devotion has the advantage of cultivating the moral virtues of love, humility and service both to Isvara himself and to our fellow human beings. Isvara is not to be identified with Brahman, but is the creator, sustainer and destroyer of the phenomenal world. He acts within and upon prakrti and is viewed as having personal qualities of which everyone can form an image or idea. As he is not subject to the law of karma, he has no beginning and no end, and as he does not suffer from ignorance, he is detached from phenomena. Human beings cannot attain a state of union with Isvara because he has personal characteristics that distinguish him from every other being. When there is union between atman and Brahman, Isvara is transcended and dissolved.

Patanjali's teachings are comprehensive and remarkably undogmatic and tolerant. Few of us can attain union with Brahman, but our efforts are not thereby wasted; what is gained from the preliminary steps of yogic practice is of value to us. The spiritual path of yoga need not be a purely intellectual one, but can take the form of moral progress and the cultivation of moral characteristics. Even the preparations we make for entry into yoga, such as compassion for the unfortunate, are of social benefit.

Notes

1. Swami Prabhavananda and Christopher Isherwood (eds), *How to Know God; The Yoga Aphorisms of Patanjali*, New York: Mentor, 1969, ch. 1 Sutra 34, ch. 2 Sutras 46 and 47.
2. *Yoga* is from the same Sanskrit root as the English word 'yoke' meaning 'join together'.
3. For further details of this debate, and the issue of whether the Patanjali of the *Yoga Sutras* is the same person as, or different from, the author of the same name who wrote a treatise on grammar, see J.H. Woods, *The Yoga System of Patanjali*, Harvard Oriental Series, Cambridge Mass.: Harvard University Press, 1927, and S. Dasgupta, *A History of Indian Philosophy*, vol. 1, Cambridge: Cambridge University Press, 1922.
4. Swami Prabhavananda and Isherwood, op. cit., ch. 1 sutra 2.
5. Swami Prabhavananda and Isherwood, op. cit., ch. 1 sutra 33.
6. Swami Prabhavananda and Isherwood, op. cit., ch. 1 sutra 9.
7. See the essay on Xunzi (Hsun Tzu), pp. 259–66 in this book.
8. Swami Prabhavananda and Isherwood, op. cit., ch. 1 sutra 7.
9. Swami Prabhavananda and Isherwood, op. cit., ch. 1 sutra 18.
10. See A. Schopenhauer, *The World as Will and Representation*, various editions,

e.g. New York: Dover, 1969, and Plato, *The Republic*, various editions, e.g. trans. F.M. Cornford, London: Oxford University Press, 1941.

11 Swami Prabhavananda and Isherwood, op. cit., ch. 1 sutras 18 and 51.
12 Swami Prabhavananda and Isherwood, op. cit., ch. 1 sutras 23 and 24.

Patanjali's writings

There are several editions of Patanjali's *Yoga Sutras*, each with a commentary, including:

Woods, J.H. (trans. and ed.), *The Yoga System of Patanjali*, Harvard Oriental Series, Cambridge, Mass.: Harvard University Press, 1927

Swami Prabhavananda and Isherwood, Christopher (trans. and eds.), *How to Know God: The Yoga Aphorisms of Patanjali*, New York: Mentor, 1969

Feuerstein, G. (trans. and ed.), *The Yoga Sutra of Patanjali*, Rochester: Inner Traditions International, 1989

Bahm, A.J. (trans. and ed.), *The Yoga Sutras of Patanjali*, Berkeley, Calif.: Asian Humanities Press, 1993

See also in this book

Badarayana, Vasubandhu, Sankara, Ramanuja, Madhva, Vivekananda, Gandhi, Aurobindo, Radhakrishnan, Milarepa, Tsong kha pa, Xunzi, Chinul.

Sources and further reading

Brannigan, Michael, *The Pulse of Wisdom*, Belmont, Calif.: Wadsworth, 1995

Dasgupta, Surendranath, *A History of Indian Philosophy*, vol.1, Cambridge: Cambridge University Press, 1922.

Dasgupta, Surendranath, *A Study of Patanjali*, Delhi: Motilal Banarsidas, 1989

Radhakrishnan, S., *Indian Philosophy*, vol. II, chs IV and V, London: Allen & Unwin, 1923

Swami Nikhilananda (ed.), *Vivekananda: The Yogas and Other Works*, New York: Ramakrishna-Vivekananda Center, 1953

BADARAYANA second century BCE

The *Upanisads* are written in the language of the seer or visionary: inspired, poetic, symbolic and of inexhaustible resonance. To this day, their words leap from the page, informed and shaped by the pressure of intense spiritual experience. What these profound texts are not is orderly or systematic, and over time the need was felt to draw together their insights into a philosophical system. The goal of Badarayana in composing the masterpiece for which he is remembered, the **Brahma Sutra**,[1] was to construct precisely such a system. Together with the

Vedas and the *Upanisads* this work forms the basis of the Indian orthodox philosophical tradition, and sets out to be a coherent statement of the philosophy implicit in the second of these works. The *Brahma Sutra* in turn has been commented on by almost every major figure in the Indian tradition and many of lesser importance also: it would be possible to trace much of the history of Indian philosophy by examining the commentaries on this work alone. Sankara, Ramanuja and Madhva, for example, all commented at length on it, finding in it confirmation of their own philosophical beliefs. The extensiveness of the body of subsequent commentary on this work is not grounded solely in its authority, however, but is also partially a result of its style. Each of the 552 propositions (each referred to as a *sutra*) in the work is terse and usually grammatically incomplete, generally such as to be not fully intelligible without accompanying exegesis. Since the *Brahma Sutra* deals with the ultimate questions of philosophy, it is not surprising that it has generated an uninterrupted stream of interpretation.

Of Badarayana nothing at all is known, and even his dates and authorship of the *Brahma Sutra* are disputed. The date of the second century BCE for the composition of the work is the one which has attracted more support among scholars than its rivals, in a range between 500 BCE and 200 CE. Internal evidence – in terms of the other schools of thought referred to in the text – make it unlikely that it could have been written before 200 BCE. The fact that Badarayana refers to himself in the third person in the work does not mean that he cannot be its author, since such a practice is not unparalleled in this tradition.[2] It is unlikely that certainty will be reached on these questions, short of a major textual discovery.

Before approaching the philosophy of the *Brahma Sutra*, it is necessary to take account of an important principle which is taken for granted in the text, and which forms one of its basic presuppositions. This principle rests on the distinction between **sruti** and **smrti**. Sruti is sacred knowledge, derived from the religious experience of the Vedic seers. It is recorded in the Vedas and the *Upanisads*. With regard to the realm beyond the **samsara**, its authority is absolute. Smrti is knowledge based on memory, tradition or inference, or a combination of these. The distinction can also be stated by saying the *sruti* is intuitional, self-evidential insight, whereas *smrti* is evidentially based ratiocination. In *sruti*, the distinction between knower and known is transcended, and the two become one. Should there arise a conflict between *sruti* and *smrti*, the former is always to be preferred, and this principle is constitutive of Vedantic orthodoxy. The nearest western analogue to *sruti* is revelation, which is accorded the same ultimate and unquestionable status in the Judaeo-Christian tradition. The parallel is not exact, however, since revelation need not involve the transcending of the distinction between knower and known.

The *Brahma Sutra* begins from the most important insight of the Vedic tradition, that reality is not the ordinary world of everyday experience, the world of individuals causally related in space and time, the world of relentless mutability which is the *samsara*, but instead is a perfect, changeless, eternal oneness or absolute, **Brahman**, from which everything (in some way to be explored) arises: '(Ultimate Reality is that) from which origin, etc., (i.e. subsistence and destruction) of this (would proceed).'[3] There is abundant authority in *sruti* texts for this, a very clear example being a passage in the *Taittiriya Upanisad*: 'That, verily, from which these things are born, that, by which, when born they live, that into which, when departing, they enter. That, seek to know. That is Brahman.'[4] Of the major questions raised by such a metaphysic, the first is to find a motive for Brahman's bringing forth of the universe. Brahman has no unsatisfied longings, is perfect and therefore lacks nothing. Why, then, does the universe come about at all? The answer begins from the assertion that, in so far as anything can be said meaningfully about the nature of Brahman, that nature is bliss (**ananda**). Badarayana is scrupulous to point out that because Brahman is an absolute unity, bliss is not an attribute of Brahman but *is* Brahman: 'If it is said (that *anandamaya*) does not (denote the highest Self) since it is a word denoting modification, it is not so on account of abundance';[5] i.e. Brahman *is* bliss immeasurable. The coming into being of the universe is the spontaneous outpouring of this bliss. The closest approximation to this in human terms is play or sport (**lila**); 'as in ordinary life, creation is mere sport (to Brahman).'[6] This should not be taken to imply that Brahman acts (so to speak) lightly: to do this is to take the notion of *lila* in too anthropomorphic a sense. The point is rather that *lila* is the least misleading way that can be found of stating why there is a universe at all.

A system of belief based on the thesis that reality is an absolute involves some of the profoundest philosophical difficulties, and it is Badarayana's chief purpose to address these, showing that the *Upanisadic* insights form a coherent and defensible whole. The central difficulty is known as the problem of the one and the many which, in the terms in which it presented itself to Badarayana, is as follows: Brahman (the absolute) is eternal, immutable and perfect (lacking nothing). How can that which is eternal, immutable and perfect be related to what is temporal, mutable and imperfect, i.e. the everyday world of human experience, the *samsara*? Is the universe a property of Brahman, or an effect of Brahman, or numerically identical with Brahman? Each of these major options involves a difficulty: if Brahman has properties, then conceptual distinctions apply to Brahman, and this is logically impossible in the case of an absolute. Again, the view that Brahman causes the universe appears to presuppose a change in Brahman, which is impossible if Brahman is eternal. Finally, if the universe is numerically identical with Brahman, then Brahman must share its imperfections, and this again is incompatible with the perfect nature of an absolute. An especially acute form of these difficulties occurs in the case of the relation of the individual soul to Brahman. The individual soul cannot be numerically identical with Brahman, since then either Brahman would be imperfect or each soul would be God, and neither is the case. Conversely, if the individual soul is distinct from Brahman, then it becomes impossible to articulate a conception of **moksa** or release, the condition of the unity of soul and Brahman: if the individual soul is distinct from Brahman, then its joining Brahman in *moksa* would constitute a change of Brahman, and this is impossible. The core of Badarayana's philosophical enterprise is to try to find a solution to these multiple dilemmas.

He begins by tackling the issue of the precise relation of Brahman and the universe, and his initial response, at first sight, appears to make this difficulty even more acute. He makes use of a standard philosophical distinction between material cause and efficient cause. The efficient cause of a clay pot is the action of the potter; the material cause of the pot is the unformed clay. Badarayana asserts that Brahman is not only the efficient cause of the universe but the material cause also: '(Brahman is) the material cause also, for this view does not conflict with the (initial) statement and illustration.'[7] The 'statement and illustration' to which he refers occur in the *Chandogya Upanisad* where it states that there is that as a result of the knowledge of which the unhearable is heard, the unperceivable perceived and the unknowable known, in the same way as 'by one clod of clay all that is made of clay becomes known, the modification being only a name arising from speech while the truth is that it is just clay'.[8] Thus Badarayana has the authority of *sruti* for the claim that Brahman must stand to the universe as clay does to things made of clay, i.e. as material cause. He addresses at once the objection that this assertion is inconsistent with other *sruti* passages which state that the universe is reabsorbed into Brahman at the end of time, and that therefore Brahman would be polluted by all the imperfections of the *samsara*.

Badarayana replies that this is not what reabsorption consists in. As gold items become simply gold when melted down, so the universe will lose its particular qualities when reabsorbed.[9] The view that Brahman is the material cause of the universe appears odd at first to westerners, but it is to be borne in mind that the idea of creation *ex nihilo* (from nothing), which is part of Christian orthodoxy, does not occur in Hindu thought.

The assertion that Brahman is the material as well as the efficient cause of the universe has, however, exacerbated the basic difficulty, since it appears to imply that both temporality and change apply to Brahman. Badarayana's reply is one of the key doctrines of the *Brahma Sutra*, and it is that cause and effect are non-different.[10] To claim that cause and effect are non-different is not the same as to say that cause and effect are identical. Later commentators on the *Brahma Sutra* explain non-difference by reference to the relation between foam, waves and bubbles on the one hand, and the sea on the other; or again, referring back to the passage from the *Chandogya Upanisad* cited above, between the clay and the clay pot, the latter being not identical with the former but equally not different from it. Since causes and effects are uniformly non-different in this way, Brahman must be non-different from the universe.

Having established to his satisfaction a sense in which Brahman can be said to cause the universe, Badarayana uses it to deal with a further important question which arises in absolutist systems. In order for a world of physical individuals to be possible, there must be space, since it is by spatial location that physical items are individuated. The question arises whether space is co-eternal with the absolute or is an effect of it: the former option is unattractive, since it is in danger of collapsing either into the view that space is a property of Brahman, or that it is co-ultimate with Brahman, and neither of these is acceptable. Granted his analysis of causality, however, Badarayana can assert that space (*akasa*; also translated as 'ether') is an effect of Brahman,[11] and can construe in this way an important statement in the *sruti*, 'From this Self [i.e. Brahman], verily, ether arose.'[12] Space is therefore not coeternal with Brahman but a non-different effect of Brahman.

Analogous questions arise over one of the central issues of Vedanta philosophy, that of the relation of the individual soul (**atman**) to Brahman. Badarayana's difficulty is all the more pressing because different *sruti* passages appear to suggest different approaches to this question. In the *Brhadaranyaka Upanisad* it is stated that 'He who dwells within the understanding, yet is within the understanding, whom the understanding does not know, whose body the understanding is, who controls the understanding from within, he is your self, the inner controller, the immortal'.[13] This passage suggests a distinction or difference between Brahman, 'the inner controller', and the understanding, an attribute of the normal self. Other passages in the *Upanisads*, however, appear to suggest a more intimate relationship between *atman* and Brahman: 'You [i.e. Brahman] are woman. You are man. You are the youth and the maiden too. You, as an old man, totter along with a staff. Being born you become facing in every direction.'[14] Badarayana cannot opt for the view that *atman* and Brahman are numerically identical, since this would entail that the *karma* of the individual soul pertains to the absolute, which is logically impossible.[15] Badarayana's solution is to propose that the individual soul is 'a part (of the Lord)',[16] not as a part of a machine stands to the whole of which it is a part, but as a spark is related to a fire. As will become clearer from later essays in this book, this question was one which continued to fascinate, and divide, later Vedantins. Sankara, for example, insists that the distinction between *atman* and Brahman cannot be absolute, but is akin to that between space and a space. By contrast, Ramanuja considers that the soul and Brahman must be different, the latter being indwelling within the former.

This issue is closely related to another serious problem in absolutist thought, the problem of evil. If reality is Brahman, then must it not follow that pain and evil are Brahman too? Put in another way, if the individual soul is identical with Brahman, then 'there would attach (to Brahman) faults like not doing what is beneficial to others and the like',[17] i.e. evil would be attributable to Brahman. Badarayana has two lines of reply to this problem, each of which has to be consistent with his view that the soul is, in his sense of the phrase, a part of Brahman. Since the soul is in his sense of the term a part of Brahman, Badarayana must adopt the position that what we call evil and pain are conditions predicable only of the individual soul in the condition of **avidya**, spiritual blindness without awareness of Brahman.[18] When the true nature of the soul is revealed in *moksa*, it is seen that it is free from what is usually called both good and evil. Elsewhere, Badarayana makes use of the doctrine of **karma**. We build up *karma* by the exercise of our free will, and we get what we deserve, be it suffering or reward, and so 'Inequality and cruelty cannot (be attributed to Brahman) for (his activity) has regard to (the works of souls)',[19] i.e. we create what we call the evil we suffer by means of our own *karma*. Brahman being eternal is independent of *karma*, which remains our responsibility. Both these lines of reply, that what we call evil appears so only because of ignorance, and that evil is a consequence of our having free will, are often used in western responses to analogous forms of this problem.

The goal of life in this philosophy is release (*moksa*), and this is identical with direct awareness or knowledge (**vidya**) of Brahman. In this type of insight, the distinction between knower and known collapses: the knower does not know Brahman, but *is* Brahman, as is stated in the *Chandogya Upanisad*:

> Where one sees nothing else, hears nothing else, understands nothing else, that is the infinite. But where one sees something else, hears something else, understands something else, that is the small (i.e. the finite). Verily, the infinite is the same as the immortal, the finite is the same as the mortal.[20]

In this condition all distinctions are transcended, including that between self and not-self: it is liberation alike from time and desire, and brings perfect inward peace. When knowledge of Brahman is attained, *karma* cease to be accumulated. Only *karma* in the process of being worked out continue to be operative, and when these are exhausted the *Brahmana* (knower of Brahman) attains the condition of **jivanmukta** (one who is free while living). Such a *Brahmana* is said to be one with Brahman.[21] Since liberation is the state of being freed from ignorance, it follows that it is not the coming into being of a new property of the soul, but rather the revealing of its original nature after being freed from the illusions of *avidya*.[22]

The means by which *moksa* is approached is meditation: while the performance of works and duties is useful, neither is sufficient to bring knowledge of Brahman.[23] That *sruti* passages differ over details of meditational technique is unimportant, for the essential message, and the end result, is the same in all cases. The only invariant recommendations are that it should be conducted in a seated position, and be repeated at any times which are propitious. The choice of symbols or other devices to still the process of ratiocination and bring the mind to one-pointedness is an area in which variation can be allowed.[24] Most importantly, meditation is to be carried on until death, since the thought that occupies the mind at the moment of death is declared in the *Bhagavad Gita* to be of determining significance for the future: 'Thinking of whatever state (of being) he at the end gives up his body, to that being does he attain . . . being ever absorbed in the thought thereof.'[25]

The *Brahma Sutra* is a work of great philosophical acumen, and the product of a tradition which was already well developed, rigorous and subtle. It articulates and faces up to the difficulties involved in one of the styles of philosophy to which the human mind feels impelled to return again and again, a monism based on the transcendental insights which haunt us. It was not, of course, the last word, and a great tradition has been devoted to refining its philosophy: the thought of Sankara, Ramanuja and Madhva each in its way shows how these ideas have been diversely criticized and interpreted. This is not surprising: if Badarayana had said the last word on the matters he considers, he would have solved most of the riddles of existence single-handed.

Notes

References to the *Brahma Sutra* are given by part, sub-section and individual *sutra*, e.g. I.4.12, as is standard. Radhakrishnan's version (London: Allen & Unwin, 1960; New York: Allen & Unwin, 1968) is used throughout.

References to relevant *Upanisadic* texts are given in the same way, preceded by the name of the *Upanisad* in question e.g. *Chandogya U.*, III.3.3. P.U. = S. Radhakrishnan (ed. and trans.), *The Principal Upanisads*, London: Allen & Unwin, 1953.

1 The text is also known as the *Vedanta Sutra*, since it sums up **Vedanta** philosophy, and as the *Sariraka Sutra* (S: *sarira* = body) since it deals with the embodiment of Brahman.
2 Badarayana refers to himself, e.g. at III.2.41; III.4.1; III.4.8; III.4.19; IV.3.15; IV.4.7; and IV.4.12.
3 I.1.2. cf. I.3.10; III.2.11–21.
4 *Taittiriya U.*, II.1, P.U., p. 553.
5 I.1.13. There is a clear statement of this in the *sruti* texts in *Taittiriya U.*, II.8.1, P.U., pp. 550–2.
6 II.1.33.
7 I.4.23.
8 *Chandogya U.*, VI.1.4, P.U., pp. 446–7.
9 II.1.8–9.
10 Discussed at II.1.14–20.
11 II.3.2.
12 *Taittiriya U.*, II.1.1, P.U., p. 542.
13 *Brhad-aranyaka U.*, III.7.22, P.U., p. 229.
14 *Svetasvatara U.*, IV.3, P.U., p. 732.
15 II.3.47 sqq.
16 II.3.43. There is a basis for this in the *Bhagavad Gita*, XV.7: 'A fragment of My own self, having become a living soul, eternal, in the world of life', etc. (Radhakrishnan's 2nd edn, London: Allen & Unwin, 1949, p. 328.)
17 II.1.21.
18 cf. II.1.22.
19 II.1.34.
20 *Chandogya U.*, VII.24.1, P.U., p. 486.
21 IV.1.13; IV.1.19; IV.2.16; IV.4.4.

22 IV.4.1. There is no real difference between *moksa* in this tradition and the *nirvana* of Buddhism.
23 III.4.26–35.
24 IV.1.1–11; III.3.1–2 and 59.
25 *Bhagavad Gita*, VIII. 6 (Radhakrishnan's 2nd edn, p. 229). The view that the thought occurring at the moment of death is vitally important occurs also in Buddhist sources, cf. *The Tibetan Book of the Dead*, ed. W.Y. Evans-Wentz, Oxford: Oxford University Press, 1980, pp. 89ff. Western parallels are also noted in this work.

Badarayana's writings

Badarayana's name is linked with a single great work, the *Brahma Sutra*.

See also in this book

The Buddha, Patanjali, Sankara, Ramanuja, Madhva, Vivekananda, Gandhi, Aurobindo, Radhakrishnan

Sources and further reading

Badarayana, *The Brahma Sutra*, ed. and trans. S. Radhakrishnan, London: Allen & Unwin, 1960; New York: Allen & Unwin, 1968

See also:

Radhakrishnan, S., *Indian Philosophy*, 2nd edn, vol. II, ch. VII, London: Allen & Unwin, 1929 and many subsequent impressions
Radhakrishnan, S. (ed. and trans.), *The Bhagavad Gita*, 2nd edn, London: Allen & Unwin, 1949 and many subsequent impressions
Radhakrishnan, S. (ed. and trans.), *The Principal Upanisads*, London: Allen & Unwin, 1953
Thibaut, G., *The Vedanta Sutras with the Commentary by Samkarasarya*, vols XXXIV and XXXVIII, Oxford: Oxford University Press, Sacred Books of the East series, Pt I, 1890, Pt II, 1896
Thibaut, G., *The Vedanta Sutras, with the Commentary of Ramanuja*, vol. XLVII, Oxford: Oxford University Press, Sacred Books of the East series, 1904

NAGARJUNA about second century CE

When Buddhism began to develop into distinct schools of thought its main division occurred between what became known as the **Theravada** (or **Hinayana**) and **Mahayana** schools. Further division then took place in both these schools. Theravada Buddhism divided into the Vaibhasika and Sautrantika schools. Mahayana Buddhism gave rise to the **Madhyamika** school and then, more than a century later, to the **Yogacara**.[1]

It is in virtue of his founding and promulgation of the Madhyamika branch of Mahayana Buddhism that Nagarjuna ranks among the greatest of the Indian Buddhist thinkers. Madhyamika teaching focuses on the Buddha's doctrine of the Middle Way, which advocates a life lived between the two extremes of a rigorous asceticism and an over-worldly indulgence, and Nagarjuna's philosophical thought provides a kind of logical counterpart to the Buddha's teaching of the Middle Way. He developed a process of dialectical reasoning which exposed contradictions in ordinary thought and which, by reducing all claims to pairs of negations, sought to dislodge thinking from such extremes, thereby freeing the mind to achieve enlightenment. According to this procedure, when it is recognized that opposing poles of thought may be negated by reasoning, the mind is able to acknowledge that reality is neither of them, and is able to experience *sunyata*, an emptiness or void which, although it defies description, is not nihilistic in its import. This experience of emptiness is regarded as the condition of a poised and perfect wisdom, *prajnaparamita*, in which intellect and intuition are united. Perhaps it is best thought of as a clarity of one's whole consciousness that permits the kind of apprehension that is not possible for a mind that thinks in terms of stark oppositions: 'the middle between these two extremes . . . is the intangible, the incomparable, non-appearing, not comprehensible, without any position . . . that verily is the Middle Path – the vision of the Real in its true form.'[2] For Nagarjuna, *sunyata* is a concept which encompasses a range of meanings and which, together with the method of dialectical reasoning, provides the framework for a visionary yet rigorous philosophy.

Nothing conclusive is known about the exact dates of Nagarjuna's life. By all accounts it seems to have been a long one. He was probably philosophically active somewhere between 50 CE and 200 CE but he has also been placed around 300 CE and these uncertainties about his dates have suggested to some commentators that more than one person may have been responsible for the doctrine and writings attributed to him. The several biographical reports that are available are not entirely consistent with each other. It seems reasonably certain that he was a **Brahmin**, born in southern India, and that his early years were strangely clouded with the threat of sin and evil, so that he appeared to be someone doomed to an early death. A biography by Kumarajiva[3] records that he was redeemed from this state in early manhood when he experienced some kind of illumination or conversion in which he recognized that desire and passion are the causes of suffering. The account relates that as a consequence of this realization he entered the Buddhist order. Some Tibetan sources tell a somewhat different story, recounting that astrologers had predicted that Nagarjuna would die at the age of 7 but that he avoided that fate by entering the Buddhist order in early childhood and undergoing instruction. Whatever his route to scholarship and spirituality, there is entire agreement concerning his remarkable aptitude for intensive study, the profundity of his insights and the compassion and care he exercised towards the community in which he lived.

Nagarjuna's thought constitutes a distillation and systematization of the *Prajnaparamita* (Perfection of Wisdom) texts. Those texts form an immense body of literature that is the source of the *sunyata* (emptiness) doctrine and that derives from those teachings of the Buddha that were meant for his more philosophically minded followers. It is no longer thought, as it once was, that Nagarjuna was the author of some of these texts but there is general agreement in attributing to him the authorship of approximately twenty-five works including a number of *sastras*, or commentaries, on the primary *Prajnaparamita* literature.[4] What is not in doubt is that he was the agent of a profound revolution in Buddhism in that he developed the Buddha's 'silence' concerning the nature of ultimate reality into a comprehensive critique of metaphysical dogmatism. In a conversation with a disciple the Buddha is reported to have described his position in the following words:

> To hold that the world is eternal or to hold that it is not, or to agree to any other of the propositions you adduce, Vaccha, is the jungle of theorizing, the wilderness of theorizing, the tangle of theorizing, the bondage and the shackles of theorizing, attended by ill, distress, perturbation and fever; it conduces not to detachment, passionlessness, tranquillity, peace, to knowledge and wisdom of Nirvana. This is the danger I perceive in these views which makes me discard them all.[5]

It is precisely this standpoint that Nagarjuna's dialectic upholds and develops.

Broadly, the method of the dialectic is fourfold: first, it considers the affirmation of something; next, its negation; then, the affirmation of both the affirmation and the negation; and, finally, the negation of both the affirmation and the negation.[6] Something of its use is exemplified in Nagarjuna's treatment of a fundamental theme in his philosophy:

the idea of 'dependent origination'. It concerns causation and has to be understood in relation to the general Buddhist principle, already described, that repudiates all polarities and affirms that reality lies in the Middle Way. In the Madhyamika *sastras* (commentaries), and repeatedly throughout Buddhist scriptures in general, the repudiation of polarities is expressed in the following words of the Buddha: 'No production nor destruction; no annihilation nor persistence; no unity nor plurality; no coming in nor going out'.[7] In accordance with this principle, when Nagarjuna considers causality, he rejects both a total determinism and a total indeterminism and espouses a Middle Way account of causation. He maintains that it is by means of an interdependence, or 'dependent origination', that the world has its being, and that a certain kind of intuitive realization of this fact of interdependency, although not dogmatically stateable in language, is essential to enlightenment and spiritual development: it is the condition of the Middle Way. He writes: 'Dependent origination we call emptiness. This is metaphorical designation and is, indeed, the middle path'.[8]

In examining causation, Nagarjuna considers three positions: first, that of identity, which holds that the effect is included in the cause; second, that of non–identity, which holds that the effect is distinct from the cause; third, a mixed view in which a cause is regarded as the consequence of a pre–existent cause and becomes so in virtue of an external combination of conditions. When subjected to Nagarjuna's dialectical logic, all three positions are shown to be untenable: the first because if an effect already exists as part of its cause then it cannot be produced; the second because if the conditions supposedly giving rise to the effect are distinct from it, then 'anything can come out of anything', and that is not what is understood by 'causation'; the third for the reasons already given for the unacceptability of the first two. Nagarjuna further points out that causality presupposes *change* and that this disposes us to adopt a view of reality as consisting of momentary events, since it is absurd to speak of change with regard to what is permanent. But as change involves a *process* of change requiring continuity, there cannot be a process of change in relation to events which are merely momentary. Deployed thus, the dialectic reduces all three accounts of causality to incoherence and there appears to be no way in which to enunciate an intelligible causal theory. The condition for the realization of *sunyata* obtains.[9]

What has to be remembered in the endeavour to grasp Nagarjuna's ideas is that when his logic has demolished a particular position or point of view it is not because he is going to assert its contrary or

opposite. That, too,will be similarly demolished in order to experience the emptiness in which it is recognized that the distinctions of
opposites are false distinctions and, more profoundly, that essentially
there are no differences between the polarities formulated by reason.

Has Nagarjuna, in exposing inadequacies in the several accounts of
causality, also destroyed the buddhistic understanding of dependent
origination that he wishes to promulgate? Some commentators have
said that he has and that his doctrine is a negating and wholly nihilistic
one in that it rules out any kind of conceptualization. Others have
defended his method on the grounds that it can bring someone to the
experience of *sunyata* and so to the central focus of Madhyamika
doctrine; that is, to the point at which polarities of thought collapse
into incoherence and it is recognized that apparent oppositions are
actually non-existent, that there is 'no production nor destruction;
no annihilation nor persistence', indeed, no oppositions of any kind,
because there is really no difference between the posited opposites.
Ultimately, Nagarjuna maintains, we come to see even that the
conditioned existence of **samsara** is not different from **nirvana**. This
does not mean that he wanted to deprive ordinary empirical
distinctions of their utility and validity. Their legitimate use, he held,
is in the transactions of daily life. However, they have to be recognized
as misleading if applied to higher or philosophical truth. What is
important is that the empirical distinctions of practical living are
understood within the context of the critical account of their
relationship to the higher reality.

Nagarjuna's discussion of dependent origination is a corollary of
the general tenet of Buddhism that everything is in flux, is becoming
rather than being, and that the notion of an enduring essential
substance as the foundation of the real is an illusion or an incorrect
interpretation of experience. His remarks on the existence of the self
are similarly consistent with this view. He held that the entities of
the world cannot be said to have enduring self-natures, or souls, and
that *prajna*, or wisdom, consists in the continuing consciousness of
the transitoriness of all things. Once again, this is not to be taken
as a refutation of claims for the existence of the self but as a critique
of all definitive assertions both of its existence and non-existence.
Thus Nagarjuna writes: 'The self is not different from the states, nor
identical with them; (there) is no self without the states; nor is it to be
considered non-existent.'[10]

It could be claimed that Nagarjuna's repudiation of all systems
and theories cannot escape being construed as yet another system or
theory. In contesting such a claim it may be pointed out that, unlike

theories and systems, his thought is not concerned to provide anything resembling an *explanation* of things according to some pattern or formula, but to generate a critical awareness of the presuppositions on which all such formulas depend and to note that our choices of such presuppositions are often entirely arbitrary or a matter of purely personal dispositions. T. R. V. Murti has likened Nagarjuna's critique to the procedures of the western philosophers David Hume and Immanuel Kant,[11] both of whom set out to be profoundly sceptical of all traditional justifications of metaphysical claims. It may also be compared, perhaps at an even more fundamental level, with the existentialist approach of Jean-Paul Sartre; in particular with Sartre's claim that free human choice is ultimately an absurd choice since it is made on the basis of nothing. Murti remarks:

> The Madhyamika method is to *de*conceptualize the mind and to disburden it of all notions . . . The dialectic is not an avenue for the acquisition of information, but a catharsis . . . It is the abolition of all restrictions which conceptual patterns necessarily impose. It is not nihilism, which is itself a stand-point asserting that nothing is. The dialectic is a rejection of all views including the nihilistic.[12]

By those who practise it, Buddhism is often spoken of as '*dharma*'. The word derives from the root *dhr*, 'to uphold', and has numerous meanings. Chiefly it refers to the ultimate reality of *nirvana*, the law or nature of the universe, the moral life, right conduct and teaching, and the insights of enlightened understanding. It is also used to speak of particular things. Terms such as 'dharma-body' and 'dharma-eye' occur frequently and there are countless other uses that have to be interpreted in relation to their particular contexts. A broad distinction is always maintained between everyday entities, which are illusory or false in some way, and '*dharmas*', which are always aspects of a deeper and more essential reality. The **bodhisattva**, the devout Buddhist who has achieved enlightenment but forgoes transition to *nirvana* for the sake of guiding others towards the same goal, is someone who has progressed even beyond *dharmas*. The mind of such a person maintains a transparency from which self-consciousness and all other forms of dualism have been banished by means of the union of intellect and intuition and its concomitant condition of complete freedom: 'Bodhisattvas do not grasp at ideas, they cling to nothing, their perfected knowledge is empty. This is the essence of supreme wisdom.'[13]

In his writings, Nagarjuna describes a sixfold path of spiritual discipline for those who aspire to this condition. His emphasis in this aspect of his teaching is always on the transcending of – although he never belittles – the everyday virtues of life. He rejects the ideal of the *arhat*, the saintly person of traditional Buddhism whose purposes were confined to the bringing about of the cessation of personal suffering and the realization of *nirvana*. Instead, his concern is with the *bodhisattva*'s dedication to the service of others and a sense of the community of all beings. His is not a discipline for the recluse. It has a moral quality not unlike that which informs Plato's account of the ascent of the human mind from illusion and shadows to a direct, intuitive knowledge of the Good. Like Nagarjuna, Plato advocates that those who achieve such knowledge should return to help those who are still struggling at the lower levels of understanding.[14]

The scope, detail and rigour of Nagarjuna's thought are not easily conveyed in a short essay; nor is its spirituality, which is at once intense and serene. His ideas have been powerfully influential in India, China, Tibet, Japan and Korea for over two thousand years and were, in particular, notably formative of Chinese Zen Buddhism.[15] Nagarjuna is closely studied in the West as well as in Asia, for occidental philosophers seem able to detect countless affinities between his views and certain elements of the western tradition. Since no more than about 5 per cent of the *Prajnaparamita* literature has so far been reliably translated and edited, this is an area of scholarship that will surely continue to develop and flourish.

Notes

1 The leading figure of the Yogacara school was Vasubandhu, *c.* fourth or fifth centuries CE. (See pp. 103–14 in this volume.) The fundamental difference in the two main schools of Buddhism is between their views of the basic elements of existence (*dharmas*). Theravadins believed in the existence of distinct entities possessing essences. Madhyamika doctrine affirmed the non-substantiality of things and the ultimate identity of *samsara* and *nirvana*.

2 Quoted from the *Kasyapaparivarta* in T.R.V. Murti, *The Central Philosophy of Buddhism*, London: Allen & Unwin, 1955, p. 210.

3 Kumarajiva (344–409/413 CE) translated into Chinese, in 100 books, Nagarjuna's commentary on the *Mahaprajnaparamita Sutra*. It was through him that Mahayana became established in China. With the help of numerous pupils he translated many *sutras* and *sastras* and comprehensively taught the practices of the Middle Way.

4 The *sutras* of the *Prajnaparamita* literature are anonymous and are held to enshrine the words of the Buddha. The *sastras* are commentaries on these primary texts. Nagarjuna is said to have brought the *Prajnaparamita sutras*

from the country of the Nagas in 100,000 *gathas* and to have produced an abridged *sastra* of 25,000 *gathas*.
5 Murti, op. cit., p. 47.
6 There is a very full discussion of Nagarjuna's dialectic in Murti, op. cit., Pt II.
7 These are the famous 'Eight Noes' of Madhyamika literature, as translated in Christmas Humphreys, *Buddhism*, Harmondsworth: Penguin Books, 1952, pp. 54, 55.
8 Ian C. Harris, *The Continuity of Madhyamika and Yogacara in Indian Mahayana*, Leiden: Brill, 1991, p. 143.
9 The process of the dialectic is sometimes described as having three stages: dogmatism, criticism and intuition. But intuition may also be achieved through moral and religious consciousness, and by the cessation of pain-causing acts.
10 Murti, op. cit., p. 206.
11 Murti, op. cit., especially ch. XII.
12 Murti, op. cit., p. 212. Murti's comparison of Nagarjuna with Kant has been examined and discussed most interestingly by Andrew P. Tuck in his *Comparative Philosophy and the Philosophy of Scholarship*, Oxford: Oxford University Press, 1991.
13 Heinrich Dumoulin, *Zen Buddhism: A History*, vol. I, *India and China*, New York and London: Macmillan, 1988, p. 31.
14 Plato's account of the ascent from the cave is in *The Republic*, bk VII.
15 The reciting of the *Diamond Sutra*, one of the best-known works in the *Prajnaparamita* literature, enabled the Sixth Patriarch, Huineng (638–713 CE), to achieve enlightenment.

Nagarjuna's writings

There is no single, definitive list of Nagarjuna's writings. A fairly comprehensive list, accompanied by bibliographical sources, is in D.S. Ruegg's *The Literature of the Madhyamika School of Philosophy in India* in *A History of Indian Literature*, vol. 7, fascicle 1, Wiesbaden: Harrassowitz, 1981. T.R.V. Murti's *The Central Philosophy of Buddhism* contains a helpful section on the Madhyamika literature (pp. 87–103) in which he attributes six main treatises and a number of smaller works to Nagarjuna. Almost all are commentaries (*sastras*) on the *Prajnaparamita sutras*.

See also:

Conze, E. (trans.), *The Perfection of Wisdom in Eight Thousand Lines and Its Verse Summary*, Berkeley, Calif., Four Seasons Foundation, 1973
Inada, Kenneth K., *Nagarjuna: A Translation of his Mulamadhyamakakarika with an Introductory Essay*, Tokyo: Hokuseido, 1970

See also in this book

the Buddha, Vasubandhu, Huineng, Tsong kha pa, Fazang, Nishitani

Sources and further reading

Garfield, J.L., *The Fundamental Wisdom of the Middle Way: Nagarjuna's Mulamadhyamakakarika*, New York and Oxford: Oxford University Press, 1995

Harris, I.C., *The Contuinity of Madhyamika and Yogacara in Indian Mahayana*, Leiden: Brill, 1991

Murti, T.R.V., *The Central Philosophy of Buddhism*, 2nd edn, London: Allen & Unwin, 1970

Radhakrishnan, S., *Indian Philosophy*, 2 vols, vol. I, London: Allen & Unwin, 8th impression, 1966, pp. 643–69

Radhakrishnan, S. and Moore, C.A. (eds), *A Source Book in Indian Philosophy*, Princeton: Princeton University Press, 1957, contains extracts from Nagarjuna's *Mahayana Vimsaka* and his *Madhyamika Sastra* (pp. 338–45)

Ramanan, K.V., *Nagarjuna's Philosophy*, Delhi: Motilal Banarsidass, 1978

Smart, Ninian, *Doctrine and Argument in Indian Philosophy*, London: Allen & Unwin, Muirhead Library of Philosophy, 1964 (discusses Nagarjuna's dialectical critique of causation)

Tuck, Andrew P., *Comparative Philosophy and the Philosophy of Scholarship*, Oxford: Oxford University Press, 1991

VASUBANDHU fourth or fifth centuries CE

In his recorded utterances, the Buddha repeatedly states that his ideas are not intended to be a *darsana* or philosophy but a *yana* or vehicle, a practical method leading to enlightenment. Consistently with this view, and with his refusal to speculate about what lies beyond or behind human experience, the Buddha made no attempt to set out a metaphysical basis for his vehicle for the relief of suffering. However, as Radhakrishnan suggests, it seems that there is in human beings an inbuilt need to speculate about ultimate questions, and for this view the subsequent history of Buddhism provides ample evidence.[1] Unable to resist the urge to fill in the deliberate omissions of the Buddha, later generations of Buddhists added their own metaphysics and epistemologies to complete the picture he left, their differences generating the various schools in the history of Buddhism. The major division is that between the **Theravada** (or Hinayana) on the one hand, and the **Mahayana** on the other. In turn, each of these major schools itself split into two, divided by philosophical differences to be touched on below. The Theravadins are divided into the Vaibhasikas and the Sautrantikas, and the Mahayanists into the **Madhyamikas** and the **Yogacarins**. The ideas of these two latter schools have been of the first importance in the development of the Mahayana, and are used as reference points not only by Indian thinkers, but also many in

Tibet, China, Korea and Japan. The greatest representative of the Madhyamika is Nagarjuna, and Vasubandhu is a leading figure of the Yogacara school.

Despite the existence of a fairly early biography of Vasubandhu by Paramartha (499–569 CE) – a leading exponent of Yogacarin doctrine in China – there is very little agreement about the facts of Vasubandhu's life. According to Paramartha's *Biography of Master Vasubandhu* (C: *Posoupandou fashih zhuan* [*P'o-sou-p'an-tou fa-shih chuan*]), Vasubandhu was born in Purusapura (Peshawar), son of a Brahmin named Kausika and younger brother of Asanga, himself to become a major figure in the Yogacarin tradition. In his earlier years, Vasubandhu is said to have been a follower of the Theravadin *Abhidharma*,[2] composing a major summary of doctrine, the *Abhidharmakosa*, in 600 verses, to be followed by a prose commentary, the *Abhidharmakosa-bhasyam*.[3] This work, together with his skill as a disputant, is said to have brought Vasubandhu a considerable reputation.

It is said that Asanga, a Mahayanist, feared that his younger brother would use his considerable powers to attack the Mahayana. Feigning illness, Asanga persuaded Vasubandhu to return to him at Purusapura. In the course of the visit, Asanga converted Vasubandhu to the Mahayana, and the latter then turned his considerable intellectual gifts to its service. Together with commentaries on major Mahayana scriptures (e.g. on the *Avatamsaka, Vimalakirti, Nirvana* and *Prajnaparamita sutras*), Vasubandhu also wrote a number of what became key texts of the Yogacarin school, notably the *Twenty Verses and their Commentary* (*Vimsatika-Karika Vrtti*), the *Thirty Verses* (*Trimsika-Karika*) and *The Teaching of the Three Own-beings [or: Natures]* (*Tri-Svahbava-Nirdesa*). Vasubandhu is said to have died in his eightieth year at Ayodhya.

Such is the outline of the biography given by Paramartha. Many scholars have been reluctant to accept this evidence, however, since other early sources give conflicting dates for Vasubandhu's life by up to two hundred years, and in addition there are several figures in Buddhist history named Vasubandhu. In an attempt to accommodate all the evidence, the scholar Erich Frauwallner proposed that there were in fact two Vasubandhus whose lives and works have been confused, one responsible for the *Abhidharmika* works, and the other Asanga's younger brother.[4] Frauwallner's thesis is accepted by some scholars and disputed by others, and it is unlikely that the issue can be settled unless new evidence comes to light. It is one of several profound disagreements in Vasubandhu studies.

One point which is beyond dispute is that the Yogacarin school of the Mahayana has accumulated more names than any other, being standardly referred to in no fewer than four ways. The terms used are worth noting, since they indicate some important features of this school of thought from which to begin. The terms are as follows:

(1) *Yogacara*, from **yoga** and *acara*, a therapeutic course of action; this is the most ancient of the terms used to designate this school, and it indicates its concern to free the mind from false beliefs (a psychological therapy) by means of yogic practices. It may also indicate that the metaphysical doctrines of the school are founded on insights derived from yogic states of meditation as much as discursive reasoning,[5] a thesis for which there is evidence, as will be seen, in Vasubandhu's works;

(2) *cittamatra* or mind-only;

(3) *vijnaptimatra* or perception-only;

(4) *vijnanavada* or consciousness- (or mind-) doctrine.

Terms (2) and (4) are roughly equivalent, and indicate the central metaphysical doctrine of the school, idealistic **monism**, i.e. the view that reality is one and not many, and the one is mental in nature, not material.[6] Term (3) indicates the principal way in which this metaphysical belief is argued for, namely by means of a philosophical analysis of perception.

The philosophy of perception had been for some time an area of dispute between the two major schools of Theravadins, among whom Vasubandhu received his intellectual training. The Vaibhasikas accepted what is termed a naive realist theory of perception, i.e. the view that what is given in perception is the external world, not a sensation caused by something in the external world. On this view, we do not in any way create the objects of which we are aware in perception, which are held to be entirely unaffected by the nature of our perceptual apparatus. Instead we simply discover the external world, as it is, via direct perception of it. By contrast, those belonging to the Sautrantika school, whilst accepting the existence of the external world, deny that it is directly experienced in perception.[7] They hold a form of what is termed a representationalist theory of perception. Common to all forms of this view is the thesis that what is immediately experienced in perception is not an object but a mental entity or datum, from which the existence of an external object must be inferred.[8] The belief in the existence of the external world, no longer itself immediately experienced, is justified as the most plausible hypothesis by means of which to account for the major features of perceptual experience, namely its coherence and its independence of our will.

Vasubandhu accepts the Sautrantika view that the immediately given in perception is something mental in nature, a sensation or sense-datum in western terminology. What he then argues is that there is no need to add the hypothesis that these sensations are caused by physical objects in an external world. All there is can be explained equally well in terms of mental events alone: hence the term *cittamatra* or mind-only as a name for this philosophy.[9] He begins his argument for this conclusion by drawing attention to the fact that perception can malfunction. We can believe ourselves to be experiencing external objects but be deceived by a malfunction in our perceptual apparatus:

> All this is perception-only, because of the appearance of non-existent objects, just as there may be the seeing of non-existent nets of hair by someone affected with an optical disorder.[10]

That is, in delusory perception something is perceived, but what is perceived is not an external stimulus, and must therefore be something mental in nature.

It may be objected that this argument can at best only establish that some and not all experiences have mental contents as their immediate data. Further, how can the coherence and involuntariness of perceptions be accounted for on the hypothesis that there is no external world to cause them? Somewhat as Descartes was to do again many centuries later when wishing to cast doubt on the trust-worthiness of the senses, Vasubandhu now turns to the experience of dreaming:

> In a dream, even without an [external] object of sense or understanding, only certain things are to be seen: bees, gardens, women, men, etc. and these only in certain places, and not everywhere. And even there in those places, they are there to be seen only sometimes, and not all the time.[11]

That is, in dreams, where there is agreed to be no external object, our mental contents exhibit coherence and involuntariness, and therefore coherence and involuntariness do not entail the existence of an external world.

This argument is by no means immune to criticism,[12] though Vasubandhu would not have been unduly troubled, since he has another and quite different type of argument to support his mind-only thesis, and this is an argument based on the insights derived from nondual awareness:

> when [people] become awakened by the attainment of a supermundane knowledge free from discriminations, which is the antidote to these [discriminations], then they truly understand the non-being of those sense objects through meeting with a clear worldly subsequently attained knowledge.[13]

'Supermundane knowledge free from discriminations' is the nondual awareness of enlightenment, direct non-conceptual awareness of being-as-is. Those who attain this level of insight have direct apprehension of the unreality of all individuals, and this Vasubandhu regards as incorrigible evidence in favour of the mind-only thesis. A 'clear worldly subsequently attained knowledge' is the state of mind of the enlightened after the enlightenment experience itself: a pure, non-clinging reflection, in which dualistic experiences are apprehended as they are, i.e. mere constructions, mental in nature.

The acceptance of monism in metaphysics generates an agenda of philosophical problems which monists must address. Just as those who accept materialistic monism (the view that what there is is matter-only) must give an account in materialistic terms of all the phenomena ordinarily called mental, so those who accept idealistic monism are faced with a corresponding set of difficulties. In the present case, Vasubandhu has to give an account of the ordinary distinction between veridical and non-veridical perception, and of the major features of our experience – How does it come about that it is ordinarily dualistic? How do causal sequences operate over time? – in ways which do not presuppose the existence either of matter or an external world. Vasubandhu sets out to do precisely this, within the context of a buddhistic framework whose ultimate goal is a practical one, the attainment of *nirvana*, the release from suffering.

The distinction between veridical and non-veridical perception is a difficult issue for idealistic monists. In the framework of a pluralistic metaphysics which accepts (roughly) the common-sense picture of the world as composed of variously related discrete individuals in space and time, this distinction can be fairly easily accommodated, in principle at least: veridical perceptions accurately reflect the way things are in the external world, and non-veridical ones do not. Vasubandhu has dispensed with the external world, however, and so cannot have recourse to this idea of correspondence or lack of it between perception and what is perceived. Instead, he recasts the distinction in terms of the mutual coherence or incoherence of perceptions: 'The certainty of perceptions takes place mutually, by the state of their sovereign effect on one another.'[14] In other words, since ordinary experience is simply a sequence of mental events, all change is change within this sequence. What we ordinarily regard as veridical perceptions are those which cohere with the rest of the sequence. We regard as non-veridical those which are incoherent with this sequence. This way of recasting the distinction is a fairly standard move in metaphysics of the kind under discussion.[15]

Next, Vasubandhu has to accommodate within his mind-only metaphysics both the major features of our mental life and the buddhistic view that our ordinary mental life is delusory and can be abrogated. The major features of our ordinary mental life which are of most pressing concern to Vasubandhu are:

(1) that it is dualistic, i.e. of a world of individuals, based on the dualism of self and not-self, articulated by means of conceptual discrimination; and
(2) that it is an ordered succession of cause and effect, not a series of random changes, and these causal sequences are independent of our volition.

In order to account for the dualistic nature of our ordinary world-picture, and to accommodate the buddhistic notion of enlightenment, Vasubandhu introduces the doctrine of the three own-beings or natures.

According to this doctrine, all the elements of consciousness can be divided into three classes, which Vasubandhu calls the inter-dependent own-being (S: *para-tantra-svabhava*); the constructed (or imagined) own-being (S: *parikalpita-svabhava*); and the fulfilled (or perfected) own-being (S: *parinispanna-svabhava*). The interdependent own-being is the play of the phenomenal world, the stream of experience. All conceptual discriminations within this stream of experience are the result of the activity of the imagination (*parikalpa*), which thus fabricates or constructs the common-sense (and delusory) world-picture, i.e. the constructed own-being. Against the views of the Madhyamikas, the Yogacarins consider that it is incoherent to suppose that such fabrication is possible except on the hypothesis of a substratum: hence their insistence that there are three basic classes of elements of consciousness rather than two. The fulfilled own-being is the absence of discrimination, i.e. enlightenment or the condition of a Buddha.

Vasubandhu describes the relations between the three own-beings in the following way:

> At first, the interdependent, which consists of the non-being of duality, is entered;
> then and there construction only, non-existent duality, is entered;
> then and there the fulfilled, the non-being of duality, is entered.[16]

This ordering is partly logical and partly psychological. The construction of the dualistic world-picture, as has been indicated, in Vasubandhu's view presupposes something out of which to construct it: thus the interdependent own-being is logically prior to the constructed. Psychologically, the attainment of nondual awareness or fulfilled own-being is posterior to the ordinary awareness of constructed own-being. Logically, however, the fulfilled own-being is prior to everything else, being reality and so the ground of all events:

> Through the non-apprehension of duality,
> There is apprehension of the Ground of events.[17]

(Strictly speaking, the fulfilled own-being cannot be an own-being at all, as Vasubandhu sometimes notes. Since it is Suchness or being-as-is, no predicates apply to it, and so it can have no own-being or nature. When he speaks in this way, Vasubandhu's views come close to those of Nagarjuna.)[18]

The next stage in Vasubandhu's account of the major features of experience involves one of the most characteristic and influential Yogacarin doctrines, the analysis of the eight types of consciousness. Within the context of idealistic monism, Vasubandhu has to explain in detail why it is that the phenomenal world appears to us to be ordered in causal sequences which operate independently of our volitions. This is an especially high priority for a Buddhist, since to do this is to explain how the law of **karma** can operate without reference to a world of material individuals to be the vehicles of causal interactions. The law of *karma* states that our past and present actions, good or bad, generate consequences of a like kind which will unfailingly be visited upon us at some time in the future. How is this possible within a purely mental universe?

Vasubandhu's answer to this difficulty is the theory of the store-consciousness (*alayavijnana*), the first of the eight types of consciousness discriminated in Yogacarin thought. The store-consciousness is an ever-changing stream of mental events which underlies *samsaric* experience. It is held that all actions leave what the Yogacarins metaphorically term seeds (S: *bija*) and these are deposited, so to speak, in the store-consciousness. They mature, i.e. return to consciousness, when required to do so by the law of *karma*. In this way, momentary mental events (which is what our actions really are), can have consequences which do not appear to consciousness until well after the event in question, independently of our conscious will:

> The residual impressions of actions, along with the residual impressions of a 'dual' apprehension,
> cause another maturation (of seeds) to occur,
> where the former maturation has been exhausted.[19]

The store-consciousness is subliminal or on the borderline of ordinary awareness, yet it has experiences, including volitions: Vasubandhu must claim this, in order to provide a motivating force for change:

> Its appropriations, states, and perceptions are not fully conscious,
> Yet it is always endowed with contacts, mental attentions, feelings, cognitions, and volitions.[20]

It is important to note that the store-consciousness is not the ultimate reality in Yogacarin thought. Indeed, the goal of Yogacarin training is to bring its operation to a halt, at which point it ceases. It ceases when no more seeds are deposited and so when no more *karma* are generated, i.e. when the condition of the **bodhisattva** (i.e. sainthood) or of a Buddha is attained.[21]

The store-consciousness forms the basis for the seven other types of consciousness identified by Vasubandhu: one type of consciousness is associated with each of the five senses, and an accompanying sixth type, *manovijnana*, is the aspect of consciousness which synthesizes the impressions of the senses and the data of introspection. The seventh type of consciousness is 'tainted mind' (S: *klistamanas*), a type of consciousness which takes the store-consciousness for its object, and mistakenly regards the latter as the true, real self. Tainted mind involves our ordinary, mistaken sense of self-consciousness, and is the source of suffering: 'It is always conjoined with four afflictions . . . known as view of self, confusion of self, pride of self, and love of self.'[22] Since the illusion of ordinary self-consciousness is removed by enlightenment, tainted mind, like the store-consciousness, ceases when nondual awareness is attained.[23]

It may seem paradoxical that, in a philosophy whose goal is the attainment of a state of awareness in which all discriminations are abrogated, Vasubandhu should spend so long, and with such evident relish, elaborating a complex idealism embodying many fine distinctions. Vasubandhu was aware of the seeming paradox, and has a consistent response to it. In one sense, the entire Yogacarin system is a therapy: its analyses are designed ultimately to free the mind from the grip of delusory conceptual thought. It is a ladder which is to be thrown away once the higher levels of awareness have been reached. Vasubandhu is careful to point out that knowledge of the Yogacarin system itself does not constitute enlightenment. To entertain the belief, '"All this is perception only" . . . involves an apprehension',[24] i.e. conceptual discriminations, and so is not enlightenment. The latter is nondual awareness, in which 'consciousness does not apprehend any object of consciousness':[25]

It is the inconceivable, beneficial constant Ground, not liable
   to affliction,
bliss, and the liberation-body called the *Dharma*-body of the
   Sage.[26]

The ultimate purpose of this elaborate and influential philosophy is to bring about a state in which all philosophizing comes to an end.

Notes

1 S. Radhakrishnan, *Indian Philosophy*, 2 vols, vol. I, London: Allen & Unwin, 1966, pp. 468–9.
2 The *Abhidharma* (P: *Abhidhamma*) is the section of the Theravadin **Tipitaka** which deals with matters of psychological and to some extent philosophical interest. A follower of the *Abhidharma* is referred to as an *abhidharmika*. To be absolutely precise, Vasubandhu's *Adhidharmakosa* is a summary exposition of the *Mahavibhasa*, itself a commentary on the *Abhidharma* treatises.
3 This major work is now available in English, trans. L. Poussin and L.M. Pruden, 4 vols, Berkeley, Calif.: Asian Humanities Press, 1988.
4 See E. Frauwallner, *On the Date of the Buddhist Master of the Law Vasubandhu*, Rome: Istituto Italiano per il Medio ed Estremo Oriente, 1951. For a

contrary view, see S. Anacker, *Seven Works of Vasubandhu*, Delhi: Motilal Banarsidass, 1984, pp. 7–28.

5 cf. Paul Williams, *Mahayana Buddhism: The Doctrinal Foundations*, London: Routledge, 1989, p. 83.

6 Even at so basic a level, the interpretation of Vasubandhu's thought is disputed. Kochumuttom in *A Buddhist Doctrine of Experience*, Delhi: Motilal Banarsidass, 1982, argues that Vasubandhu embraces pluralistic realism, and is much closer to the *abhidharmikas* than is generally realized. Radhakrishnan, op. cit., pp. 624–43, accepts the idealist monist interpretation. For a detailed survey of the whole issue, see T.E. Wood, *Mind Only*, Honolulu: Hawaii University Press, 1991. In my view, the idealist monist view makes more sense of the arguments put forward in Vasubandhu's later works than any other, though the influence of *abhidharmika* views is marked in some other works. It is not difficult to construe all the works attributed to Vasubandhu as those of one thinker who began as an *abhidharmika*, was converted to the Yogacara, but by no means abandoned all his former ideas. Thus in certain of his works Vasubandhu adopts the key Yogacarin doctrine of the store-consciousness – a term explained later in the present essay – but combines it with an *abhidharmika* metaphysics in which the ultimate realities are moment-events (cf. e.g. *A Discussion of the Five Aggregates/Pancaskandhaka-Prakarana*, in Anacker, op. cit., pp. 51 ff.). In this theory, the store-consciousness is said to be only momentary in duration, replaced in the next moment by a further momentary store-consciousness, and so on. It is a question of some interest, though too big to be pursued here, whether this doctrine of moment-events, a direct consequence of the Buddha's doctrine of aggregates (*skandhas*), is easily compatible with the nondualism of the Mahayana, in which ultimate reality is neither momentary nor an event.

The present exposition of Vasubandhu's philosophy is based on late works which are manifestly Yogacarin.

7 The term Vaibhasika is used because this group of Theravadins accept as their key scriptural text the *Vibhasa*, a commentary on the *Abhidharma*. The origin of the term Sautrantika is disputed: it perhaps indicates that this group chose as their scriptural authority the *Suttapitaka*, adjuring the other two sections of the *Tipitaka*: cf. Radhakrishnan, op. cit., p. 619, n. 2. Both Vaibhasikas and Sautrantikas are standardly classified as adherents of the Sarvastivada. A Sarvastivadin is one who accepts the metaphysics of plural-istic realism, i.e. the view that reality is composed of a number of discrete, independent substances.

8 In western versions of representationalist theories of perception, the immediate data of sense-experience have been referred to in a number of ways: 'ideas' (Locke); 'impressions' (Hume); or 'sensa' or 'sense-data' in more recent variants of this same view.

9 Vasubandhu's development of the Sautrantika viewpoint was to be paralleled very closely some 1,300 years later in the West in Berkeley's reaction to Locke's philosophy; cf. the articles on these philosophers in D. Collinson, *Fifty Major Philosophers*, London: Routledge, 1988.

10 *Twenty Verses*, Anacker, op. cit., p. 161.

11 *Twenty Verses*, Anacker, op. cit., p. 162. cf. Descartes, 1st *Meditation*.

12 e.g. some centuries later the Vedantin Sankara objected to Yogacarin dream arguments: 'the things of which we are conscious in a dream are negated by

our waking consciousness . . . Those things, on the other hand, of which we are conscious in our waking state, such as posts and the like, are never negated in any state' (Sankara, *Commentary on the Vedanta Sutras*, II.2.29, in S. Radhakrishnan and C.A. Moore (eds), *A Source Book in Indian Philosophy*, Princeton: Princeton University Press, 1957, p. 534). Sankara argues that we regard dream-experiences as non-continuous and incoherent with waking experiences, and so no conclusions can safely be drawn about the latter on the analogy of the former. Sankara is following Badarayana's criticisms of analogous dream-arguments, cf. *Brahma Sutra*, II.2.29 and III.2.3.

13 *Twenty Verses*, Anacker, op. cit., p. 173.
14 Ibid., p. 172.
15 It has a close parallel in the coherence theory of truth, adopted by western philosophers like Hegel who also adopt idealistic monism.
16 *The Teaching of the Three Own Beings*, Anacker, op. cit., p. 294.
17 Ibid., p. 295. In the two-truth theory of the Madhyamikas, the constructed and interdependent own-beings are reduced to one (S: *samvrti satya*); the fulfilled own-being is retained, being called *paramartha satya* (profound, ultimate, or absolute reality). Cf. Nagarjuna.
18 e.g. *Thirty Verses*, vs 24, Anacker, op. cit., p. 188.
19 Anacker, op. cit., vs 19. The *Thirty Verses* became the most widely read and commented on of all Yogacarin treatises.
20 Anacker, op. cit., vs 3, p. 186.
21 Hence Vasubandhu writes of the store-consciousness, 'Its de-volvement [i.e. cessation] takes place in a saintly state' (Anacker, op. cit., vs 5). Some commentators have wrongly taken the store-consciousness to be the ultimate reality in Yogacarin thought, cf. J.D. Willis, *On Knowing Reality*, New York: Columbia University Press, 1979, pp. 23ff.
22 *Thirty Verses*, vs 6, Anacker, op. cit., p. 186.
23 Anacker, op. cit., vs 7. The eightfold analysis of consciousness proved influential in the later development of Mahayana Buddhism. It was accepted, for example, by many Zen thinkers, cf. Hakuin, and by many Tibetan thinkers, cf. Padma-Sambhava and Milarepa.
24 Anacker, op. cit., vs 27, p. 189.
25 Ibid., vs 28.
26 Ibid., vs 30.

Vasubandhu's writings

The major Yogacarin works of Vasubandhu are:

Madhyanta-Vibhaga-Bhasya (Commentary on the Separation of the Middle from Extremes)
Trimsika-Karika (The Thirty Verses)
Tri-Svabhava-Nirdesa (The Teaching of the Three Own-beings)
Vimsatika-Karika Vrtti (The Twenty Verses and their Commentary)

See also in this book

the Buddha, Badarayana, Patanjali Nagarjuna, Padmasambhava, Milarepa, Tsong kha pa, Fazang, Hakuin

Sources and further reading

Anacker, S., *Seven Works of Vasubandhu*, Delhi: Motilal Banarsidass, 1984 (contains the major Yogacarin works with extensive notes and introductory matter)

Frauwallner, E., *On the Date of the Buddhist Master of the Law Vasubandhu*, Rome: Istituto Italiano per il Medio ed Estremo Oriente, 1951 (sets out the arguments for the 'two Vasubandhus' theory)

Haldar, A., *Some Psychological Aspects of Early Buddhist Philosophy based on the Abhidharmakosa of Vasubandhu*, Calcutta: Asiatic Society Monograph, vol. 25, 1981

Kochumuttom, T.A., *A Buddhist Doctrine of Experience*, Delhi: Motilal Banarsidass, 1982

Radhakrishnan, S., *Indian Philosophy*, 2 vols, vol. I, London: Allen & Unwin, 8th impression, 1966

Radhakrishnan, S. and Moore, C.A., *A Source Book in Indian Philosophy*, Princeton: Princeton University Press, 1957 (contains a further translation of the *Twenty Verses and their Commentary* and the *Thirty Verses*)

Vasubandhu, *Abhidharmakosabhasyam*, trans. L. Poussin and L.M. Pruden, 4 vols, Berkeley, Calif., Asian Humanities Press, 1988

Vasubandhu, *Karmasiddhiprakarana* (Treatise on Action), trans. E. Lamotte and L.M. Pruden, Berkeley, Calif., Asian Humanities Press, 1988 (there is another translation of this work in Anacker, op. cit., 1984)

Williams, P., *Mahayana Buddhism: The Doctrinal Foundations*, London: Routledge, 1989

Willis, J.D., *On Knowing Reality*, New York, Columbia University Press, 1979 (a translation of a key section of the major Yogacarin work of Vasubandhu's brother Asanga)

Wood, T.E., *Mind Only*, Honolulu: Hawaii University Press, 1991

HADANTACARIYA BUDDHAGHOSA fifth century CE

Of the several members of the Buddhist order who have borne the name 'Buddhaghosa' the one who flourished towards the latter half of the fifth century CE is the most renowned and influential. The reputation of this Buddhaghosa rests on his detailed and comprehensive synthesis of the doctrines enshrined in the classics of the Pali Canon, the body of literature that defines **Theravada** Buddhism.[1] His commentaries on these classics are copious, treating not only of the broad scope of Buddhist doctrine but also of a wide range of social customs, folklore, and literary, commercial, cultural and philosophical matters. His best-known work, the *Visuddhimagga* (The Path of Purification), has been described as 'a compendium of all Buddhism in three books'.[2] It comprises a comprehensive work of reference and analysis, and a complete manual of meditational practice.

Reliable information about Buddhaghosa's life is scant. A few details have been culled from his own writings at points where he has mentioned in passing his sojourn in a particular place or a meeting with a particular person. There is also a thirteenth-century account, composed in thirty-three couplets, of his life and work.[3] A third source is a life of Buddhaghosa, *Buddhaghosuppatti*, written in Pali in the middle of the fifteenth century by Maha Mangala, a Burmese **bhikshu**, or mendicant disciple.[4] This last source has been described as 'of a legendary and edifying character and of little independent value'.[5] Along with the thirteenth-century account it must be read with caution, in the light of the fact that it was written many centuries after Buddhaghosa's lifetime.

What does seem to be reasonably certain is that Buddhaghosa, after ordination into the Buddhist priesthood, travelled from India to Sri Lanka to live monastically and study the abundant Theravada literature which had been steadily accumulating there since missionaries began taking Buddhism to Sri Lanka in the first century after the Buddha's death. This source material was written for the most part in Sinhala, the major language of Sri Lanka and, as part of his project, Buddhaghosa set himself and accomplished the task of translating much of it into Pali.[6] He remained in Sri Lanka, living either in or near the Mahavihara monastery in Anuradhapura, the royal capital, until the political peace of the area was destroyed by invaders. During his time in the monastery he seems to have astonished the monks with his wide learning and knowledge of texts, his prodigious memory and his unfailing intellectual energy.

Buddhaghosa's significance as a commentator and synthesizer has to be understood in the historical context of the development of Buddhism. After the death of the Buddha a series of councils was called in order to establish and clarify the main elements of the **Tripitaka**, or Three Baskets, those remembered sayings and sermons of the Buddha and the established practices that had been memorized and collected together by his first followers and disciples.[7] Inevitably, divisions of opinion erupted at the councils, chief among them a disagreement between the orthodox Elders, who maintained that buddhahood was achieved by a strict adherence to the discipline of laid-down rules of conduct, and a group of more unorthodox thinkers who held that buddhahood is potentially present in everyone and needs only to be nurtured in order to manifest itself. This latter, minority group detached itself from the Elders and eventually generated the numerous sects which became known as **Mahayana** Buddhism, or the Greater Vehicle. The Elders, or Theravadin, regarded Mahayana as an erroneous departure from the Buddha's true teaching, or **dharma**, but the Mahayanists declared their own doctrine to be an extension or development rather than a repudiation of Theravada doctrine and they gave the Buddhism of the Elders the name of **Hinayana**, or the Lesser Vehicle.[8]

As the division between these two groups became more sharply delineated, the Theravada ideal of the **arhat**, the person who by stringent self-discipline achieves a personal salvation, gave way in Mahayana teaching to the ideal of the **bodhisattva**, the self-denying and compassionate person who willingly delays personal salvation in order to love and serve all sentient beings. A further difference between the two groups concerns the question of the divinity of the Buddha. Theravada doctrine resolutely refused to regard the Buddha as God. Mahayana, on the other hand, invoked the concept of a transcendental Buddha, not identical with the historical Buddha, who is accessible through worship and prayer to all who need solace, mercy and support in the difficulties of life. Yet another area of contention between the two groups lay in the difference between the Theravada avowal that reality is the plurality of distinct things that we apprehend in ordinary perception, and the Mahayana rejection of pluralism in favour of a doctrine that asserted ineffable Emptiness (**sunyata**) to be the ultimately real.

Buddhaghosa's consolidation of Theravada teaching is entirely faithful to the basic tenets of Buddhism as propagated by the Elders. Thus he treats at length of the task, taken by Buddhism to be incumbent on everyone, to seek salvation in the context of impermanence, change, the cycle of decay and renewal, and the belief that life is a continual flux that takes place in accordance with a universal causality. He rejects, just as Buddhism in general rejects, the idea of an individual, immortal soul and fosters instead the buddhistic belief in the unity and interdependence of living things and the possibility of a harmony, achievable by means of compassion, that is able to supersede the suffering that permeates much of human existence. Equally important in his work is an emphasis on the essential practicality of Buddhism that is evident in the Buddha's enunciation of the Four Noble Truths. These Truths are: that suffering is everywhere; that misplaced desire is the cause of suffering; that its cure lies in removal of the cause; and that the cause may be removed by following the Noble Eightfold Path, the guide to life offered by the Buddha when he exhorted his followers to engage in right beliefs, right thought, right speech, right conduct, right vocation, right effort, right attention and right concentration.[9] Buddhaghosa's concern is always to set out the exact means to achieve understanding and, eventually, enlightenment and accession to **nirvana**, the condition of being which is at once a negation of all ordinary conditions and yet wholly positive in its sublimity and unsurpassed bliss.

Debate about the concept of *nirvana*, its coherence or incoherence and its significance in Buddhist thought and practice, is unending among Buddhists and non-Buddhists alike. It has been described as

> not endless space, not infinite thought, nor nothingness, neither ideas nor non-ideas. Not this world nor that is it . . . nor death, nor birth . . . It is the ending of sorrow. There is . . . an Unbecome, Unborn, Unmade, Unformed . . . there is release.[10]

But the literal meaning of *nirvana* is 'blown out', in the sense in which a fire goes out when its fuel is exhausted, and from this meaning some commentators have argued that to attain *nirvana* is to sever connections with the ordinary things of life and to become indifferent to ordinary human tasks and difficulties.

The negative interpretation of *nirvana* outlined above is one that Buddhaghosa, in his promulgation of authentic Theravada doctrine, is much concerned to deny. He maintains that the 'blowing out' or 'extinction' meaning of *nirvana* must be taken metaphorically and that it should not be regarded as a state of 'nothingness'. He distinguishes between the Path or way to *nirvana* and *nirvana* itself. The Path, he holds, can be described, but not the destination. He says: 'it [*nirvana*] can only be reached, not produced, by the Path . . . it transcends the intrinsic nature of matter . . . being attainable through special insight effected by strong effort.'[11] This account of *nirvana* is consistent with the actual life and conduct of the Buddha who, in the forty-five years he lived after his enlightenment, did not withdraw from the ordinary activities of daily living but spent his time in the midst of people, teaching them and sharing his thoughts with them, treading a middle way between extreme asceticism and the pursuit of pleasure, and refraining from making definitive pronouncements concerning the nature of *nirvana*. It is to this examplar, provided by the Buddha, of continuing participation in the life of the world rather than to any subsequent theorizing about *nirvana* that Buddhaghosa adheres in his doctrinal exegeses.

In Buddhaghosa's best-known work, *The Path to Purification*, the purity that is sought and to which the Path leads is *nirvana* itself. Buddhaghosa first systematically examines the nature and constituents of Virtue, raising a series of questions which he proceeds to answer in painstaking detail, and exploring a range of possible meanings for almost every word used in the canonical sources. In the course of his analyses, and in presenting anecdotal examples or illustrations of the points he wants to make, he provides a vivid picture of the social customs and sensibilities of his society and a mass of definitions of mundane as well as lofty concepts. Some of the distinctions he draws are fine almost to the point of triviality. For example:

> *Disparaging* is contemptuous talk. *Reproaching* is enumeration of faults such as 'He is faithless, he is an unbeliever'. *Snubbing* is taking up verbally thus 'Don't say that here'. Snubbing in all ways, giving grounds and reason, is *continual snubbing*. Or, alternatively, when someone does not give, taking him up thus 'Oh, the prince of givers!' is *snubbing*; and the thorough snubbing thus 'A mighty prince of givers!' is *continual snubbing*.[12]

For the dedicated *bhikshu*, such minutiae provided precise and certain instruction for the conduct of meditation concerning what is to be avoided in the search for virtue.

Buddhaghosa's writing is unfailingly penetrating in respect of every topic he examines. When he turns to the subject of concentration he deals comprehensively with numerous forms of meditational practice including a step-by-step method for remembering and dwelling on each moment of one's past life and previous incarnations. The *bhikshu* who succeeds in these practices, he writes,

> immerses himself in voidness and eliminates the perception of living beings. Since he does not entertain false notions about wild beasts, spirits, ogres, etc., because he has abolished the perception of living beings, he conquers fear and dread and conquers delight and aversion.[13]

The result of engaging in this intense concentration at the highest level is that a person achieves Direct Knowledge of a complex and transforming kind, and 'arrives at blissful perception and light perception'. Buddhaghosa continues:

> that same perception should be understood to be called 'perception of lightness' too because it is liberated from hindrances and from the things that oppose it . . . But when

he arrives at that state, his physical body too becomes as light as a tuft of cotton. He goes to the Brahma World thus with a visible body as light as a tuft of cotton wafted by the wind.[14]

Such a person has obtained supernormal powers and although to enter the Brahma world is not to achieve complete release, it marks arrival at a significant stage on the path leading to *nirvana*.

The scope and comprehensiveness of Buddhaghosa's scholarly ordering and analysis of Theravada thought are not easily made clear in a short essay. Historians and commentators, even when they have disagreed about the details of his life or the attribution to him of certain works, are unanimous in acclaiming his six major commentaries as masterly and his philological and exegetical discrimination as unsurpassed in Buddhist literature. His influence on subsequent commentators was profound and far-reaching. He set the highest standards concerning accuracy, authenticity and respect for the texts he studied and there can be no doubt that his systematic organization and presentation of Theravada teaching have guaranteed its dissemination and widespread acceptability. His aim was always to understand and transmit the Buddha's teaching in its purest and most illuminating form.

Notes

1 Theravada Buddhism is the 'Teaching of the Elders'. It differs doctrinally from the less orthodox Mahayana Buddhism developed by such thinkers as Huineng.

2 T.W. Rhys Davids, 'Buddhaghosa', in J. Hastings (ed.), *Encyclopaedia of Religion and Ethics*, Edinburgh: T. and T. Clarke, 1908–26, and New York: Scribner, 1951.

3 There is a translation of this account of Buddhaghosa's life in Buddhaghosa, *The Path of Purification*, trans. Bhikkhu Nyanamoli, vol. I, Berkeley, Calif.: and London: Shambala, 1976, pp. xxi, xxii.

4 A précis of this account, described as a 'popular novel', is given in *The Path of Purification* (see note 3 above), pp. xxiv–xxvi.

5 In Mircia Eliade (ed.), 'Buddhaghosa', *Encyclopaedia of Religion*, London and New York: Collier Macmillan, 1987, p. 886.

6 Pali is 'the text language', that is, the language traditionally known as *Magadhi* which from around the first century BCE was developed for the presentation of Theravada scriptures. In 1881 the Pali Text Society was founded by T.W. Rhys Davids. It has published most of the Pali Canon in the Roman alphabet.

7 The Baskets have distinct subject-matters. The first, the *Vinayapitaka*, treats of the discipline and history of the Buddhist Order. The second, the *Suttapitaka*, contains discourses and sayings attributed to the Buddha. The

third, known as the *Abhidhammapitaka*, covers the philosophical and psychological aspects of Buddhist doctrine. (These are the Pali names for the Baskets.)

8 Because the term 'Hinayana' means 'Lesser Vehicle' it has a derogatory tone and is therefore rarely used nowadays to refer to Theravada Buddhism.

9 For a more detailed account of these important elements of Buddhism see R.C. Zaehner (ed.), *Encyclopaedia of Living Faiths*, London: Hutchinson, 1978, pp. 263–92.

10 See Keith Ward, *Images of Eternity*, London: Darton, Longman & Todd, 1987, pp. 59, 60.

11 Ibid., p. 61.

12 *The Path of Purification*, pp. 30, 31.

13 Ibid., p. 405

14 Ibid., p. 442.

Buddhaghosa's writings

Buddhaghosa's works fill over thirty volumes in Pali Text Society editions. His major commentary is:

Visuddhimagga (The Path of Purification), 2 vols, trans. Bhikkhu Nyanamoli, Berkeley, Calif. and London: Shambala, 1976

See also in this book

the Buddha, Vasubandhu, Huineng, Fazang

Sources and further reading

Conze, E., *A Short History of Buddhism*, London: Allen & Unwin, 1979
Dasgupta, S., *A History of Indian Philosophy*, 5 vols, vol. I, Cambridge: Cambridge University Press, 1922
Law, B.C., *Buddhaghosa*, Bombay: Royal Asiatic Society, 1946
Ward, Keith, *Images of Eternity*, London: Darton, Longman & Todd, 1987, ch. 3.

SANKARA *c.*788–*c.*820 CE

Among the most highly revered of the sages of India, Sankara ranks second only to Gautama Buddha.[1] He represents the flowering of the Vedanta school of Hindu philosophy, the last of the six schools which developed from extremely ancient foundations.[2] Sankara's system of thought is known as **Advaita**, a term that classifies it as nondualistic. Its central theme is an examination of the relation between **Brahman**, the divine power of the cosmos, and *atman*, the individual human self.

Sankara held that reality is ultimately one and that the apparent plurality of the individual selves and entities of empirical existence is illusory: what seems to be an individual self, or *atman*, is in fact not essentially different from the one Self (*Atman*), just as the space contained in an individual jug or pitcher is not different from space as a whole. The one Self, he maintains, is identical with Brahman and the aim of the individual human being must be to obtain release from the illusory conceptions of the differentiated self by achieving a full realization of the identity of Self with Brahman. The western understanding of Hinduism is largely derived from Sankara's Vedantic thought.

Sankara was born in Kaladi, in what is now Kerala state, in southern India. His family was of the priestly class, the **Brahmin**, and in due course he became a disciple of Govindapada, a well-known teacher. The details of Sankara's short lifetime are few, although it is evident that during it he achieved much, exerted a charismatic influence on his followers and became widely revered. Like other **gurus**, he is regarded by his biographers as having supernormal, though not supernatural, powers. He was a highly skilled dialectician, a religious reformer and a gifted writer of devotional hymns. He regarded all these activities, along with ritual, meditation and other religious practices, as stages of an ascent to a higher experience that would transcend not only personal existence but also traditional Hindu thought and customs.

The foundation of Hindu thought is the unquestioning acceptance of its tripartite doctrine of **samsara**, **karma** and **moksa**. Briefly, *samsara* is the wheel of continual rebirth or transmigration of souls; *karma* is the principle, or law, of action and consequence, a kind of causal destiny, believed to condition the types of rebirth an individual undergoes; *moksa* is the liberation or salvation from *samsara*, achieved by means of union with Brahman. It is on the basis of this doctrine that Sankara built his philosophical conception of the nature of things.

The source of many of Sankara's ideas was the **Brahma Sutra**, a collection of writings that dates from the first century CE and that provides an interpretation of the **Upanisads**. The *Upanisads* are the reputedly 'secret' or 'hidden' teachings that are attached to the primary Hindu scriptures, the **Veda**, which are regarded as infallible. Sankara derives much of his account of the nature of things from parts of the *Upanisads* that assert that there is a sense in which Brahman and *atman* are one. But within this fundamental unity he develops the notion of comprehending the world at two levels or from two points of view. This distinction permeates all his thought and provides the basic structure for his account of the nature of reality and human experience. At the higher level of comprehension, he maintains, it is possible to comprehend the ultimate oneness of reality; at the lower level, everyday experience leads us to think of reality as a multiplicity of individual persons and things and at this lower level there is no escape from *samsara*. *Moksa*, the release from *samsara*, is obtained only by an experiential realization of oneness at the higher level of comprehension.

According to Sankara, the lower level of experience is **maya**, often translated as 'illusion'. It is important to understand exactly what is meant by this. The Indian philosopher R. Puligandla has pointed out that the word *maya* has at least three meanings which have to be understood in relation to each other. In a psychological sense *maya* is the human tendency to regard appearance as reality and reality as appearance. In an epistemological sense it signifies human ignorance concerning the difference between appearance and reality. In an ontological sense it refers to the creative power of Brahman. *Maya* is, Puligandla says, the creative power of reality by virtue of which the world of variety and multiplicity comes into existence. Sometimes *maya* as the creative power of reality is referred to as 'the sheer cosmic playfulness (**lila**) of reality'.[3] On this understanding of *maya*, Sankara's 'illusory' world of individuated phenomena is not without a foundation in reality, for the illusion that is *maya* refers to the way in which reality appears from the lower-level point of view. It is not a deception, nor is it a falsehood, but rather an erroneous or inadequate conception of reality, the result of a misunderstanding which vanishes when it is ousted by knowledge. Sankara maintains that the world of appearances is neither real nor unreal. It is simply an incorrect conception of the true reality.

Sankara employs the concept of sublation in order to develop his account of the human person's progress from error to truth, or from appearance to reality. Sublation is a process of correcting errors of judgement. An erroneous conception of something is sublated when experience enables it to be replaced by a less erroneous conception. Thus a person draws closer to reality through successive sublations of appearances. For Sankara, appearances are of three kinds of existents: real existents, existents and illusory existents. To experience a mirage of an oasis in the desert is to experience an illusory existent, and the perception is sublated by the discovery, on arrival at the place, that there is no such oasis. Existents are items of common sense or conventional knowledge which may be sublated by more general or more scientific principles, as when the conception of a rainbow as a coloured arc in the sky is sublated by a description of it in terms of the prismatic refraction of light through drops of water. This scientific principle, along with other general principles such as the law of contradiction, is a real existent. Real existents are sublatable only by reality itself; that is, by being wholly transcended in the experience of an ultimate unity that obliterates all subject–object distinctions. Reality itself, since it is one and undifferentiated, and since sublation requires distinct objects, is unsublatable. At the other end of the scale is unreality, or non-being. Unreal objects are contradictions such as square circles, married bachelors and so on. Unreality cannot be sublated because it cannot be experienced.

Some difficult questions are generated in reflecting on Sankara's philosophical point of view; in particular, in connection with the relationship of his notion of two levels of knowledge to his claim concerning the ultimate oneness of reality. For how is it that *maya*, the world of particular, individual entities, can have come into existence? The oneness of reality precludes any attribution of *maya* to an alien or separate power and Sankara clearly did not want to think of it as some sort of wilfully deceptive act of Brahman. He therefore describes it briefly as without beginning and concentrates his attention on an analysis of how things are rather than on how they came to be as they are. Perhaps *maya* is best thought of by reference to the description of it as the generative power of Brahman; as a kind of spontaneous creativity that provides the *possibility* of the phenomenal world, and that is the necessary condition of any kind of human experience of a subject–object sort. Thus Sankara points out that Brahman is the 'basis of this entire apparent world . . . while in its true and real nature . . . it remains unchanged'.[4] Essentially, Brahman is formless and beyond description. It is a totality of pure knowledge and the variety and flux of the phenomenal world 'are names only . . . in reality there exists no such thing as modification'.[5]

Further difficulties arise concerning the relation of the individual self, or *atman*, to the one Self. Sankara holds that each person is a being who is essentially and fundamentally an aspect of the changeless Self, arguing that this is so because when we are conscious of the empirical self it is the Self in us that is aware. But at the lower level of understanding, a person takes herself or himself to be an individuated being, subject to karmic destiny and reincarnation, and inhabiting a world of individual and perishable entities. But the task of each person, Sankara maintains, is to aspire to a participation in the oneness of Brahman. This cannot be a matter of becoming a radically different being, for it already is the case that the apparently individual self is really Self or Brahman. It must therefore be a matter of dispelling *maya*; of shedding one's illusory conception of things by means of a progression of successive experiences of sublation, and thereby proceeding from an inadequate conception of reality to knowledge of it. Yet the achievement of this higher state does seem to embody something of a contradiction. For the loss of individuality involved means that there can be no sense or awareness of the achievement of union. There is release from the thraldom of the desires and propensities of the empirical self and from the possibility of a continuing cycle of rebirth; but if such release is total then it can only be lived and not contemplated as an object, since there remains no subject capable of the awareness *that* one exists in the bliss of union with Brahman. Multiplicity, change and individuation constitute the conceptual conditions that make experience possible. These conditions are abolished by the notion of oneness with Brahman, so that it is impossible to conceive of the experience other than in terms of a total negation or nothingness.

Various affinities between Sankara's ideas and those of western thinkers have been pointed out by commentators on his philosophy. His notion of a progress from illusion to knowledge is reminiscent of Plato's account, in *The Republic*, Bk 7, of the ascent from the illusions and appearances of the cave to the direct, intuitive knowledge that is *noesis*. There are clear affinities, too, in Sankara's philosophy, with Spinoza's account of inadequate and adequate ideas; with Kant's distinction between the noumenal and the phenomenal; and, in the claim that it is the universal Self, or *Atman*, in us that is aware of the empirical self, with Descartes's argument for his existence as a thinking substance or consciousness. But the western philosopher whose thought has most in common with Sankara's is Arthur Schopenhauer (1788–1860). In particular, Schopenhauer's doctrine of the quieting of the individual will and the resulting attainment, through the nullification of individual striving, of ecstasy, rapture, illumination, union with God, bears a very close resemblance to Sankara's views concerning the recognition and experience of unity with Brahman. For Sankara, the attainment of *moksa*, through a discipline of asceticism, study, reflection and meditation, had similar results, effecting a transformation of one's relationship with the world and an intuitive realization that one's essential being is imperishable, and untouched by either life or death.

Sankara's thought became extremely influential during his lifetime and has remained important in the Indian tradition through subsequent centuries. But its unequivocal nondualism provoked a reaction: an interpretation of Vedanta that argued the necessity for differentiation within the unity that is Brahman. In this new interpretation, *atman* (the personal self) and Brahman were regarded as capable of union and so of being one, but also as able to be distinguished one from the other.

Notes

1 See the essay on the Buddha in this book, pp. 74–81.
2 The Vedantic school was founded by Badarayana (see pp. 87–95 in this book). Vedanta is a Sanskrit word meaning 'the end of the Veda', the Veda being the primary revealed text of the orthodox Hindu tradition. The *Upanisads*, the hidden, or secret, teachings, were added to the hymns and rituals of the Veda, and Vedanta doctrine is an exegesis of the *Upanisads*. There are three main Vedantic schools, each of which lays claim to a correct exposition of doctrine: see Ramanuja and Madhva in this book for accounts of the other two main schools, the Visistadvaita (qualified nondualism) and the Dvaita (dualism).
3 In R. Puligandla, *Fundamentals of Indian Philosophy*, New York: Abingdon Press, 1975, p. 217.
4 Quoted in Keith Ward, *Images of Eternity*, London: Darton, Longman & Todd, 1987, p. 11.
5 Ward, op. cit., p. 12.

Sankara's writings

Sankara wrote commentaries on the following:

The Brahma Sutra
The Upanisads
The Bhagavad Gita
See: Leggett, Trevor, *The Complete Commentary by Sankara on the Yoga Sutras* (a full translation of the newly discovered text), London: Kegan Paul, 1990

Sankara's philosophical standpoint is clearly expressed in:
Johnston, Charles (trans.), *The Crest Jewel of Wisdom*, London: John M. Watkins, 1925 (a translation of Sankara's *Viveka Cudamani*)

See also in this book

Badarayana, Patanjali, Ramanuja, Madhva

Sources and further reading

Lott, E.J., *Vedantic Approaches to God*, London: Macmillan, 1980
Pande, G.C., *Life and Thought of Sancaracarya*, Delhi: Motilal, Banarsidass, 1994
Radhakrishnan, S., *Indian Philosophy*, 2 vols, London: Allen & Unwin, 1923–7
Zaehner, R.C., *Hinduism*, Oxford: Oxford University Press, 1962

RAMANUJA *c.*1016–1100(?) CE

Ramanuja was a Hindu philosopher and theologian who exerted considerable influence on the tradition of thought known as **Vedanta**[1] and who led a community that revered him for his saintly example and inspiration. His philosophy is a questioning and critical development of the monistic teaching of Sankara[2] and is described as **Visistadvaita**, or qualified nondualism.

Ramanuja espouses nondualism in so far as he maintains that the soul and God are fundamentally one but he qualifies that claim in holding that the soul retains self-consciousness and so is capable of an external relationship with God. His views provided an impetus for theism[3] and the development of 'the way of devotion', in contrast to 'the way of knowledge' which had been established two and a half centuries earlier by Sankara. A century after his death, Ramanuja's thought was developed by Madhva into an unequivocal dualism and theism. These three philosophers, Sankara, Ramanuja and Madhva, represent the most influential doctrines of medieval Vedantism.

Ramanuja was the last in a succession of three great *acaryas*, or teachers, the first being Nathamuni, and the second Yamuna, grandson of Nathamuni. There are sources that attribute a life of 120 years to Ramanuja and there is some uncertainty about the date of his birth, but it is likely that he was born around 1016 at Bhutapuri in southern India. He was married at 16 and then went to Kanci (Conjeevaram) to study. He was to have sat at the feet of Ramuna in Srirangam, but Ramuna died before Ramanuja arrived. Ramuna's disciples taught him the five aspects of Yamuna's doctrine and then, after being sworn to secrecy on eighteen separate occasions, Ramajuna ceremonially received the secret knowledge of the meaning of the *mantra*, or ritual, of his community, the Sri Vaisnavas. Tradition has it that on the day after he had sworn the final vow of secrecy, Ramanuja ascended to the balcony of the temple and shouted the secret to the Sri Vaisnavas assembled below. Subsequently he acknowledged to his teacher, Yadavaprakasha, that his disobedience should be rewarded by condemnation to hell; at the same time he remarked that the people to whom he had revealed the secret would be saved by their contact with the more faithful of Ramuna's disciples. This observation so impressed his teacher that Ramanuja was immediately recognized as a leader capable of reforming and inspiring his community. Ramanuja's subsequent work of transforming and reconstructing the tradition he inherited was based on scholarship, wide consultation and practical reorganization. At around the age of 30 he renounced domestic life and began to travel as a religious teacher, working in both northern and southern India and founding a monastery at Puri. He was persecuted by a Saivite king, Rajendracola, and so fled to the Hoysala region, but in due course he was able to return to Srirangam where he remained until his death.

Ramanuja's thought is best understood as a kind of loosening of Sankara's somewhat rigid monism. Sankara had maintained that **Brahman**, the Supreme Power of the universe, is without form and that all differentiations and cognitional forms imposed on Brahman are illusory and false: they are appearances that are generated by ignorance and that vanish once a knowledge of true reality is achieved. Ordinary, everyday experience, according to Sankara, is flawed and is inferior to knowledge of the one because it is made up of distinctions, differences and separations. His condemnation of the pluralism of ordinary experience is summed up in the following declaration:

> Eternal, absolutely non-changing consciousness, whose nature is pure non-differentiated intelligence, free from all distinctions whatever, owing to error illusorily manifests itself . . . as broken up into manifold distinctions – knowing subjects, objects of knowledge, acts of knowledge.[4]

As already indicated, Ramanuja's challenge to Sankara's view does not take the form of a direct opposition to it; his doctrine is not dualistic but a 'qualified nondualism'. He maintains that Brahman, matter and the individual souls of the cosmos are indeed an ultimate unity, since matter and souls constitute the body of Brahman and have no existence apart from Brahman. But matter and souls, he says, are essentially different from, even though not independent of, Brahman. There is not a dualism of Brahman and the world, but a nondualism that is qualified by a certain kind of plurality. He rejects Sankara's doctrine of *maya*, or illusion, concerning reality and maintains instead that the world of change and distinctions is entirely real.

Ramanuja offers some detailed and systematic criticism of Sankara's doctrine. He argues that there can be no proof of Sankara's claim that Brahman is unqualified, because all proof depends on the making of qualifications and on the necessarily qualified experience of the experiencer. He argues that to say that Brahman is pure consciousness, infinite, and so on, *is* to ascribe properties to Brahman. When we assert something – for example, 'This is a basin' – we assign characteristics; perception necessarily reveals something that has characteristics and there is no source of perception or knowledge that can reveal something that has no characteristics.

Ramanuja names three sources of knowledge: perception, inference and scripture. He distinguishes between indeterminate and determinate perception. The former is the first perception of something, in which its characteristics are not fully grasped; the latter is subsequent perception in which previously discerned features are reconsidered and more fully comprehended. He argues that perception cannot, as Sankara had maintained, provide us with knowledge of unqualified being because

> if perception made us apprehend only pure being, judgements clearly referring to different objects – such as 'Here is a jar', 'There is a piece of cloth' – would be devoid of all meaning. And if through perception we did not apprehend difference . . . why should a man searching for a horse not be satisfied with finding a buffalo? . . . If all acts of cognition had one and the same object only, everything would be apprehended by one act of cognition.[5]

Ramanuja points out that inference, understood as knowledge derived from a principle, is founded on perception and accordingly is as much dependent on qualities and characteristics as perception is: 'its object is only what is distinguished by connection with things known through perception and other means of knowledge'.[6] Scripture, although absolutely authoritative, is similarly grounded in distinctions. It is an arrangement of words; and a word, Ramanuja writes, 'originates from the combination of a radical element and a suffix, and as these two elements have different meanings it necessarily follows that the word itself can convey only a sense affected with a difference'.[7] Thus, according to him, none of the forms of knowledge can provide us with knowledge of the unqualified oneness of pure being asserted by Sankara. Knowledge involves distinctions and discrimination and can never be of an undifferentiated object.

Ramanuja makes a careful analysis of the concept of the self. He argues that the self always persists in its own being, never losing its identity in pure consciousness. Once again, this is a view that is contrary to that of Sankara, who had maintained that the entity referred to as 'I' has two parts of which one is pure consciousness and the other the individual 'ego' which is dependent on the pure consciousness. Ramanuja, in contrast, denies that there is a self that is also pure consciousness. He argues that the self is simply the individuated ego that persists through times of consciousness and unconsciousness, and that consciousness itself cannot also be the subject that is sometimes conscious, sometimes unconscious. He writes:

> we clearly see that this agent [the subject of consciousness] is permanent [constant], while its attribute, i.e. consciousness, not differing here from joy, grief, and the like, rises, persists for some time, and then comes to an end . . . The judgement 'I am conscious' reveals an 'I' distinguished by consciousness; and to declare that it refers only to a state of consciousness – which is a mere attribute – is no better than to say the judgement 'Devadatta carries a stick' is about the stick only.[8]

Ramanuja's insistence not only on the reality of the distinction between subject and object but also on their fundamental non-duality means that he has to demonstrate both the logical feasibility of that conception of reality and its consonance with holy writ. He has to show that Brahman is transcendent as well as immanent and that such conclusions are derivable from the scriptures, which, he holds, are fully coherent and consistent when properly understood.

He therefore starts by affirming the supreme reality of Brahman. We cannot comprehend the glory of Brahman, he says, because it is infinite; it is free from limitation and from any constraints of substance, time and place, and it is unchangingly perfect. The world is the body of Brahman and the texts that deny Brahman's possession of attributes are denying only false or finite attributes. What such texts are repudiating, he points out, is the notion of any reality that is separate from the unified reality of Brahman. At the same time he rejects the interpretation of the famous scriptural pronouncement 'That art thou' (*Tat tvam asi*)[9] that takes it to be a declaration of the absolute oneness of Brahman with the individual soul. He argues that if there were not some difference between the two it would not be possible to assert their union: they are two meanings belonging to one substance. This kind of thinking is the basis of Ramanuja's theism. The distinction between Brahman and the individual soul ascribes personhood to the power that is Brahman and provides a basis for a devotional relationship between God and the souls of the world.

Ramanuja makes it clear that the individual soul is to be thought of not as a falsity or aberration but as something real, unique and eternal. It is distinct from the body although, in its human manifestation, it is bound to a body as knower and agent. It remains essentially unchanged even though it is born or reborn many times into the sensible world. It is an aspect of, though not identical with, Brahman. God, he argues, bestows free will on souls but also acts according to laws that are the expression of his own nature. These laws relate to the rewarding of virtue and the punishment of evil in accordance with righteousness. **Karma**, the law governing the kind of rebirth a soul must undergo as a consequence of its previous existence, is not independent of God but expresses his will. God is therefore the source of everything, but not the cause of evil. In discussing this aspect of Ramanuja's theology, the twentieth-century Indian philosopher Radhakrishnan cites the following scriptural passage:

> The divine being . . . having engaged in sport befitting his might and greatness and having settled that work is of a twofold nature, good and evil, and having bestowed on all individual souls, bodies and sense organs enabling them to enter on such work and the power to control their bodies and organs, and having himself entered into their souls as their inner self, abides with them . . . The souls endowed with all the powers imparted to them by the Lord . . . apply themselves on their own part and in accordance with their own wishes to work out good and evil . . . The Lord then recognizing him who performs good acts as one who conforms to his commands, blesses him with piety and wealth, happiness and release, while he makes him who transgresses his commands experience the opposites of all these.[10]

According to Ramanuja, **moksa**, or the soul's release from the body, is not the end of the self but the disappearance of limitations that were barriers to community with God. When release is obtained, all desire goes, so that return to **samsara**, the wheel, is impossible. The capacity for intelligence and holy joy is unimpeded and all souls become alike in that they are freed from the egoism of particular bodies. This does not mean that a soul loses its individuality but that the distinctions between animals, plants, men and gods no longer obtain. The liberated soul is able to give to its nature without the impediment of a body, thereby perfecting itself as an element in the whole which is at once a unity and an interrelated community of souls. The soul never becomes absorbed into God. For Ramanuja it is an atomic entity that retains its individual nature eternally, even in its ultimate perfection. He regards the longing of the mystic for a complete loss of personality in a union with God as an impossibility. Radhakrishnan has remarked:

'In the nature of things, Ramanuja contends, evidence of such absorption into God is impossible. He who has become God cannot return to tell us of his experience: he who narrates his story cannot become God.'[11]

Ramanuja's philosophy is a timely reminder of the fact that Hindu thought does not, as many are inclined to believe, adhere uniformly to a theory of abstract monism, which is the general view that only one substance is real and that the total absorption of the individual into the one is the only true value. In place of such a monism he expounds the theistic conception of a relationship between God and souls which allows for the full reality of both and the complete dependence of the latter on the former while denying the possibility of their identity.

Ramanuja's theism exhibits the difficulties to which theism in general is subject: those of giving an account of the exact nature of the relationship of God's attributes to God and of the relationships obtaining between the attributes themselves; that of describing the relationship between individual souls and God; in short, the difficulty of setting out the relationship between the finite and the infinite, the changing and the changeless. But his arguments commanded intellectual respect as well as intuitive agreement. His doctrine made room for the worship and adoration of the Supreme Power without abandoning either the possibility of union with the Lord or the fundamental monism so strongly asserted by Hindu scripture. At the same time he was able to offer a philosophical structure that many must have found more satisfying, more comprehensively explanatory, than the austere conclusions of Sankara.

Notes

1 Vedanta is one of the six main systems of Hindu philosophy. It is based on the *Upanisads*, the oldest Hindu scriptures.

2 For a fuller understanding of this development the essay on Sankara (pp. 120–5) should be read before or immediately after this essay.

3 The word 'theism' refers to any philosophical position that affirms a belief in a transcendent and personal God.

4 S. Radhakrishnan and Charles A. Moore (eds), *A Source Book in Indian Philosophy*, Princeton: Princeton University Press, 1957, p. 543.

5 Ibid., p. 545.

6 Ibid.

7 Ibid., p. 544.

8 Ibid., p. 547.

9 There are numerous interpretations of the meaning of the Sanskrit phrase '*tat tvam asi*' ('That art thou'), from the *Chandogya Upanisad*. It was invoked by Sankara to endorse his monistic doctrine. For a fuller exposition of

Ramanuja's arguments opposing a monistic interpretation see Radhakrishnan and Moore, op. cit., pp. 551–5.
10 S. Radhakrishnan, *Indian Philosophy*, 2nd edn, 2 vols, vol. II, London: Allen
& Unwin, 1929, p. 694, footnote.
11 Ibid., p. 712.

See also in this book

Badarayana, Patanjali, Sankara, Madhva

Ramanuja's writings

Sribhasya (Great Commentary on the Vedanta Sutra)
Vedanta Sara (Essence of the Vedanta)

There is an Indian edition of Ramanuja's works:

Sri-Bhagavad-Ramanuja-Grandha-Mala, ed. P.B. Annangara-charya Swamy,
Kanchipuram, 1956

See also:

Thibaut, G. (trans.), *The Vedanta Sutras, with the Commentary of Ramanuja*, vol.
XLVIII, Pt III, Oxford: Oxford University Press, Sacred Books of the East
series, 1964; Delhi: Motilal Banarsidass, 1956

Sources and further reading

Carman, J.B., *The Theology of Ramanuja: An Essay in Interreligious Understanding*,
New Haven: Yale University Press, 1974
Dasgupta, Surendranath, *A History of Indian Philosophy*, 5 vols, Cambridge:
Cambridge University Press, 1922–55; repr. Atlantic Highlands, NJ:
Humanities Press, 1975; Delhi: Motilal Banarsidass, 1976
Lipner, J., *The Face of Truth: A Study of Meaning and Metaphysics in the Vedantic
Theology of Ramanuja*, Albany: State University of New York Press, 1986
Puligandla, R., *Fundamentals of Indian Philosophy*, Nashville, NY: Abingdon
Press, 1975
Radhakrishnan, Sarvepalli, *Indian Philosophy*, 2 vols, vol. 2, London: Allen &
Unwin, 1923–7
Sharma, C., *Indian Philosophy: A Critical Survey*, New York: Barnes & Noble,
1962, ch. xvii
Ward, Keith, *Images of Eternity*, London: Darton, Longman & Todd, 1987

MADHVA *c.*1199–1278 CE[1]

Madhva's thought marks the third stage of the development of Indian
Vedantic philosophy as it moved from the monism of Sankara to the

qualified nondualism of Ramanuja and thence to Madhva's own conception of a fundamental dualism of God and souls and a plurality of world substances.[2]

Madhva maintained that God created all souls and substances and that each soul is changeless and uniquely different from all others. He held that although souls may exhibit some properties which they share with some other souls, there is no universal property that serves as the basis of all souls. He saw reality as consisting of an infinite number of substances, each uniquely different from all others. Accordingly, his thought is much concerned with drawing distinctions and this feature of it established the conditions for a theology of a devotional relationship between God and individual souls, thereby imparting to his philosophy a characteristic not found in the earlier Vedantic tradition as exemplified by Sankara.

Madhva wrote thirty-seven works of various kinds, known collectively as *Sarva-Mula*. Among them are commentaries on the *Bhagavad Gita*, on the **Upanisads**, and on the first forty hymns of the **Rig Veda**.[3] His metaphysics, logic and epistemology are expounded in ten short monographs, *Dasa-Prakaranas*. There is general agreement that his style is somewhat terse, but the difficulties of understanding his works have been eased by commentaries written by Jayatirtha[4] in the fourteenth century.

Madhva was born near Udipi, not far from Mangalore on the west coast of India south of Bombay. As a young man he was famed for his prodigious gift for reciting the scriptures and for his inspirational teaching and intepretation of them. He travelled extensively in southern India, debating theological and philosophical issues and developing his own stringent opposition to the monistic doctrine of Sankara. Subsequently he toured in North India where he endured a measure of persecution for his views, including the burning of his books. He established a temple at Udipi and with it a doctrinal tradition that has been passed down through a long line of disciples and successors and that flourishes still.[5] Many commentators have detected a Christian element in his life and teachings and have sought, without success, to discover evidence of some contact with Christian influences.[6] There is little doubt that he was a charismatic teacher who was profoundly devout, learned and inspiring. His death has been described as follows:

> Charging his disciples with his last message in the closing words of his favourite *Upanisad*, the *Aitareya*, not to sit still but to go forth and preach and spread the truth among the

deserving, Sri Madhva disappeared from view, on the ninth day of the bright half of the month of Magha.[7]

The monistic doctrine of Sankara which Madhva rejected had postulated an ultimate reality that was an undivided and spiritual whole. Sankara had explained the variety and multiplicity of the physical universe by describing it as the appearance, rather than the reality, of God, or Brahman. In rejecting this account, Madhva did not deny that reality was one in the sense that the world is Brahman's world but, in opposition to Sankara, he maintained that the physical universe and its individual beings are ultimately and fully real, and not merely appearances of Brahman: there is a dualism of God and God's universe, yet, at the same time, an ultimate unity that is grounded in the fact that the physical order is entirely dependent on God. He says: 'There are two orders of reality, the independent and the dependent.'[8]

Madhva develops his metaphysical system by employing a series of distinctions. He first identifies three main elements of reality: God, souls and matter, the latter two together comprising the dependent element in a fundamentally dualistic reality. He then names a fivefold set of differences that obtain between the three elements. These differences are between God and the individual soul, between God and matter, between individual souls and matter, between soul and soul, and between material thing and material thing. Again, these differences are not merely apparent, as Sankara would have deemed them to be, but are willed by God and are therefore real and perceivable. The profound difference between souls and God is that souls are wholly dependent on God while God is an entirely independent reality. Madhva cites some words from the *Garuda Purana*:

> There is no equality in experience between the Lord and the self; for the Lord is all-knowing, all-powerful, and absolute; while the self is of little understanding, of little power and absolutely dependent.'[9]

Souls and God are nevertheless alike in that, despite the material and external aspects of the former, both are fundamentally unchanging. God determines what each individual soul is and from the unique constitution of each soul there flow the particular life and events that follow logically from it: the course of an individual life is the necessary consequence or realization of what God has ordained. This aspect of Madhva's thought bears a resemblance to the philosophy of the seventeenth-century western philosopher Leibniz, who held that each individual is an aggregate of unique monads each of which necessarily unfolds in a way already contained within its constitution.

Madhva's pluralistic ontology, which sees reality as consisting of an infinite number of different things or substances, gave rise to a doctrine known as the theory of relative particulars. Madhva rejected the view that universals are real entities and explained the use of universal terms such as 'round' or 'triangular' by saying that such terms serve to indicate similarities between things. Accordingly, he maintained, qualities are to be understood as aspects of substances rather than as distinct entities. However, this suggests that a quality is actually identical with the substance of which it is an aspect, and that if the quality disappears then the substance also disappears. Madhva counters this difficulty by saying that any substance is a conglomeration of an indefinite number of particulars, particulars being the kind of features we refer to when we say, 'This is triangular', 'This is red', and so on. Those particulars referred to in a description of a substance depend on the point of view from which the substance is described; thus they are particulars that are *relative* to the point of view. This theory is part of Madhva's doctrine of *visesa*, or particularity, an ontological principle through which he sought to give an account of identity and difference in things. He wanted to maintain that there is no real inconsistency between affirming, on the one hand, a unique particularity for each thing and, on the other, a capability for identity within inseparable wholes, as in the case of a substance and its attributes. *Visesa* is the principle that accommodates such claims. In particular, it goes some way to providing a resolution of problems that assail theism concerning the exact relationship between God and God's unlimited attributes.

In common with other schools of Indian philosophy, Madhva nominates three sources, or *pramanas*, of knowledge: sense-perception, inferential reasoning and scripture. Knowledge, he maintains, requires both a knower and an object that is known, and it is possible to have knowledge of things as they actually are. Truth is the exact agreement of knowledge with its object. He argues that we must accept that there is genuine knowledge, pointing out that if we do not, then we have nothing with which to contrast falsity and illusion. There is no reason to suppose that the truth of things is other than our tested views and the words of the scriptures affirm it to be, and he cites a passage from the *Gita* XVI.8.:

> Without beginning or end (through eternity) this world has continued to exist as such. There is nothing here to be questioned. In no place or time was this world ever observed otherwise by anybody in the past, nor will it be, in the future.[10]

He further maintains that when we are mistaken or deluded in our beliefs about the physical universe this does not mean that the physical universe is an illusion, but only that we are in error: we are making a mistake about something that does exist, thinking it is something it is not rather than conjuring something out of nothing. He describes ignorance, or *avidya*, as a kind of negative substance that clouds natural intelligence. It is not uniformly similar for everyone but is peculiar to each individual, the *avidya* of one person being different from that of another. Similarly, each person who is able to seek release from *samsara*, the wheel of life, has a particular way of apprehending Brahman and, accordingly, traverses an individual path to knowledge and salvation. For Madhva, sense-perception, although limited in that it is able to yield knowledge only of a certain kind, is a valid form of knowledge provided that it is acquired under the correct conditions. He points out that it is absurd to name perception as a source of knowledge and then try to insist, as some Advaitins did, that it is ultimately falsifiable. However, he concedes that perception requires a final arbiter and invokes the notion of what he calls the 'the inner witness', or *saksi*, the intuitively perceiving agent capable of comprehending both the knowledge and its validity. We have to think of the *saksi* as a fundamental structure of the human mind: that element of consciousness that includes awareness of space, time and self, that can conceptualize the processes of perception and inference, and comprehend the validity of knowledge. The *saksi* itself is infallible and not subject to sublation or any other kind of correction;[11] it is that which corrects the discrepancies of sense and memory. However, the *saksi* is not always able to be active. It includes the capacity to perceive space and distance; but if, for example, a particular distance is such that it affects the integrity of an individual's perception then the judgement of the *saksi* is held in abeyance, thereby creating the condition we call doubt: it is unable either to confirm or disconfirm what is being perceived.

Inference, according to Madhva, is a process that can organize, test and reinforce knowledge but cannot extend it. Like perception, it is unable to understand or penetrate the mysteries and meanings of the universe. For knowledge of the profundities of reality itself we must rely absolutely on the Vedic literature which Madhva regards as infallible and wholly authoritative in virtue of being uncreated by any personal author.

Madhva's distinctions between independent and dependent reality provide the conditions of a devotional relationship between God and human souls. We know, he maintains, even though we cannot perceive God, that we are different from God; we declare the difference in acknowledging that God is to be worshipped. He cites the scriptures: 'the Lord is said to stand (to be merely present) shining; while the self is subject to the experience of the consequences of his works: (thereby the difference between the Lord and the self is declared).'[12] Since all individual souls are eternal, and since God, or Brahman, is eternal, the differences are also eternal. It follows that no individual soul, in achieving release from the wheel of life (*samsara*), can ever be identical with God in the way described by Sankara; that is, as an undifferentiated unity that precludes the possibility of a relationship between a soul and God.

Madhva's rejection of the doctrine of the soul's absorption into Brahman constitutes a radical and controversial element in his thought. It had significant implications for the way in which the scriptures were to be understood. In particular, it meant that Madhva must show that he was not denying what was declared in that best known of all scriptural pronouncements, '*Tat tvam asi*' (That art thou), in which '*Tat*' is generally taken to refer to Brahman so that the words are understood as an affirmation of the identity of the human soul with Brahman.[13] Madhva's treatment of this difficulty is an extended one, not to be explored in detail here but, broadly, he claims that '*Tat tvam asi*' is not an assertion of the identity of God and soul but a statement that points out that the essence of the soul has qualities that resemble God's qualities. His interpretations of other passages that seem to suggest that undifferentiated union is possible are similarly emendatory; they reject or qualify apparent claims to absolute oneness and offer instead an understanding of them in terms of close fellowship or devotional accord with Brahman. Madhva draws attention to scriptural passages and to commentaries on them, such as the following, that lend support to his view:

> The supreme Lord is absolutely separate from the whole class of selves; for He is inconceivable, exalted far above the selves, most high, perfect in excellences and he is eternally blessed, while from that Lord this self has to seek release from bondage.[14]

Madhva is unique among the great Hindu thinkers in holding that not all souls, or *jivas*, are able to find release. He describes three kinds of *jiva*. The first kind comprises those that are eternally free; the second, those who have achieved release from *samsara*. The third kind includes both those destined to find release eventually and those who will never achieve it. These last will enter hell or darkness or be bound in continual rebirth to the wheel of *samsara*. According to Madhva, release is not the mere cessation of suffering but a positive experience of joy and liberation. Through the grace of Brahman it may be succeeded by *moksa*, the salvation that is possible once desires and ignorance have fallen away, and which restores the soul to its primordial condition of bliss.

Knowledge and devotion are the means by which the soul may aspire to *moksa*, and Madhva issues numerous prescriptions for the acquisition of knowledge and the practice of devotional meditation. Yet his advocacy of the life of striving and aspiration has to be seen in the context of his account of God as the maker and controller of the cosmos and as the one supreme Lord who determines the monadic constituents, and hence the development and destiny, the *karma*, of everything, including that of the souls who are to be eternally ignorant and irredeemable. Thus there is a tension in Madhva's theology between his concept of a loving and devotional relationship linking a God of grace and human souls, and his predestinarian concept of God's exertion of supreme power. The twentieth-century Indian philosopher Sarvepalli Radhakrishnan has commented on this tension in the following way:

> the theory of election is fraught with great danger to ethical life . . . The moral character of God is much compromised and the qualities of divine justice and divine love are emptied of all meaning and value. Individual effort loses its point, since whether one believes oneself to be the elect or the non-elect, one is bound to lapse into indifferentism or apathy . . . In the absence of knowledge we may at least have hope. But this theory will overwhelm us in despair and raise the question: Is not God playing a practical joke on us, when he implants in us a desire for heaven while making us unfit for it?[15]

Madhva's philosophy of dualism, realism and empiricism, although less widely known than Sankara's spiritual monism, marks a high intellectual point in Vedantic thought and his teaching concerning the devotional aspects of Hinduism has been significantly influential. After his death his writings generated a profusion of dialectical literature which, over the centuries, has fostered and sustained a continuing interest in his philosophy and theology, and a critical appreciation of his scholarship, not only in the Madhva community of southern India but, increasingly, among a much wider community of scholars.

Notes

1 I have given a traditional birth date of 1199 CE for Madhva but there is considerable uncertainty about it and about the length of his life. Some have attributed to him a life of 95 years; more usually he is reported to have lived to the age of 79. There is also some evidence to suggest that he may have been born in 1238 CE.

2 A broad outline of the development of Vedantic philosophy may be obtained by reading the essays in this book on Sankara, Ramanuja and Madhva in that order. See also the Introduction to Indian philosophy (pp. 63–8).

3 For further detail of the Hindu scriptures see the Introduction to Indian philosophy in this book (pp. 63–8). In general, the Vedantan thinkers regarded the Vedas as primary texts and all subsequent writings as secondary, but Madhva does not observe this distinction.

4 Jayatirtha (1365–88 CE) dedicated many years of his life to the scholarly interpretation of Madhva. His commentaries are systematic, detailed and stylistically superb, and he possessed great dialectical skill. An account of his life and work is in B.N.K. Sharma, *History of the Dvaita School of Vedanta and Its Literature*, Delhi: Motilal Banarsidass, 1981.

5 Twentieth-century followers of Madhva are to be found in Karnataka. Many of them have the surname of Rao.

6 Ninian Smart, in *Doctrine and Argument in Indian Philosophy*, London: Allen & Unwin, Muirhead Library of Philosophy, 1964, pp. 118–19, has noted that there are legendary accounts of Madhva's life that describe him as walking on water and as figuring in other incidents reminiscent of events recounted in the New Testament. The association is strengthened by the fact that there were early Christian settlements in the Mangalore area. A doctrine of predestination, otherwise uncharacteristic of Indian thought, is also attributed to Madhva and has been taken to be an indication of Christian influence. Nothing conclusive emerges from these conjectures.

7 Sharma, op. cit., p. 83.

8 See M. Sivaram, *Ananda and the Three Great Acaryas*, New Delhi: Vikas Publishing House, 1976, p. 132.

9 Sarvepalli Radhakrishnan and Charles A. Moore (eds), *A Source Book in Indian Philosophy*, Princeton: Princeton University Press, 1957, pp. 558–9.

10 Ibid., pp. 562–3.

11 Sublation is a concept employed by Sankara to describe the progress from error to truth that takes place when experience gradually corrects errors of judgement. See the essay on Sankara in this book (pp. 120–5).

12 Radhakrishnan and Moore, op. cit., p. 560.

13 *Tat tvam asi* ('That art thou') is a Sanskrit phrase used as a *mantra* in Hinduism. *Tat* refers to Brahman, and *tvam* (thou) to the individual soul when it is understood as an aspect of Brahman and, as such, is known as *Atman*. The phrase is found in the *Chandogya Upanisad* VI.8.6.

14 From the *Kausitaki Upanisad*, quoted in Radhakrishnan and Moore, op. cit., p. 565.

15 Sarvepalli Radhakrishnan, *Indian Philosophy*, 2 vols, vol. II, London: Allen & Unwin, 1932, pp. 750–1.

Madhva's writings

Of his thirty-seven works the following are the most important:

(1)   commentaries on the *Brahma Sutra*, ten of the *Upanisads* and the *Bhagavad Gita Annvyakhana*, a justification of his commentary on the *Brahmasutras*;
(2)   *The Dasa-Prakaranas*, ten monographs presenting his logic, epistemology and ontology and some dialectical reasonings;
(3)   notes and short commentaries on the *Bhagavata Purana* and some interpretations of the *Rig-Veda*.

For a translation of some of his writings see *Vedanta-sutras with the Commentary of Sri Madhwachanya*, trans. S. Subba Rao, Tirupati: Sri Vyasa Press, 1936.

His minor works include verses in praise of Krishna, works on ritual and a compendium of daily conduct and religious practice.

See also in this book

Sankara, Ramanuja, Patanjali and the Introduction to Indian philosophy

Sources and further reading

Dasgupta, Surendranath, *A History of Indian Philosophy*, 5 vols, vol. IV, Cambridge: Cambridge University Press, 1973

Lott, Eric, *Vedantic Approaches to God*, London and Basingstoke: Macmillan, 1980

Radhakrishnan, Sarvepalli, *Indian Philosophy*, 2 vols, vol. II, London: Allen & Unwin, 1932

Radhakrishnan, Sarvepalli and Moore, Charles A. (eds), *A Source Book in Indian Philosophy*, Princeton: Princeton University Press, 1957

Sharma, B.N.K., *History of the Dvaita School of Vedanta*, Delhi: Motilal Banarsidass, 1981

Sharma, B.N.K., *Philosophy of Sri Madhvacarya*, Delhi: Motilal, Banarsidass, 1986

VIVEKANANDA 1863–1902 CE

In 1893, the distinguished representatives of the world's leading religions met at the World's Parliament of Religions in Chicago. A young Swami named Vivekananda, only 30 years of age, electrified this audience by his direct, forceful and moving oratory, and almost single-handedly began a movement to make the world aware of modern Hinduism, a movement which has lasted to this day. Vivekananda combined in one personality an unusual range of qualities: the intense spirituality which had attracted him to the path of the Hindu *samnyasin* or renunciant, counterbalanced by real concern for social reform in his native India; great philosophical competence, especially with regard to the ideas of Sankara, combined with insights gained from yogic, religious experience; and added to these enormous energy, powers of persuasion and oratorical skill. Vivekananda believed with absolute sincerity that the Hindu outlook had much to offer the world, and devoted much of his short life to a brilliantly successful attempt to make these ideas known in the West.

Vivekananda ('bliss of discerning knowledge') is the religious name adopted in the early 1890s by Narendranath Datta. Born on 12 January 1863, son of a successful lawyer in the Calcutta High Court, Vivekananda was at first destined to follow his father into the legal profession. He was duly entered at college in Calcutta between 1878 and 1884. During these college years, his concern for social reform led Vivekananda to become a member of one of the liberal Indian reform organizations of the time, the Brahmo Samaj, though this movement was ultimately unable to satisfy his profound spiritual needs.

The search for that satisfaction had caused Vivekananda in 1881 to seek out the great Hindu visionary Sri Ramakrishna (1836–86 CE), who at once recognized in the younger man a hunger and aptness for spiritual experience. Vivekananda, though he recognized the spiritual genius of Ramakrishna, found him insufficiently interested in the social issues which had led him to the Brahmo Samaj. It was not until 1885, after his father's death, that Vivekananda finally accepted Ramakrishna as his *guru*. He remained as Ramakrishna's disciple, undergoing intensive spiritual training and attaining profound religious experience, until the latter's death in August 1886. Appointed his successor by Ramakrishna, Vivekananda acted as leader to the other disciples for three years, but left them in 1890 as a result of a crisis of belief. During the extended pilgrimage in India which followed, Vivekananda worked out his own philosophical and religious outlook, based on the **Advaita Vedanta** of Sankara, combining it with elements both from Buddhism and the beliefs of Ramakrishna. It was with these convictions, to which he refers in his works as 'practical Vedanta', that Vivekananda set out for Chicago in 1893.

Following his success at the World's Parliament of Religions and offers of academic appointments in America (which he declined), Vivekananda began work to realize his vision of a worldwide movement based ultimately on Hinduism. The Vedanta Society of New York was founded in 1895, soon followed by a London branch, and Vivekananda returned to India in 1897 to carry on his work. By May of that year he had founded the Ramakrishna Mission, which within two years established itself worldwide. By this time, the intensity of his programme of work had begun to undermine Vivekananda's health. After one further brief visit to the West, he died in India on 4 July 1902.[1]

The metaphysical basis of Vivekananda's thought is Advaita or non-dual Vedanta, derived to a considerable degree from the philosophy of Sankara. Being-as-is or reality is not the phenomenal world of individual beings and entities, causally reacting in space and time. Reality or **Brahman** is a unity, oneness or absolute, changeless, eternal, and such that no predicates can apply to it:

> in the Absolute there is neither time, space nor causation. The idea of time cannot be there, seeing that there is no mind, no thought. The idea of space cannot be there, seeing that there is no external change. What you call motion and causation cannot exist where there is only one.[2]

Vivekananda himself had attained mystical awareness of Brahman during his period of discipleship to Ramakrishna. Aware, however, that western audiences were by and large innocent of such experiences, Vivekananda uses a number of arguments to support this view. Of these, the one he uses most frequently begins from an analysis of perception.

Perception, he argues, is a complex process. It begins with sensations produced as a result of stimulation of a sense organ, and transmitted along neural pathways to the brain. Perception does not occur, however, unless we are paying attention to sensation, and attention is a property not of the brain but of the mind, which in Vivekananda's view is not identical with the brain. Yet even the joint occurrence of sensation and attention is not sufficient for perception. The mental event which results from attended-to sensation is not a perception unless it is a property of a self, or, in other words, there cannot be a perception which is not *someone's* perception. Human experience presupposes *self*-consciousness. The process of perception 'will not be completed unless there is something permanent in the background, upon which the picture, as it were, may be formed, upon which we may unify all the different impressions'.[3] This unifying, constant background, the precondition of all experience, Vivekananda calls the soul or **Atman**. The *Atman*, he contends, is distinct not only from the body but also from the mind.

The next stage in the argument leads back to the concept of Brahman. The *Atman* or soul has no shape or form, and if it has neither shape nor form, it must be omnipresent, since whatever is without shape or form is without limit, and whatever has no limit or boundary logically cannot be located in a particular place. Again, time, space and causality, the preconditions for and generators of the phenomenal world of individuals, pertain to the mind but not to the soul. If *Atman* is beyond space, time and causality, it must be infinite. If *Atman* is infinite it must be One. If *Atman* is omnipresent, infinite One, *Atman* and Brahman must be one and the same:[4] thus Vivekananda returns to the classic doctrine of the *Upanisads*.

This metaphysics of nondualism generates a number of profound philosophical difficulties, of which the first is this: why did the one manifest itself as the many? Why did the eternal become temporal, the infinite become finite, the immutable become mutable? Many thinkers in the orthodox Hindu tradition argue that the answer is delight (S: **ananda**): the universe is Brahman's expression of delight in creation. Vivekananda's reply is different: the question why the Absolute became finite cannot be answered because it is a logically incoherent question. It is an incoherent question because it applies to the Absolute concepts which cannot apply to it, and an answer would likewise have to be given in terms of human conceptual systems inapplicable to it:

> To ask this question we have to suppose that the Absolute also is bound by something, that it is dependent on something. Thus we see that the very question as to why the Infinite became the finite is an absurd one, for it is self-contradictory.[5]

Even if it is not possible to say why Brahman manifested itself, it is possible to say a good deal, in Vivekananda's view, about a closely related issue: how does it come about that the phenomenal universe takes the form it does, composed of causally interacting individuals in space and time? The Advaitist answer is that the phenomenal universe is an appearance only, an appearance which can be dispelled by appropriate spiritual discipline. The illusion of division is a product of ignorance (**avidya**). It functions through our ordinary patterns of conceptual thought, to which Vivekananda summarily refers by means of classic formulation 'name and form' (**nama-rupa**). The operation of *nama-rupa* generates the categories of space, time and causality (*desa; kala; nimitta*) and with them the whole phenomenal universe. To take the universe of *nama-rupa* for reality is to be in the grip of **maya** or illusion. The operation of *maya* Vivekananda likens to what is now called seeing-as: when a rope is seen as a snake, the rope is really there, unchanged by the delusory perception, and the snake is not. Analogously Brahman is always what is really there, unaffected by the operation of *nama-rupa*.[6] *Maya* is no less than a way of describing the entire condition of those ignorant of the true nature of reality:

> The whole of human knowledge is a generalization of this *maya*, an attempt to know it as it appears to be . . . Everything that has form, everything that calls up an idea in your mind, is within *maya*; for everything that is bound by the laws of time, space and causation is within *maya*.[7]

One of the most far-reaching of the errors we entertain in the condition of *maya* concerns the nature of the self. Vivekananda's nondualist metaphysic entails that our ordinary concept of the self as a limited individual is merely an instance of *nama-rupa*. Our real nature, our true individuality, does not reside either in bodily identity or a set of memories or a congeries of habits. All these are mutable, and could form the basis only for a frail, inconstant individuality. The truth concerning our real nature is quite otherwise: 'There is no individuality except in the infinite . . . We are not individuals yet. We are struggling towards individuality; and that is the Infinite. That is the real nature of man.'[8] The real self is the *Atman*, and the *Atman* and Brahman are one and the same. The real self is divine.

This belief in turn entails a particular view concerning the nature of immortality. The real self or *Atman* is eternal: it is beyond death, and so also can never be said to have lived: 'That which does not die cannot live. For life and death are the obverse and reverse of the same coin.'[9] This is a consequence of the identity of Brahman and *Atman*, for, if no predicates (like 'living' or 'dead') apply to the former, no more can they apply to the latter. It follows that the immortality which is a consequence of nondualism is not personal: it is immortality of the *Atman*, the One. Moreover, it follows also that, if the real self is to continue to manifest itself, it must do so by means of reincarnation in a number of mortal bodies. Thus Vivekananda regards reincarnation as 'the only logical conclusion that thoughtful men can arrive at. If you are going to exist in eternity hereafter, it must be that you have existed through eternity in the past; it cannot be otherwise.'[10] It is often objected to the doctrine of reincarnation that we cannot recall past lives, but this, Vivekananda contends, is merely because we live only on the surface of the psyche. There are depths of memory which can be tapped by yogic training, and memories of past lives can be recovered.[11]

There are further important consequences of nondualism in the area of moral philosophy. There is one belief, Vivekananda contends, which is common to all moral systems, which is to put others before oneself. The question arises at once: why should I be moral in this sense? What reason have I to put others before myself? The principle of utility, much discussed in the nineteenth century, can provide no convincing answer to this question, in Vivekananda's view. At the time when he was writing, the most commonly advanced form of the principle of utility was: so act as to maximize the greatest happiness of the greatest number.[12] Vivekananda objects first: 'If happiness is the goal of mankind, why should I not make myself happy and others unhappy? What prevents me?'[13] Secondly, utilitarianism is an ethical system designed very specifically to suit society in its present stage of evolution. There is no reason to regard our current social structures as other than transient, and when they are swept away by time the destroyer, utility will cease to have any relevance to moral decision making. The only philosophical system which can supply an answer to the question of why I should be moral, and indeed the only system which makes intelligible the central moral recommendation to put others before myself, is Advaita Vedanta. The truth behind the imperative to altruism is the nondualist assertion, the 'eternal truth that "I am the universe; this universe is one". Or else where is the explanation? Why should I do good to my fellow men? . . . It is sympathy, the feeling of sameness everywhere.'[14] I do good to others because they are myself.

A second important moral consequence of nondualism is that it allows Vivekananda to give an answer to the serious philosophical issue of the problem of evil: how does it come about that Brahman manifests itself in such a way as to bring manifold pain and suffering into the phenomenal world? Brahman is pure delight (*ananda*), so how can this be? Vivekananda's answer follows from the doctrine of *maya*: the concepts of good and evil, pleasure and pain are instances of *nama-rupa*, and have no counterpart in Brahman, to which no predicates apply. Hence, 'throughout the Vedanta philosophy there are no such things as good and bad; they are not two different things; the same thing is good or bad, and the difference is only in degree'.[15] All the universe is Brahman, manifesting itself both as what we call good and what we call evil. For those who attain to knowledge of the real self, that is, those who attain direct awareness of Brahman, the distinction between good and evil dissolves. Thus Vivekananda remarks with only apparent paradox that such a person realizes 'How beautiful is good and how wonderful is evil',[16] for in reality nothing corresponds to this distinction.

Advaita has further important consequences in the philosophy of religion. As with other nondualisms – Zen is also an example – it follows that the kernel of religion lies not in adherence to a given set of beliefs or the practice of specific rituals but in direct awareness of the One. The path to religious truth is a voyage inward: 'only the man who has actually perceived God and the soul is religious . . . religion is not in books and temples. It is in actual perception',[17] and this conviction led Vivekananda to believe in the possibility of a universal religion. Further, Vivekananda believed that just as the imperative to altruism is common to all moral systems, so all religions embody one common presupposition, 'the knowledge that we are all advancing towards freedom',[18] and freedom consists in awareness that God and real self are one and the same. This belief, combined with his belief in the impersonal divinity of nondualism, leads Vivekananda to advocate extreme mutual toleration between the various religions of the world. Each is in its own way a valuable vessel of truth, and that adherents of diverse religions should persecute each other on the ground of disagreement over the less profound areas of belief struck him as madness. To those who have realized the truth of nondualism, all violence and all competition are against oneself, and so are pointless.[19]

In the light of this profound tolerance of the variety of religious belief, it is not surprising – and here he follows an ancient tradition in Hindu thought – to find that Vivekananda contends that there is no single form of discipline (or, as he would put it, **yoga**) suitable to lead all human beings to a realization of the truth of Vedanta. In his view, there are four major types of personality, and for each an appropriate *yoga*. To each of these *yogas* he devoted one of his major works. The approach to Vedanta via philosophy is the *jnana-yoga* which has been outlined above, and which is suitable for the person in whom reason is the dominant feature of the personality. Others are primarily given to action (**karma**) or work, and for them *karma-yoga* is appropriate, outlined in a work with this title. The goal is to act or work whilst maintaining absolute non-attachment to the work or its fruits: 'let us do good because it is good to do good . . . Any work that is done with even the least selfish motive, instead of making us free, forges one more chain for our feet.'[20] In others, emotion is the strongest aspect of the personality, and for these adoration (*bhakti*) is the natural attitude to God. Yet the emotion of which this is typical usually creates bonds which bind us to this world of *maya*, rather than freeing us from it. In his work *Bhakti-yoga*, Vivekananda describes how emotion can be controlled for spiritual ends, the ultimate goal being to love God because it is good to love God, entirely without ulterior motive. Finally, there are those who aspire to direct awareness of Brahman in mystic experience, and the discipline for them is *raja-yoga*, the king of *yogas*. Vivekananda's work with this title is his commentary on the classic *Yoga Aphorisms* of Patanjali, describing the path to the ultimate religious experience.

The difficulties in Vivekananda's philosophy are those of the Advaita of which it is a fine recent example, difficulties which centre on the possibility of articulating a satisfactory nondualist account of the relation of the one and the many, both in metaphysics and the ethical form of the problem of evil. That the West knows of this philosophy in such detail is in no small measure due to Vivekananda's work, and in this connection he has with respect to Advaita a position somewhat analogous to that of Suzuki regarding Zen. This is the result not only of lucidity and rhetorical skills, but of the appeal of the transparently sincere and tolerant personality which informs all his works.

Notes

Unless otherwise indicated, references to Vivekananda's works are to the compendium volume, ed. Swami Nikhilananda: *Vivekananda: The Yogas and Other Works*, New York, 1953 (hereafter cited as VYOW).

1 Vivekananda's life is well documented: cf. the works in the Bibliography by Swami Nikhilananda (1953) and Isherwood (1986), together with the Swami's letters and autobiographical passages scattered throughout his works.

2 *Jnana-Yoga*, VYOW, p. 244. *Jnana* is knowledge or reality attained by means of philosophical reasoning, and *jnana-yoga* is the spiritual discipline based on this reasoning. The book by Vivekananda issued under the title *Jnana-Yoga*, in which most of his philosophical views are concentrated, is made up, like nearly all his works, of lectures transcribed by a stenographer. Granted the pace of Vivekananda's life in his last decade, he would have had no time to write down and assemble such books himself. The lectures in *Jnana-Yoga* were given in the USA and the UK between 1896 and 1900. All Vivekananda's works are written in excellent English.

3 Ibid., p. 325.

4   Ibid., p. 212.
5   Ibid., p. 245. The view that the Universe is a manifestation of Brahman's
    delight is found throughout the Hindu tradition, from the earliest times to
    Aurobindo.
6   'The Vedanta philosophy' (1896) in *Miscellaneous Lectures*, VYOW, p. 725.
7   *Jnana-Yoga*, VYOW, p. 233.
8   Ibid., p. 214.
9   Ibid., p. 307.
10 Ibid., p. 296.
11 cf. 'Hinduism' in *Chicago Addresses* (1893), VYOW, p. 187.
12 cf. the essays on Bentham and Mill in D.J. Collinson, *Fifty Major Philosophers*,
    London: Routledge, 1988.
13 *Jnana-Yoga*, VYOW, p. 204.
14 Ibid., p. 215.
15 Ibid., p. 266.
16 Ibid., p. 275.
17 Ibid., p. 264.
18 Ibid., p. 241.
19 Ibid., pp. 335–6 and the essay 'The ideal of a universal religion' (in *Jnana-
    Yoga*), *passim*.
20 *Karma-Yoga*, VYOW, p. 507.

Vivekanda's major writings

Bhakti-Yoga
Chicago Addresses
Inspired Talks
Jnana-Yoga
Karma-Yoga
Raja-Yoga

See also in this book

Badarayana, Patanjali, Sankara, Ramanuja, Madhva, Gandhi, Aurobindo,
Radhakrishnan

Sources and further reading

Chakrabarti, M., *Swami Vivekananda: A Study on Aesthetics*, New Delhi: Atlantic
    Publishers, 1993
Datta, B., *Swami Vivekananda, Patriot-Prophet: A Study*, Calcutta: Nababharat
    Publishers, 1954
Isherwood, Christopher, *Ramakrishna and His Disciples*, Hollywood, Calif.:
    Vedanta Society of Southern California, 1986
Nehru, J. *Sri Ramakrishna and Swami Vivekananda*, 2nd edn, Almora: Advaita
    Ashrama, 1953
Sil, N.P., *Swami Vivekananda: A Reassessment*, Selinsgrove, Pa. and London:
    Susquehanna University Press and Associated University Presses, 1997

Swami Nikhilananda, *Vivekananda: A Life*, New York: Ramakrishna–Vivekananda Centre, 1953

Swami Nikhilananda (ed.), *Vivekananda: The Yogas and Other Works*, New York: Ramakrishna–Vivekananda Centre, 1953 (contains all the items listed above under *Major Works*, together with some letters and poems; the same organization also issues Vivekananda's *Complete Works* in eight volumes)

Williams, George M., *The Quest for Meaning of Swami Vivekananda*, Chico, Calif.: New Horizons Press, 1974

MOHANDAS KARAMCHAND GANDHI 1869–1948 CE

In each period of history, a few human beings change the course of events not by political machination or military conquest but through leading lives of absolute purity and resoluteness of moral purpose. Such a one was Gandhi, who altered the direction of Indian history with no weapon beyond an inflexible adherence to his moral, political and economic goals. Gandhi did not claim to be either a philosopher or a mystic, but there can be no doubt that behind his programme of action there lies a comprehensive world-view. Though this system of ideas does not follow exactly any of the classical patterns of Indian thought, it is clear that Gandhi's deepest insights tend towards **Advaita** (nondual) **Vedanta**, blended with a profound admiration for the ethics of the *Bhagavad Gita*. On the basis of these beliefs, Gandhi formulated an ethical, political and economic programme which touched every aspect of life. Though he wrote and spoke in favour of this programme extensively – his *Collected Works* run to over seventy volumes – he never simply preached it at others. Everything he advocated he did: he believed firmly that the best recommendation for a philosophy or a religion is not a book, but the life it inspires.[1]

Gandhi was born on 2 October 1869 at Porbandar, capital of the principality of Gujarat in western India. His father was chief minister of Porbandar, while his mother Putlibai divided her time between care for her family and religious devotion. Gandhi grew up in a religious ambience which compounded the worship of the Hindu god Vishnu with a strong element of Jainism, and thus from childhood was acquainted with the principle of *ahimsa* (love of all things or non-violence). After a local schooling in which he did not shine, and a child marriage at the age of 13, Gandhi's family decided that he should become a barrister. To qualify he had to carry on his education in England, for which he set sail in late 1888, and where he remained until 1891.

Back in India, Gandhi found that his qualification did not open the door to a successful career. His natural diffidence did not help him to make a mark in an overcrowded profession. Offered a one-year post by an Indian law firm in Natal, Gandhi moved to South Africa in 1893, where his experiences were to change the course of his life. The racial oppression to which the Indians in South Africa were subjected by its European citizens transformed Gandhi into a political activist. He stayed there not for a year but until 1914, tirelessly campaigning against the legalized inequalities of the South African system, developing his technique of *satyagraha* or non-violent resistance. True to his principles, however, during the Boer War Gandhi argued that Indians had a duty to the colony of Natal and organized an ambulance corps of over a thousand volunteers.

For the first few years after his return from South Africa, Gandhi took little part in Indian politics. He was finally provoked into action in 1919, in opposition to proposed legislation allowing the British to imprison without trial those accused of sedition. From that time until the end of his life, Gandhi was never to be far from the centre of the struggle for Indian independence. He used his technique of *satyagraha* on a number of occasions to great effect, and transformed the Indian National Congress into a major political force. Not even he, however, could heal the rifts between Hindus and Muslims, and one of the greatest disappointments of his life was the creation of the state of Pakistan. His subsequent attempts to reconcile the conflicting elements in society did have some success, but equally attracted suspicion from both parties. It was a Hindu fundamentalist who shot him dead on 30 January 1948 in Delhi.[2]

At the base of Gandhi's system of beliefs is his view of the nature of ultimate reality. This he refers to not as Brahman (as is usual in advaitism) but as **Satya** (S: Truth), a term derived from **sat**, or Being. *Satya* or Truth alone can truly be said to be real:

> It is That which alone is, which constitutes the stuff of which all things are made, which subsists by virtue of its own power, which is not supported by anything else but supports everything that exists. Truth alone is eternal, everything else is momentary.[3]

Being-as-is or Truth or God is nondual, and so beyond description in conceptual terms. Being nondual, it follows that it is false to assert that God has any properties since the possession of properties implies analysability and so non-unity. Hence Gandhi stresses that Truth is not a *property* of God, but is *identical* with God: 'it is more correct to say that Truth is God, than to say that God is Truth.'[4] Further, where there is Truth there is knowledge (for which Gandhi uses the term: S: *chit*), and where there is knowledge there is bliss (S: **ananda**), and so Gandhi can accept the classic Hindu description of ultimate reality as *sat-chit-ananda*.

Since Truth is nondual, it cannot be an object of normal human sense-experience or ratiocination, because both these modes of awareness are conceptual, and if it is to be experienceable at all, it must be so in some other way. Gandhi, unlike, for example, Vivekananda and Aurobindo, denied that he had had direct, mystical awareness of Truth, but he did claim to have had 'glimpses' of it,[5] and these glimpses were by means of what he termed faith. By this term, he did not mean pure trust in authority or belief founded on no possible evidential experience, but rather a mode of awareness independent of either reason or the senses: 'There is an indefinable mysterious Power that pervades everything. I feel it, though I do not see it. It transcends the senses . . . [and] Where there is realization outside the senses it is infallible.'[6] Again, 'Faith . . . does not contradict reason but transcends it. Faith is a kind of sixth sense which works in cases which are without the purview of reason.'[7] Reason and the senses are inadequate to the Truth: in their attempt to grasp it they must limit the illimitable. Any mode of awareness which bypasses them is more to be trusted and not less.[8]

The intuitions of faith are not awareness of something outside us but within us. Gandhi accepts the advaitin doctrine that the **atman** or soul within us is identical with God: 'God is not some person outside ourselves or away from the universe. He pervades everything and is omniscient as well as omnipotent . . . *Atman* is the same in every one of us.'[9] A consistent advaitin metaphysic of this kind has implications for every other area of thought. Its fundamental consequence is that, if reality is one and divine, then to do harm to anyone or anything is to do harm to God, and this thought underlies the whole of Gandhi's ethical and political stance.

The goal of life, in Gandhi's ethics, is to serve God, and the only sure way to do this is to practise **ahimsa**: this means literally non-violence (S: *himsa* = violence), but a better English term for it is love, used in much the same sense as in the Christian injunction to love one's neighbour as oneself. It is not correct to regard *ahimsa* as a means with realization of Truth as its goal. The distinction between means and ends is for a nondualist as unreal as other conceptual distinctions, and so Gandhi regards them as intersubstitutable notions:

when you want to find Truth as God the only inevitable means is Love, i.e. non–violence, and since I believe that ultimately the means and end are convertible terms, I should not hesitate to say that God is Love.[10]

In practice, to follow the path of *ahimsa* is to serve others: God is present in everyone, and so all must be the object of our service.[11] If I am to serve others, I must eliminate attachment to my own ego and its desires. In other words, I must put myself absolutely last,

I must reduce myself to a zero. So long as a man does not of his own free will put himself last among his fellow creatures, there is no salvation for him. *Ahimsa* is the farthest limit of humility.[12]

To put oneself last inevitably involves a good deal of self-discipline and self-restraint. One who has conquered the ego and is free of attachments Gandhi describes in the terms of the *Gita* as *Sthitprajna* or *Samadhista* (one stable in spirit). Such a one is unrufflable in adversity, and does not hanker after happiness.[13]

To follow the path of *ahimsa* will lead to the realization of one of Gandhi's most cherished goals, *sarvodaya* or the good of all, an ideal which follows directly from nondualism and *ahimsa*:[14] since all there is is God, one must strive for the good of all. This doctrine brought Gandhi into conflict with many beliefs and institutions, both western and Indian, and he announced his views with a typical and unflinching regard for truth. *Sarvodaya* entails, for example, that utilitarianism must be rejected as an inadequate moral system, since it seeks to promote the good only of the greatest number, not of all:

[Utilitarianism] means in its nakedness that in order to achieve the supposed good of fifty-one percent, the interest of fortynine percent may be, or rather, should be, sacrificed. It is a heartless doctrine and has done harm to humanity.[15]

Again, *sarvodaya* entails a strict egalitarianism with regard to the treatment of others, and Gandhi was therefore bound to oppose all forms of unequal treatment of human beings. His campaign against racism in South Africa is one instance of this, but he had no more patience with the forms of inegalitarianism built into the institutions of his own country. It follows from the doctrine of the unity of *atman* that women are to be valued as much as and are entitled to the same treatment as men, and this was far from being the case in Indian society:

> My own opinion is that, just as fundamentally man and woman are one, their problem must be one in essence. The soul in both is the same. The two live the same life and have the same feelings. Each is a complement of the other.[16]

This does not mean that they have the same roles: Gandhi advocates a traditional division of labour with women as home-based raisers of the family and men as bread-winners, but he insists on the absolutely equivalent value of these roles, and on the need for chastity on the part of each partner. Again, *sarvodaya* entails that Gandhi had to oppose the caste system in India, which relegated millions of his countrymen and women to the status of untouchables. These outcasts he preferred to call *Harijans* (children of God), and he argued tirelessly that this systematized inequality could not be ended quickly enough.[17]

The same absolute even-handedness moulds Gandhi's views on religion. To anyone convinced of nondualism, the outward forms of the various religions are matters of little consequence. The same reality informs them all, no matter what names and forms are used to describe and worship it, and so such a metaphysic is a perfect ground for religious toleration. Any religion which binds us to Truth is of value, and this, in Gandhi's view, is the function of them all:

> I believe in the fundamental truth of all great religions of the world. I believe that they are all God-given, and I believe that they were necessary for the people to whom these religions were revealed. And I believe that, if only we could all of us read the scriptures of different faiths from the standpoint of the followers of these faiths, we should find that they were at bottom all one and were all helpful to one another.[18]

A further consequence of nondualism is that religion is not an optional component in human life: *atman* and Brahman/*sat-chit-ananda* are identical, and so God is part of our essence; therefore, 'no man can live without religion. There are some who in the egotism of their reason declare that they have nothing to do with religion. But it is like a man saying that he breathes but that he has no nose.'[19] The same *atman* is present in us all: to deny the essentiality of religion is therefore blindness and error. Further, it follows from the principle of *ahimsa* and the goal of *sarvodaya* that religion must function for the good of all. Gandhi could not approve of any system of belief which recommended withdrawal from the ordinary world: 'Religion which takes no account of practical affairs and does not help to solve them, is no religion.'[20]

From this in turn it follows that politics, which has a considerable bearing on the well-being of individuals, cannot be independent of religion, and this is precisely Gandhi's view. Positions in political thought follow from beliefs about metaphysics, ethics and religion in combination with beliefs about forms of government, the nature of the state, and related concepts. Gandhi believes in nondualism (and so the omnipresence of God), in *ahimsa* and *sarvodaya*. Therefore politics were of great concern to him:

> For me, politics bereft of religion are absolute dirt, ever to be shunned. Politics concern nations and that which concerns the welfare of nations must be one of the concerns of a man who is religiously inclined, in other words, a seeker after God and Truth . . . Therefore in politics also we have to establish the Kingdom of Heaven.[21]

The Kingdom of Heaven on earth would come about if all people lived in the light of Truth. They would consistently put the desires of their own egos last, and therefore there would be no conflict of interests. Where there is no conflict of interests, there is no need for any political institution, including that of the state, and so Gandhi's political ideal turns out to be an anarchy, i.e. the condition of society in which there is no government: 'A society organized and run on the basis of complete non-violence [i.e. *ahimsa*] would be the purest anarchy.'[22] Such a social order would not be anarchic in the secondary sense of the term, i.e. chaotic, since all its members would, in western vocabulary, be saints, and the interests of saints do not conflict.

Gandhi of course realized that this vision is an ideal only, and that in practice a political system based on the notion of a state will be needed for the foreseeable future. Consistently with his ideal, however, Gandhi subscribed to Thoreau's view that the best form of government is that which governs least, i.e. because it has least need to do so. The more extensive and interventionist the state, the worse it is, Gandhi argues, for the further it intrudes into personal life, the less morally developed are its citizens, since they are invited to become lazy and less self-reliant.[23] This combined set of moral and theological presuppositions informed Gandhi's support for *Swaraj* (self-rule) on democratic lines for India. *Swaraj*, for him, was not a means whereby

India could maximize its political power and set about bullying its neighbours, but on the contrary was to be informed by the ideals of *ahimsa*. Self-rule would increase the self-reliance of all Indians, and so develop them morally in the direction of Truth. *Swaraj* based on *ahimsa* involves absolute egalitarianism towards all citizens (and so total religious toleration), and beneficent relations with other states.

The political technique which Gandhi developed, from his South African years onward, to allow him to further these goals was *satyagraha*. This means literally 'Truthforce', or, more idiomatically, 'holding fast to Truth'. In practice, it is a technique of absolutely non-violent resistance: Gandhi coined the term to differentiate his technique from that of passive resistance. This latter was a phrase in vogue in English in the early years of the century, having been used, for example, by the suffragettes. The technique was unacceptable to Gandhi since it did not entirely forswear violent means, and the suffragettes had, on occasion, resorted to violence.[24] Any violence is incompatible with *ahimsa* and *sarvodaya*, and is entirely excluded from *satyagraha*. The aim of *satyagraha* is to wean one's opponent from error by patience and sympathy. The only way genuinely to change someone's convictions is to touch them emotionally by taking suffering on oneself. The essential procedure of the *satyagrahi* is to refuse to submit to unjust laws or other objectionable institutions and to take the consequences without flinching, whether they involve deprivation of property, rights, liberty or even of life itself.

Such a technique is not for the fainthearted, and in Gandhi's view required a long period of spiritual training. The *satyagrahi* must become indifferent to pain, imprisonment and poverty, and so to the features of life dearest to the ego. One who is indifferent to the ego is one who realizes Truth and so satisfies a further condition for the *satyagrahi*, perfect religious faith: Gandhi is at one with the classical Hindu and Buddhist traditions in holding that only those who do not live in the ego are fearless.[25] Gandhi also contended that celibacy (*brahmacharya*) is a necessary part of the conduct of a *satyagrahi*, since without it there will be a deficiency of inner strength.[26] The ideal of the *satyagrahi* is in effect identical with that of the ideal human being or *sthitprajna* (man of steady wisdom) described above. In Gandhi, metaphysics, theology, ethics and politics are inseparable: the good man, the saint and the ideal political activist are the same, the seeker after Truth.

From a technical point of view, this set of beliefs no doubt involves some difficulties: no real consideration is given to the problem of the one and the many, or the issue of the status of the ordinary world or the question of evil, beyond cursory remarks that God has left us free to make our own moral choices.[27] Gandhi would probably have smiled at such considerations, since they would have appeared to him, not unjustly, rather remote from the urgent business of addressing sharp injustice. The focus of Gandhi's interest is in the area of practical morality, and here the grandeur and sincerity of the vision is beyond question. Philosophy for him was dead as soon as it became merely academic: 'All our philosophy is dry as dust if it is not immediately translated into some act of living service.'[28]

Notes

Works frequently cited in the notes are *The Selected Works of Mahatma Gandhi*, ed. Shriman Narayam, 6 vols, Ahmedabad: Navajivan Publishing House, 1968, hereafter cited as SW + vol. number + page; and Gandhi's *In Search of the Supreme*, ed. V.B. Kher, 3 vols, Ahmedabad: Navajivan Publishing House, 1931, hereafter cited as ISS + vol. number + page.

1 As he puts it, 'A rose does not need to preach. It simply spreads its fragrance . . . The fragrance of religious and spiritual life is much finer and subtler than that of a rose.' SW, VI, pp. 270–1.
2 Gandhi's own version of his life is set out in his *An Autobiography*, SW, I and II.
3 SW, VI, p. 96.
4 Ibid. The same is true of any other alleged 'properties' of God, cf. 'goodness is not an attribute. Goodness is God, (ibid., p. 102); cf. also ISS, II, pp. 10–24.
5 SW, VI, pp. 95–6; cf. pp. 123ff.
6 Ibid., pp. 103–5.
7 Ibid., p. 106, cf. pp. 115ff.
8 This thesis in epistemology is more or less unavoidable in advaitism. cf. e.g., Radhakrishnan's concept of intuition, which is very close to Gandhi's notion of faith.
9 SW, VI, pp. 101 and 113.
10 SW, VI, p. 100, cf. ISS, II, pp. 25–59 *passim*.
11 SW, VI, p. 114.
12 Ibid., p. 125.
13 Ibid., p. 146, cf. *Bhagavad Gita*, Bk II, sections 55ff.
14 *Sarvodaya* is the term Gandhi used as the title for his Gujurati translation of Ruskin's essay in economics *Unto This Last* (1860–2), which he read as a young man and which crystallized many convictions to which he was to adhere for the rest of his life. cf. SW, IV, pp. 229–30; cf. also SW, IV, pp. 41–80; and *An Autobiography*, Pt IV, ch. xviii, SW, II, pp. 443–7.
15 SW, VI, p. 230; cf. a similar condemnation of utilitarianism by Vivekananda.
16 SW, VI, p. 480, cf. *Constructive Programme*, ch. 9, SW, IV, pp. 353–5.
17 cf. e.g. ISS, III, pp. 146ff.
18 SW, VI, p. 264, cf. ISS, III, pp. 3–60 for a detailed treatment of this issue. There are very similar views in the works of some other modern Hindus like Vivekananda and Radhakrishnan.

19 SW, VI, p. 117.
20 SW, VI, p. 264.
21 SW, VI, p. 435, cf. ISS, II, pp. 308ff.
22 SW, VI, p. 436.
23 cf., e.g. SW, VI, p. 438. For another defence of minimalist government, cf. the essay in this book on Laozi (pp. 240–8). Thoreau's point of view is set out in his essay 'Civil disobedience' (1849 and 1866).
24 cf. *Satyagraha in South Africa*, SW, III, ch. xiii: '*Satyagraha* v. passive resistance'.
25 cf. e.g. ISS, I, p. 53; SW, VI, p. 189.
26 cf. *An Autobiography*, SW, I, pp. 305–15; ISS, II, pp. 66–98; SW, VI, p. 198.
27 cf. e.g. SW, VI, p. 101.
28 *Selected Letters*, SW, V, p. 496.

Gandhi's major writings

Note: unless otherwise stated, these works were all issued by the Navajivan Publishing House, Ahmedabad. Some are themselves composed of smaller pieces, which are again collected in the major selections listed below in 'Sources and further reading'.

All Men are Brothers, UNESCO, 1958
Caste Must Go, the Sin of Untouchability, 1964
Discourses on the Gita, 1960
Ethical Religion, 1969
Fasting in Satyagraha, its Use and Abuse, 1965
In Search of the Supreme, 3 vols, ed. V.B. Kher, 1931
Non-violence in Peace and War, 2 vols, 1960–1962
Satyagraha, Non-violent Resistance, 1951 and 1958
Truth is God, ed. R.K. Prabhu, 1955 and 1969

See also in this book

Vardhamana, Badarayana, Patanjali, Sankara, Ramanuja, Madhva, Vivekananda, Radhakrishnan, Laozi

Sources and further reading

Gandhi's *Collected Works*, Government of India, Publication Division (publication began 1958, and is continuing), extend to more than seventy volumes, and most readers prefer to approach him via the several sets of thematically edited extracts now available. Principal among these are:

Bose, Niral Kumar, *Selections from Gandhi*, Ahmedabad: Navijivan Publishing House, 1948
Kher, V.B. (ed.), *In Search of the Supreme*, 3 vols, Ahmedabad: Navajivan Publishing House, 1961 (1st edn 1931)
Narayam, Shriman (general ed.), *The Selected Works of Mahatma Gandhi*, 6 vols, Ahmedabad: Navajivan Publishing House, 1968

Of the many books about Gandhi, the following dealing principally with his philosophy may be mentioned:

Barathi, K.S., *The Social Philosophy of Mahatma Gandhi*, New Delhi: Concept Publishing, 1991

Datta, Dhirendra Mohan, *The Philosophy of Mahatma Gandhi*, Madison, Wis.: University of Wisconsin Press, 1953

Richards, Glyn, *The Philosophy of Gandhi*, London and Atlantic Highlands, NJ: Curzon Press/Humanities Press, 1991

Shukla, Chandrashankar, *Gandhi's View of Life*, Bombay: Bharatiya Vidya Bhavan, 1956

Verma, Surendra, *Metaphysical Foundations of Mahatma Gandhi's Thought*, New Delhi: Orient Longman, 1970

SRI AUROBINDO 1872–1950 CE

The surest sign of the profundity of a philosophical idea, in any tradition, is that it permits and stimulates repeated reinterpretations which are themselves of philosophical value. Of no idea can this be more fittingly said than of the **Upanisadic** doctrine of **Brahman** and its identity with *Atman* (cf. the Introduction to this section on Indian philosophers). In essence, the philosophy of Aurobindo is a modern reinterpretation of this belief, in which it is combined with an optimistic version of evolutionism:[1] Aurobindo argues that history has a direction, and is the unfolding of an evolutionary manifestation of Brahman which will end in universal perfection. Behind this assertion there is more than logic: Aurobindo was a yogic adept, whose thought is firmly based on his own repeated religious experiences in meditation. These experiences furnished the ground of a philosophy which aims to do no less than explain why there is a universe at all, and the significance of human existence within it.

The works in which this philosophy is expounded are all written in excellent English, a fact explained by Aurobindo's education. Aurobindo Ghose[2] was born on 15 August 1872 in Calcutta, the sixth child of a doctor who had been trained in England. Aurobindo's father had his son brought up in ignorance of Indian tradition, and sent him to England to be educated. At St Paul's High School and later at King's College, Cambridge, Aurobindo acquired an excellent knowledge of contemporary western ideas, together with mastery of Latin, Greek, French, German and Italian. He returned to India in 1893 after fourteen years in the West. The effect of the return was to trigger at once the first in a long series of spiritual experiences, 'a feeling of the Infinite pervading material space and the Immanent inhabiting material objects and bodies'.[3]

After his return, Aurobindo occupied a number of college teaching posts, and became closely associated with the cause of Indian nationalism. He also began to practise yoga, and in so doing had further spiritual experiences of an Advaitic Vedantic kind. He later commented that these experiences 'made me see with a stupendous intensity the world as a cinematographic play of vacant forms in the impersonal universality of the Absolute Brahman'.[4] These experiences continued during the year Aurobindo spent in gaol following his arrest by the British in 1908 for suspected complicity in a fatal bomb plot. Finally acquitted, Aurobindo briefly rejoined political life, but inner voices urged him to move instead to Pondicherry to devote himself to the religious life, and this he did in 1910.

There he established his *ashram* or religious community, and soon underwent the third of the four major spiritual experiences of his life, a vision of the Supreme Reality as both one and many. This began the period of his greatest literary productivity, corresponding roughly to that of the First World War in Europe. During these years, as well as the first version of his major philosophical work, *The Life Divine*, Aurobindo published *The Synthesis of Yoga, The Ideal of Human Unity, The Human Cycle, The Future Poetry, Essays on the Gita, The Secret of the Veda* and essays on the *Upanisads*.

In 1914, Aurobindo had met the Frenchwoman Mira Richard. She returned to Pondicherry in 1920 and took over the running of the *ashram*, leaving Aurobindo free to seclude himself. The fourth great spiritual experience of Aurobindo's life occurred on 24 November 1926. This he described as the descent of the Overmind (a term clarified below), a state in which all other points of view can be experienced as one's own. The rest of Aurobindo's life was spent in meditation in his *ashram*. He died there on 5 December 1950.

The ambitious philosophical framework which underlies the whole of Aurobindo's thought is set out in *The Life Divine*. His aim in this book is no less than 'to discover what is the reality and significance of our existence as conscious beings in the material universe and in what direction and how far that significance once discovered leads us, to what human or divine future'.[5] To do this involves answering the profoundest of philosophical questions: why there is a universe at all; why it has the properties it has; and what is the place of human existence within it. To each of these questions Aurobindo has an answer.

He begins with his view on the nature of reality or what there is, and this, following the Upanisadic tradition, he calls Brahman, the omnipresent, ultimate pure being, a predicateless unity, beyond all conceptual description: 'pure existence, eternal, infinite, indefinable, not affected by the succession of Time, not involved in the extension of Space, beyond form, quantity, quality – Self only and absolute'.[6] Many thinkers in the Indian tradition would accept such a view, but Aurobindo develops this idea in an unusual way, which can be made clear, by contrasting his view with the Advaita (nondual) Vedanta of Sankara. Accepting the reality of Brahman, Sankara argues that it must follow that the material world and ordinary self must be an illusion (*maya*) brought about by ignorance (*avidya*). To put it in traditional philosophical language, Sankara holds that only Being (Brahman, the one) is real, and that Becoming (the material world of mutable individuals, the many) is unreal. Aurobindo, by contrast, interprets differently the Upanisadic doctrine 'All This is Brahman'[7] which is usually held to justify the Advaitin position. If All This is Brahman, then in Aurobindo's view, it follows that Matter too is real, and Matter too is Brahman. A right understanding of the universe must not only include a belief in the reality of spirit but must also 'accept Matter of which it [i.e. the universe] is made'.[8] It is this insistence that Matter as well as Spirit is real which shapes much of Aurobindo's thought, and which generates a number of the profound difficulties he has to face.

The first of these is the question of why Brahman chose to manifest itself at all. The major option facing a metaphysician at this point is to contend either that the universe is in some sense a necessary manifestation of the one, or that it is the result of what, in the human context, we would call free will. The first option entails that the one is not free to do other than manifest itself, and this Aurobindo rejects on the grounds that Brahman cannot lack the property of freedom. He is then faced with the corresponding difficulty facing those who opt for the thesis that the universe is the result of a free act, i.e. why should the one, self-sufficient, perfect, free, lacking and desiring nothing, choose to manifest itself at all? Aurobindo's answer is a traditional one in Indian thought:

> If, then, being free to move or remain eternally still, to throw itself into forms or retain the potentiality of form in itself, it indulges its power of movement and formation, it can be only for one reason, for delight. (S: *ananda*)[9]

Brahman delights in realizing the infinity of possibilities inherent in its nature.[10]

Having established the reason for the existence of the universe,

Aurobindo must now explain its most pervasive feature, i.e. mutability or change, a second aspect of the classic philosophical problem of relating one and many in metaphysical systems which include these concepts. If Brahman is a pure, eternal, changeless existent, how is temporal change possible? His answer is again a traditional one in Indian thought. Brahman not only has the aspects of pure immutable being (S: *sat*) and of delight, but also of Consciousness-Force (S: *cit* or *chit*), and this Force underlies all change. It is to be stressed that Being, Consciousness-Force and Delight are not distinct properties of Brahman, for Brahman is beyond all conceptual distinctions. Only the forms of our language necessitate that we divide up these aspects which in reality are one and the same. Aurobindo combines the Sanskrit terms for these aspects into the form Sachchidananda, a synonym for Brahman,

> a Triune Existence-Consciousness-Bliss . . . In everything that is, dwells the conscious force and it exists and is what it is by virtue of that conscious force; so also in everything that is there is the delight of existence and it exists and is what it is by virtue of that delight.[11]

The stress on delight, combined with his acceptance that all there is is Brahman, entails that Aurobindo has to face a particularly acute form of the problem of evil: 'If the world be an expression of Sachchidananda . . . of existence that is also infinite self-delight, how are we to account for the universal presence of grief, of suffering, of pain?'[12] The acuteness of the problem for Aurobindo is a consequence of his assertion that absolutely all that exists is Brahman, and so pain and evil must, it seems, be predicable of Brahman also: 'how came the sole and infinite Existence-Consciousness-Bliss to admit into itself that which is not bliss, that which seems to be its positive negation?'[13] An analogous problem arises with respect to ignorance, since it is initially difficult to see how perfect knowledge (Brahman) can manifest itself in a form which involves less than perfect knowledge. These are serious difficulties to which Aurobindo devotes a great deal of attention.

With regard to evil, Aurobindo adopts one of the classic philosophical positions, one which has close analogies in, for example, Christian responses to this question. He contends that our ideas of good and evil are consequences of our extremely limited viewpoint with regard to the universe. The ethical point of view is a human construction, and is simply inapplicable to Brahman or the universe as a whole. It will be transcended as evolution proceeds, and is merely an inevitable step in the progress of Sachchidananda towards universal delight.[14] Again, concerning pain, Aurobindo argues that its apparent contrariety with universal bliss is a product of human limitation:

> pain is a contrary effect of the one delight of existence resulting from the weakness of the recipient, his inability to assimilate the force that meets him . . . it is a perverse reaction of Consciousness to *Ananda*, not itself a fundamental opposite of *Ananda*: this is shown by the significant fact that pain can pass into pleasure and pleasure into pain and both resolve into the original *Ananda*.[15]

The question of the possibility and nature of ignorance (*avidya*) is a further area in which Aurobindo's belief in the reality of matter necessitates a sharp divergence from the Mayavada of Sankara. Since he accepts that the material universe is real, Aurobindo cannot hold that all perception (and so perceptually-based knowledge) is an illusion (*maya*). Instead, in Aurobindo's epistemology, the common-sense picture of the world as composed of discrete spatio-temporal individuals has a real if extremely limited validity:

> Each form [in the universe] is there because it is an expression of some power of That [i.e. Brahman] which inhabits it; each happening is a movement in the working out of some Truth of the Being in its dynamic process of manifestation. It is this significance that gives validity to the mind's interpretative knowledge, its subjective construction of the universe.[16]

As with evil and pain, 'ignorance' is a term whose ground is not a contradiction in reality, but human limitation:

> what we call Ignorance is not really anything else than a power of the one divine Knowledge-will; it is the capacity of the One Consciousness similarly to regulate, to hold back, measure, relate in a particular way to the action of its Knowledge.[17]

Moreover, Aurobindo argues that evil, pain and ignorance are only temporary features of the universe, destined to vanish as time passes. His thought is profoundly optimistic, in a philosophical sense, and this is a consequence of another of his most striking beliefs, namely that the universe is evolving in a direction whose goal he has identified. The manifestation of Brahman we call the universe has evolved from a state which Aurobindo calls subconscient to its present state in which ordinary human and animal consciousnesses are present. The direction of its future evolution is towards 'the Infinite and the Supreme'.[18] What we now regard as human nature will be transcended, replaced by 'a supreme consciousness and an integral awareness',[19] and those who will live in this way will live what Aurobindo calls the Life Divine. This belief is the ground for Aurobindo's central moral imperative. Even with our limited consciousness we can so conduct ourselves as to live in alignment with the direction of Brahmanic evolution. To do this we must seek a 'complete and radical transformation of our nature . . . [to make] spirit our life-basis'.[20] What this means is explained by Aurobindo in some detail.[21]

The complete transformation of human nature takes place in three major stages, with some further subdivisions. Though practice may speed up this evolution, Aurobindo contends that none of its steps can be omitted.[22] The first stage is the psychic transformation, a formulation in which the term 'psychic' is used in a technical sense. In common with many eastern thinkers, Aurobindo contends that the ego of ordinary experience is a superficial construct, often baneful in its influence.[23] Behind it, as it were, is the real self or 'subliminal psychic entity, a pure power of light, love, joy and refined essence of being'.[24] This true or psychic self is 'that which endures and is imperishable in use from birth to birth, untouched by death, decay or corruption, an indestructible spark of the Divine'.[25] The psychic transformation is a major shift in consciousness such that direction of the individual passes from the surface ego to the psychic or true soul. This event has two major consequences: it results first in a complete harmonization of all aspects of our being and, secondly, permits a free inflow of spiritual experience of all kinds.[26]

Great though the psychic transformation is, it is only the first step on the path to the Life Divine. The next stage is the spiritual transformation, which Aurobindo epitomizes as follows:

> What we see by the opening of vision is an Infinity above us, an eternal Presence or an infinite Existence, an infinity of consciousness, an infinity of bliss − a boundless Self, a boundless Light, a boundless Power, a boundless Ecstasy.[27]

Generally, such experiences have to be repeated until the whole being lives in them, as it were, normally and habitually. In such a case, awareness of the Eternal in everything is normal. No limit can be set to this change, 'for it is in its nature an invasion of the Infinite'.[28]

Even this, in Aurobindo's view, is not the ultimate spiritual condition. Beyond this lies what he calls the supramental trans-formation or descent of Supermind, a condition not attainable by the exercise of human will.[29] No language is adequate to describe this condition, and Aurobindo attempts to hint at its nature by describing the stages of spiritual evolution discernible between the spiritual and supramental transformations. The first of these stages is Higher Mind, which is still a mode of conceptual awareness, 'a mind of spirit-born conceptual knowledge'.[30] It also has will, the exercise of which prepares us for the next stage, Illumined Mind, 'a Mind no longer of higher Thought, but of spiritual light'.[31] Both thought and vision are derived from what Aurobindo calls Intuition, and the third stage on the ascent to Supermind he calls Intuitive Mind, 'a power of true automatic discrimination of the orderly and exact relation of truth to truth'.[32] When Intuition is stabilized, what Aurobind terms Overmind begins to emerge, and it is at this point that our ordinary sense of selfhood disintegrates:

> When the Overmind descends, the predominance of the centralizing ego-sense is entirely subordinated, lost in large-ness of being and finally abolished; a wide cosmic perception and feeling of a boundless universal self and movement replaces it.[33]

Finally comes the supramental, or, as Aurobindo alternatively terms it, the gnostic transformation to which conceptual description is entirely inadequate. The gnostic being is free from our current form of individuality, which presupposes barriers between the self and others. Rather, at each moment, the gnostic being will have 'the sense of the whole movement of an integral being and the presence of its entire and integral bliss of being, *Ananda*'.[34] Gnostic life involves an entirely new relation of mind and body, the latter being filled with the energy of the Consciousness-Force, banishing pain and bringing instead pure delight. Again, our present mode of conceptual knowledge would be replaced by an intuitive awareness 'able to see and grasp things by direct contact and penetrating vision'.[35] Such awareness is beyond the need for what we term morality. Morality is a consequence of our ignorance. The gnostic being has perfect knowledge and for such a being no conflict of good and evil can arise. To use a Kantian term for what Aurobindo is describing, the gnostic being has a holy will; i.e.

such a being will spontaneously and with delight do what is 'right'. In Aurobindo's view, the future belongs to the gnostic beings who will inevitably evolve. Few at first, their numbers will grow. Though no indication of time-scale is given, Aurobindo is certain that human nature as we know it will be transcended as the Brahmanic evolution takes its unalterable course towards universal perfection.

This philosophy involves a number of unresolved difficulties. Aurobindo does not show conclusively why Brahman chose a manifestation which would involve so much suffering; nor can the view that evil, suffering and ignorance are a consequence of our frailty and ultimately destined to disappear be of much consolation to those presently in their grip. One cannot doubt, however, the grandeur and evident sincerity of Aurobindo's thought, nor its grounding in a wealth of genuine spiritual experience. And his philosophy has the enormous merit of tackling head-on most of the deepest of metaphysical problems. This is no technical exercise, but a genuine attempt to solve the profoundest riddles of existence.

Notes

Unless otherwise stated, references to Aurobindo's works are to the relevant volume of the Sri Aurobindo Birth Centenary Library, 30 vols, Pondicherry: Sri Aurobindo Ashram, 1970–2.

1 This is an instance or a repeated phenomenon in the history of philosophy, i.e. the impact of scientific ideas. Behind the thought of Descartes, Spinoza and Leibniz is the profound influence of mathematics, the successful science of the time, just as behind that of Locke, Berkeley and Hume lies that of Newtonian experimental science. Analogously, evolutionism made a deep impact on thought at the time of Aurobindo's education in the West, cf. the ideas of Bergson, Dewey, William James and Whitehead.
2 The title 'Sri' ('Lord') indicates that Aurobindo is regarded as an incarnation of the divine.
3 *Letters on Yoga*, vol. 22, p. 121.
4 *On Himself*, vol. 26, pp. 83–4; quoted in Joan Price, *An Introduction to Sri Aurobindo's Philosophy*, Pondicherry: Sri Aurobindo Ashram, 1982, p. 9.
5 *The Life Divine (LD)* 1 vol. edn, p. 1015.
6 Ibid., pp. 77–8.
7 cf. e.g. *Mandukya Upanisad*, vs 2: 'All This Universe is the Eternal Brahman', in Aurobindo's *The Upanisads*, vol. 12, 1988 edn, p. 319.
8 *LD*, p. 6.
9 Ibid., p. 91.
10 Ibid., p. 110.
11 Ibid., p. 92.
12 Ibid., pp. 92–3.
13 Ibid., p. 95.
14 Ibid., pp. 95–9.

15 Ibid., p. 497.
16 Ibid., p. 646.
17 Ibid., pp. 497–8.
18 Ibid., p. 626.
19 Ibid., p. 627.
20 Ibid.
21 The practical means by which the transformation described by Aurobindo can be achieved is a special system of yoga, which lies outside the scope of the present work. It is described in great detail by Aurobindo in *The Synthesis of Yoga*, vols 20–1, and *Letters on Yoga*, vols 22–4.
22 LD, p. 931.
23 cf. e.g. the Zen concept of 'original self' in Dogen and Hakuin.
24 Ibid., p. 220.
25 Ibid., p. 225.
26 Ibid., pp. 907–8.
27 Ibid., p. 911.
28 Ibid., p. 913.
29 Aurobindo's philosophy contains a number of terms with the prefixes 'super-' or 'supra-', e.g. '-mind', '-nature', '-consciousness' and their cognates. The prefix is meant to indicate that the nouns they modify denote states or entities of nature entirely other than those denoted by the unmodified nouns. Thus supermind is not to be conceived of as like, though more powerful than, a human mind; but rather as something as far beyond ordinary consciousness as it in turn is beyond and other than unconsciousness. Aurobindo faces the common difficulty of all mystics, namely that there is no vocabulary adequate to their experiences.
30 LD, p. 939.
31 Ibid., p. 944.
32 Ibid., p. 949.
33 Ibid., p. 950.
34 Ibid., p. 977.
35 Ibid., p. 924.

Aurobindo's writings

(limited to works of primarily philosophical interest)

Essays on the Gita
The Life Divine
The Secret of the Veda
The Supramental Manifestation and Other Writings
The Upanisads: Texts, Translations and Commentaries

See also in this book

Badarayana, Patanjali, Sankara, Ramanuja, Madhva, Vivekananda, Gandhi, Radhakrishnan

Sources and further reading

Unless otherwise indicated, references to works by Aurobindo cite their volume number in the Sri Aurobindo Birth Centenary Library, published by the Sri Aurobindo Ashram, Pondicherry, 1970–2, in thirty volumes.

Sri Aurobindo, *Essays on the Gita*, vol. 13
—— *Letters on Yoga*, vols 22 and 23
—— *The Life Divine*, 1 vol. edn
—— *The Supramental Manifestation and Other Writings*, vol. 16
—— *The Upanisads*, vol. 12; repr. with additional material, 2nd edn 1981, same publisher
Bruteau, Beatrice, *Worthy is the World: The Hindu Philosophy of Sri Aurobindo*, Rutherford, Madison and Teaneck: Fairleigh Dickinson University Press, 1971
Chakravarty, S., *The Philosophy of Sri Aurobindo*, New Delhi and New York: Sterling Publishers, 1991
Chaudhuri, Haridas and Spiegelberg, Frederic (eds), *The Internal Philosophy of Sri Aurobindo: A Commemorative Symposium*, London: Allen & Unwin, 1960
McDermott, Robert (ed.), *Six Pillars: Introductions to the Major Works of Sri Aurobindo*, Chambersberg, Pa, Anima, 1964
Pandey, S. *Sri Aurobindo and Vedanta Philosophy*, New Delhi: Deep and Deep Publications, 1987
Price, Joan, *An Introduction to Sri Aurobindo's Philosophy*, Pondicherry: Sri Aurobindo Ashram, 1977, repr. 1982
Rafique, M., *Sri Aurobindo and Iqbal: A Comparative Study of Their Philosophy*, Aligarh: Aligarh Muslim University, 1974

SARVEPALLI RADHAKRISHNAN 1888–1975 CE

Of all the distinguished thinkers in the modern Indian tradition, few may claim so wide a range of achievement as Radhakrishnan. Not only did he produce a range of philosophical works demonstrating creative thought, depth of scholarship and powers of assimilation which are rarely equalled, but combined this with a career in politics culminating in his appointment as President of India. Moreover, all the facets of his life are informed by breadth of culture, a deep knowledge not only of Indian but also of western thought and institutions, and a willingness to review each in the light of the other. If his own philosophy is a modified version of **Advaita Vedanta**, with a great and acknowledged debt to Sankara,[1] his adherence to it is not to be thought of as an instance of cultural determinism, but a reasoned preference in the light of a thorough awareness of the alternatives. His philosophy, which he came to refer to as the religion of the spirit, is developed in a long series of distinguished works. Nondualism and a reinterpreted doctrine of *maya* form the basis for a complete system embracing ethics, aesthetics and the philosophy of religion, this last culminating in a form of spiritual life lived not in retreat but in service to the world.

The roots of Radhakrishnan's intellectual cosmopolitanism are to be found in the circumstances of his early life. Born in the town of Tirutani (near Madras) in 1888, Radhakrishnan attended schools run by Christian missionaries until 1908. During school hours he was educated in a Christian setting, whilst his home life was one of traditional Hindu piety. The contrast between the two traditions sparked an interest which never left him, becoming the driving motive for his many essays in comparative thought. The first was the two-volume *Indian Philosophy* (1923 and 1927) which, despite its title, employs a comparative approach.

By the time this work was published, Radhakrishnan had begun the academic career which was to last until 1962; from 1953 to 1962 he was chancellor of the University of Delhi. From 1946 onwards, senior university posts were combined with diplomatic appointments, e.g. headship of the Indian delegation to UNESCO (1946–52) and Indian Ambassador to the Soviet Union (1949–52). His career culminated in Indian politics: he served as Vice-President of India from 1952 to 1962, and President from 1962 to 1967.[2]

Throughout this period, Radhakrishnan issued a series of major philosophical works. Some are scholarly editions of classics of Hindu and Buddhist thought: *The Bhagavad Gita* (1948); *The Dhammapada* (1950); *The Principal Upanisads* (1953) and *The Brahma Sutra* (1968). In other works, Radhakrishnan develops his own philosophy and draws out its consequences when applied to the thought and institutions of the West, e.g. *The Hindu View of Life* (1926); *An Idealist View of Life* (1932) and *Eastern Religions and Western Thought* (1939). By common consent, the second of these is regarded as the most complete and accessible statement of Radhakrishnan's own views. At the end of a long and varied life, during which he had travelled widely and lived in many countries other than India, Radhakrishnan was optimistic about human nature and its future:

> There are no fundamental differences among the peoples of the world. They have all the deep human feelings, the craving for justice above all class interests, horror of bloodshed and violence. They are working for a religion which teaches the possibility and the necessity of man's union with himself, with nature, with his fellow men, and with the Eternal Spirit of which the visible universe is but a manifestation.[3]

At the philosophical base of Radhakrishnan's thought lies the metaphysics of Advaita (nondual) Vedanta. Being-as-is or reality is not the phenomenal world of discrete entities in space and time, but a oneness, Supreme, Brahman or Absolute (all these terms are used in Radhakrishnan's works) to which no conceptual categories apply. Brahman is

> nondual, free from the distinctions of subject and object . . . [it is] before all phenomena, before all time and . . . is equally after all phenomena and all time. Yet it is neither before nor after. It is that which is, real, unhistorical being itself. We cannot think it, enclose it within categories, images and verbal structures.[4]

The question arises at once as to how the oneness of Brahman, eternal and divisionless, is related to the many, the world of spatio-temporal individuals. Three major answers have been given to this question, and Radhakrishnan follows Sankara in dismissing them all: (1) *creation*: to say that Brahman created the universe presupposes that Brahman was once alone and then decided (so to speak) to have company, but no reason can be given for such a decision; (2) *manifestation*: this concept is no help, since it is utterly unclear how the infinite can manifest itself in a finite form; (3) *transformation*: this view involves a dilemma: either Brahman is wholly transformed into the universe or only a part of Brahman is thus transformed. If the former, then there is no Brahman beyond the universe, and if the latter it follows that Brahman can be partitioned and is not a unity. In Radhakrishnan's view, the problem of the one and the many in metaphysics and theology is insoluble: 'The history of philosophy in India as well as in Europe has been one long illustration of the inability of the human mind to solve the mystery of the relation of God to the world.'[5] We have the universe of individuals which is not self-sufficient and in some sense rests on Brahman, but the exact nature of the relation between them is a mystery.

Advaitism involves not only the question of the relation of one and many, but also that of the status of the many. Brahman alone is real, and to many thinkers it has seemed to follow that the many (the ordinary world) are unreal, even an illusion (*maya*) and so unworthy of attention. Radhakrishnan was deeply conscious that nondualism has sometimes been so interpreted as a justification for ignoring the world and its suffering, and this he regarded as morally unacceptable:

That human suffering will be healed, that the whole world will vanish like a pitiful mirage, that all our trouble is of our own making, and that in the world's finale all people will find that absolute oneness which will suffice for all hearts, compose all resentments and atone for all crimes, seem to many to be pious assumptions. The entranced self-absorption which arms itself with sanctity, involves a cruel indifference to practical life hardly acceptable to average intelligence.[6]

In Radhakrishnan's view, the doctrine that the status of the phenomenal world is that of *maya* (which he accepts) is not to be construed as the view that it is a dismissible illusion. The correct understanding of *maya* is this:

The world is not a deceptive façade of something underlying it. It is real though imperfect. Since the Supreme is the basis of the world the world cannot be unreal. *Maya* has a standing in the world of reality . . . In Hindu thought, *maya* is not so much a veil as the dress of God.[7]

The world is not merely an illusion, and there is no justification for ignoring it.

The next serious philosophical issue involved in Advaitism arises in the area of epistemology or the theory of knowledge. All ordinary human experience is conceptual in nature, i.e. is organized under the categories in which we ordinarily think. However, Brahman is said to be predicateless, or, in other words, such that in principle no concepts apply to it: concepts presuppose division, and Brahman is a unity. How, then, is any form of awareness of Brahman possible for human beings? Radhakrishnan's reply is that the assumption on which this objection is based, namely that all human knowledge is derived either from sense-experience or reasoning, is false, since it misses out a third mode of knowing. This third possibility he calls intuition or intuitive apprehension.

Intuition, like sense-experience, is immediate, but it is not conceptual. In intuition, there is no distinction between knower and known, no mediation of the object of experience by any concepts. Rather, it is knowing by fusion of subject and object:

This intuitive knowledge arises from an intimate fusion of the mind with reality. It is knowledge by being and not by senses or symbols. It is awareness of the truth of things by identity. We become one with truth, one with the object of knowledge. The object known is seen not as an object outside the self, but as a part of the self.[8]

The example of intuitive apprehension most frequently given is self-awareness. We are aware of our self, as we are aware of emotions like love or anger, not by any process of inference but by being it. Radhakrishnan contends that everything known by sense-experience or the use of reason can in principle be known by intuition. Since intuitive grasp of an object is complete, intuitive knowledge of that object cannot grow: it is final, unlike other forms of knowledge which can be added to. It is not to be confused with imagination, since intuition is direct awareness of reality, and so always coheres with truths derived from sense-experience or reason. (Radhakrishnan assumes, in accordance with advaitist metaphysics, that there is no contradiction in reality, and so that all truths are compatible.) Whilst this is so, because of its non-conceptual nature, the findings of intuition can be uttered only obliquely in linguistic terms: the vocabulary of intuition is that of myth and art, not science. Again, no intuitive finding can be doubted: all carry a feeling of absolute finality and satisfaction.[9] Where the object (so to speak) of this mode of knowing is Brahman, what Radhakrishnan calls intuition coincides precisely with what is usually termed mystical experience.[10]

His analysis of mystical experience follows the classic Advaitist line. He begins by distinguishing the empirical self or ego from what he calls the true subject – in traditional Hindu terminology, this is the distinction between the **jivatman** and the **atman**. The empirical self is the subject of psychology, the congeries of thoughts, emotions and sensations of which we are aware by introspection. The true subject, by contrast, cannot be introspected, since it is the precondition for introspection. It is what Kant termed the '*Ich denke*' ('I think'), that in virtue of which a given experience is mine and not anyone else's, the precondition of self-conscious experience. It is studied in metaphysics, not psychology. This true subject Radhakrishnan identifies with spirit: it is 'the simple, self-subsistent, universal spirit which cannot be directly presented as the object . . . While the empirical self includes all and has nothing outside to limit it.'[11] If the true self has no limit, then it is identical with Brahman, 'the Universal Self active in every ego even as it is the universal source of all things.'[12] Brahman and *atman* are one and the same.

This view that human nature is tripartite, involving not only body and mind but also *atman* or spirit, is one of the key presuppositions of the law of *karma*. This law states that we will reap what we sow and entails that the universe is ultimately just. Our actions build our character which in turn influences further decisions as to action: every decision we take is morally significant because every decision shapes our destiny. This doctrine is not compatible with the view that human nature is limited to mind and body:

> If man were a mere object of study in physiology, if he were a mere mind described by psychology, his conduct would be governed by the law of necessity . . . [but] There is in us the Eternal different from the limited chain of causes and effects in the phenomenal world.[13]

Body and mind are subject to causal laws, but the *atman* is not.

It may be objected to the law of *karma* that it is false to the facts: that the wicked often prosper at the expense of the good. This difficulty is accommodated by the doctrine of reincarnation: we will inevitably reap what we sow, if not in this life then in a future one. Not to accept the hypothesis of reincarnation, Radhakrishnan argues, would mean accepting a meaningless element in an otherwise orderly cosmos: 'In an ordered world, sudden embodiment of conscious life would be meaningless and inconsequential. It would be a violation of the rhythm of nature, an effect without a cause, a fragmentary present without a past.'[14] However, the doctrine of reincarnation is in turn open to a powerful objection: why do we not remember our past lives? Of what benefit is it to us to suffer if we do not know why we are suffering? If we are not aware that our present suffering is retribution, how will it help us avoid misdeeds in the future? Radhakrishnan replies that we do not ordinarily conclude from the fact that we have forgotten many experiences that it was not we who had them. Personal identity does not depend on memory of individual events. Rather, our past shapes us by forming dispositions, and it is these that are carried over between incarnations. What is reborn is not the same personality, but the results of experience: we take with us our character.[15]

The views set out above have far-reaching consequences, notably in ethics, asethetics and the philosophy of religion. In ethical theory or metaethics, Radhakrishnan's metaphysics and epistemology leave him little choice but to accept a form of intuitionism, i.e. the view that our awareness of what is good or what it is right or dutiful to do is not furnished by deductions from moral principles, but by (in his special sense of the term) intuition: 'In our ethical life . . . intuitive insight is essential for the highest reaches . . . Mere mechanical observance of rules or imitation of models will not take us far. The art of life is not a rehearsal of stale parts.'[16] Those in touch with the reality of Brahman rarely have need of moral rules, and often appear unconventional to the mass of humanity, lacking this insight and forced to rely on moral codes.

The libertarianism which is part of Radhakrishnan's interpretation of the law of *karma* is also used by him in his response to the problem of evil, his answer to the question why Brahman or God has permitted the existence of evil in the universe. Evil is permitted by God because it can be excised from the universe only if human beings are denied freedom of the will. We are made in the image of God insofar as we are creative, and

> While animals are creatures we are creature-creators. There is no animal delinquency. Evil is not passivity but activity. Without creative freedom man cannot produce either a paradise or desolation on earth. God permits evil because he does not interfere with human choice.[17]

The themes of intuition and creativity lead Radhakrishnan to an interest in aesthetics, where they combine with his metaphysics in an analysis of the nature of artistic creativity and of what works of art can do for us. Creativity is a form of intuition, and so is characterized by oneness of artist and subject-matter:

> In poetic experience we have knowledge by being as distinct from knowledge by knowing. The mind grasps the object in its wholeness, clasps it to its bosom, suffuses it with its own spirit, and becomes one with it.[18]

It follows further that the outcomes of artistic creation, works of art, are not vehicles for pleasure but for the profoundest of truths:

> Art as the disclosure of the deeper reality of things is a form of knowledge . . . [the artist] discerns within the visible world something more real than its outward appearance, some idea or form of the true, the good and the beautiful, which is more akin to the spirit itself than to the visible things . . . Poetic truth is a discovery, not a creation.[19]

The artist is akin to the mystic and the seer: the beauty manifested in art is the beauty of reality revealed, not a confection invented by the artist's imagination.

The intuition involved in artistic creativity or in the moral life is a pale reflection of the ultimate form of this experience, mystical union or direct apprehension of Brahman. It is this experience, Radhakrishnan argues, which underlies all religion: 'Religion means conscious union with the Divine in the universe, with love as its chief means.'[20] Such experience has no connection with adherence to a specific set of dogmas or religious practices. The great figures in the history of religion do not enforce belief or ritual, but seek to bring about a change of heart: 'They invite the soul to its lonely pilgrimage and give it absolute freedom in the faith that a free adaptation of the divine into oneself is the essential condition of spiritual life.'[21] This belief leads Radhakrishnan to advocate religious toleration in a very generous form, an attitude he associates particularly with Hinduism.[22]

Whatever the rites and beliefs involved, the goal of all religious practice is the same: release (S: *moksa*), which is the same as eternal life. Release is not a mode of being which will be had after death in a special place or heaven. It consists in the transformation of the inner life which occurs after mystic union with the one. It is not the destruction of the world but the shaking free from the false view of it which is *avidya*. It is an ego-less mode of existence, and utterly satisfying: 'Release is not a state after death but the supreme status of being in which spirit knows itself to be superior to birth and death, unconditioned by its manifestations, able to assume forms at its pleasure.'[23] Such a state can be achieved via many routes during life[24] and those who attain it are said to be *jivanmukti* (free while living). Those who have achieved this peak of spiritual development work for the goal of the ultimate release of all (*sarvamukti*). When this condition has been achieved, the cosmic process ceases, and the universe lapses back into Brahman.

Radhakrishnan's philosophy is by no means free from difficulties. Some are those of advaitism in general – the problem of finding a way to characterize the relation of one and many, or of finding a reason for the manifestation of Brahman as the universe – while others are peculiar to his version of it, e.g. the assumed identity of the Kantian 'I think' with *atman*. Its virtues, however, are very considerable: comprehensiveness, seriousness, sincerity and a basis of formidable learning. There can be no doubt that this system deserves its honoured place in modern Indian thought.

Notes

The titles of works most frequently cited are abbreviated as follows: *BS* = *The Brahma Sutra*; *ERWT* = *Eastern Religions and Western Thought*; *HVL* = *The Hindu View of Life*; *IP* = *Indian Philosophy*; *IVL* = *An Idealist View of Life*; *PU* = *The Principal Upanisads*.

1 He writes of Sankara, transliterated by him as Samkara, as follows: 'Samkara's system is unmatched for its metaphysical depth and power . . . It is a great example of monistic idealism which it is difficult to meet with an absolutely conclusive metaphysical refutation . . . Even those who do not agree with his general attitude to life will not be reluctant to allow him a place among the immortals.' *IP*, II, pp. 657–8).

2 During his life, Radhakrishnan refused all requests to write autobiographical statements. There is now, however, an excellent biography by his son: Sarvepalli Gopal, *Radhakrishnan: A Biography*, Delhi: Oxford University Press, 1989.

3 'The religion of the spirit and the world's needs', repr. in Whit Burnett (ed.), *This Is My Philosophy*, London: Allen & Unwin, 1958, p. 366. This piece was first printed in P.A. Schilpp, *The Philosophy of Sarvepalli Radhakrishnan*, New York: Tudor Publishing Co., 1952.

4 *BS*, pp. 118 and 176, cf. *PU*, pp. 52 sqq; *IVL*, pp. 271 sqq.; *ERWT*, pp. 20 sqq.

5 *HVL*, p. 49; cf. *IVL*, pp. 140 sqq; *BS*, p. 150; *ERWT*, pp. 90 sqq.

6 *IP*, II, p. 657. cf. *ERWT*, ch. iii, esp. pp. 84 sqq.

7 *BS*, pp. 156–7. Consonantly with this interpretation of *maya*, Radhakrishnan construes *avidya* not as intellectual ignorance but as spiritual blindness, lack of awareness of the reality of spirit, cf. *BS*, p. 21.

8 *IVL*, p. 109.

9 *IVL*, pp. 101–12, cf. *BS*, pp. 105 sqq.

10 cf. *BS*, pp. 109 sqq.

11 *IVL*, p. 215.

12 *BS*, p. 147, cf. *PU*, pp. 77–8.

13 *BS*, p. 195.

14 *BS*, p. 190, cf. *IVL*, pp. 227 sqq.

15 cf. *BS*, pp. 190–207; *PU*, pp. 113–17; *IVL*, pp. 227–39.

16 *IVL*, p. 155.

17 *BS*, p. 155.

18 *IVL*, p. 145.

19 *IVL*, p. 152. This interpretation of the artist as penetrative to the truth of things often forms part of philosophies incorporating a one and a many, e.g. most of the English Romantic poets accepted a very similar set of views, cf. C.M. Bowra, *The Romantic Imagination*, Oxford: Oxford University Press, 1950.

20 *IVL*, p. 161.

21 Ibid., cf. *HVL*, pp. 6–7.

22 cf. e.g. *BS*, p. 170; *HVL*, pp. 28 sqq; *ERWT*, ch. viii.

23 *BS*, p. 215, cf. *PU*, pp. 117–31; *IVL*, pp. 97–9. This idea is not peculiar to the Hindu tradition. There are very close parallels in Buddhist literature, and the Sufi mystics of Islam also write of release in a similar way, e.g. Farid al-din 'Attar (1119–1230?): 'Whoever leaves this world behind him passes

away from mortality, he attains to immortality. If thou dost desire to reach this abode of immortality . . . divest thyself first of self (F.C. Happold, *Mysticism*, Harmondsworth: Penguin Books, 1970, p. 258).

24 Radhakrishnan adopts a traditional analysis (as does e.g. Vivekananda) of different paths to release: by work (*karma*); devotion (*bhakti*); or meditation (*dhyana*); cf. *BS*, pp. 151–83.

Radhakrishnan's writings

The Philosophy of Rabindranath Tagore, 1918
The Reign of Religion in Contemporary Philosophy, 1920
Indian Philosophy, 2 vols, 1923 and 1927
The Hindu View of Life, 1926
An Idealist View of Life, 1932
Gautama – The Buddha, 1938
Eastern Religions and Western Thought, 1939
Religion and Society, 1947
The Bhagavad Gita, 1948
The Dhammapada, 1950
The Principal Upanisads, 1953
The Brahma Sutra, 1968

See also in this book

Badarayana, Patanjali, Sankara, Ramanuja, Madhva, Vivekananda, Gandhi, Aurobindo

Sources and further reading

Arapura, J.G. *Radhakrishnan and Integral Experience*, New York: Asia Publishing House, 1966
Bowra, C.M., *The Romantic Imagination*, London: Oxford University Press, 1950
Burnett, W. (ed.), *This is My Philosophy*, London: Allen & Unwin, 1958
Gopal, S., *Radhakrishnan: A Biography*, Delhi: Oxford University Press, 1989
Happold, F.C., *Mysticism*, Harmondsworth, Penguin Books, 1970
Radhakrishnan, S., *Indian Philosophy*, vol. I and vol. II, London: Allen & Unwin, 1923 and 1927
—— *Eastern Religions and Western Thought*, 2nd edn, Oxford: Oxford University Press, 1940; 1st edn, 1939
—— *The Bhagavad Gita*, 2nd edn, London: Allen & Unwin, 1949
—— *Comparative Studies in Philosophy in Honour of his Sixtieth Birthday*, London: Allen & Unwin, 1951
—— *The Principal Upanisads*, London: Allen & Unwin, 1952, repr. 1969
—— *The Brahma Sutra (of Badarayana)*, London: Allen & Unwin, 1960
—— *The Dhammapada*, Madras: Oxford University Press, 1966; 1st edn, 1950
—— *The Hindu View of Life*, London: Allen & Unwin, 1988; a reprint of the 2nd edn, 1937; 1st edn 1932

—— *New Essays in the Philosophy of Sarvepalli Radhakrishnan*, Delhi: Sri Satguru Publications, 1995

Schilpp, P.A. (ed.), *The Philosophy of Sarvepalli Radhakrishnan*, New York: Tudor Publishing Co., 1952

Sinha, H.P., *Religious Philosophy of Tagore and Radhakrishnan*, Delhi: Motilal Banarsidass, 1993

Part 4

TIBETAN PHILOSOPHY

INTRODUCTION

Until the recent military occupation of Tibet by the Chinese, the history of Tibetan thought is to all intents the same as the history of Tibetan Buddhism, which has greatly overshadowed the native Tibetan religion of Bönism. Buddhism was diffused in Tibet over a long period, from the eighth to the thirteenth centuries CE, generally subdivided by its historians into two phases. The first phase, dated approximately from the founding of the first Buddhist monastery at Bsam-yas in the late eighth century, involved influences from both India in the West and China in the East. This process was disrupted by the political disintegration of the country in 842 CE. It was only when stability returned with the establishment of a new royal dynasty towards the end of the tenth century that the 'second diffusion' of Buddhism in Tibet could begin. This phase differed from the first in that the influences were entirely Indian in origin.

This interrupted development has left its mark on Tibetan thought, chiefly in respect of the canons of scriptures accepted as authoritative by the various sects of Tibetan Buddhism which have evolved over the centuries. The most ancient sect, the *rNying ma pa* (the Old Ones, also called the Red Hats), who trace their history back to Padmasambhava, accept different scriptures from sects which arose during or after the second diffusion. Of these, the most important are the *bKa' brygud pa* (Whispered Transmission school) of which Marpa and Milarepa are the most famous representatives, and the *dGe lugs pa* (the Orthodox or Reformed school, also called the Yellow Hats). This latter sect, though originating in the eleventh century, became dominant in Tibet only in the time of Tsong kha pa (1357–1419 CE). It is this school of which the Dalai Lama is the head.[1] It should be stressed that in speaking of 'sects' or 'schools' of Tibetan

Buddhism, what is intended is analogous to the relation of different religious orders (Franciscan, Dominican, and so on) within the Catholic Church, and not a difference as marked as that, for example, between Catholic and Protestant. The agreement on fundamental beliefs between the schools is very considerable.

These fundamentals are drawn from the two great metaphysical systems of the **Mahayana** (T: *theg chen*), the **Madhyamika** and the **Yogacara**. (The ideas of the **Theravada** (T: *theg dman*) were never a living force in Tibetan life, being known of only as matters for study, not for lived religious practice.) From the Madhyamika school of Nagarjuna Tibetan thinkers take a fundamental thesis concerning the nature of reality. Nagarjuna argues that since all individual things arise dependently, i.e. come into being because of the causal interactions of other things, they are without essence or empty. Being-as-is or reality does not arise dependently, and its nature is voidness (S: *sunyata*), that is, a predicateless unity, not nothingness. From the Yogacarin school (cf. in this book the essay on Vasubandhu), is taken the assertion that although the phenomenal world of the *samsara* is unreal, yet the consciousness which produces this world is real. Thus, in a Tibetan text edited in the seventeenth century (CE) but whose doctrinal sources date from many centuries earlier, it is said:

> Whatever be seen during sleep is not something apart from mind. Similarly, all phenomena of the waking-state are but the dream-content of the Sleep of Obscuring Ignorance [i.e. *avidya*]. Apart from the mind (which giveth them illusory being) they have no existence.[2]

This assertion is blended with the Madhyamika doctrine of the Voidness: 'As waves are produced from water itself, so, in like manner, is to be understood how all things are the offspring of the mind, which, in its own nature, is Voidness.'[3] This makes it clear that one must take care not to mistake the meaning of the term 'mind' in these texts by construing it in a western fashion: it is being-as-is, not merely individual consciousness as it is understood in western thought. The reason for the Yogacarin preference for this way of putting the basic metaphysical doctrine is perhaps, as Edward Conze suggests, that it makes clear where reality is to be sought, i.e. within us, in the deepest recess of our own consciousness, a point made repeatedly in the Tibetan texts.[4]

In the Tibetan context, these beliefs are combined with further ideas and practices from the esoteric form of Buddhism called

Tantrism (T: *rGyud*), also called the **Vajrayana** or Diamond Vehicle (T: *rDo rje theg pa*). The relationship of the Vajrayana to the Mahayana is the subject of debate, some holding that Tantrism is a sub-school of the Mahayana, others that it is a third, distinct, major form of Buddhism. The scriptures of this school are called *tantras* as distinct from *sutras*, the usual generic term for such writings in Buddhism, and Tantrists maintain that their scriptures contain doctrines even more advanced than those to be found in the *prajnaparamita* (S: Perfection of Wisdom) *sutras* of the Mahayana. Tantric Buddhism is a subject in itself, its doctrines and practices being both intricate and complex. The remarks that follow address only a few points which are taken for granted by the thinkers to be considered, and do not pretend even to be an outline of the subject as a whole.

First, in common with adherents to a number of other esoteric forms of religion, Tantrists maintain that their founder (in this case, of course, the Buddha himself) put forward more than one set of doctrines: the exoteric, for those of lesser spiritual ability, and the esoteric or secret for spiritual adepts. These esoteric doctrines and practices are not transmissible by means of the written word alone; they can be realized by the aspirant (S: *shishya*) only in the context of study with a master or *guru* (T: *bla ma*), and full transmission of the Tantric insights occurs only in this context. Not surprisingly, the role of the *guru* is central in Tantric practice, and the *guru–shishya* relationship is of the first importance. Once the *shishya* has been accepted by the *guru*, the student must submit entirely and unquestioningly to the teacher's direction, however harsh or perverse it may appear. The *guru* will gauge the *shishya's* progress towards the goal, will suggest suitable practices, and will gradually unfold the deeper Tantric mysteries as the *shishya* becomes fit to receive them. (For an analogous attitude to the master–student relationship, and of face-to-face transmission of doctrine, cf. the essays on the Zen thinkers Dogen and Hakuin.) The relationship of Milarepa to his *guru* Marpa is the most famous example of such in Tibetan thought. It will be no surprise that all the leading thinkers in the Tibetan tradition have the title '*guru*' or 'great *guru*', as is the case with Padmasambhava.

Second, although the metaphysics underlying Tibetan Tantrism is that of the Mahayana, it has been blended with further beliefs and practices from more popular types of Buddhism. Thus Tantrism has taken over the Buddhist pantheon of one hundred deities, and construes them as personifications of spiritual forces which can be mobilized as aids on the road to enlightenment. Further, the means by which the assistance of the deities can be secured are highly evolved, partly by dance and ritual gesture, and partly by the use of **mantras** (T: *sNags*). '*Mantra*' is the Sanskrit for 'spell' (from *man* = mental process, and *tra* = protect), and the theory underlying the construction of these incantations is a science on its own. The syllables used are held to have the power to put the aspirant in touch with cosmic forces by addressing their personifications. Each *mantra* corresponds symbolically to a divine plane, itself symbolically represented by a deity. The essence of a god can be expressed by a pure sound, and the syllables contain this essence. The best known in the West is probably '*Om-Mani-Padme-Hum*', a *mantra* very widely used in Tibetan Buddhism.

Third, the blending of the doctrine of the Voidness with the Buddhist pantheon results in Tantric meditation being based on beliefs and practices not found elsewhere in Buddhism. The use of *mantras* permits the meditator to conjure up the deity in question. As the meditation proceeds, a conception of the external form of the deity is formed in the mind, this appearance following a specification hallowed by tradition and set down in the texts known as the *Sadhanas* (*c*.500 CE). As a further aid in this phase of the meditation, **mandalas** may be used, a *mandala* being a depiction, circular in form, of the deity in question. However, it follows from the Mahayanist metaphysics that the deities thus invoked must be unreal or empty, since being-as-is is a divisionless, predicateless One. Tantrism is made consistent by the thesis that the conjured deities are created by the conjuration, having no being independent of it. Thus it is held that in the advanced stages of meditation, meditator and deity become one: this is possible because both are empty. This condition, in which deity and wor-shipper are one, constitutes **samadhi** for the Tantrist. In the present context, the point to fix on is that references to multiple deities are not to be construed in a polytheistic fashion, which would contradict the underlying Mahayanist nondualism.

One further point needs to be noted before approaching the Tibetan thinkers themselves. Many major works in the Tibetan tradition include the word *yoga* [T: *rnal 'byor*] in their title, e.g. *The Yoga of the Great Symbol*; *The Yoga of the Six Doctrines*; *The Yoga of Consciousness Transference*, and the like. This is *yoga* in the sense in which the term is used in the *Yoga Sutras* of Patanjali, i.e. a full programme of techniques to assist spiritual development, their goal being the freeing of the subject from the illusions of ordinary consciousness. (Thus, though not usually described as such, the Zen practice of **zazen** and the device of the **koan** are *yogas*.) The *yogas* to be discussed in the following pages, and which are described here only in their philosophical aspect, are of the most advanced kind, their final results being achievable, if at all, only after many years of training.

Notes

1 'Dalai' is the Mongolian word for 'ocean', and the title was first bestowed by a Mongol Khan in the sixteenth century. All Dalai Lamas are regarded as incarnations of the god Avalokitesvara.
2 *The Yoga of the Great Symbol*, in W.Y. Evans-Wentz (ed.), *Tibetan Yoga and Secret Doctrines*, Oxford: Oxford University Press, 1958, p. 146.
3 Ibid., p. 148.
4 Edward Conze, *Buddhism*, Oxford: Bruno Cassirer, 1957, p. 166.

PADMASAMBHAVA eighth century CE

Padmasambhava (T: Padma-'byun-gnas, also known as *Guru Rinpoche* [Precious Guru] and Padmakara) is one of the most renowned and revered figures in the religious history of Tibet: one of his many honorific titles is no less than 'Second Buddha', and it is partly as a result of his influence that Tantric Buddhism took so firm a hold in that country. He is said to have founded the first Buddhist monastery in Tibet (bSam-yas), and his followers formed a school of Buddhism which has endured to the present, the *rNying ma pa* (the Old Ones), more popularly called the Red Hats. The members of this school hold that Padmasambhava and other masters buried sacred texts in secret locations, these buried texts (T: *gter-ma*) to be found by 'takers-out of the treasures' (T: *gter-ston*, pron. ter-ton) when they are needed to help the world towards enlightenment. (A taker-out is always a person of the highest spiritual attainments, and never more than one incarnates at a given time.) Again, the *rNying ma pa* have preserved the doctrine of the **bardo**, i.e. the experience a person undergoes between death and the next reincarnation. *The Tibetan Book of the Dead* (*Bardo Thodol*), on which Padmasambhava wrote a commentary, contains a detailed description of the experiences of the individual on the *bardo* plane. In the present context, however, the principal concern will be the Mahayanist metaphysics and associated *yogas* set out in Padmasambhava's work *The Yoga of Knowing the Mind, called Self-Liberation*, a subsection of the work *The Profound Doctrine of Self-Liberation by Meditation Upon the Peaceful and Wrathful Deities* (T: *Zab chos zhi khro dgongs pa rang grol*), together with recommendations for practice set out in certain *gter-ma* texts.[1]

Though there is an almost contemporary biography of Padmasambhava, very little can be gleaned from it concerning the historical facts of his life, much of the content being myth, legend or religious allegory. Thus he is said to have had an immaculate birth, emerging not from the womb but from a lotus blossom; to have developed yogic powers to the extent of mastery of shape-changing, mind-reading, understanding the language of animals, raising the dead, and becoming invisible.[2] He is said to have lived for centuries, to have taught the **dharma** both to humans and to spiritual beings in various heavens, and to be a reincarnation of the Buddha, returned to the flesh for the special purpose of spreading Tantric doctrine.

The biography does, however, refer to one or two incidents which scholars agree to be historical. Padmasambhava was probably Indian by birth, and spent many years studying under *gurus* in his native country,

Burma, Afghanistan and Nepal. He achieved mastery of many *yogas* and acquired a considerable reputation as a **siddha** or Tantric adept. The contemporary king of Tibet, Khri srong lde brtsan (reigned 740–86? CE) was concerned that Buddhism was not taking as firm a hold in his country as he wished, and enquired who could remedy the situation. His advisers recommended Padmasambhava, who was duly invited to Tibet in 746 and arrived in the spring of 747. How long he stayed in Tibet is unknown, as are the circumstances of his departure. In a sense, these details are unimportant by comparison with the achievement attributed to him. He has a unique place in Tibetan religious history, in some ways analogous to that of Bodhidharma, another semi-legendary figure, in the development of Zen in the Far East. It is held that the effect of his presence was the establishment of Buddhism in Tibet, and further that his example set the direction for its development.

The Yoga of Knowing the Mind epitomizes the philosophical basis of Padmasambhava's Buddhism. He begins at once with the fundamental metaphysical assertion that the world of ordinary sense-experience and introspection (the **samsara**) is an illusion and that being-as-is or reality is One Mind: 'There being really no duality, pluralism is untrue. Until duality is transcended and at-one-ment realized, Enlightenment cannot be attained. The whole *Sangsara* and Nirvana, as an inseparable unity, are one's mind.'[3] The One Mind is a predicate-less unity, and this assertion has far-reaching consequences, as becomes clear if the implications of the following description of it are followed through:

> In its true state, mind is naked, immaculate; not made of anything, being of the Voidness; clear, vacuous, without duality, transparent; timeless, uncompounded, unimpeded, colourless; not realizable as a separate thing, but as the unity of all things, yet not composed of them; of one taste (i.e. homogeneous), and transcendent over differentiation.[4]

The whole of *The Yoga of Knowing the Mind* is an amplification of this statement.

It follows first that the mode of being of the One Mind cannot be characterized as either existence or non-existence, since these concepts apply only in the *samsara*: 'Although the One Mind is, it has no existence'[5] since 'there are no two such things as existence and non-existence'.[6] Moreover, the One Mind must of necessity be 'timeless', i.e. eternal. Eternity is the mode of being outside time or, put another way, to which in principle no temporal predicates apply.

Time is the framework in which all events or changes are located: there logically cannot be an event which is not in time, and conversely, if there is time, there must be events. Now the One Mind is predicateless: it is unchanging and must therefore be eternal.

A further consequence flows from this conclusion, namely that our ordinary time-consciousness, our awareness of time as having a unidirectional flow from past to present to future, must be a *samsaric* illusion to be overcome by the practice of appropriate *yogas*. If this is not done,

> The yoga concerning past and future not being practised, memory of the past remains latent. The future, not being welcomed, is completely severed by the mind from the present. The present, not being fixable, remains in the state of the Voidness.[7]

Enlightenment or Liberation consists in part in transcending normal time-consciousness: it is the condition in which there is no past, present, or future. Further, since birth and death are changes which occur in time, they must be *samsaric* and so illusory, and do not pertain to the One Mind: 'Not having known birth, it knows not death.'[8]

Again, since the One Mind is indeed one, i.e. 'transcendent over differentiation',[9] it follows that the distinction which lies at the root of all human consciousness, that between the self and everything which is not the self, is an illusion, since it is an instance of duality, and all dualities without exception are unreal. If enlightenment or the Great Liberation (as it is referred to in this work) is attainable, it is realized that this distinction is inapplicable:

> Although [the One Mind] is Total Reality, there is no perceiver of it ... When exhaustively contemplated, the teachings merge in at-one-ment with the scholarly seeker who has sought them, although the seeker himself when sought cannot be found.[10]

'The seeker cannot be found' because after enlightenment, normal self-consciousness is absent, and so in an important sense the person who set out on the road to liberation no longer exists.

Normal experience, then, is a tissue of illusions which we must seek to overcome. What ordinarily passes for knowledge of the world, information concerning the nature and interactions of all the individual entities into which we erroneously subdivide it, is accordingly knowledge of an illusion and so worthless. What we must seek is not such knowledge but wisdom or acquaintance with being-as-is. Since what commonly passes for knowledge is unconnected with reality, it is unconnected with wisdom. There is no link between extensive learning and enlightenment, and indeed the former is likely to get in the way of the latter. Thus Padmasambhava stresses that 'Even a cowherd [i.e. an illiterate] may by realization obtain Liberation'.[11] Padmasambhava is careful to point out, however, that this distinction between wisdom and ignorance is merely a device to help us along the Path to the Great Liberation. Like all dualities, it is inapplicable to being-as-is: 'Although the Wisdom of Nirvana and the Ignorance of the Sangsara illusorily appear to be two things, they cannot truly be differentiated.'[12]

Having indicated the nature of reality and the extent of *samsaric* illusion, the next stage is to indicate the Path the aspirant must follow in order to attain the Great Liberation. As the title of the treatise indicates, the path to reality lies inwards, via the *yoga* of knowing the mind. The bedrock **Yogacarin** insight is that reality is One Mind. We too have mind, and the route to Liberation is to free our mind from its fetters. We must seek to rid the mind of all the illusions of the *samsara*, to control it by means of various *yogas*, and to restore it to its primal nakedness, i.e. the condition of non-conceptual awareness of reality. Over and over again, Padmasambhava enjoins the aspirant to seek the truth by turning inwards: 'The *Dharma* being nowhere save in the mind, there is no other place of meditation than the mind . . . Again and again look within thine own mind.'[13]

As is to be expected from one of the greatest Tantric **gurus**, Padmasambhava has much to say about meditational technique, its stages and benefits, from the first steps to the farthest reaches of **mahasandi** (S: Great Perfection; T: *rDzogs chen*) *yoga*. The first essential is to find a qualified *guru*, one who has attained full enlightenment, and who is motivated by compassion for all sentient beings:

> You should know that the master is more important
> Than the buddhas of a hundred thousand aeons,
> Because all the buddhas of the aeons
> Appeared through following masters.
> There will never be any buddhas
> Who have not followed a master.[14]

Failure to follow a qualified *guru* will result in disaster, the tragedy of indefinite deferment of enlightenment.

The next step for the aspirant is to arouse **bodhicitta**, the desire for enlightenment, not just for oneself but for all sentient beings. As Milarepa was to do later, Padmasambhava makes use of one of the consequences of the doctrine of reincarnation: in the past, we have all had countless lives, and every sentient being has been at some time our father and our mother. To entertain this belief helps to reinforce in us the desire to act for the sake of others. The arousing of *bodhicitta* in this way is a necessary condition for gaining enlightenment: 'Unless you cultivate *bodhicitta*, you will not attain enlightenment, even though you gain mastery of **mantra** and be very powerful.'[15]

When *bodhicitta* is aroused, it is appropriate to proceed to practise meditation. The central element in Tantric *yoga* is the visualization of a deity by the meditator using *mantras*, and Padmasambhava gives careful recommendations as to how this may be achieved by persons of differing aptitudes: most must begin by concentrating on a physical image of their *yidam* (i.e. personal) deity, and practise until this external stimulus is no longer necessary. Throughout his detailed prescriptions on method, Padmasambhava stresses, consistently with his nondual metaphysics, that the deity thus visualized is non-separate from the mind of the meditator, having no real, discrete existence: 'Realize that you and the *yidam* deity are not two and that there is no *yidam* deity apart from yourself . . . Do not become fascinated or overjoyed by such visions since they are only the manifestations of your mind.'[16] It follows further from nondualism that, since reality is a oneness, all distinctions between deities are illusory, and so it does not matter which one is chosen as a focus for meditation: 'if you practise one you will be practising them all.'[17]

As in other schools of Buddhism, the aim of this method of meditation is to bring conceptual thought to a halt and so facilitate enlightenment or direct awareness of being-as-is. One who reaches this level of insight is a *vidyadhara* (S: knowledge-holder). Again in common with other systems of *yoga*, there is more than one degree of insight to be attained, and Padmasambhava discriminates four *vidyadhara* levels.[18] The first is that of maturation (T: *rnam smin rig 'dzin*):

When you attain stability [as a result of meditation] . . . without discarding your body, it will be matured into a deity . . . Although your body remains as an [ordinary] human being, your mind is matured into a deity. This is like an image formed in the mold.[19]

At this first level, conceptual thought is stilled, the divine nature of the mind is revealed, and so the mind has 'matured into a deity'. At the second *vidyadhara* level, that of life-mastery (T: *tshe dbang rig 'dzin*) the yogi, though still linked to the body, begins to acquire special powers, such as extension of the life-span at will, and that of shape-changing, the ability to manifest as 'myriad things through three incalculable aeons'[20] and act for the welfare of all sentient beings. Such a one is said to be beyond life and death, and so, equally, to be beyond the point at which it is possible to fall back into an unenlightened state.

The third *vidyadhara* level is that of *mahamudra* (T: *phyag chen rig 'dzin*)[21] and at this level the practitioner is said to be able to leave the body at will: 'When leaving your body in the *bardo* state, you become that particular deity just like the image coming out of the mold . . . the moment the body is discarded, the practitioner becomes the form of the *yidam* deity.'[22] *Bardo* (literally 'between two'; S: *antarabhava*) is a term used to refer to any intermediate state of being, notably where the soul is separate from the body. Descriptions of this kind are not unusual in the context of advanced mystical experience: the Zen master Dogen, for example, when attempting to describe union with the infinite, speaks of body and mind 'dropping away'. At such times, the distinctions between mind and body, self and other, are transcended, and a way has to be found to gesture at the nature of this state using conceptual descriptions.

The final *vidyadhara* level is that of spontaneous presence (T: *lhun grub rig 'dzin*) which, like the analogous stages of other *yogas*, is effectively beyond description. Padmasambhava suggests the nature of this condition as follows:

> Gathering regents and giving teachings, you attain the consummation, the *vajra* [= diamond]-like **samadhi**, and accomplish the welfare of self and others through effortless magical powers . . . Meeting the *dharmakaya* [= reality] face to face, you receive teachings through blessings and purify the subtle obscuration of dualistic knowledge.[23]

He describes at some length the nature of the consciousness of the yogi who has arrived at this rare peak of attainment. This condition he epitomizes as 'mirror-like wisdom': 'all phenomena appear like reflections in a mirror while having no self-nature, and are cognized while having no conceptual thinking.'[24] Discriminations are made, but the phenomena discriminated appear as they truly are, as illusions of the *samsara*. Moreover, since the yogi has transcended the surface ego and its desires, the discriminated phenomena are simply reflected in consciousness: none is desired, since desire has been overcome. Hence the use of the classic Buddhist image of the mirror, for a mirror simply reflects what is before it, and desires nothing. Such a yogi 'will naturally progress beyond meditation and post-meditation and will be free from holding a conceptual focus or conceiving of attributes, just as clouds and mist spontaneously clear in the vast expanse of the sky'[25] Meditation is no longer an activity which takes place, as it does during the years of training, at set times, but is the state in which all actions are performed.[26]

Further, Padmasambhava considers that this condition is the only sure basis for moral action. So long as an agent is innocent of non-dual awareness and therefore cognizes in ordinary self-conscious, conceptual terms, there is a constant danger that good deeds (to which he refers as 'virtuous roots' or 'roots of virtue') will be done for the wrong reason:

> In general, a virtuous root is unerring when embraced by nonconception. To think in conceptual focus, I did a virtuous action!, and to dedicate your virtuous deeds toward material gain or good reputation, is perverted dedication.[27]

Padmasambhava presupposes that an action is truly virtuous only if it is spontaneous, not done with a view to any possible gain of good reputation or other benefit for the agent, and the only condition in which it is certain that self-regarding motives are absent is that after enlightenment. In this state, there is no ego in the normal sense, and action is the spontaneous manifestation of compassion. For those who have yet to reach this state, Padmasambhava recommends that 'In all cases [of doing good deeds], completely let go of all focus on dedication, object of dedicating, and dedicator, while leaving no trace behind'.[28] When conceptual distinctions are dropped, the innate Buddha-nature can manifest itself; when the ego is dispersed and with it all selfish desires, what remains is the will of God.

This philosophy is open to the objections which beset nondualism: to find a motive for the manifestation of the absolute as the *samsara*; to give an account of how the eternal can be related to the temporal, the changeless to the mutable, the perfect to the imperfect. Padmasambhava would reply that these are problems only for those unable to transcend a conceptual focus. The accomplished *vidyadhara* knows the mind of God, and for such a one all problems are resolved.

Notes

The titles of works cited in these notes are abbreviated as follows: *DT* = Erik Pema Kunsang (trans.), *Dakini Teachings*, a selection of *gter-ma* texts attributed to Padmasambhava, Boulder, Colo.: Shambhala, 1990; *TBGL* = W.Y. Evans-Wentz (ed.), *The Tibetan Book of the Great Liberation*, London: Oxford University Press, 1954.

1 Whether the attribution of these works to Padmasambhava himself is secure is a matter for scholars: the issue is very difficult to settle in connection with a figure like this around whose life there has gathered a nimbus of legend. What matters in the present context is that those texts set out a consistent form of *rNying ma pa* Tantrism.

2 The same powers are attributed to other advanced Tantric yogis, e.g. Milarepa.

3 *TBGL*, pp. 206–7.

4 *TBGL*, p. 211.

5 *TBGL*, p. 208.

6 *TBGL*, p. 225.

7 *TBGL*, p. 222.

8 *TBGL*, p. 219.

9 *TBGL*, p. 211.

10 *TBGL*, pp. 219 and 224.

11 *TBGL*, p. 237.

12 *TBGL*, p. 229.

13 *TBGL*, p. 217.

14 *DT*, p. 103. This work is a translation of parts of *gter-ma* texts said to have been dictated by Padmasambhava to his biographer and most faithful disciple Lady Yeshe Tsogyal, who also concealed them. They were discovered by the *gter-stons* Nyang Ral Nyima Oser (1124–92) and Dorje Lingpa (1346–1405).

15 *DT*, p. 7.

16 *DT*, pp. 105 and 107.

17 *DT*, p. 105.

18 cf. analogous distinctions in Hakuin's Zen, Aurobindo's Hinduism, and the four stages of the *Mahamudra* yoga of Milarepa.

19 *DT*, p. 109.

20 *DT*, p. 130.

21 This sense of the term *Mahamudra* is distinct from that in which it is used as a generic description of the *yoga* of Marpa and Milarepa.

22 *DT*, p. 130.

23 Ibid.

24 *DT*, p. 132; cf. Dogen's description of the same condition as the 'ocean seal concentration [= *samadhi*]', in which the enlightened mind is likened to the surface of a calm ocean.

25 *DT*, p. 145.

26 Analogously, Zen master Hakuin suggests that for the adept, the whole of life becomes a *koan*.

27 *DT*, p. 148.

28 Ibid.; cf. Zen master Bankei's description of post-enlightenment action in his advice to layman Gesso.

Padmasambhava's writings

The attribution of texts to a figure like Padmasambhava is a complex matter. Philosophically, the most central of those thus attributed is *The Yoga of Knowing the Mind, called Self-Liberation*. The *gter-ma* texts used here originate chiefly in Nyang Ral's *Jomo Shulen* (The Questions and Answers of the Lady) i.e. Lady Yeshe Tsogyal.

See also in this book

the Buddha, Nagarjuna, Vasubandhu, Milarepa, Tsong kha pa

Sources and further reading

Blofeld, J., *The Tantric Mysticism of Tibet*, Boulder, Colo., Shambhala, 1970

Douglas, K. (trans.), *The Life and Liberation of Padmasambhava* (by Lady Yeshe Tsogyal), Berkeley, Calif: Dharma Publishing, 1978

Evans-Wentz, W.Y. (ed.), *The Tibetan Book of the Great Liberation*, London: Oxford University Press, 1954 (contains the text of *The Yoga of Knowing the Mind*, and a condensed version of Lady Yeshe Tsogyal's biography of Padmasambhava)

Evans-Wentz, W.Y. (ed.), *The Tibetan Book of the Dead*, 3rd edn, Oxford: Oxford University Press, 1957

Freemantle, F. and Chogyam Trungpa (trans and eds), *The Tibetan Book of the Dead*, Boulder, Colo., Shambhala, 1975

Guenther, H.V., *The Teachings of Padmasambhava*, Leiden and New York: Brill, 1996

Padma-Sambhava, *Dakini Teachings*, trans. Erik Pema Kunsang, Boulder, Colo.: Shambhala, 1990

Sogyal, Rinpoche, *Dzogchen and Padmasambhava*, 2nd edn, Santa Cruz: Rigpa Fellowship, 1990

MILAREPA 1052–1135 CE

There is no figure in the history of Tibetan Buddhism who inspires more affectionate devotion amongst his countrymen and women than the **yogi** Milarepa. He is the ideal Tantric adept, possessed of the supernormal powers associated with the most advanced yogic practice – flying; shape-changing; multiple physical manifestation, and so on – yet devoted to the path of the *bodhisattva*: a being who has achieved buddhahood yet remains by choice in the realm of the *samsara* in order to assist more sentient beings towards the goal of enlightenment. Milarepa's life perfectly exemplifies the path of the ascetic yogi: after years of discipline with his *guru*, the formidable Marpa the Translator (1012–96 CE),[1] Milarepa withdrew to meditate in the icy mountain fastnesses of Tibet, gaining the fullest enlightenment. Thereafter, he lived the life of a mendicant yogi, abjuring all property, living in caves in the most absolute poverty, and refusing to try to found any organization of which he might be made head. He devoted his life to seeking to bring enlightenment to others, chiefly by his own example and by explaining to them the path of the Buddha. His explanations often took the form not of prose sermons but of songs, recorded both in his biography, the *Jetsün-Khabum*, and in the long collection of stories about him, the *Mila Gurbum*,[2] both major Tibetan classics.

As is the case with a number of western saints, Milarepa's life did not at the beginning have the appearance of that of a holy man. His father died not long after his birth in 1052,[3] and his mother was unable to prevent the ruthless theft of her husband's estate by her relatives. Humiliated and reduced to poverty as a result, Milarepa was persuaded by his mother to learn black magic. This he used to take revenge on his enemies: by means of sorcery he accomplished the deaths of many of his relatives, and in addition destroyed the harvest in his native valley by inducing violent hailstorms.[4]

These misdeeds were soon followed by repentance: 'I longed so for religion that I forgot to eat',[5] and he vowed to spend the rest of his life following the Buddha Way. An enlightened lama initiated him into the doctrines and practices of the Great Perfection,[6] but he still failed to make significant spiritual progress. Perceiving this, the lama sent him to a great *guru* recently returned from India, Marpa the Translator. Marpa realized at once Milarepa's potential, but before accepting him as a disciple set out to destroy all the faults of character which could impede spiritual progress. One of Marpa's chief techniques was back-breaking and pointless physical labour: thus Milarepa was made to build and then tear down a number of houses on a desolate mountain. The goal of all these techniques was to subdue the selfishness of the ego, and only when Marpa judged him ready was Milarepa accepted as a disciple and given initiation into the teachings of the sect of which he was to become the greatest member, the *bKa' brygud pa* or Whispered Transmission school.[7] Milarepa then meditated alone in a cave for eleven continuous months, finally achieving his first experience of enlightenment.

His training under Marpa had kept him away from home for many years, and in a dream Milarepa saw the bones of his mother lying in the ruins of his family home. He took leave of Marpa, returned home and found that his dream had been accurate. His sense of the evanescence of life became overwhelming, and reinforced his desire to renounce the world completely in order to seek absolute Liberation (i.e. enlightenment: the term 'Liberation' is often preferred in Tibetan texts). He meditated alone in a cave for twelve years, in conditions of the greatest hardship, finally achieving complete enlightenment. His fame began to spread, and he earned the title *re.pa* (= cotton-clad) in recognition of his perfection of the heat yoga, the means whereby an advanced yogi can keep warm, dressed only in a cotton shift, in near-Arctic temperatures.[8] Thereafter, Milarepa spent his life preaching the **dharma** and initiating those he found able into the secrets of Tantric yoga. His goal was that of the *bodhisattva*:

> May none of living creatures, none e'en of insects,
> Be bound unto *sangsaric* life; nay, not one of them;
> But may I be empowered to save them all.[9]

Milarepa died as a result of taking poisoned food, administered by the concubine of an envious lama. He knew that he was being poisoned, but his compassion for his poisoner forbade him to do otherwise than accept the food. No other course of action would have been consistent with his *bodhisattvic* vows.[10]

The Tantric yogas of which Milarepa was the master rest on a philosophy typical of Tibetan thought in its blend of the concepts furnished by the **Madhyamika** and **Yogacara**. Ultimate reality, the eternal, changeless one-ness or absolute underlying the temporal world of change, is characterized by Milarepa as follows:

> I, the Yogi who developed by his practices
> Know that outer hindrances are but a shadow-show,
> And the phantasmal world
> A magic play of mind unborn.
> By looking inward into the mind is seen
> Mind – nature – without substance, intrinsically void.[11]

This description, echoed in many places in Milarepa's songs, combines the characterization of the absolute as mind – the Yogacarin view – with the thesis that its nature is that of a void, this latter being the essential teaching of the Madhyamika. The Yogacarin thesis emphasizes that reality is to be found not in the outside world of individuals and objects which constitute the *samsara*, but by turning inward and stripping away the layers of the surface ego. The Madhyamika view emphasizes that reality is beyond conceptual description, an absolutely undivided unity: it is a voidness (S: **sunyata**) because nothing can be said of it, not because it is nothingness. Milarepa acknowledges this often with his view that Reality is 'beyond Playwords', 'Playwords' being any form of conceptual characterization.

A consequence of this metaphysics to which Milarepa draws attention more than once concerns time. In the song just quoted, he refers to reality as 'unborn',[12] and by this he means that the absolute or being-as-is exists in an atemporal or eternal manner. Time and the changes whose individuation it permits are illusions of the *samsara*, and have no real existence:

> In the beginning, nothing comes;
> In the middle, nothing stays;
> At the end, nothing goes.
> Of the mind there is no arising and extinction![13]

What exists outside time can neither come into being nor cease to be.

This metaphysics has profound implications concerning the nature of true knowledge, and the veracity of the ordinary human experiences of perception and introspection. Milarepa analyses them by means of the concept of **bardo** [T: literally 'between-two']: this notion is often used to refer to the mode of being of the soul between the death of one body and reincarnation in the next, but can be used (as here) to refer to any type of intermediate state:

> you should know that this life is merely part of the Bardo of Birth-Death; its experiences are unreal and illusory, a form of reinforced dreaming. Mental activity in the daytime [creates a latent form of] habitual thought which again transforms itself at night into various delusory visions sensed by the [semi-consciousness]. This is called the deceptive and magic-like Bardo of Dream, and the whole of ordinary human experience can be described as 'the Bardo of Samsara.[14]

All conceptual knowledge is therefore *samsaric*, and an impediment to experience of reality. To have contact with reality is not to know anything about it, but to experience it:

> all manifestations [i.e. the *samsara*] [consist in] Mind, and Mind is the illuminating-Voidness without any shadow or impediment. Of this truth I have a decisive understanding; therefore not a single trace of inference or deduction can be found in my mind.[15]

To be exact, it is inaccurate (in this case) to speak of knower and known as if they were distinct. In awareness of reality, which is Liberation, this distinction, in common with all others, collapses:

In the Realm of Illumination
Where subject and object are one,
I see no cause, for all is Void.
When acting and actor disappear,
All actions become correct.[16]

If ordinary experience is delusive, and the use of reason a hindrance to Liberation, it follows that a special technique is needed to bring us to enlightenment. This technique is Tantric *yoga* practised, as long as necessary, under the guidance of a *guru*. In the case of the *bKa'brygud pa*, the key practice is the *yoga* of the Great Symbol (S: **Mahamudra**; T: *phyag-chen*). Milarepa stresses repeatedly that this is a stern undertaking:

Great faith, reliance
On a wise and strict Guru,
Good discipline,
Solitude in a hermitage,
Determined, persevering
Practice, and meditation –
These are the Six ways that lead to Liberation.[17]

Of these, Milarepa lays greatest stress on unrelenting practice. The path to reality cannot (surely) be followed in any other way, certainly not by means of book-learning or intellection. The true yogi is a disciplined ascetic in whose life everything is sacrificed to the goal of Liberation: 'See what hardships I have undergone. The most profound teaching of Buddhism is "*to practise*". It has simply been due to this persistent effort that I have earned the Merits and Accomplishment.'[18] There is no short or easy path.

The *Mahamudra yoga* has four stages, of which the first is the Stage of One-Pointedness. In this stage, the flow of thought is brought to a halt by concentrating the mind on one object, physical or mental, animate or inanimate. The goal of this stage is inner quiescence:

To realize that non–clinging and illuminating Self-awareness
Is unborn and immanent,
Is the consummation sign of the Stage of One-Pointedness.[19]

This realization, however, is still at least partly conceptual in nature. It is only at the second level, the Stage of Away-from-Playwords, that nondual awareness begins. To be 'Away-from-Playwords' is to leave conceptual thought behind. When conceptual thought ceases, the true nature of Mind, the Buddha-nature or reality, is experienced directly:

> In realizing that the non-clinging and illuminating mind,
> Is embodied in bliss and transcends all playwords,
> One sees his mind's nature as clearly as great Space.[20]

It is to be stressed that to *see* the true nature of the Mind is not to *know* anything about it: it is to experience it directly and to be at one with it; and to compare the experience to that of 'great Space' is to hint, however inadequately in conceptual terms, that the experience of reality is the experience of the infinite.

As is the case in other mystical traditions such as Hinduism, and in other branches of Buddhism, e.g. Zen, this first tradition of nondual awareness is not the ultimate Liberation, but only a step, if a significant one, on the way.[21] The follower of the *Mahamudra* has two further levels of awareness to which to penetrate. The next is the third step in the Yoga of the Great Symbol, the Stage of One Taste. At this point, all hindrances are overcome. The true nature of all things is clear to the yogi: this is the stage

> In which Samsara and Nirvana are felt to be the same.
> It is a complete merging of Buddha and sentient beings.[22]

In this stage, the presence of the infinite (i.e. reality or the Buddha-nature) is apparent in everything: hence the identity of *samsara* and *nirvana* and hence the description 'One Taste'.[23] Once again, Milarepa is careful to note that this is not the same as entertaining the belief that the infinite is present in all things: it is experiencing it:

> He who says that 'all is one',
> Is still discriminating;
> In the Stage of One Taste,
> There is no such blindness.[24]

The fourth and ultimate degree of insight is the Stage of Non-Practice, and the yogi who reaches this peak has attained buddhahood. It is called the Stage of Non-Practice because in this condition the distinction between meditator and meditative practice is no longer meaningful: there is no practice and no one practising. All dualistic distinctions have collapsed, and the state of awareness of the few who reach this condition is ineffable.[25]

Those who do reach this state have attained the Great Liberation or enlightenment, and Milarepa has much to say about this condition and its benefits. Strictly speaking, nondual awareness is ineffable, but, like all mystics, Milarepa tries to convey something of this experience:

It is pure and bright as a flower,
It is like the feeling staring in the vast and empty sky.
The Awareness of Voidness is limpid and transparent, yet
vivid.[26]

This state is characterized further by the absolute inward tranquillity which is a consequence of complete freedom from desire. The surface ego is dispelled, and with it all its varied wants and needs and the suffering they bring:

No Hope, no Fear, and no Confusion
Are the quintessence of Accomplishment.[27]

This might seem to be a state merely of absolute indifference to all things, simply an affectless condition. However, Milarepa, like all Buddhists, stresses that when buddhahood is reached, the enlightened person is filled with a boundless compassion for all beings still trapped in the prison of *samsaric* suffering. The *bodhisattva* is absorbed in 'the Compassion of Non-discrimination',[28] a compassion derived not from the limited sympathies of the surface ego but from the perspective of a Buddha, at one with the infinite. Milarepa does not present this arising of compassion simply as a datum or a mystery, but explains it by means of the doctrine of reincarnation:

From beginningless time in the past until now, we all have taken myriads of bodily forms in our past incarnations, comparable only to the total sum of grains of sand in the great Universe ... [and so] all the sentient beings in the Six Realms are either my mother or my father.[29]

and, conversely, he is theirs. Everyone has stood to everyone else in the relation of father, mother, son and daughter, and so the occurrence of universal compassion is less surprising than it looks.

Further, after Liberation, the way in which the realm of the *samsara* is experienced is irreversibly changed:

After Enlightenment, one sees all things and objects
As but magic shadow-plays,
And all objective things
Become his helpful friends.[30]

The 'shadow-plays' seen to be unreal include death, and in consequence a further benefit of enlightenment is a complete freedom from fear:

Since I know the Illuminating Void,
I fear not life or death.[31]

Finally, the mode of behaviour of a Buddha cannot properly be called action in the sense in which unenlightened persons act. In the state of buddhahood the claims of the surface ego are nullified, and the only remaining motive for 'action' in such a condition is compassion. The deeds of a Buddha are the spontaneous manifestations of this feeling. when Milarepa states, of a Buddha, that 'The absence of act and deed appears without'[32] he means not that a Buddha remains in a state of indifference, but that the deeds of such a one are not the actions of an individual ego, but the manifestations of a holy will.

As with all philosophies derived from mystical insights, Milarepa's thought involves a number of intractable logical difficulties, notably why the *samsara* exists at all, and why it should involve so much suffering, or again whether, in the presence of so much pain, one can justify a life of ascetic retreat which if it does no harm in most cases appears to do little good. Milarepa, who was anything but solemn or unctuous and laughed a great deal, would certainly have smiled at these problems, dismissing them as trivialities typically produced by those lost in the realm of playwords. The experiences for which he lived are beyond words of any kind:

. . . in [the realm of] Absolute Truth
Buddha Himself does not exist;
There are no practices and no practisers;
No Path, no Realization, and no Stages,
No Buddha's Bodies and no Wisdom
There is then no Nirvana,
For these are merely names and thoughts.[33]

Notes

References to C.C. Chang's translation of *The Hundred Thousand Songs of Milarepa*, 2 vols, Boulder, Colo.: Shambhala, 1962, are given as *HTSM* + vol. number + page. References to the classic biography of Milarepa, the *Jetsün-Khabum*, W.Y. Evans-Wentz (ed.), *Tibet's Great Yogi Milarepa*, Oxford: Oxford University Press, 1928, are given in the form *TGYM* + page number.

1 'The Translator' because of his extensive Tantric learning.
2 *Jetsün-Khabum* = The Hundred Thousand Words [about] the Holy [Milarepa]; Milarepa is often referred to simply as the *Jetsün* or Holy One. *Mila Gurbum* = The Hundred Thousand Songs of Mila[repa]. In neither case is the figure of one hundred thousand to be taken literally, indicating instead simply a substantial work.
3 Some Tibetan sources give Milarepa's dates as 1040–1123 CE. I have followed the dates 1052–1135, which are those given (in the Tibetan calendar) in the *Jetsün-Khabum* Both sets of dates place Milarepa's *nirvana* in his 84th year, said also to have been the age of the Buddha at the time of his *nirvana*.
4 cf. *TGYM*, pp. 41–81.
5 *TGYM*, p. 84.
6 *rDzogs. Pa. Chen. Po*, the major yogic doctrine of the *rNying ma pa* ['The Old Ones'], founded by Padmasambhava. *rDzogs Chen* is the *rNying ma pa* version of the *Mahamundra* [Great Symbol] yoga of the *bKa'brygud pa*.
7 In another popular system of transliteration of Tibetan, this school emerges as the Kargyütpa. Its yoga is based largely on that of the Indian sage Naropa; cf. *The Yoga of the Six Doctrines*, in W.Y. Evans-Wentz (ed.), *Tibetan Yoga and Secret Doctrines*, London: Oxford University Press, 1958, pp. 155–252; and *The Yoga of the Great Symbol*, in Evans-Wentz, pp. 101–54.
8 The heat yoga is the first of Naropa's six yogas; cf. Evans-Wentz, *Tibetan Yoga and Secret Doctrines*, pp. 172–209.
9 *TGYM*, p 257.
10 cf. *TGYM*, pp. 244–304.
11 *HTSM*, I, pp. 18–19.
12 As does the Zen master Bankei, q.v.
13 *HTSM*, I, p. 102.
14 *HTSM*, II, pp. 487–8.
15 *HTSM*, II, p. 390.
16 *HTSM*, I, p. 29.
17 *HTSM*, I, p. 32.
18 *HTSM*, II, p. 495, cf. p. 469. Professor Chang justly points out that in his stress on practice Milarepa resembles the Zen master Huineng, q.v.
19 *HTSM*, I, p. 98.
20 Ibid.
21 On stages of mystical awareness, cf. the Hindu Aurobindo and the Zen master Hakuin.
22 *HTSM*, I, p. 99.
23 The same state occurs in other forms of Buddhism. Thus, for example, in Zen, to 'solve' Hakuin's *koan*, 'What is the sound of one hand clapping?' is to experience (not to *understand*) the presence of the Absolute in one hand in the same way as in two.

24 *HTSM*, I, p. 99.
25 There is a more detailed statement of *Mahamudra* practice, based on a different text, not by Milarepa but identical in essentials with his views, in Evans-Wentz, *Tibetan Yoga and Secret Doctrines*, pp. 101–54.
26 *HTSM*, I, p. 128.
27 *HTSM*, I, p. 70.
28 *HTSM*, I, p. 275.
29 *HTSM*, I, p. 304.
30 *HTSM*, I, p. 308.
31 *HTSM*, I, p. 302.
32 *HTSM*, I, p. 132.
33 *HTSM*, I, p. 325.

Milarepa's recorded thoughts

Milarepa did not write any books himself. His thought was recorded by disciples in two major works:

Jetsün-Khabum (The Hundred Thousand Words [about] the Holy [Milarepa])
Mila-Gurbum (The Hundred Thousand Songs of Mila[repa])

See also in this book

the Buddha, Patanjali, Nagarjuna, Vasubandhu, Padmasambhava, Tsong Kha pa

Sources and further reading

Chang, C.C. (ed. and trans.), *The Hundred Thousand Songs of Milarepa*, 2 vols, Boulder, Colo.: Shambhala, 1962
Chang, C.C. *Six Yogas of Naropa and Teachings of Mahamudra*, Ithaca, NY: Snow Lion Books, 1986
Evans-Wentz, W.Y. (ed.), *Tibet's Great Yogi Milarepa*, London: Oxford University Press, 1928, and many reprints (an edition of the *Jetsün-Khabum*)
Evans-Wentz, W.Y. (ed.), *Tibetan Yoga and Secret Doctrines*, Oxford: Oxford University Press, 1958.
Mi-la-ras-pa, *The Message of Milarepa* (a selection of his poems), Allahabad: Rupad Co. 1998
Tsang Nyon Heruka, *The Life of Marpa the Translator*, Boulder, Colo.: Shambhala, 1983

Some of Milarepa's songs have been incorporated in electronic music composed by Eliane Radigue: 'Songs of Milarepa', New York: Lovely Music LCD 2001 (two CD set)

TSONG KHA PA 1357–1419 CE

One of the most respected and influential religious leaders to emerge from the Second Diffusion[1] of Buddhism in Tibet was Tsong kha pa, originally known as Losang Drakpa. He is generally acknowledged to have been the founder of the dGe lugs pa, or 'Yellow Hats',[2] school of Buddhism, to which the fourteenth Dalai Lama belongs. In his attempt to return to the original teachings of the Buddha, and of other major Indian thinkers such as Nagarjuna, Tsong kha pa produced a comprehensive interpretation and development of Buddhist philosophy and practice. In 1409, he founded the great monastery of dGa'ldan [Ganden], where he instituted a strict monastic discipline and a high standard of academic learning and scholarship. His disciples, including Gendun Druba (retrospectively recognized as the first Dalai Lama) disseminated his teachings, and the backing by a succession of powerful Mongol Khans in the sixteenth and seventeenth centuries CE ensured the spiritual and political supremacy of the sect until the Chinese occupation of Tibet in 1950 and the flight of the Dalai Lama, together with many of his followers, in 1959.

Legendary accounts of the life of Tsong kha pa surround his birth with a number of auspicious events. Padmasambhava is said to have prophesied the birth of a spiritually gifted boy named Losang Drakpa, who would become a great religious teacher in Tibet. Tsong kha pa's parents are reported to have had a number of dreams whereby they believed that their son was an emanation of two buddhas: Manjusri, who embodies wisdom, and Avalakitesvara, the manifestation of compassion.

More prosaically, Tsong kha pa was born in the Amdo province of north-eastern Tibet, adjacent to China. He showed early signs of spiritual progress and took his monk's novice vows at the age of 7. He travelled widely throughout Tibet, though never beyond its borders, in search of sources of Indian Buddhism and allegedly authentic teachings of the Buddha,[3] which he claims in his autobiography to have found in the **Tantras**,[4] or esoteric doctrines of Buddhism. From time to time, he went into meditative retreats and from the age of 32, he produced an impressive series of commentaries on earlier Buddhist texts, besides original works of his own. After a long period of ill health, he died at his monastery of dGa'ldan and his cremated remains were there interred in a *stupa*, or funerary mound, which became an important centre of pilgrimage.

In common with other Tibetan thinkers, Tsong kha pa combined various features of two schools of **Mahayana** thought. From the

Yogacara, he took the therapeutic method of yogic practice, which according to its adherents frees the mind from both intellectual ignorance and injurious emotions, and thus enables its practitioners to escape from the cycle of reincarnation or *samsara* by allowing them to gain insight into the *dharmas*, or what constitutes ultimate reality.[5]

From the teachings of Nagarjuna, the founder of the **Madhyamika**, itself based on the *prajnaparamita* (Perfection of Wisdom) texts, Tsong kha pa derives his metaphysical system. A general belief of Buddhism is that everything is caught up in an endless process of flux; a true account of reality is one of becoming, not being. Thus nothing has fixity nor endurance; in other words, nothing has an essence or permanent nature. In keeping with this doctrine, Tsong kha pa introduces the distinctive Madhyamika teaching of 'dependent origination'. All things are transitory and changing, and they arise and disappear through causal interaction. Whatever is caused has dependent origination, and thus has no independent existence and no essence. The true condition of all things is that of emptiness or voidness (*sunyata*), which is neither a positive nor a negative attribute. Instead, it indicates an absence of attributes, but is not thereby nihilistic.[6] Whatever is empty is beyond the realm of conceptualization, and without such an intellectual tool, there is no distinction between particular things. Such things are swallowed up in, but not distinguished from, ultimate reality, which again is held to be empty, having no fixed nature nor permanence.

Of particular interest to Tsong kha pa and other dGe lugs pa thinkers was the doctrine of *sunyata* in relation to the human mind. This was held to be one of the genuine, though esoteric, teachings of the Buddha. Our own minds, too, have no independent existence, nor can there be any fundamental differentiation between them. They consist of a continuous flow of mental experiences. As such experiences change, they can do so for the better. Each of us thus has the potential to achieve buddhahood, as our minds (or, more strictly, the stream of mental experiences) can become pure, tranquil and transparent, like a 'clear light', instead of being polluted by the imperfections of defilement and ignorance.[7]

The insistence that our minds are not truly differentiated, and consist only of a stream of experiences, is similar to the radical empiricism and philosophical scepticism of David Hume. Whilst Hume did not mention the possibility of moral improvement, he tried to find a basis in our experiences, or perceptions, for our concept of a permanent self. Such perceptions, which consist of sensations, emotions and thoughts, are momentary and fleeting and thus there is nothing to which our notion of an enduring self underlying our experiences can correspond. Hume's theory is often referred to as the 'bundle' theory of the self, but there are no 'ties' by which one bundle (or self) can be distinguished from another. In other words, there are no lasting entities to which different streams of transitory experiences can be assigned.

A further concern of Tsong kha pa is to be found in his insistence that discursive thought is the means of, or a necessary condition for, achieving wisdom (*prajna*) and enlightenment, or escape from the cycle of reincarnation (*samsara*). This issue was one which separated the teachings of the **Zen** [C: Ch'an] school of Buddhism from those of other sects, and Tsong kha pa was no doubt anxious to prove his adherence to the Indian tradition. Zen claims that enlightenment can be reached by instantaneous direct insight into ultimate reality, thus avoiding conceptualization altogether. The contemplation of ultimate reality is, according to Buddhism, non-discursive, but Tsong kha pa maintained that it could only be reached gradually, through discursive thought. Such thought can be seen as a critical approach to inadequate propositions and their replacement by other, more adequate ones: thus, the view that human beings should each seek their own pleasure is to be replaced by the more appropriate proposition that we should all work for the benefit of others.

As Tsong kha pa realized, the belief that ultimate reality cannot be conceptualized has implications for language, as the latter cannot then be used to describe the former. Language is based on the distinction between different things, their processes and interrelationships but it cannot be stretched to cover insight into the *dharmas*, or what constitutes undifferentiated ultimate reality.

Tsong kha pa maintained that humanity can be divided into three groups, the *sravakas*, the *pratkeyabuddhas* and the *bodhisattvas*. In keeping with the universal human capacity for buddhahood, all three groups can attain wisdom primarily by following the precepts of the *prajna-paramita* texts, and thus can be liberated from *samsara*. The *sravakas* and *pratkeyabuddhas*, however, can only become **arhats**; they can achieve a release from merely personal suffering and existence by their entry into **nirvana**. The *bodhisattvas*, by contrast, through studying the teachings of the Tantras by the Yogacara method, can have the Thought of Enlightenment, the vow to forgo individual liberation in favour of dedicating themselves to the escape from *samsara* of all sentient beings. Thus they delay their own transition to *nirvana*. Tsong kha pa regards it as a religious duty to do so; as he records in his autobiography, 'I have written this personal narration [of my study of the Tantras] so as to greatly increase my own virtue, and so as to teach methodically and errorlessly the entrance gate to many fortunate persons of discrimination . . . [to] enter the path [of the *bodhisattva*].'[8]

There is a similarity between the *bodhisattvas* and Plato's Guardians or philosopher-kings. The latter, too, after an intensive period of training, gain direct and intuitive insight into the Form of the Good, or an objective, independent and transcendent standard of goodness. If they were to consult only their private interests, the Guardians would remain in contemplation of the Good, but they sacrifice their individual desires and return to the task of providing guidance for the whole of the community, who look to them for leadership.

What distinguishes the *bodhisattvas* from the other two groups within society is compassion, on which Tsong kha pa places great emphasis. Wisdom and compassion are not entirely separate characteristics, but are usually found together.[9] *Sravakas* and *pratkeyabuddhas* are not devoid of compassion, but do not act upon it for the benefit of all sentient beings. Tsong kha pa illustrates this point in a story taken from a Buddhist text:

> A certain merchant-housekeeper had one son . . . That boy, whilst playing in the mode of a child, fell into a cess-pit. Thereupon, the mother and kinsfolk of that boy . . . sighed deeply, were sorrowful and uttered lamentations, but they did not enter the cess-pit and bring out the boy. Then, the father of the boy . . . descended into that cess-pit and brought out his only son. . . . [T]he boy is a metaphor for the sentient beings; the mother and kinsfolk [are the *sravakas* and *pratkeyabuddhas*] who, seeing the sentient beings fallen into the cyclical flow, are sorrowful and utter lamentations but are incapable of bringing them out; and the merchant-housekeeper is a metaphor for the Bodhisattva.[10]

The path to compassion is long and difficult, and the way to attain and keep within it takes up most of the *bodhisattva* section of Tsong kha pa's *Lam Rim Chen Mo*. The aspirant to the path must try to find a **guru**, or teacher, who is to be regarded as a vehicle for the transmission of the teachings of the Buddha. If there is none available, the student should read the Tantras. To prepare for compassion, we must rid our minds of negative feelings and distractions, of which Tsong kha pa maintains there are many. If we concentrate on the evil deeds of sentient beings, we become afraid and there is thus no place in our minds for compassion and its development. We must rid ourselves of self-serving thoughts, and there is even a risk involved in progress in virtuous thoughts and deeds, because we must not become proud of them nor wish to make them known. We should renounce our possessions and clear our minds of worldly thoughts, including the attachment to our homes and even our bodies, as all of these are hindrances to spiritual growth.

In cultivating compassion, we must first rid ourselves of the distinction between friends and family, whom we love; enemies, whom we hate; and 'neutral' beings, towards whom we have no feelings at all. If we consider the sufferings of an enemy who is caught up in *samsara*, we might well wish for their increase. If, however, we initially concentrate on an image of the sufferings of a friend or family member (Tsong kha pa recommends the mother) we feel sorrow. We should then think of past and future reincarnations; there must be some time when each sentient being was or will be a friend or member of our family, so we can feel sorrow towards everyone trapped in the suffering of the cycle of rebirth. Thus the original distinction between different groups of people is broken down.

A more advanced stage on the path to compassion is what Tsong kha pa characterizes as the 'interchange mentality'. We must not only eliminate distinctions between different classes of people, but between different individuals. This can be done by considering ourselves to be in the place of others and taking on their sufferings as our own. Thus we avoid the distractions of self-cherishing in the realization that we are not separate from others, but that there is a continuum between all sentient beings.

Compassion is not to be tainted with the admixture of any other feeling. It has 'equipoise' or 'evenness': that is to say, it must be distributed equally and impartially to all living things. There are several components to compassion, including meditation, or the holding of a succession of particular images of sentient beings, and a cognitive element consisting of the discursive thought of wishing to bring about the release of all beings from their suffering. We should cultivate steadfastness in compassion by continually practising the methods by which it is reached, instead of making only sporadic efforts to achieve it. We should consistently endeavour to cultivate compassion, as only then will it be spontaneous and instantaneous, and deserving of the name 'Great Compassion'. This treatment of compassion is one of gradual development, and is similar to the growth of the Aristotelian virtues. Aristotle maintained that the more we practise the virtues, the more easily we can continue to do so.

Buddhism has always had a strong ethical component and the ethical teachings which Tsong kha pa puts forward are complex and fascinating. Both his works and those of other Tibetan thinkers are certainly worthy of the intensive study which they have received in the West in recent decades.

Notes

1 The First Diffusion of Buddhism in Tibet took place in the eighth century CE and was mainly Indian in origin, with some Chinese influence. The depth of penetration of Buddhism into Tibetan society during this period is a matter of debate. The Second Diffusion began in the eleventh century CE.

2 The dGe lugs pa school, especially its meditative practices, grew out of the Kha dam pa sect, the first school of Buddhism founded in Tibet. The dGe lugs pa are thus sometimes known as the 'new Kha dam pa' movement.

3 As Edward Conze acerbically remarks, to regard all the claims to esoteric teachings of the Buddha as true would yield 'a rather elastic conception of the Buddha'. See *A Short History of Buddhism*, London: Allen & Unwin, 1980.

4 See A. Wayman (trans. and ed.), *The Ethics of Tibet: Bodhisattva Section of Tsong kha pa's Lam Rim Chen Mo*, New York: State University of New York Press, 1991, pp. 17–22.

5 See the essay on Vasubandhu in this book, pp. 103–14.

6 See the essay on Nagarjuna in this book, pp. 95–103.

7 For details of the dispute between this esoteric doctrine and the orthodox Buddhist doctrine, see Paul Williams, *Mahayana Buddhism: The Doctrinal Foundations*, London and New York: Routledge 1989.

8 Wayman, op. cit., p. 22.

9 Tsong kha pa suggests that there can be compassion without wisdom. See Wayman, op. cit., p. 28.

10 Wayman, op. cit., p. 43.

Tsong Kha pa's writings

The best-known works of Tsong kha pa are *sNags rim chen mo (Great Exposition of Secret Mantra)*, a study of esoteric teachings of the Buddha recommended for Tantric aspirants, and *Lam Rim Chen Mo (Great Exposition of the Stages of the Path)* which contains his version of Tantrism. Other works include: *Legs bshad gser pheng (Golden Rosary of the Good Explanations), Lam gtso rnam gsum (Three Principal Aspects of the Path), dRang ba dang nges pa'i don rnam par phye ba'i bstan bcos legs bshad snying po (Essence of the Good Explanations, Treatise Differentiating the Interpretable and the Definitive)* and *dbu ma la 'jug pa'i rgya cher bshad pa dgongs pa rab gsal (Illumination of the Thought: Extensive Explanation of the 'Entry into the Middle Way')*, his interpretation of the tenets of Madhyamika.

See also in this book

The Buddha, Patanjali, Nagarjuna, Vasubandhu, Padmasambhava, Milarepa.

Sources and further reading

Hopkins, J., *Compassion in Tibetan Buddhism*, London: Rider 1980
—— *Meditation on Emptiness*, London: Wisdom, 1983
Thurman, R.A.F. (ed.), *Life and Teachings of Tsong Kha Pa*, Dharamsala: Library of Tibetan Works and Archives, 1982
—— *Tsong Kha Pa's Speech of Gold in the Essence of True Eloquence*, Princeton: Princeton University Press, 1984
Wayman, A. (trans. and ed.), *Ethics of Tibet: Bodhisattva Section of Tsong Kha Pa's Lam Rim Chen Mo*, New York: State University of New York Press, 1991
Williams, P., *Mahayana Buddhism: The Doctrinal Foundations*, London and New York, Routledge, 1989

Part 5

CHINESE PHILOSOPHY

INTRODUCTION

Until the twentieth century three major traditions dominated Chinese culture. These three, Confucianism, Daoism [Taoism] and Buddhism, coexisted for the most part without conflict for over two and a half thousand years, often receiving intellectual and spiritual incentive from each other and sharing a range of moral and social values. At the time of the Hundred Days Reform of 1898, western influence was already strong, and by 1911, when the Qing [Ch'ing] dynasty was overthrown by Sun Yatsen and the Republic of China was founded, the three traditions were beginning to confront serious threat and disruption. Thirty-eight years later, in 1949, Mao Zedong established China as a communist state, the People's Republic of China. The new regime sought to eradicate long-established values, closing down many traditional and religious institutions and persecuting those who clung to them. At the millennium China is still changeful and restless. It remains to be seen just how profoundly the Chinese people's distinctive traditional cast of mind has been altered by its latterday upheavals.

Although there are fragments of writings dating from the very early years of the Zhou [Chou] dynasty (*c.*1122–249 BCE), the first Chinese philosophers to emerge as individuals were men of the sixth and fifth centuries BCE. It was they, and in particular the best-known of them, Confucius (551–479 BCE), who formulated the thoroughly humanistic character of Chinese philosophy and established an enduring system of values that embraced ideals, of harmony, wisdom, filial piety and the enactment of rites conducive to ethical conduct.

Confucius and his followers were men of considerable education but lacking in political power. They were deeply troubled by the decadence and disorder of the society in which they lived and looked back with admiration to what they knew of the early years of the Zhou dynasty and a past that seemed to have been better than the present. Rulers, they maintained, had come to abuse the mandate to govern bestowed by heaven, frittering resources on their own high living and on vicious squabbles with other small powers, and showing scant concern for the communities under their rule. Confucius did not urge revolution and rebellion as a way to counter this state of affairs, but rather argued for a change of heart and mind that would make room for humane government, political stability, a generous education for all and the cultivation of inward virtue and public integrity. The concepts and values that he and his followers espoused and the kinds of debates in which they engaged were always closely related to the daily lives of people, having to do with the exact and practical detail as well as the guiding principles of social and personal conduct. In consequence, Chinese philosophical thought has informed and permeated almost every aspect of the national culture.

The origins of Daoism, the second of the great Chinese traditions, are obscure and the dates of Laozi [Lao Tzu], the person traditionally acknowledged as its central figure, are uncertain. He is sometimes placed in the sixth, sometimes in the fourth century BCE. There is some evidence to suggest that he may on at least one occasion have met and instructed Confucius. What is not in doubt is that the book attributed to him, the **Dao** De Ding [*Tao Tě Ching*] (The Way and Its Power), is held in the highest regard, not only in China but in many parts of the world. Daoism is generally regarded as a balance to Confucianism rather than something that is in opposition to it. It seeks a harmony with the nature of things through a quiet submission to the Way Dao [*Tao*] which, for Daoists, is the ultimate metaphysical principle of being. Confucianism also aspires to harmony with nature, but by means of the enactment of carefully prescribed rituals and ceremonies deemed conducive to it. It is not difficult to see how the controlled ceremonial of Confucianism acts as a balance to the intuitive wandering of Daoism. The metaphysics of Daoism became the basis of the splendid flowering of Chinese science.

The Zhou dynasty (*c.*1122–249 BCE), which encompasses the rise of both Confucianism and Daoism, is regarded as the Classical or Golden Age of Chinese philosophy, but as Zhou political power waned, so did its intellectual and social life fragment, first into a phase known as the Hundred Schools and then into an era called the Time of the Warring States (403–222 BCE). Eventually, unity was reimposed with the founding of the shortlived Qin [Ch'in] dynasty (221–206 BCE), a regime which was backed up by the philosophy of Legalism, a doctrine of ruthless control that rejected Confucian morality in favour of a form of positivism that accepted only the authority of the ruler and rigorously imposed a uniformity of conduct on the people.

Buddhism, the third great philosophico-religious movement in China, was founded in northern India through the life and work of Sidhartha Gautama. It began to take root in China around 60 BCE, its literature having been transmitted and translated by monks and scholars and its interpretation facilitated by the application to it of Chinese philosophical concepts. Buddhism steadily gained sympathy and support in China and soon became part of a cross-fertilization of ideas with Confucianism and Daoism that was to establish it as a major religious and cultural influence. The development of Chan Buddhism, known in the West by its Japanese name, **Zen**, and numerous other forms of Chinese Buddhism, as well as neo-Confucianism, are testimony to these fertile interactions. In India, Buddhism had already divided into two main doctrinal schools, the **Mahayana** and the **Theravada**, and it was, by and large, the Mahayana movement that became the dominating influence in Chinese Buddhism. Within the metaphysical framework furnished by the **Madhyamika** and **Yogacarin** thinkers of India for the Mahayana, a number of sub-schools evolved in China and Japan. Among these are Huayan [Hua-yen] (J: Kegon), Tiantai [T'ien t'ai] (J: Tendai), and **Pure Land** (J: Jodo, C: Jingdu [Ching-t'u]). Of these, it is Zen that has become most widely known in western cultures.

When the Early, or Former, Han dynasty succeeded the Qin in 206 BCE, a time of more settled government ensued. In the four hundred years of Han rule, an era noted for a burgeoning of intellectual endeavour, Confucianism was consolidated by state sponsorship, Daoism flourished and evolved, and Buddhism became securely established. The end of the Han dynasty in 220 CE brought with it a reaction against Confucianism and a surge of fresh ideas in Daoist thought. Thereafter, Buddhism gained in vitality, reaching a peak in the Tang dynasty (618–907 CE) with the emergence of the Zen doctrines promulgated by the Sixth Patriarch, Huineng (638–713 CE). Subsequently, Buddhism fell into some disfavour and towards the end of the eighth century intellectual energies began to be channelled into a revival of Confucianism which culminated during the Song dynasty (960–1279 CE) in the profoundly influential neo-Confucianism of Zhuxi [Chu Hsi] (1130–1200). Zhuxi brought about a remarkable synthesis of the whole gamut of Confucian ideas. His written output was prodigious, totalling about sixty-two volumes. He wrote commentaries on the Four Books, the Confucian classics, and presented them in the form in which they became the set texts for the Chinese civil service examinations which were set up in 1313 and not abolished until the early years of the twentieth century. Subsequently, various versions of neo-Confucianism, ranging from developments of the idealism of Zhuxi [Chu Hsi] (1130-1200 CE) to the critical empiricism of Dai Zhen [Tai Chen] (1724–1777), dominated Chinese philosophy until the end of the nineteenth century; although they never ousted either Buddhism or Daoism. As already noted, the interaction of the three great traditions, whether combative or co-operative, seemed in the long run to result only in their mutual survival, regeneration and benefit.

China underwent profound change in the latter part of the nineteenth century, experiencing political troubles that were severe enough to dominate her entire cultural and intellectual life. The Opium War of 1840–2, in which she suffered defeat at the hands of the British, and the Sino-Japanese War of 1894, focused thought on the practicalities of national survival and generated a critical approach to entrenched and inflexible political processes and to a Confucianism which had become rigid and lifeless. The burgeoning influx of western ideas began to inject a new style of thought not only into China's mainstream of political theorizing but into every aspect of her cultural life. In philosophy, the works of Plato, Kant, Schopenhauer, Darwin, Nietzsche, J.S. Mill, Dewey, Bergson and many other European intellectuals began to make their impact on the Confucian tradition. With the ascent to power in 1949 of Mao Zedong and the thoroughgoing adoption of Marxist-Leninist principles, philosophy and politics began to interact in new ways. During this first half of the twentieth century China produced many important philosophers who drew on a wide range of western doctrines and exhibited a remarkable diversity of intellectual capabilities. But in the climate of unrelenting criticism and of the wholesale espousal of science and technology, Confucianism suffered widespread condemnation and repudiation, even while it continued to inform attitudes and assumptions at the very deepest levels. At the same time, the translation and study of western philosophy developed apace, although always within the perspective of an entrenched and dogmatic Marxism which classified and interpreted western philosophical systems according to their perceived political dispositions and evaluated them by reference to their per-ceived tendencies to reinforce or undermine the dominant Marxist ideology. The cry of the 1950s to 'let a hundred flowers blossom and let a hundred schools of thought contend' was uttered from within a framework of assumptions already securely bolted into place.

In the late twentieth century, in the aftermath of the political upheavals that culminated in the Peking Massacre of 4 June 1989, Chinese philosophy confronted many complexities. Its prime task for the future, is to define itself as a scholarly endeavour which is honoured and at ease not only in the international community of scholars but also in its own home, and in awareness of a tradition that has never seen philosophy as something distinct from the daily lives of people.

CONFUCIUS (KONGFUZI, K'UNG FU-TZU)
551–479 BCE

The wise words and doctrines attributed to Confucius and his followers informed the moral, social and political structure of Chinese life for two and a half thousand years, from some time in the sixth century BCE until the overthrow of the Qing [Ch'ing] dynasty in 1911. Almost all the institutions of imperial China, its customs, purposes and aspirations, were founded on Confucius' conceptions of the virtuous individual and the virtuous society. Until the early years of the twentieth century, almost every aspect of Chinese education was designed in accordance with Confucian principles. The Confucian writings known as the Four Books were required reading for the Chinese civil service examinations first set up in 1313 and not abolished until 1905.

Confucius' thought did not become known to the western world until the Jesuit missionaries who established themselves at Peking in 1583 had absorbed Chinese culture and learning and conveyed their new knowledge to Europe. It was they who latinized his name so that the great Sage became known to much of the world as Confucius.[1]

Confucius was born in the state of Lu, now Shandong province, and lived during the Zhou [Chou] dynasty (1027–256 BCE) about five hundred years before the Christian era. He was brought up in humble circumstances by his mother, his elderly father having died when he was very young. He worked first as a keeper of granaries and director of public pastures but his ambition was to promulgate the moral virtues that characterized the earlier years of the Zhou dynasty and to revive the ideals of the kings Wen and Wu who ruled during its founding era. But the times were difficult. The political unity and strength that had been notable features of Zhou in former years had been greatly undermined by conflicts between its own constituent city states, by expansionist attacks from non-Zhou states and by raids from nomadic groups coming from the mountains and wilder regions. Confucius' own state of Lu had fallen under the control of usurpers and he was unable to obtain the kind of public office that would have given authority and influence to his teaching. Like others with similar aspirations and difficulties he therefore set out to teach peripatetically, offering his services to the courts and rulers he visited, accompanied by his small group of disciples and followers.

It is impossible to verify either the story of Confucius' life and character or the details of the doctrines attributed to him. We have only the composite accounts that were developed after his death and that were worked over, enriched and no doubt rearranged in numerous ways by his followers. In spite of some internal inconsistencies and variations of emphasis in the material available, it is possible to discern a coherent picture of a man who believed passionately in the pursuit of knowledge and moral virtue and who retained his integrity and an unswerving dedication to teaching throughout his life. Similarly, it is impossible to establish the authenticity or inauthenticity of the written sayings attributed to Confucius. We have to accept a general and hybrid account of Confucian doctrine rather than the authenticated thought of the individual man. We have to study the movement he began, looking at the stages of its development in relation to what is known about Confucius himself, and in that way arrive at a critical understanding of the ideas that have been so profoundly influential in the lives of many millions of human beings.

Many of the words and thoughts attributed to Confucius are contained in a collection of writings known as the *Analects*. In 1687 four Jesuit missionaries published *Confucius Sinarum Philosophus, sive Scientia Sinesis*. This book included not only the *Analects* but also two shorter works, the *Great Learning* and the *Doctrine of the Mean*. These works, along with the writings of Mencius,[2] constitute the Four Books that were the texts for the Chinese civil service examinations, already mentioned. The Four Books belonged to a larger body of writings known as the Thirteen Classics, which formed the enduring source literature not only for Confucianism but also for Daoism [Taoism] and Buddhism in China.

Confucius' philosophy was predominantly a moral and political one. It was founded on the belief that heaven and earth coexist in harmony and balanced strength whilst maintaining a perpetual dynamism. Human beings, he taught, are sustained by these conditions and must strive to emulate the cosmic model. In the *Doctrine of the Mean* we read that 'This equilibrium is the great root from which grow all the human actings in the world, and this harmony is the universal path which they all should pursue'.[3]

Confucius' exhortation to live harmoniously did not mean that an individual's passions and feelings were to be entirely repressed for the sake of maintaining a kind of bland and undisturbed tenor of life. He upholds an important distinction between equilibrium and harmony. Equilibrium, we are told, is to have 'no emotion of pleasure and anger, sorrow and joy, surging up', but harmony is 'to have these emotions surging up, but all in due time'.[4] The *Doctrine of the Mean* is the elaboration of the way of harmony; it furnishes the details of the kind of life that, in its recognition of due degree, will be in accordance with the principle of equilibrium, the root of all things. These ideas of harmony, justice and balance in both the cosmos and the individual provided a focus for political theory and practice. A belief that was well established long before Confucius' lifetime was that an earthly ruler held a mandate from heaven, a mandate that would be forfeited if the ruler did not pursue the objectives of maintaining peace and harmony. The Zhou dynasty so much admired by Confucius was established by men who, he believed, had gained the approval of Heaven and who therefore had a right to oust the tyrannical Shang dynasty that had preceded the Zhou. Confucius regarded the early years of Zhou, five hundred years before his own lifetime, as a golden age. He saw a revival of its ideals as the way to restore China's unity in a time of conflict and schism and he thought of himself as the transmitter of those former values rather than the maker of new ones.

For Confucius, all social and political virtues were simply personal virtues writ large. Education was a matter of acquiring moral knowledge. But this was not simply knowledge *that* certain actions and attitudes were good; it was also knowledge acquired in practice and through experience; by being good and by doing good. One learned from the example of one's teacher and then taught others by being an example for them. Such education, Confucius maintained, began in a person's early years and continued throughout life. At the core of his concept of moral goodness is the notion of *ren* [*jen*], that is, benevolence or love of humankind. The Chinese word *ren* is difficult to translate exactly. It is sometimes rendered as 'benevolence', sometimes as 'humaneness', in order to suggest the kind of relationship that ideally should obtain between human beings. *Ren* is a distinctively human capacity, the development of which depends on the individual's own efforts towards self-cultivation rather than on the straightforward exercise of an innate ability. In the *Analects* Confucius says of *ren*, or benevolence, that 'If we really wished for it, it would come'.[5] It is the most important single attribute of what he called 'the gentleman' or 'the superior man'. This is the person who loves learning so much that in eager pursuit of it he 'forgets his food' and 'does not perceive that old age is coming on'.[6] Benevolence demands that self-interest and self-gratification are overcome and the way to it is in observing rites, or *li*, a body of rules or principles governing every aspect of human conduct and designed to guide a person towards exemplary action. The details of the rites are copious. They relate to gesture, demeanour, dress, movement and facial expression as well as procedures, actions and whole ceremonies. The following is part of a description of the behaviour appropriate to the gentleman:

In bed he does not lie in the posture of a corpse . . . When he sees anyone in mourning, even if he knows him well, he must change countenance; and when he sees anyone in sacrificial garb, or a blind man, even if he is in informal dress, he must be sure to adopt the appropriate attitude. On meeting anyone in deep mourning he must bow across the bar of his carriage; he also bows in the same way to people carrying official tablets. When he is given a dish of delicacies, he must change countenance and rise to his feet. At a sudden clap of thunder or a violent gust of wind he must change countenance.[7]

It should not be thought that the Confucian rites were merely a behavioural façade or had only superficial importance. Confucius was a member of the *ru* [*ju*], the class of teachers who specialized in the ceremonies taught in the households of rulers. Under his tutelage these rituals acquired profound moral significance. He insisted that true benevolence or humaneness requires an integrity of the person in which the heart and mind are at one with the outward conduct. The rites are never trivial. They show what the inner disposition should be like, just as a true inner disposition of benevolence finds expression in appropriate rites. The performing of rites can be a training for benevolence, a way of making all things propitious for the cultivation of right-mindedness. Confucius described the act resulting from a proper moral integrity as *i* [*yí*], that is, morally fitting and in accord with the complete benevolence that consists of the cultivation of a personal morality that always aims to benefit and teach others. Love of learning was an essential element in the acquisition of the kind of discernment needed here. Confucius remarks that 'To love benevolence without loving learning is liable to lead to foolishness':[8] it is not enough to be well intentioned. For example, it is not enough to express one's generous impulses by giving to others indiscriminately.

Knowledge and learning help to develop a moral acumen so that one can see how to deploy one's generosity towards a true good. Knowledge, learning and experience help a person to recognize what is unalterable in life and to distinguish it from what may be changed by endeavour. At the end of the *Analects* we read: 'Confucius said, "A man has no way of becoming benevolent unless he understands Destiny".'[9] Destiny, in Confucian doctrine, governed the unalterable and so had to do with such things as the length of human life, mortality, and so on. Reflection concerning these unalterable necessities made a person recognize the futility of trying to change them and realize that it is better to direct effort into working on what can be improved, namely, one's moral capacities and understanding.

Confucius regarded the sage as the very best kind of person but he did not consider himself to be one and he thought that very few people managed to become sages. In the *Analects* he remarks: 'I have no hopes of meeting a sage.'[10] The gentleman is next in excellence to the sage and it is the gentleman who wields most influence in daily life. He is the man who, 'in his dealings with the world . . . is on the side of what is moral',[11] and whose exemplary role is described in detail in the *Analects*. The gentleman is able to command and to receive obedience because of his own moral excellence which shows itself in a sincere concern for the welfare of others. Confucius believed that, as a ruler, 'If you desire good the people will be good'.[12] He also maintained that the people must remain as the people, that 'the nature of the gentleman is like the wind and the nature of the small people is like the grass; when the wind blows over the grass it always bends',[13] so that government is always conducted by a ruling group that benevolently exerts its powers over a society in which there is a well-defined role for every member. This did not preclude promotion for those who merited it. Confucius advocated and practised a system of education that was open to all and in which the actual practice of what a person had learned was the test of genuine ability. It did not suffice merely to adopt the ways of a gentleman; one must retain and practise them by ruling well, by guiding others and establishing correct rites by one's own example. Those who diligently followed the exemplary ruler were participating fully in good government and also benefiting from it. Confucius believed that men are equal at birth and it was this conviction that underlay all his views on education and that influenced Chinese educational policies over subsequent centuries.

It is not difficult to see how Confucius' ideas about personal morality cohere with his vision of the nature of reality: the moral activity of the individual who is seeking to achieve social harmony contributes to the cosmic shifts of balance which, through harmonious interaction, find equilibrium. Nor is it difficult to detect broad affinities between Confucian thought and some of the ideas of the pre-Socratic philosophers who flourished in the sixth and fifth centuries BCE in classical Greece. Among these latter, Anaximenes (585–528 BCE) taught that human souls and the natural world are sustained as a unity within one medium; Pythagoras (571–496 BCE) devised ritualized modes of conduct to maintain purity and held that there should be a consonance between a mathematically conceived heavenly harmony and the human soul; Heraclitus (fl. *c*.504–501 BCE) propounded the idea of the Logos, a principle of balanced give and take which worked to preserve a kind of cosmic justice or equilibrium. Confucius' own character, his modest wisdom and his dedication to teaching others, have been compared with similar characteristics in Socrates, and the Socratic Golden Rule of conduct which enjoins one 'not to do to others what one does not want done to oneself' is one that is ubiquitous among moralists.[14]

Confucius did not engage in elaborate metaphysical speculation; nor did he advance any theory about the nature or possibility of human knowledge. Yet he was sensitive to the limits of what the human intellect might claim to know and, concomitantly, was reluctant to make claims that were not securely grounded in what would commonly count as experiential knowledge. To a man who once spoke to him somewhat rashly he is reported to have said, 'Where a gentleman is ignorant, one would expect him not to offer any opinion'.[15] To his follower, Zili [Tzu-lu], he remarked: 'Shall I tell you what it is to know? To say you know when you know, and to say you do not know when you do not, that is knowledge.'[16]

A Confucian doctrine referred to in the *Analects* as 'the rectification of names' has interesting philosophical implications. Confucius was greatly concerned because those called 'gentlemen' in his own time were failing to behave in ways that had formerly warranted the description. He asks, 'If a gentleman abandons humaneness, how can he fulfil the name?'[17] and he declares that government is easy if it is in the hands of those who behave correctly so that 'the prince is a prince, the minister a minister, the father a father, the son a son'.[18] It was not, it seems, the names that Confucius wanted 'rectified' but the conduct of those who assumed the names. It is rather as if he saw names, or concepts, such as 'gentleman', 'sage', 'prince', and so on, as if they were absolutes; certainly as having been precisely defined and fixed by the golden age of Zhou that he took for his model.

Reverence for the past and for ancestors, a profound concern with ritual and a strong emphasis on the importance of filial duty and of the father–son relationship, are aspects of Confucianism that have perhaps made it seem somewhat alien to the western tradition. Yet the West is familiar to some extent with all these concerns: with the bonds of family and respect for one's elders; with the valuing of customs, conventions and ceremonies; with the moral importance of moderation, reserve and proper modesty. And so it is by no means impossible to understand the Confucian stance and to recognize a universality in many of its values and practices.

After Confucius' death in 479 BCE, his disciples quietly continued his teaching. Two of his major followers, Mencius and Xunzi [Hsun Tzu], established themselves as teachers of eminence, contributing their own ideas and emphases to Confucian thought. This was a time when intellectual discussion about many moral and political matters flourished in the courts of rulers. Debates were arranged and the learned were invited to participate. All this was taking place in a setting of political turmoil and continual conflict between the Chinese states, so that the era became known as the Time of the Warring States. The strife culminated in the ascendancy of the Qin [Ch'in] dynasty (221–206 BCE). Its ruler, Qin Shi Huang Di [Ch'in Shih Huang Ti], unified China. He declared himself its emperor and built the Great Wall to defend his empire from invaders from the north. In 213 BCE, in order to reinforce his totalitarian power, he ordered the 'Burning of the Books', a conflagration that destroyed not only much Confucian literature but numerous other classics as well. During the Han dynasty (206 BCE–9 CE) a revival of Confucian thought took place. The fragments of the old writings were gathered together and restored, and Confucian ideas became widely re-established in spite of the arrival of Buddhism in the early years of the Christian era. Thereafter Confucianism or, more precisely, various forms of neo-Confucianism, continued to be part of the mainstream of Chinese culture, disseminated to people through the education in the classics.[19] In this way Confucianism united millions of people spread over a vast and varied territory. It endured because it provided both personal and public ideals, and forged a clear link between the two. Its rites and ceremonies laid down exact practices that were meaningful to simple people yet capable, at the same time, of infinite refinement by the intellegentsia. It honoured the conception of the family, the social condition known to all levels of Chinese society, and it regarded the well-wrought family life as the model for a harmonious and unified society and the fulfilment of heavenly law. It saw the arts and the cultivation of the emotions not only as delightful in themselves but as valuable to the development of cultural and political cohesion and to the fostering of the profoundly moral civility that characterized the truly humane person.

The China of the mid-twentieth century rejected almost every aspect of Confucianism. Former criticisms of its rigidity, its backward-looking ideals and its obsession with hierarchy and ceremony were revived as China began to measure itself against the western world. In his book about Confucius, Raymond Dawson has drawn attention to the way in which the revolutionary spirits of the 1960s made

Confucius responsible for every aspect of the state of affairs they wished to repudiate:

> It was Confucius who was to blame for the rigid and hierarchical society of the past: when the young wanted to assert themselves, they pointed the finger of scorn at the Confucian subordination of children to their parents; when women's rights were at issue, reformers could blame Confucian Literature for the fact that the traditional female role was first and foremost to bear children . . . so as to ensure the continuity of ancestor worship . . . Those who marvelled at the wonders of Western science and technology saw that China was helpless against the military strength of Western nations . . . The ancient criticisms of Confucius as a pedlar of ritual and a trickster who duped rulers with his moralistic nonsense resurfaced in the work of leading twentieth-century writers.[20]

It is not easy to dispose of attitudes that are part of the cultural bloodstream. Although the Cultural Revolution of the 1960s intensified the anti-Confucian criticisms of the earlier People's Republic, the innovations that were meant to oust Confucianism were nevertheless imbued with its flavour and style. It is often pointed out that the communist aim of remoulding one's personality to conform with proper proletarian attitudes closely resembles the Confucian exhortation to cultivate oneself and that the veneration accorded to the words of Chairman Mao was akin to that previously felt for Confucius.

Ideas of harmony, unity and equilibrium have always been the instinctive presuppositions of Chinese thought. This has meant that although Daoism and Buddhism have been as much a part of Chinese culture as Confucianism has, there has been very little rivalry between these three powerful movements. Their mutual relationships are accurately described in the Chinese saying 'Three religions, one religion'. Each seems to complement the other two and each is used in those situations to which it is deemed to be most appropriate. Daoism and Buddhism have supplied dimensions of mysticism and spirituality that Confucianism largely neglects. Confucianism has supplied inspiration for public life and the conduct of affairs of state.

Notes

1 During the Jesuits' stay in China they pursued a policy of establishing cordial relations with the imperial government whilst steeping themselves in knowledge of the culture. Their resulting version of Confucianism, when disseminated to the West, was greatly admired.
2 See the essay on Mencius in this book, pp. 233–40
3 *Doctrine of the Mean*, ch. 1.
4 Ibid.
5 *Analects* 7:29 trans. by A. Waley in *The Analects of Confucius*, London: Allen & Unwin, 1938.
6 Confucius' remarks about learning are scattered throughout the *Analects* but see especially ch. 7.
7 *Analects* 10:16.
8 Ibid., 17:8.
9 Ibid., the final sentence.
10 Ibid., 7:26.
11 Ibid., 4:10.
12 Ibid., 12:19.
13 Ibid.
14 For accounts of these thinkers see Diané Collinson, *Fifty Major Philosophers*, London: Routledge, 1992 (reprint).
15 *Analects* 13:3.
16 Ibid., 2:17.
17 Ibid., 4:5.
18 Ibid., 12:11.
19 For accounts of later forms of neo-Confucianism see the essays on Zhuxi and Dai Zhen in this book pp. 278–83 and pp. 288–95
20 Raymond Dawson, *Confucius*, Oxford: Oxford University Press, Past Masters series, 1986, pp. 85, 86.

Major Confucian writings

The writings known as the Classics were in existence before Confucius' lifetime. Nothing of certainty is known about how much he contributed to them. They are:

Shijing [Shi Ching] or the Book of Odes, verses from the early Chou period
Shujing [Shu Ching] or the Book of History, records from 7000–2000 BCE
Yijing [I Ching] or the Book of Changes, formulae to explain nature, used for divination
Lijing [Li Ching] or the Book of Rites, rules of social conduct, probably compiled during or after Confucius' lifetime but recording earlier customs
Chunqin [Ch'un Ch'in] the Spring and Autumn Annals, records from 722–464 BCE

Confucius drew on the Classics for his teaching. His own ideas, and developments of them, are contained in the Four Books, the writings used as basis for the Chinese civil service examinations. The Four Books are:

Lunyu, or the Analects of Confucius, the sayings of Confucius
Daxue [Tu Hsueh] or the Great Learning, on politics

Zhongyong [Chung Yung] or Doctrine of the Mean, on moral precepts
Mengzi [Meng Tzu] the Book of Mencius

See also in this book

Mozi, Mencius, Laozi, Zhuxi, Dai Zhen, Xunzi, Kang Youwei, Mao Zedong, Yi Yulgok

Sources and further reading

Allinson, Robert E., *Understanding the Chinese Mind: The Philosophical Roots*, Oxford: Oxford University Press, 1996

Chan Wing-tsit, *A Source Book in Chinese Philosophy*, Princeton: Princeton University Press, 1963

Cleary, Thomas, *The Essential Confucius: The Heart of Confucius' Teachings in Authentic I Ching Order*, San Francisco: Harper, 1993

Dawson, Raymond, *Confucius*, Oxford: Oxford University Press, Past Masters series, 1986, 1993

Eber, Irene (ed.), *Confucianism: The Dynamics of Tradition*, New York: Macmillan, 1986

Fung Yu-lan, *A Short History of Chinese Philosophy*, trans. D. Bodde, 2 vols, vol. I, New York: Free Press; London, Collier Macmillan, 1968

Hughes, E.R., *Chinese Philosophy in Classical Times*, London: Dent, 1942

Lau, D.C., *The Analects*, Harmondsworth: Penguin Books, 1979

Legge, James, *The Chinese Classics*, Hong Kong: Hongkong University Press, 1961 (reprint)

Shaughnessy, Edward, L., *I Ching: The Classic of Changes*, New York: Ballantyne Books, 1997

MOZI (MO TZU) fifth century BCE

Early Chinese philosophy was dominated by three traditions: Confucianism, Daoism and Mohism. Of these schools of thought, it was Mohism, based on the teachings of its founder Mozi (also known by the latinized Micius) which proved to be the least durable, but during the fifth and fourth centuries BCE, it was the major rival to Confucianism. Whereas Confucius and his followers looked back upon the early years of the Zhou dynasty (c.1122–1249 BCE) as a model of social orderliness, stratification and political stability based on principles of propriety, Mozi regarded the earlier Xia dynasty (c.2183–1752 BCE) as having put into practice, at least intermittently, the ideals of peace and equal regard for everyone. In opposition to Confucius, Mozi's philosophy was that of utilitarianism. This ethical doctrine holds that actions are neither intrinsically right nor wrong;

instead, they are to be judged by their consequences. Actions are right or virtuous if and only if they either increase benefit or decrease harm, and wrong if and only if they either decrease benefit or increase harm. Mozi thus condemned war as destructive, and advocated universal, impartial love or brotherhood. The Mohist school waned in importance during the third century BCE. One reason for this was that its tenets were incompatible with the political conflict and instability which characterized the Warring States period (403–222 BCE) of Chinese history, when the several states which were to compose China vied for political ascendancy and power. In the twentieth century, there has been a revival of interest in the doctrines of Mozi and his followers, partly because they form an indigenous corpus of beliefs comparable to the western philosophical tradition of utilitarianism, and partly because of the current official hostility towards Confucianism.

Details of Mozi's life are scarce. Even his dates are uncertain, although it is known that he was active from about 470 to 438 BCE. He was born either in Lu, Confucius' native state, or in Song, both now in Shandong province on the North China plain. In the *Shi Chi* [*Shiji*] (Historical Records, a compilation from the first century BCE), the historian Ssu-ma Ch'ien [Sima Qian] writes, 'Mo Ti [Mozi] seems probably to have been a great officer in the state of Sung [Song]. He was skilful in maintaining military defences'.[1] Further suggestions have been made about his career: that, when young, he was a follower of Confucius, and for a period he was a member of the *xie*, a quasi-military group which could be hired for protection; and that he was an artisan, because he frequently uses measuring instruments such as compasses and set-squares as metaphors in his writings.[2] Later in life, he led a frugal existence and travelled from province to province, seeking audiences with rulers in order to try to dissuade them from waging war on neighbouring states. By the time of his death, he had attracted about three hundred followers, probably not of aristocratic status. They were split into three groups, each with its own Elder; they practised asceticism and continued to travel in the causes of universal brotherhood and peace.

The source for the doctrines of Mozi and his followers is the text *Mozi* [*Mo Tzu*], part of which is now lost. Many of the sections contain three separate essays on the same subject, and it has been suggested that each of the three was written by a different branch of the early Mohists. There are six chapters, chs 40–5, that are generally held to be the work of the later, post-Mencian, members of the movement. These parts of the *Mozi* show a shift in interest away from ethics and social philosophy to epistemology and logic, and Mencius does not attack them in his comprehensive critique of the teachings of the school. Another strong condemnation of the Mohists was delivered by the Confucian Xunzi [Hsun Tzu].[3]

Although in their writings the Mohists presented Mozi as having been bitterly hostile to Confucius and his followers, they shared many beliefs. Both Mozi and Confucius maintained that all societies were inevitably stratified, though there should be opportunity for upward mobility by the able. Both held that there should be political stability and social order. However, the two were diametrically opposed on the source of moral values. Confucius held that such values were based on society and tradition. Families formed the nuclei of society and personal virtues could be taught and cultivated by encouraging people to follow the rules of propriety, or principles guiding human conduct (*li*). Such rules constituted an elaborate set of rituals which governed one's relationships, whether familial, social or professional, with others. By following *li*, a person would become a *zhunzi*, or 'superior gentleman'.[4] By contrast, Mozi advocated the way of the *xiaoren*, or 'inferior person', whose actions were prudential. He believed that Confucian ritual was practised for its own sake, and custom and tradition yielded only an unreflective morality.

Mozi looked to *tian*, nature or heaven, not to society, to provide us with the basis for objective, trans-social moral standards for human behaviour. His was a straightforwardly consequentialist view, though not one which involves the subjective mental states of happiness or misery, nor the hedonistic standards of pleasure and pain. Instead, he maintained that good or right actions are those which bring about an increase in material prosperity, and wrong actions are those which cause a decrease in the material standard of living. This issue of the origin of moral values was a point of controversy between the Mohists and the Legalists; the latter believed that the only moral standards acceptable in a state were those sanctioned by the laws.[5] For Mozi, nature also provides sanctions for right and wrong behaviour; it usually rewards the agent of good actions with prosperity in this life, and the undertaker of wrong actions with poverty, sickness or early death. It is not necessary, according to Mozi, for each member of society to understand that nature provides the standards for proper moral conduct. The natural human characteristic of emulation means that each stratum of society looks to the one above it for moral guidance. The peasantry are guided by the 'gentlemen', who look to the ministers, who take their moral lead from the ruler. Thus it is ultimately the responsibility of the ruler to set an example of correct moral behaviour for the rest of society. This is done partly by the proper use of language, which Mozi considered to be a public, trans-social means of discourse with two major functions. The first is that it can and should correctly describe the objective standards of social utility, and the second that it can encourage people to behave according to such standards.

The appeal to nature as a crucial part of his philosophy enabled Mozi to contrast the social with the pre-social human condition. Before society, there existed a state of conflict, in which each person held to his or her own subjective set of moral values. Nature, or the will of Heaven, selected as ruler he who had the wisdom to understand the moral order, and gave him the power to govern society in accordance with its requirements. The social and political philosophy of Mozi is an interesting combination of theories also found in the western philosophical tradition. In the ideal society advocated by Plato (427–347 BCE) in *The Republic*, the philosopher–ruler would have a direct knowledge of objective and unchanging moral standards, whereas the theory of a pre-social condition of conflict in which everyone followed their own set of moral standards is to be found in the work of the social contractarian Thomas Hobbes (1588–1679).[6]

In his repudiation of offensive warfare and state expansionism, Mozi advocated that objective and universal moral values should govern political life, thus implicitly rejecting any political philosophy which is based solely on power. He blamed aggressive rulers for promulgating the false conception that correct moral values can be promoted by war, and showed sympathy for the soldiers at whom that message is aimed. Warfare is destructive, both for the aggressor nation and the country attacked. War means that a state loses its fittest manpower to the army. Even non-combatants must leave the useful task of food production to supply the needs of the army, such as the manufacture of weapons. The crops of a conquered nation will be destroyed, thus reducing its population to destitution and starvation. Like many thinkers in both the eastern and the western philosophical traditions up to the end of the eighteenth century CE, Mozi was concerned about population levels: the scarcest resource for the improvement of material conditions was human labour. In the *Mozi*, there are also scattered references to defensive warfare; there is the practical recommendation that the proper maintenance of state defences is ultimately the responsibility of the ruler.

Burton Watson[7] maintains that Mozi's doctrine of universal love is the most revolutionary and innovative of his whole teaching.

Confucian rules of propriety and ritual enjoin upon each of us special duties only towards certain people, in keeping with our familial or social positions. Thus we are required to behave with filial piety, reverence and respect to our parents and to care for them in their old age, or to show deference towards our older siblings or social superiors. By contrast, Mozi advocated that such partial duties should be replaced by universal love, in accordance with the universality of the moral order. This does not mean that filial piety would be abandoned; instead, the obligation of care, for example, would not be confined to our parents alone, but would be extended to anyone who needed it. The crucial criterion for the promotion of universal love is material benefit, and this condition is easily met. The doctrine can be considered as a rudimentary policy of social welfare: in the words of the *Mozi*,

> Those who are old and without . . . children will find means
> of support and be able to live out their days; the young and
> orphaned who have no parents will find someone to care for
> them and look after their needs.[8]

Similarly, we should love members of other societies in the same way that we love members of our own. The requirements of universal love are thus stringent. Offensive war is totally prohibited, and helping others in need or refraining from causing them harm would be a global, not merely a local, moral duty.

One doctrine that Mozi considered would be destructive of, because incompatible with, his own was that of fatalism, the view that our futures are inevitably mapped out for us and we cannot avoid them whatever we do. Thus a student who is fated to pass her examination will do so, whether or not she studies for it. A belief in fate would sever the perceived links between correct behaviour (*ren*) and benefit or profit, good deeds and reward, and evil deeds and punishment. A state's wealth or poverty would not be seen as dependent on the industriousness or laziness of its people, nor the ability nor incompetence of its rulers. An increase in the population level or in the length of people's lives could not be achieved if fate decreed otherwise.

The concept of fate that Mozi condemns is particularly crude. The 'many gentlemen' whom Mozi accuses of propounding a belief in fatalism, and who thickly populate certain sections of the *Mozi*, are almost certainly the Confucians, but it is unlikely that they held the doctrine of fatalism attributed to them. It is much more probable that, following Confucius, they equated destiny with natural, unavoidable processes such as ageing and dying, which we may be able to delay by our own efforts but not prevent altogether.[9]

Mozi especially condemned music, on two grounds. First, it was part of an aristocratic lifestyle, and second, it distracted people from engaging in their proper occupations. In ancient China, music was accompanied by dance, and performances took place at sumptuous banquets in the homes of the aristocracy. In order to finance such luxuries, rulers acted against the interests of their subjects by the imposition of high taxation. The sage-kings of the Xia dynasty 'likewise laid heavy taxes on the people, but this was for the purpose of making boats and carts . . . [which] would be used for the benefit of the people'.[10] The peasantry, according to Mozi, had only three concerns, food, clothing and shelter, and taxation diverted resources from the provision of these necessities. Dancers often demanded delicate food and fine clothing, which was an additional expense. Artisans were required to make musical instruments instead of useful farming machinery such as ploughs and carts. Performances on the bells, which were 'like huge cauldrons', needed strong young people with keen senses, who should have been employed in the more useful task of food production. Rulers should rule and government ministers should see to the affairs of state, instead of allowing themselves to be distracted into attending musical performances.

Mozi's treatment of music reveals certain significant tendencies of his thought, particularly the narrow and puritanical character of his utilitarianism. He consistently criticizes the aristocracy and their retainers, whilst strongly championing the material advantage of the peasantry. However, it could be maintained that music provides less tangible benefits to the whole of society. Music, without its luxurious trappings, could be one of the ways of providing rest and relaxation so that people would return to their jobs with renewed energy and enthusiasm. Public performances of music might also promote a sense of social cohesion.

In Mozi's time, music was a feature of elaborate funerals. According to the *Mozi*, custom dictated that the corpse was to be buried in fine clothing and jewellery, with drapery over the several inner and outer coffins, in a deep grave. The funeral of a member of the royal family or senior minister was to be marked by human sacrifice. Ritual also specified that the chief mourners were, for a period of up to twenty-five months, to live in mourning huts, provided only with what was needed to sustain life. Burton Watson[11] says that, with the exception of human sacrifice, the whole of this ritual was advocated by the Confucians. Mozi introduced three tests for funerals, none of which was based on custom: do elaborate funerals enrich the poor, increase the population, or bring order and stability to the state? It is clear that they do not help to fulfil any of these goals. The poor are impoverished because their assets are buried with the corpse, and during the period of mourning the farmer and the artisan cannot attend to their proper occupations. Likewise, the fulfilment of their roles as mourners would prevent rulers and ministers from engaging in affairs of state, and engineers from ensuring that the defences of their territories are adequately maintained. Mozi recommends that grieving should be done at the graveside, with a return to useful occupations immediately afterwards, but this betrays a shallow understanding of human psychology; people do not mourn only for a short fixed period of time. Sexual abstinence during a period of mourning was often enjoined on man and wife, which prompted Mozi's acerbic remark: 'To hope in this way to increase the population is like ordering a man to fall on his sword and wishing him long life'.[12]

According to Chad Hansen, Mozi's philosophical objections to Confucianism prompted the Confucians into backing up their own position by philosophical argument. In Hansen's words, Mozi's 'attack on Confucian traditionalism is the catalyst of Chinese philosophical development'.[13] Mozi's philosophy is not merely of historical curiosity. It is an interesting combination of hard-headed practical considerations, particularly with his concern for the material considerations of the poor, and the visionary ideals of universal peace, love and brotherhood, all still of vital importance in today's world. Advocates of peace, non-violence and universal fraternity are to be found in both western and eastern philosophical thought, from Leo Tolstoy to Gandhi.

Notes

1 Quoted in Fung Yu-lan, *A History of Chinese Philosophy* trans. D. Bodde, 2 vols, vol. I, Princeton: Princeton University Press, 1983, p. 76.

2 Michael Brannigan, *The Pulse of Wisdom*, Belmont, Calif.: Wadsworth, 1995, p. 30, and Hansen, C., *A Daoist Theory of Chinese Thought*, New York: Oxford University Press, 1992, ch. 4.

3 See Fung Yu-lan, op. cit., pp. 80–1; Watson, Burton, *Basic Writings of Mo Tzu, Hsun Tzu and Han Fei Tzu*, New York and London: Columbia University Press, 1967, pp. 2–3, and the essays on Mencius, pp. 233–40 and Xunzi, pp. 259–66 in this book.

4 See the essay on Confucius, pp. 217–26 in this book.

5 See the essay on Hanfeizi, pp. 254–8 in this book.

6 See Plato, *The Republic*, many editions, and Thomas Hobbes, *Leviathan*, many editions, ch. 13.

7 Watson, op. cit., Pt I, p. 9.
8 Watson, op. cit., Pt I, p. 41.
9 See the essay on Confucius, pp. 217–26 in this book.
10 Watson, op. cit., Pt I, p. 111.
11 Watson, op. cit., Pt I, p. 68.
12 Watson, op. cit., Pt I, p. 69.
13 Hansen, op. cit., ch. 4, pp. 95–6.

Mozi's writings

All essays in the extant *Mo Tzu* have been translated into German in Alfred Forke, *Me Ti des Sozialethikers und seiner Schuler philosophische Werke*, Berlin: Kommisionsverlag der Vereinung Wissenschaftlicher Verlager, 1922. Selections are in Wing-tsit Chan, *A Source Book in Chinese Philosophy*, Princeton: Princeton University Press, 1963; Michael Brannigan, *The Pulse of Wisdom*, Belmont, Calif., Wadsworth, 1995; and Burton Watson, *Basic Writings of Mo Tzu, Hsun Tzu and Han Fei Tzu*, New York and London: Columbia University Press, 1967.

See also in this book

Confucius, Mencius, Laozi, Hanfeizi, Xunzi, Kang Youwei.

Sources and further reading

Brannigan, Michael, *The Pulse of Wisdom*, Belmont, Calif.: Wadsworth, 1995
Chan Wing-tsit, *A Source Book in Chinese Philosophy*, Princeton: Princeton University Press, 1963
Fung Yu-lan, *The Spirit of Chinese Philosophy*, trans. E.R. Hughes, London: Kegan Paul, Trench, Trubner, 1947
—— *A History of Chinese Philosophy*, trans. D. Bodde, 2 vols., vol. I, Princeton: Princeton University Press, 1983
Hansen, C., *A Daoist Theory of Chinese Thought*, New York: Oxford University Press, 1992
Lowe, Scott, *Mo Tzu's Religious Blueprint for a Chinese Utopia: The Will and the Way*, New York: Edwin Mellin Press, 1992
Watson, Burton, *Basic Writings of Mo Tzu, Hsun Tzu and Han Fei Tzu*, New York and London: Columbia University Press, 1967

MENCIUS (MENGZI, MENGE K'E) 371–289 BCE

Mencius, like his predecessor, Confucius, is better known by the latinized version of his name than as Mengzi [Menge K'e]. He developed Confucian doctrines and introduced ideas of his own into the body of Confucian thought.[1] His recorded sayings, known as the *Mencius*, are one of the Four Books, the collection of classical writings that for many centuries formed the basis of Chinese education. The Four Books were the main texts studied for the Chinese civil service examinations which were first instituted in 1313 CE and held annually for six centuries. The literary style of the *Mencius* is regarded as exemplary.

Little is known of the events of Mencius' life. A history called the *Shi Chi* [*Shiji*] (Historical Records), written at the beginning of the first century BCE, contains a brief biography but tells us no more than can be sifted from Mencius' own writing. He was born in the state of Zou [Tsou] in the province of Shandong [Shangtung]. From the age of 3, when his father died, he was brought up by his mother who worked as a weaver and who dedicated herself to providing an exemplary moral education for her son. Mencius was taught for a time by Tzu Ssu, the grandson of Confucius. He became a teacher and after brief service as an official in the state of *Qi* [Ch'i] in the east of China took to travelling between the courts of rulers, advising them on the practices of human government and kingship. But the political unrest that had thwarted Confucius on similar missions prevailed still – indeed, had increased – and was equally thwarting to Mencius.[2] He eventually went into retirement with a number of disciples, probably to work on the composition of the *Mencius*, but it is not entirely clear whether the book was written by Mencius himself or put together by his followers. Even if he did write it, it is evident from the names and titles of some of the people who feature in it that the version that has come down to us was not completed until after his death.

China underwent profound change during Mencius' lifetime. Her states were in continual conflict as feudalism gradually gave way to a more centralized kind of government. The era became known as the Time of the Warring States (403–222 BCE) and during it there developed a doctrine known as Legalism which regarded human beings as egotistic in nature and responsive only to reward and punishment. Mencius had scant sympathy with this view. His thought is steeped in the Confucian concepts of human benevolence **ren** [*jen*] and justice, or right conduct *i* [*yi*], and he held that there is an element of goodness in human beings that is as much part of human nature as the appetites for food and sex.

As well as maintaining Confucian views on benevolence and right conduct, Mencius developed Confucius' concept of 'the gentleman' or 'superior man', the person who is deeply humane in both his inward thoughts and outward conduct and who will never do to others what he would not wish to have done to himself. Mencius wrote: 'Slight is the difference between man and the brutes. The common man loses this distinguishing feature, while the gentleman retains it.'[3] What the gentleman retains and develops is the power to think and to rule his life by reason. He is not governed by the attractions and repulsions of the senses; he can engage in moral reflection. Mencius speaks of the heart as the organ of thought and of its having the role of a kind of reflective conscience which should govern one's life. Unlike many western thinkers, he did not believe in a sharp dualism of mind and body in human beings. He regarded human beings as organic wholes that flourished best when the most valuable elements of the body ruled the lesser ones. In his scheme of things the heart takes precedence because it is the most important organ. However, the heart is not essentially different from the rest of the body so its activity does not generate any problems of interaction between itself and what it governs.

The underpinning of Mencius' views on human nature is a conception of how things are in the cosmos. The general belief at the time was that the universe consisted of *qi* [*ch'i*], a fundamental substance which varied in consistency, its heavier parts forming earth, its lighter and more refined aspects rising to form the sky. A human being was regarded as comprising a mixture of the two, the finer *qi* constituting the heart and the animating breath of the body. In Mencius' hands this notion of *qi* was developed into something of great moral significance for each individual. At a personal level one's *qi* was to be thought of as one's essential being spiritual personality, the source of human individuality and character. Mencius spoke of his own *qi* as 'flood-like' and as 'in the highest degree, vast and unyielding'.[4] His advice concerning *qi* was:

> Nourish it with integrity and place no obstacle in its path and it will fill the space between Heaven and Earth. It is a *ch'i* which unites rightness and the Way . . . It is born of accumulated rightness and cannot be appropriated by anyone through a sporadic show of rightness . . . Whenever one acts in a way that falls below the standard set in one's heart, it will collapse . . . You must work at it and never let it out of your mind. At the same time, while you must never let it out of your mind, you must not forcibly help it grow either.[5]

To foster one's *qi*, that finer part of oneself, is to connect what is earthly with what is heavenly. It is to find the Way, **Dao** [*Tao*], the right life for a human being and one in which the ultimate harmony of the cosmos is celebrated, communicated and shared. This requires the cultivation of a steady disposition of goodwill that is not super-ficial and is never over-zealous. Virtue is the cultivation of natural propensities. Mencius quotes Confucius as saying of natural goodness: 'Hold on to it and it will remain; let go of it and it will disappear. One never knows the time it comes or goes, neither does one know the duration.'[6]

Mencius appeals to ordinary human experience to support his claim that human nature contains some innate goodness. He points out that all children are naturally aware of how to love their parents and that anyone seeing a child about to fall into a well will spontaneously endeavour to effect a rescue. He identifies four germs or seeds of innate goodness in human beings. These are the feelings of compassion and shame, courtesy, and a sense of right and wrong. If nurtured properly these seeds grow into the four cardinal virtues of benevolence, dutifulness, decorum and wisdom. Mencius remarks: 'Man has these four germs just as he has four limbs. For a man possessing these four germs to deny his own potentialities is for him to cripple himself.'[7]

In Mencian as in Confucian ethics, personal morality is the necessary condition of social and political morality. The benevolence and right conduct practised in personal relationships must manifest themselves in the larger context of compassionate and fair govern-ment. Mencius speaks of King Wen, a former ruler of Zhou and one who was greatly revered by Confucius, as caring so much for his people that he treated them 'as if he were tending invalids'.[8] He maintains that people will loyally serve a humane ruler, imitating his good example and uniting to produce a peaceful and prosperous state: 'When the prince is benevolent, everyone else is benevolent.'[9] He quotes words thought to have originated in a lost chapter of the *Shiji*, China's Book of History: 'Heaven sees with the eyes of its people. Heaven hears with the ears of its people',[10] and this seems to encompass, once again, the ideas of a natural, innate goodness in people and of the connection of these natural propensities with heaven. The ruler who recognizes all this will foster the natural virtues in his people and so enable them to share more fully in the happiness of heaven.

Mencius consistently asserts the superiority of the thinking person over the one whose life is predominantly given to physical activity. But this is not simply a crude class-division based on occupation. It stems from the view, already mentioned, that true virtue consists in giving precedence to the organ of thought, the heart, rather than to those organs to do with the appetites and senses. Mencius, like Confucius, believed that anyone might become a sage or a ruler or a gentleman; it was a question of cultivating one's potential for moral goodness.

All Confucianism is deeply imbued with conceptions of orderliness, gradations and appropriateness in all things, and Mencius' endorsement of those conceptions is particularly apparent in his teaching concerning love and dutifulness within the family. His thought here has to be seen as a response and an opposition to that of Mozi [Mo Tzu], a teacher who became widely influential early in the fourth century BCE and who rejected many features of Confucian doctrine.[11] Mozi's ideas were utilitarian in character; actions, customs, pursuits and objects were valued, he maintained, for the benefits or good consequences they yielded. Like the Confucians, Mozi advocated benevolence and righteousness (*ren* and *i*) but his conceptions of them were quite different from those of the Confucians. He maintained that our love for others should be bestowed equally and without discrimination upon everyone whereas Mencius, following the pattern established by Confucius, averred the primacy of love for one's parents and, thereafter, a graduated bestowal of love from one's family outwards to society at large. Mencius regarded it as perfectly proper that we should love those close to us more than those who are distant. At the same time he maintained that we should always be extending the scope of our love. 'Treat your own young', he says, 'in a manner befitting their tender age and extend this treatment to the young of other families.'[12]

Mozi had also criticized Confucianism for its humanistic denial of gods and spirits, arguing that this displeased God and the spirits. He pointed out that the Confucian practice of mourning the death of a parent for three years wasted human life and human resources, as did the playing of music. He maintained too that the Confucian belief in a destiny or fate had the effect of making people lazy, since they thought it useless to struggle against what they saw as a pre-ordained and unchangeable course of events. These are strongly utilitarian themes that exhibit some of the fundamental differences between Mencius and Mozi. Mencius' view was that it is heaven, rather than gods or spirits, that is important. Heaven is the source and ideal for all that is best in human morality. Heaven is also attainable, at any rate to some extent, since one's *qi* connects one with it and since all human beings have the seeds of its virtues within them. This contrasts sharply with the Mohist belief that benevolence and virtuous conduct have to be superimposed on human nature and developed by means of rewards and sanctions. With Mozi we are not so much connected with heaven as under the rule of its inhabitants; virtue is to be practised because it produces rewards and benefits, but it is not practised for its own sake.[13]

Mencius differentiated carefully between kinds of human relationship. He held that father and son should love each other; ruler and subject should be just to each other; husband and wife should distinguish their respective spheres; elder and younger brothers should have a sense of mutual precedence; and between friends there should be good faith.[14] These distinctions form the basis of his political thought: society is these relationships writ large and the task of the state is to foster and maintain them, providing the conditions for a moral community. Political life is essentially the life of morality, the development of all those qualities and propensities that distinguish the human world from the world of creatures. The ideal ruler is the sage-king, the wise ruler whose aim is to impart the finest moral education to the people. This is always to be done by example and teaching that win the voluntary allegiance of subjects rather than by the physical force and intimidation characteristic of a military leader. Mencius remarks: 'When people submit to force they do so not willingly but because they are not strong enough. When people submit to the transforming influence of morality they do so sincerely, with admiration in their hearts.'[15] And: 'It is not by boundaries that the people are confined, it is not by difficult terrain that a state is rendered secure, and it is not by superiority of arms that the Empire is kept in awe. One who has the Way will have many to support him; one who has not the Way will have few to support him.'[16]

Mencius maintained not only that the people were the most important element in government but also that they had a right to rebel against a ruler to whom the description 'kingly' could not be correctly applied. This is a familiar element in the thought of numerous political theorists, ancient and modern, and it has particularly strong affinities with the view of the seventeenth-century English philosopher Thomas Hobbes. Hobbes maintained that a sovereign might legitimately be rebelled against if he failed to protect his subjects and preserve peace; in short, if he no longer acted in the way implied by the name 'sovereign'. In a comparable way, both Confucius and Mencius insisted on 'the rectification of names', that is, on the conformity of things and persons to the names or titles given them. Interestingly, the philosophical foundations of these similarities are markedly dissimilar. Confucians seem to have believed in the existence of ideal essences which have to be discovered and which give words and terms their meanings. Hobbes, in contrast, completely rejected the notion that there are ideal essences having an existence of their own. His starting point was in the fact that we give names to particular things and that a general term such as 'sovereignty' or 'redness' is no more than a name 'imposed on many things for their similitude in some quality'.[17]

Those familiar with the history of western philosophy often see the relationship between Mencius and Confucius as being much like the relationship between Plato and Socrates. There is a range of similarities. Both Confucius and Socrates were loved for their personal integrity, practical wisdom and incorruptibility. Both had a down-to-earth approach to life and both were predominantly concerned with understanding and developing the moral nature of human beings. Both were succeeded by thinkers – Confucius by Mencius, Socrates by Plato – who developed their ideas into richer and more complex philosophical systems: there are metaphysical and mystical dimensions to the thought of both Mencius and Plato that are not present in that of the predecessors they revered. Mencius' doctrine concerning the possibility of one's *qi* finding an affinity with heaven by filling the space between earth and heaven certainly reminds one of Plato's famous allegory of the cave, in which he pictures the human being as struggling from the shadowy perceptions of a cave-bound life upwards to the sunlit heights where everything is clear in the light of the sun, seen as the symbol of Good.

Notes

1 See the essay on Confucius in this book, pp. 217–26
2 There is an excellent account of the general political and social background of this era in Fung Yu-lan, *A History of Chinese Philosophy*, trans. D. Bodde, vol. I, Princeton: Princeton University Press, 1983, ch. 2.
3 In D.C. Lau (trans.), *Mencius*, Harmondsworth, Penguin Books, 1970, IV.B.19.
4 Ibid., II.A.1 (p. 77).
5 Ibid., II.A.2 (pp. 77, 78).
6 Ibid., VI.A.8.
7 Ibid., II.A.6.
8 Ibid., IV.B.20.
9 Ibid., IV.B.5.
10 Ibid., V.A.5.
11 See the essay on Mozi in this book, pp. 226–33.
12 Lau, op. cit., I.A.7 (p. 56).
13 There is a full account of Mozi's thought and the Mohist school in Fung Yu-lan, op. cit., ch. v.
14 *Mencius*, III.A.4 (p. 102)
15 Ibid., II.A.3.
16 Ibid., II.B.1.
17 Thomas Hobbes, *Leviathan*, ch. 4 (many editions).

Mencius' writings

Mencius, trans. D.C. Lau, Harmondsworth, Penguin Books, 1970
Collie, David, *The Four Books*, Gainsville, Scholars' Facsimiles and Reprints, 1970

See also in this book

Confucius, Mozi, Laozi, Zhuangzi, Hanfeizi, Xunzi, Huineng, Dai Zhen, Kang Youwei, Yi, Yulgok

Sources and further reading

Chan Wing-tsit, *A Source Book in Chinese Philosophy*, Princeton: Princeton University Press, 1963
Fung Yu-lan, *A History of Chinese Philosophy*, trans. D. Bodde, vol. I, Princeton: Princeton University Press, 1983
Fung Yu-lan, *The Spirit of Chinese Philosophy*, trans. E.R. Hughes, London: Kegan Paul, Trench, Trubner, 1947
Kwong-loi Shun, *Mencius and Early Chinese Thought*, Stanford, Calif.: Stanford University Press, 1997

LAOZI (LAO TZU) probably fourth century BCE

Little is known about Laozi [Lao Tzu]. His enigmatic but deeply venerated figure represents the rise of **Daoist** [Taoist] thought in China. Daoism is one of the three philosophical and ethico-religious systems that dominated Chinese culture until the early years of the twentieth century. The other two great systems, Confucianism and Buddhism, used the word '*dao*' [*tao*] (pronounced 'dow') to refer to a way to right living or to spiritual development within the universe, but in Daoism the *Dao* is *the* Way and also the universal principle that is in all things. It is the unchanging source of the universe and of all that takes place in it.

The *Shiji* [*Shih-Chi*], the Chinese Historical Record compiled by Sima Qian [Ssu-ma Ch'ien] in the second century BCE, is not clear concerning Laozi's dates. It tells us that his family name was Li, his given name Erh and his public name Tan. His birthplace was a village then known as Chu Jen in the Chinese province now called Honan. Laozi was an archivist at the court of the Zhou [Chou] rulers and is reported in some sources to have had a part in teaching Confucius the rites that were so vital a part of Chinese education and life. When the Zhou dynasty began to weaken, Laozi departed the court but before leaving China he wrote, at the request of Yinzi [Yin Hsi], the guardian of the frontier pass, a treatise on the Dao. The work, known as the *Dao De Jing* [*Tao-te Ching*] (The Way and Its Power), has eighty-one short sections or chapters and consists of around five thousand Chinese characters. Because of this it is sometimes called Laozi's Five Thousand Words.

There is no record of what Laozi did after his departure from China, allegedly riding on a blue water buffalo. Most sinologists believe the *Shiji* account to be legendary and the *Dao De Jing* a compilation, made over many decades, of the words and thoughts of a number of Daoist thinkers. More than forty English translations of the *Dao De Jing* have been made and many hundreds of commentaries, in numerous languages, have been written on it. In *A Source Book in Chinese Philosophy*, Wing-tsit Chan remarks that 'No one can hope to understand Chinese philosophy, religion, government, art, medicine – or even cooking – without a real appreciation of the profound philosophy taught in this little book'.[1]

Many attempts have been made to translate the term '*dao*' in a way that conveys its full and exact meaning. The Jesuits who made the first translations of the *Dao De Jing* equated *Dao* with the Supreme Reason of the Divine Being, but this understanding of the term was inadequate in two ways. First, it failed to capture that sense in which the word refers to Nature, or the universe, as a whole. Second, it neglects the central meaning of *Dao* as the Way, and of the Way as being that of Nature as a whole rather than of a specific way within the natural order. *Dao* is a word for what is ultimate and ineffable and the *Dao de Jing* makes this clear in its opening pronouncements:

> The Tao (Way) that can be told is not the eternal Tao;
> The name that can be named is not the eternal name.
> The Nameless is the origin of Heaven and Earth;
> The Named is the mother of all things.[2]

And in the twenty-fifth paragraph we read:

> There was something undifferentiated and yet complete,
> Which existed before heaven and earth.
> Soundless and formless it depends on nothing and does not
>   change.
> It operates everywhere and is free from danger.
> It may be considered the mother of the universe.
> I do not know its name; I call it Tao.[3]

Many of the important tenets of Laozi's teaching are best understood by comparing or contrasting them with Confucian teachings. Confucius' doctrine derives from the importance he placed on each individual's capacity for moral improvement and the development of a comprehensive benevolence towards one's fellow beings and to society in general. Laozi's thought has a somewhat different emphasis. For him, the *Dao*, or Way, is found in the achievement of a harmony or union with Nature. This union is not secured by striving to achieve specified aims but rather by a kind of letting go, by a relinquishing of desire, by a reduction of needs and by a subduing of busy acquisitiveness. The *Dao De Jing* rejects the rigorous practising of rites, so vital in the Confucian system of moral education, and proposes instead a submission to and a gentle exploration of all that is natural. It advocates a wandering discovery of the Way, much as a stream of water will find a course between the irregularities of the land through which it flows. What results is a kind of lived understanding; a knowing-how rather than a knowing-that. Living becomes effortless, yet abundant. The requirement is to inhabit rather than use Nature; to immerse oneself in it rather than distinguish oneself from it.

Confucius' solution to the problem of living justly, righteously and in a state of sociability involved the elucidation of a well-defined system of morality and a carefully circumscribed education for realizing that system. Laozi shared these ideals of social harmony but not Confucius' method for realizing them. To him it was a mistake to separate out virtues and excellences and to hold up the idea of morality as a condition towards which one should struggle. He maintained that the multiplication of moral rules and conventions of conduct increased strife and competition and produced a highly artificial system of virtue that ignored Nature. We read in the *Dao De Jing* that:

> When the great Tao declined,
> The doctrines of humanity and righteousness arose.
> When knowledge and wisdom appeared
> There emerged great hypocrisy.[4]

And:

> . . . only when Tao is lost does the doctrine of humanity
> arise. Only when humanity is lost does the doctrine of
> righteousness arise.[5]

Laozi's advice for attaining virtue is to find it 'the easy way'; that is, to reject the highly articulated constructs of formalized knowledge. He says: 'Abandon sageliness . . . abandon learning, and there will be no sorrow', and he counsels rulers to 'administer the empire by engaging in no activity' because:

> The more taboos and prohibitions there are in the world,
> The poorer the people will be.
> The more sharp weapons the people have.
> The more troubled the state will be.[6]

It should not be thought from all this that Laozi advocated a kind of anarchical individualism. He held that there are immutable laws of nature and that it is through understanding the character of the laws that one finds the Way for oneself through life. Finding one's own path in the Way depends on *wuwei*, the practice of non-intervention that is in accordance with the laws of nature in that one never seeks to impede the enaction of the universal laws that constitute the Dao of Heaven. But *wuwei* is not a mere negation or opting out. It is presence in the right place and a willingness to go along with the real nature of things. Again it is water that is the ideal symbol of this conception of strength through gentleness:

> The great rivers and seas are kings of all mountain streams
> Because they skilfully stay below them . . .
> There is nothing softer and weaker than water,
> And yet there is nothing better for attacking hard and strong
>   things.[7]

Rulers and leaders were not exempt from the *wuwei* principle. Laozi remarks that 'ruling a large kingdom is like cooking small fish'; that is, the less stirring around the better the result will be. Many of the observations of the *Dao De Jing* contain specific advice to rulers to exemplify Daoism in all they do. It is pointed out that:

> Tao invariably takes no action, and yet there is nothing left
>   undone.
> If kings and barons can keep it, all things will transform
>   spontaneously.
> If, after transformation, they should desire to be active,
> I would restrain them with simplicity, which has no name.
> Simplicity, which has no name, is free of desires.

Being free of desires it is tranquil.
And the world will be at peace of its own accord.[8]

Laozi advocates a similar attitude even in the soldier who, he says, uses arms only when he cannot do otherwise:

> A skilful leader of troops is not aggressive with his military
> strength.
> A skilful fighter does not become angry . . .
> This is called the virtue of not-competing.
> This is called the strength to use man.
> This is called matching Heaven, the highest principle of old.[9]

The somewhat paradoxical finding of strength in non-violence and supremacy in lowliness illustrates a fundamental law of *Dao* expressed in the words:

> Reversion is the action of the Tao.
> Weakness is the function of the Tao.
> All things in the world come from being.
> And being comes from non-being.[10]

Another such law, derived from the essential character of the *Dao*, is the **yinyang** principle of the opposites of feminine and masculine, dark and light, activity and passivity, which are united within and, indeed, constitute the wholeness and comprehensiveness of the *Dao*. Laozi advocated the cultivation of an unaggressive receptivity, traditionally thought to be characteristic of the female, in any person seeking holiness and completion:

> He who knows the male (active force) and keeps to the female
> (the passive force or receptive element)
> Becomes the ravine of the world.
> Being the ravine of the world,
> He will never depart from eternal virtue . . . [11]

The invocation of the *yinyang* principle and the importance accorded to its feminine element are entirely consistent with the attitude of *wuwei* and a general search for balance and harmony. Laozi's commendation of female qualities was probably contrary to the conventional thought of his day, though it would have been consistent with a good deal of ancient myth and folklore current at the time. His concern was with finding a balanced vitality in which the contributory elements were never in conflict but always complemented and were nourished by each other to produce a harmonious unity. So for him, feminine and masculine were of equal importance and indispensable to each other. Moreover, in their reciprocity and mutuality they partook of the nature of the cosmos as a whole, of the universal forces of being and non-being which are elemental in the *Dao*.

The American philosopher, Arthur C. Danto has observed that Daoistic knowledge is practical rather than conceptual and that Laozi's teaching is 'deprecation of one sort of knowledge in favour of another'.[12] Danto also remarks that 'the [Daoist] thought that political felicity consists in permitting things to find their natural course is optimistic and radically naive',[13] and he cites Confucius' remark that 'If the Dao prevailed in the world, I should not be trying to alter things'.[14] Daoism does not seem fully to confront the problem of how it can begin to yield its proper consequences in a world that largely ignores its teaching. An even more serious problem is that which arises when we reflect on how things must be if or when the Daoist ideal of a mystical union with Nature is achieved, so that the individual self is lost in that it is absorbed into the life of the universe at large. For Daoism this is the supreme condition, the ultimate moral achievement; but the closing of the gap between the self and the world renders all ordinary conceptions of morality and virtue useless for, as Danto points out, 'exactly that space that Daoism intends to collapse is what makes morality possible at all'.[15] The conditions we ordinarily take as necessary for morality seem to disappear once the individuated consciousness is wholly lost.

In spite of these kinds of difficulties Daoism offers a conception of human life and the cosmos that is profoundly appealing. Its concerns are ones that are perennial and ubiquitous in human thought: What is the source of all things? Is there a meaning to life? What is Good? How should human life be lived? Its responses to these questions are not characteristic only of an oriental cast of mind; they also embody many of the presuppositions, conjectures and conclusions that are familiar in western philosophy and they express thoughts and ideas common to mysticism wherever it is found in human speculation. In Daoism it is always a union with nature that is sought. It teaches that such a union yields freedom, vital equilibrium and longevity. The person who lives the *Dao* avoids all excesses and never has a need to burn himself out and deplete his energy. Laozi thought that those who have a proper affinity with the natural world, who have a *de* [*te*], or spirit, that is in harmony with the universal *Dao*, are virtually invulnerable to what are often thought of as natural dangers:

A man endowed with plentiful *de* is comparable to a newborn infant: poisonous insects will not sting him, wild animals will not seize him in their claws, birds of prey will not carry him off in their talons; his bones are weak, his sinews supple, but his grasp is firm.[16]

Suppleness of body and breath control are important for the prolongation of life and for the maintenance of a serenity and openness which guarantee a mind so clear that it reflects and illumines the world. This is the condition of inner holiness and of longevity: Laozi has no belief in physical immortality. What he seems to advocate is a gradual purification of the mind so that, in old age, the death of the body is simply the culmination of a prolonged return to a union with all things.

Much of the *Dao De Jing* reads like a treatise on the personal and spiritual life but it has to be remembered that a part, at least, of its intention must have been to serve as a political manual for rulers during the Time of the Warring States (403–222 BCE), that unstable period in which the great states preyed on their lesser neighbours before pitting their enhanced strengths against each other, and which culminated in the third century BCE in the triumph of the Qin over the Zhou dynasty and the founding of an empire that endured for over two thousand years. It has been suggested that in these conflicts Daoism may have been invoked as a king of magic against crude, physical aggression. Its exponents might have been thought to have an insuperable and unassailable strength, drawn from their union with the strength of Nature as a whole, and a spiritual power of insight and influence derived from the same source.

When a man disappears by riding out of the life where he is known, much may be imagined or conjectured about what he does thereafter. Interest in Laozi developed into a cult and he eventually became revered as a god. A scroll discovered in a walled-up library at Dun Huang [Tun-huang] relates Laozi's transition from sage to god, describes his reappearances as the counsellor of successive emperors and quotes him as exhorting his followers to learn and recite *Dao De Jing*. The doctrine ascribed to him has developed in various ways since the Time of the Warring States, but it has unfalteringly retained and promulgated the ideal of a mystical union with Nature as its central concept. It has inspired the beautiful and dreamlike style of much Chinese landscape painting and its ethos of order and tranquillity has informed the architecture and patterns of many Chinese temples. The profound changes of twentieth-century China have not destroyed

Daoism. The China Daoist Association was officially established in Beijing [Peking] in 1957. Its aims are to unite all Chinese Daoists, to promote world peace, and to support Chinese socialism and a policy of religious freedom. Daoism is the leading religion in Taiwan, where it became firmly established in the seventeenth century and where many of its ancient practices have been retained in their traditional forms. There too, since 1964, at the instigation of a Dutch scholar, K.M. Schipper, careful research into the history of Daoism in all its forms has been conducted. Laozi and his book, the *Dao De Jing*, are now known all over the world.

Notes

1 Chan Wing-tsit, *A Source Book in Chinese Philosophy*, Princeton: Princeton University Press, 1963, p. 136.
2 *Tao-te Ching*, ch. 1, in Chan, op. cit., p. 139.
3 Ibid., ch. 25, p. 152.
4 Ibid., ch. 18, p. 148.
5 Ibid., ch. 38, p. 158.
6 Ibid., ch 57, p. 166.
7 Ibid., chs 66 and 78, pp. 170 and 174.
8 Ibid., ch. 37, p. 158.
9 Ibid., ch. 68, pp. 171, 172.
10 Ibid., ch. 40, p. 160.
11 Ibid., ch. 28, p. 154.
12 Arthur C. Danto, *Mysticism and Morality*, Harmondsworth: Penguin Books, 1976, p. 107.
13 Ibid., p. 114.
14 Ibid.
15 Ibid., p. 120.
16 *Tao-te Ching*, ch. 55, in Chan Wing-tsit, op. cit., p. 165.

Laozi's writing

The authorship of the *Dao De Jing* (Classic of the Virtue of the Tao) is attributed to Laozi although it is thought by some to be a compilation of the words and sayings of a number of Daoist thinkers. There are numerous translations of the work. See, for instance:

Chang Chung-yuan, *Tao: A New Way of Thinking. A Translation of the Tao-te Ching, with an Introduction and Commentaries*, New York: Harper & Row, 1975.
Waley, Arthur, *The Way and Its Power*, London and Sydney: Unwin Paperbacks, 1977.
Henricks, Robert G. (trans.), *Lao Tzu: Te-Tao Ching A New Translation based on the Recently-Discovered Ma-Wang-Tui Texts*, New York: Ballantyne, 1989.

See also in this book

Confucius, Mozi, Mencius, Xunzi, Huineng, Zhuxi, Dai Zhen, Mao Zedong, Xiong Shili

Sources and further reading

Chan Wing-tsit, *A Source Book in Chinese Philosophy*, Princeton: Princeton University Press, 1963

Chang Chung-yun, *Creativity and Taoism*, New York: Harper & Row, 1970

Danto, Arthur C., *Mysticism and Morality*, Harmondsworth: Penguin Books, 1976

Fung Yu-lan, *A History of Chinese Philosophy*, trans. D. Bodde, 2 vols, vol. I, Princeton: Princeton University Press, 1983

Hansen, C. *A Daoist Theory of Chinese Thought*, New York: Oxford University Press, 1992

Kaltemark, Max, *Lao Tzu and Taoism*, Stanford, Calif.: Stanford University Press, 1969

Needham, Joseph, *Science and Civilization in China*, 2 vols, vol. 2, Cambridge: Cambridge University Press, 1969

Watts, A., *Tao: The Watercourse Way*, Harmondsworth, Penguin Books, 1979

ZHUANGZI (CHUANG TZU) 369–286 BCE

Zhuangzi is regarded as the co-founder, with Laozi [Lao Tzu], of **Daoism** [Taoism], that distinctive style of philosophical thought that along with Confucianism and Buddhism has been a defining element in Chinese culture for more than two millennia.

The two thinkers espoused a common core of ideas, but their writings reveal differences of attitude and sensibility that not only define their individual characteristics but also enrich Daoist thought. In place of the often visionary and dreamlike nature of the *Laozi*, Zhuangzi's writings provide a commentary on the life of the world, a critique of Confucianism and a shrewd examination of language and knowledge. At the same time, his fundamental concerns are the personal experience and spiritual life of the seeker of Daoist reality. A tenet that pervades his thought is: 'There first must be a True Man before there can be true knowledge'.[1] His views are frequently expressed in allegories, fables and satirical anecdotes that are full of charm and humour, and he has been described as 'perhaps the most delightful writer in any literature'.[2]

Accounts of Zhuangzi's life are fragmentary and most of them have little more than the status of legend. The historian, Sima Qian [Ssu-ma Ch'ien], writing in the closing years of the second century BCE, informs us that Zhuangzi was born in the province of Meng, south of the Yellow River, and that he worked as a government official. This was in China's feudal age when the country consisted of a number of states whose allegiance was to the royal house of Zhou [Chou]. Sima Qian tells us that Zhuangzi is eventually renounced all involvement in public affairs, refusing in forthright terms King Wei's invitation to become his chief government minister. He is reported to have greeted the king's messengers with good-humoured contempt saying 'Go away, do not defile me . . . I prefer the enjoyment of my own free will.'[3] The story may not be strictly accurate in detail, but it vividly conveys to us the characteristic picture of an oriental sage: a person of independent mind, prepared to reject worldly success and conventional wisdom in order to engage in a way of life that is satisfying to his personal vision and spirituality.

Certainty concerning the authenticity of writings attributed to Zhuangzi is as elusive as that relating to accounts of his life. The extant text consists of thirty-three chapters believed to have been reduced from fifty-two that were in existence in the fourth century CE. Of these thirty-three, seven are known as the Inner Chapters and are regarded as the work of Zhuangzi. The remainder, the Outer Chapters, have many features characteristic of Zhuangzi's cast of mind but also show developments and interpretations that were probably introduced by early commentators. It has been pointed out that the Inner Chapters, although shrewd and penetrating, have a more benign approach than the somewhat acerbic and condemnatory Outer Chapters.

Although Zhuangzi's frequent intent is to point out failings in Confucian teaching, his representation of Confucius is not always consistent and can be confusing to the reader. Sometimes Confucius is made straightforwardly to deliver his own teaching so that it can be confounded by a Daoist protagonist, but at other times he is made the actual mouthpiece of Daoist confutations of his own pronouncements. Both Zhuangzi and Confucius believed that life was to be lived in accordance with the **Dao** [Tao], or Way, but they differed significantly in their views of what was required to do that. According to Confucian doctrine, human and social well-being are achieved by the development of personal qualities through strict adherence to numerous clearly-defined rules of both private and public conduct. The chief virtues sought are compassion, or 'human-heartedness' (**ren**, *jen*); a sense of duty and justice (**i**, *yi*); the ability to act supremely well within the rules of one's tradition and culture (**li**); and a wisdom (**zhi**, *chih*) that accrues from a lived understanding of and spontaneous obedience to 'the Dao of Heaven'.[4] The Confucian Dao is a kind of complex moral principle wrought from fundamental elements of human social and ethical propensities, and Confucian teaching is based on the presupposition that right effort will result in attainment of a personal, social and cosmic harmony appropriate to the Confucian ideal of the 'Superior Man'.[5] In contrast with the objective clarity of Confucianism, Zhuangzi rejects the whole idea of attempting to achieve a defined and public end by defined and overt means. He is comprehensively sceptical about the imposition of orderliness or method on what he sees as the amorphous and unrestricted flux of reality. For him, the unceasing transformations of Nature are themselves the Dao, and the Dao is not found through the practice of certain disciplines and rituals; indeed, it is everywhere, and is not *found* or striven for at all, because 'the Way is to man as rivers and lakes are to fish, the natural condition of life'.[6] Participation in Dao requires an immersion in that natural condition and a recognition of its multiplicity and its unity so that the differences and contrasts of daily living, on which so much importance is commonly placed, are experienced as mere superficialities. The sage, we are told, 'embraces things. Ordinary men discriminate among them and parade their discriminations before others'.[7] For the person who realizes all this there are, according to Zhuangzi, no profound dualities or opposites. Instead, there is a lively awareness of the interconnectedness and wholeness of things. Thus Zhuangzi writes: 'Heaven and earth were born at the same time I was, and the ten thousand things are one with me.'[8]

Underlying this metaphysic is the conception, derived from Laozi, of the relationship between Dao and De, On this conception, Dao is the fundamental and formless One that is the ground of De, all the countless, particular forms. In chapter 12 we read: 'in the great beginning there was nonbeing; there was no being, no name. Out of it arose One; there was One but it had no form. Things got hold of it and came to life and it was called Virtue.'[9]

The implications of Zhuangzi's participatory mysticism are manifold, not least in respect of a person's inner life and attitude to the world. When differences and oppositions are dissolved there is no pursuit of particular, defined aims or ambitions. Decisions about how to act are not reached by calculation; rather, they emerge as a kind of natural necessity or inevitability from one's state of harmony with the cosmos. Zhuangzi says: 'The world can't decide what is right and what is wrong. And yet inaction can decide this.'[10]

But the burning question is: How exactly is the condition of spiritual lightness and freedom described by Zhuangzi to be reached?

It is clear that, in his view, zealous striving and endeavour will achieve nothing. What seems to be required is much more like a letting go, the creation of a mental space or emptiness in which an awareness of the nature of the Dao can develop. Zhuangzi's True Man has to 'unlearn' the ordinary ways of living and must cultivate a consciousness that perceives the world afresh through a minute-to-minute questioning of every presupposition that has bound him or her in a false relationship with the world. Such a person is liberated from those unthinkingly acquired assumptions and is able to abandon the constructed social self, becoming free to inhabit nature as an element in it rather than as a separate entity pitted against it.

It should not be thought that this kind of affinity with the world necessitates a simple passivity. Proper action, we are told, is a form of inaction; it is **wuwei**, conduct that exhibits an awareness of the qualities and modes of existence of things. This means that actions are performed with a sensibility that reveals a care and respect for all forms and ways of being. Zhuangzi's story of the cutting of the carcass an ox vividly exemplifies what is meant by this. In the story, the butcher, Cook Ting describes how, through many years of careful practice, he has acquired the skill of slipping his knife in just the right hollows and interstices of a carcass, never blunting his blade and working in such a way that 'the whole thing falls apart'. Perception and understanding, he says, have come to a stop 'and spirit moves where it wants. I go along with the natural make-up . . . I never touch the smallest ligament or tendon'. Wenhui, for whom Cook Ting is cutting the ox, sees this as a parable for living. He declares: 'I have heard the words of Cook Ting and learned how to care for life!'[11]

Zhuangzi rejected conventional methods of ruling a nation or society. Like Laozi, he advocated government through non-government, maintaining that if the people are left alone their De will function naturally and truly. His advice to rulers consists largely of a series of stories that illustrate the hurt, confusion and discontent that result from meddling in the lives of others. The ruler, he urges, should be a man who 'makes sure of himself first and then [he] acts. He makes absolutely certain that things can do what they are supposed to do, that is all.'[12] Rulers are advised to look at everything in relation to the Dao: 'Look at words in the light of the Way – then the Sovereign of the world will be upright. Look at distinctions in the light of the Way – then the duty of sovereign and subject will be clear. Look at abilities in the light of the Way – then the officials of the world will be well ordered. Look everywhere in the light of the Way – then the response of the ten thousand things will be complete.'[13]

Zhuangzi's critique of knowledge is thoroughly consonant with his fundamental stance concerning the unity of all things. He points out that what is generally counted as knowledge is knowledge of *differences* in the world. Such distinctions, he holds, are superficial and misleading and, moreover, they generate dissent and division by separating things instead of recognizing their oneness. He points out that we each make our claims to knowledge from a particular and finite point of view, and that each individual believes in the rightness of his or her own assertions. But, he argues, all these views are in fact merely relative and partial. What has to be understood is that there is a higher point of view that transcends all particular, finite and partial views and from which there are no final judgements about the rightness and wrongness of anything, but only the understanding that there are just a great many ever-shifting views. The individual who never realizes this and who continues to insist on the rightness of his own assertions is like the frog at the bottom of a well who sees only a small patch of sky above and therefore takes the sky to be only as large as the patch he can see.

Zhuangzi directed a similarly penetrating scrutiny on language and words. He saw words as attempts to pin down things and classify them, to make static and crystalline what is changeful and fluid. In short, he deemed words inadequate to the task of describing the true nature of things. Thus he endorses Laozi's view that if the Way is made clear, it is not the Way.

The richness of Zhuangzi's thought defies summary or encapsulation. If it has a single, dominant characteristic it must be his pervasive aspiration to dissolve the habits of thought that ordinarily limit our experience. Everything he says manifests a freshness of vision that rejects all dogma and nourishes a sensibility to the living, thriving, ever-transforming natural world. Typically, this vision is achieved by a transmutation of passion or striving into a yielding to an elemental way of inhabiting reality. This conception of the true nature of things exerted considerable influence on Chinese culture. In particular, Chinese painters and artists developed an intimate awareness of the qualities of their materials and their aptness for depicting the fluid harmonies of natural things. But of course, Daoist affinities are evident in many philosophies and cultures: in Zen Buddhism, especially in the near-mystical illumination of the *satori*; in Indian philosophy and religion; in the Heracleitan notion of flux; in Platonism, Neo-platonism and in many other mystical veins of thought too numerous to be listed.

A distinctive characteristic that often imbues Zhuangzi's writing with a happy radiance is his humorous lightness of touch. He had the capacity to temper the solemnity of cosmic wonder with a reminder of the absurdity of human intellectual constructions. 'Where', he once cried, 'can I find a man who has forgotten words so that I can have a word with him?'[14]

Notes

1 Watson, Burton (trans.), *The Complete Works of Chuang Tzu*, New York: Columbia University Press, 1968, p. 77.
2 Danto, Arthur C., *Mysticism and Morality*, Harmondsworth: Penguin Books, 1972, p. 106.
3 Giles, Herbert A., *Introduction to Chuang Tsu*, New York: Paragon Books, 1964.
4 For an interesting account of these virtues see the *Companion Encyclopaedia of Asian Philosophy*, eds Brian Carr and Indira Mahalingam, London: Routledge, 1998, pp. 522–5.
5 See the essay on Confucius in this book.
6 Watson, op. cit.
7 Ibid., p. 44.
8 Ibid., p. 43.
9 Ibid., p. 131.
10 Ibid., p. 191.
11 Ibid., pp. 50, 51.
12 Ibid., p. 93.
13 Ibid., p. 126.
14 Ibid., p. 302.

Zhuangzi's writings

There are numerous translations and editions of Zhuangzi's writings. The translation chiefly used in this essay is:

Watson, Burton (trans.), *The Complete Works of Chuang Tzu*, New York: Columbia University Press, 1968.

See also in this book

Confucius, Laozi, Xunzi

Sources and further reading

Carr, Brian and Mahalingam, Indira (eds), *Companion Encyclopaedia of Asian Philosophy*, London and New York: Routledge, 1997, Part IV
Danto, Arthur C., *Mysticism and Morality*, Harmondsworth: Penguin Books, 1972
Fung Yu-lan, *A History of Chinese Philosophy*, trans. D. Bodde, Princeton: Princeton University Press, 1953, vol. I

HANFEIZI (HAN FEI TZU) *c.*280–233 BCE

The Master Hanfei is the last and philosophically most sophisticated member of the important school of ancient Chinese philosophy known as Legalism. Legalism, like a number of the other major schools of Chinese thought considered in this book, is a product of the violent and unstable but philosophically inventive period in Chinese history known as the Time of the Warring States, 403–222 BCE. During this period, China as a unified state did not exist. The territory which was eventually to become China was divided into seven powerful and fifteen less powerful states, all vying with each other for political advantage. The history of the period is one of constant alliance, counter-alliance, of treaties made and broken, and above all of warfare. What was chronically absent was political stability. The central question on the minds of rulers and philosophers alike was that of how to gain and then retain real political power. Legalism, developed for somewhat over a century, was formulated as an answer to this question: it is an example of a philosophy that is the exact reverse of armchair speculation. It is an attempt to answer an urgent, practical problem of real seriousness.

Hanfei was unusual among ancient Chinese philosophers in being of noble birth, a prince of the ruling family of the state of Han. It is said that he studied under the eminent Confucian Xunzi and that one of his fellow students was Lisi (Li Ssu, d. 208 BCE), the man destined to be the cause of Hanfei's death. Hanfei was greatly concerned by the insecurity of the state of Han. Because he did not speak well – he suffered from a bad speech impediment – he committed his concerns to writing, firstly in the form of remonstrances to the ruler of Han, and then in the form of the book that bears his name, the *Hanfeizi*. The ruler of Han, King An, was unimpressed. Far more impressed was Qin Shih-huang-di [Ch'in Shih-huang-ti], the ruler of the powerful state of Qin [Ch'in] and the man destined ultimately to unify China and end the Time of the Warring States. In the pursuit of political supremacy for Qin, Qin Shih-huang-di invaded Han in 234 BCE, and the Han ruler sent Hanfei to Qin as an envoy. Before he could see the Qin ruler, however, Lisi, by this time Prime Minister of Qin, persuaded the latter that Hanfei could not be trusted, since his loyalties must always be suspect. Accordingly, Hanfei was imprisoned and sent poison by Lisi. Having no way to defend himself, Hanfei took the poison (233 BCE).

Hanfei's philosophy is the culmination of Legalism. He takes the ideas of earlier writers in this school – notably the writers of the compilation we know as *The Book of Lord Shang* (probably put together over almost a century and complete by the end of the third century BCE), Shen Pu-hai (d. 337 BCE) and Shenzi (350–275 BCE?) – and, adding his own emphases, produces from them a comprehensive set of political recommendations. Like *The Book of Lord Shang* and in the western tradition Machiavelli's *The Prince*, the *Hanfeizi* is a manual for rulers: it sets out policies and guidelines for producing a strong and stable state and a secure position for its ruler. Success in politics, according to Hanfei, will come only if the ruler pays full attention to three features of political life: the law (*fa*); statecraft (*shu*, i.e. the art of conducting political business and of handling people) and power (*shih*).

As in all political and moral philosophies, the policies and values advocated by Hanfei rest on a set of assumptions about human nature. Not unexpectedly – being both of an admirer of *The Book of Lord Shang* and a pupil of Xunzi – Hanfei regards human beings, generally, as very unpleasant creatures indeed. In his view, human beings are naturally idle, greedy, cowardly, treacherous, unwise and inconsistent. No one can be trusted, from the rulers of other states to one's own family and intimates. As he notes, 'Consorts and concubines long for the early death of the ruler'[1] and history supplies an abundance of examples of sons who have betrayed their fathers. Quite typical is the conclusion: 'Prepare as you may against those who hate you, calamity will come to you from those you love.'[2]

How then is the ruler, with this unpromising raw material to work with, to achieve his goals of hegemony for his state and security for himself? The prime means, as the name of the school of thought might suggest, is by the use of the law. The ruler must establish a clear and comprehensive body of law, to be administered – at least in theory – absolutely even-handedly to persons of all ranks in society. (When first announced, this policy was little short of revolutionary: prior to Legalism, each state in China was in practice governed by the noble families in each of its states in a feudal manner. There were no public laws in any modern sense, only the customs (*li*) of the noble families. It can be assumed that these customs were favourable to those in power, and were anything but even-handed.) Human beings can be controlled and made useful to the state only by the use of what Hanfei calls 'the two handles', i.e. rewards and punishments, and these rewards and punishments are to be embodied in the law. As he puts it: 'for correcting the faults of superiors, chastising the misdeeds of subordinates, restoring order, exposing error, checking excess, remedying evil, and unifying the standards of the people, nothing can compare to law.'[3] Of the many benefits claimed for this system, one of the most significant is that it has political stability (the longed-for goal of those alive during the Warring States period) built in: when the state is run in accordance with the laws, there is no need to rely on finding men of talent or goodness, who are exceedingly rare, to occupy the important posts in the administration. Instead, the legalist system is designed to run itself: 'the way of the enlightened ruler is to unify the laws instead of seeking for wise men, to lay down firm policies instead of longing for men of good faith. Hence his laws never fail him, and there is no felony or deceit among his officials.'[4]

The law is to be the only source of values permitted in the state. Any alternative value systems – which in practice meant the other philosophies current at the time, notably Mohism but especially Confucianism – are not to be tolerated. The reason for the venom with which Hanfei (in common with other Legalists) attacks Confucianism is that the latter includes values – righteousness or benevolence (*ren*), filial piety and so on – which may cause those who hold them to put a personal or family interest before that of the state. Hanfei is clear that 'the interests of the state and the individual are mutually at odds, and both cannot prevail at the same time.'[5] Hence the major values and practices of Confucianism are characterized by Hanfei as 'the five vermin', and he regularly describes as parasites and hangers-on those literati who sought to make a living by advising rulers along Confucian lines.[6] Such people are breeders of sedition and political weakness, and should be treated accordingly. The only paths to reward in the state should be military service or agricultural work, since these are the two essential contributors to a strong state. Anyone not engaged in either of these forms of activity is a passenger.

The ruler, then, manifests *shih* or power via a rigorously enforced system of rewards and punishments; the latter are to be especially severe, with death or mutilation as their almost invariant forms. Yet there is more to being a successful ruler than simply establishing a legal system which makes service to the state in some form the only acceptable value and punishes any divergence from the law with great brutality. The ruler must also have a firm grip on *shu*, the methods of government: ways to handle people so as to accomplish his own purposes and thwart those of his enemies, both outside the state and within it. Almost since its inception, Legalism had been influenced by Daoist ideas, and this is specially pronounced in Hanfei's description of what it is like to be a master of *shu*: he manifestly has in mind the Taoist concept of **wuwei** or actionless activity, an utterly spontaneous and masterly reaction to the prevailing situation. Thus he advises the ruler in Daoist vocabulary: 'Do not let your power be seen; be blank and actionless. The sage holds to the source and the four quarters come to serve him. In emptiness he awaits them, and they spontaneously do what is needed.'[7] He also gives some more straightforward advice on *shu*: for example, the ruler must take care not to enrich any citizen to so great an extent that the latter can afford to turn against him. Again, he must be sure to destroy any group or clique within the power structure without compunction, since, 'The only reason the ministers do not assassinate their sovereign is that their parties and cliques are not strong enough.'[8]

A further aspect of *shu* on which Hanfei lays some stress he terms 'forms and names' (*xing-ming*: Hanfei borrowed the terminology from another of the schools of philosophy of the Warring States period, the School of Names, *ming jia*, but has given the terms a purely political meaning rather than the logical sense of their original context). By 'name' he means the name of a political office, the duties attached to it and any proposals made by its holder, and by 'form' he means the actual performance of the holder of the office. The ruler is to ensure that name and form exactly coincide, and any deviation of form from name is to be punished. Such a policy, Hanfei argues, will bring uniformity and stability, or as he puts it, 'Use the single Way and make names the head of it. When names are correct, things stay in place; when names are twisted, things shift about.'[9] Knowing that this is the policy in force, officials will be punctilious in carrying out their duties but will not overreach themselves, and the ruler will know exactly what is going on.

The efficacy of these policies for a certain period of time is beyond doubt, since the practice of them by the state of Qin resulted in that state overwhelming its neighbours and uniting China in 210 BCE under Qin Shih-huang-di. This first emperor of a unified China was careful to observe the Legalist injunction to tolerate no sources of value in the state beyond the law, since it was in the name of that doctrine that he ordered one of history's most notorious Burnings of Books, in 213 BCE. Yet the fact that his dynasty fell three years after his death, to be replaced by the Han in 206 BCE, indicates the real source of difficulty in this philosophy. It makes the assumption that there is effectively no limit to the amount of oppression and brutality which the populace will bear nor to the length of time for which they will bear it, and this assumption is false. No subsequent Chinese dynasty sought to base its administration on undiluted Legalism. Yet this sort of totalitarian thinking is manifestly of far more than historical interest. The history of the twentieth century alone, for example, makes it clear how readily *realpolitik* of this kind based on a single ideology can take hold and at what cost. Legalism is a paradigmatic example of the sort of state-centred politics which recurs only too readily when the appropriate conditions arise.

Notes

(All page references are to Burton Watson's *Basic Writings of Han Fei Tzu*, full details of which are given below.)

1 *Hanfeizi*, section 17, p. 85.
2 Ibid., sect. 17, p. 86.
3 Ibid., sect. 6, p. 28.
4 Ibid., sect. 49, p. 109.
5 Ibid., sect. 49, p. 107.
6 e.g. Ibid., sect. 49, *passim*.
7 Ibid., sect. 8, p. 35.
8 Ibid., sect. 8, p. 40.
9 Ibid., sect. 8, p. 36.

Hanfei's writings

The Complete Works of Han Fei Tzu, trans. W.K. Liao, 2 vols, London: Probsthain, 1939 and 1959
Basic Writings of Han Fei Tzu, trans. Burton Watson, New York: Columbia University Press, 1963.

See also in this book

Confucius, Mozi, Mencius, Laozi, Xunzi

Sources and further reading

Ames, R.T. *The Art of Rulership: A Study of Ancient Chinese Political Thought*, Albany: SUNY Press, 1994
Fung Yu-lan, *A History of Chinese Philosophy*, vol. I, ch. XIII (See General Bibliography at the end of this book for full details of this work.)
Hsiao Kung-chuan, *A History of Chinese Political Thought*, trans. F.W. Mote, Princeton: Princeton University Press, 1979
Wu Kuo-cheng, *Ancient Chinese Political Theories*, Shanghai: Commercial Press, 1933
'Shang Yang', *The Book of Lord Shang*, trans. J.J.L. Duyvendak, London: Probsthain, 1928. Reissued with Sun Tzu's *The Art of War*, intro. by R. Wilkinson, Ware: Wordsworth, 1998

XUNZI (HSUN TZU) *c.*320–*c.*230 BCE

Xunzi [Hsun Tzu] (also known as Hsun K'uang, Hsun Ch'ing or Ch'ing Tzu) was a Confucian who lived during the second half of the Warring States period (403–222 BCE), a time when the states that were later to compose China vied with each other for political power and ascendancy. This era was characterized by political instability and violence. Paradoxically, there were also huge developments in intellectual and civic life and trade and, predictably, in the techniques of warfare. China became unified in 221 BCE under the ruling house of the state of Qin [Ch'in] in western China. Given this historical background, it is unsurprising that there is in Xunzi's writings a moderate strain of Legalism, a group of political theories which, at their most extreme, advocated complete and unquestioning obedience to the state and its laws, however oppressive, as the only source of moral standards.[1] According to Xunzi, the promulgations of a true ruler should be obeyed, as he alone has access to true knowledge. Xunzi attempted to synthesize the various strands of philosophical thinking current during his time. As a Confucian, he advocated training in and obedience to *li*, the elaborate code of ritual which governed familial, social and professional relationships. He endorsed certain aspects of **Daoism**, the teachings on the ultimate, unchanging an ineffable Way, or source or principle of the natural and moral orders. His interests extended to the logical aspects of language, including a philosophical issue which is known as the 'rectification of names'.[2] The thought of Xunzi forms a highly integrated philosophical system, and in the course of his writings he comprehensively criticizes the work of earlier philosophers, particularly Mencius, Mozi [Mo Tzu] and Zhuangzi [Chuang Tzu].

There is little information about the life of Xunzi. Even his dates are uncertain, although it is known that he was active between 298 and 238 BCE. In the *Shi Chi* [*Shiji*] (Historical Records, a compilation from the first century BCE), the historian Sima Qian [Ssu-ma Ch'ien] says that Xunzi was born in Zhao [Chao] in northern China, now the province of Shanshi and Henan. At the age of about 50, he travelled east to the coastal state of Ji where, a generation earlier, the newly-emergent ruling dynasty had begun to attract many of the leading Chinese intellectuals. In Ji, Xunzi's talents were recognized, and he was three times given the important ceremonial duty of pouring the sacrificial wine. As a result, he was slandered and in order to avoid confrontation with his enemies he moved to the vast southern state of Chu, an area now including the provinces of Hunan and Hubei and the seaport of Shanghai. In Chu he was appointed to the magistracy of the city of Lanling, only to lose his post on the overthrow of the ruler. For the times, Xunzi seems to have lived a quiet and unremarkable life of study and teaching. Amongst his students were the Legalist Hanfeizi [Han Fei Tzu], and Lisi [Li Ssu], afterwards as Prime Minister of Qin to play a leading part in the unification of China.

The text which bears his name was probably written partly by Xunzi and partly by other scholars contemporary with him. Xunzi had as an example of philosophical writing the *Mozi* [*Mo Tzu*], which included several self-contained essays each written on a different theme, a structure which he followed. The style of the *Xunzi* [*Hsun Tzu*] is less repetitive and more sophisticated than that of the *Mozi*. With its careful analysis of the key terms used, which is a reflection of the absorption in issues of language, the *Xunzi* has a strikingly modern ring to it.

Although Xunzi and Mencius were both Confucians, one issue of fundamental controversy between the two was that of what human nature is really like. Mencius had maintained that humankind is innately good: virtue is the fulfilment of natural capacities. Human beings become evil when they lose their natural tendency towards goodness.[3] In total contrast, Xunzi declared: 'Man's nature is evil; goodness is the result of conscious activity.'[4] He uses both a metaphor and an argument to say that human beings are basically evil. The metaphor, which employs an analogy between goodness and straightness, is that of a warped piece of wood which must be steamed and hammered to become straight; it can never become so of its own accord. The argument is the following: we lack what we desire; in our original state, we can only desire to be and to do good; therefore, goodness is not part of our original nature. According to Xunzi, human nature is always and everywhere the same, and it consists of whatever we do spontaneously or instinctively. All human beings are born with unreflective, unlimited, self-centred and indiscriminate desires such as envy and hate, and the urge to have sensations. If the satisfaction of these impulses were pursued in an unregulated way, the result would be wantonness, irresponsibility, strife and disorder. The achievement of moral goodness is dependent on the development of our reflective conscious activity or intellectual faculties, which can restrain, though not suppress, our destructive desires and emotions. Both intellectual development and good government can best be encouraged through education or training in and obedience to *li*, the elaborate Confucian principles of propriety which govern every aspect of human behaviour and lead to the practice of **ren** [jen]; that is, benevolence or humaneness.[5] Xunzi thus sets up a bipolar opposition between nature and culture. Whatever is natural is evil and undirected, and can be restrained only by cultural forces. Our moral values are grounded in culture, not nature. He challenges Mencius' evidence for innate natural goodness, particularly in Mencius' example that each one of us would rescue a child if it were about to fall down a well, on the grounds that the illustration is not decisive. The rescue could be the result of training, not spontaneity. If, as Mencius maintained, human beings were naturally good, there would be no need for political authority and social ritual, nor for rewards and punishments, which are the final sanction used to curb the destructive natural tendencies of human beings.

The issue of human nature is one of absorbing interest to many philosophers in both the western and the eastern traditions, and serves as the foundation for much subsequent philosophical theorizing, particularly in political and social thought. However, there are problems with any claim that certain human characteristics are natural, whereas others are due to culture. No satisfactory way has yet been found to separate what is natural from what is the result of socialization. More extreme positions, favoured by many recent western philosophers, are based on the view that human beings have no essence or nature; we are either wholly a product of socialization, or we have a wide choice about what we are to become.

Xunzi regards moral goodness in purely humanistic terms. Unlike Mencius, he does not consider morality to be a component part of the balance or harmony of the cosmos, nor does he engage in Mencian metaphysical speculation about *qi* [*ch'i*], that spiritual part of us which is responsible for our individuality.[6] Moral goodness, for Xunzi, is wisdom. We are all theoretically capable of becoming perfectly wise, just as we are all physically capable of walking to the ends of the earth, but none of us has done or will do so, because we lack the willpower. The sage-kings have the best-developed intellectual faculties and thus the most wisdom. It is they who institute rituals and laws for their subjects to follow. Thereafter, wisdom decreases with social rank, through the 'man of breeding', the 'petty man' and the 'menial'.[7]

Xunzi gives vital importance to the role of the teacher, who functions in much the same way as the guru in Buddhist or Hindu tradition. We do not become wise through the acquisition of a body of propositional knowledge, or 'knowledge-that', but by knowing how to act or, more fundamentally, how to be. Our teachers are our guide to wisdom, and we should follow their example. We should also choose morally good friends and companions, as their loyalty, respect and benevolence will enhance our own. Xunzi quotes with approval a text that contains the advice, 'If you do not know a man, look at his friends; if you do not know a ruler, look at his attendants'.[8]

Mozi criticized music as being a waste of time, effort and resources,[9] but Xunzi considered some music to have a useful social function. Performances can create a sense of cohesion between the members of the audience. In the words of the *Xunzi*,

> When [music] is performed within the household, and father and sons, elder and younger brothers listen to it together, there are none who are not filled with a spirit of harmonious kinship. And when it is performed within the community, and old and young together listen to it, there are none who are not filled with a spirit of harmonious obedience . . . And yet Mo Tzu [Mozi] criticises it. Why?[10]

Music, according to Xunzi, can act as a channel for the emotions, so that they are not used in a manner harmful to society. When tranquil, it promotes obedience to the laws, and when stern and majestic, it promotes social order. Wild or licentious music should be censored, on the grounds that it is detrimental to society: it leads to disorder, depravity and rebellion. Music can be a reflection of Dao, or the Way; the diversity of the sounds made by different instruments blend into a unity, just as all particulars have their place in an all-encompassing, unified structure or pattern.

The social effect of art has been of pervasive interest in the western philosophical tradition from Plato to Tolstoy and the Marxists. Plato (427–347 BCE) gave the first case in the west for censorship. He, like Xunzi, believed that wild music would encourage licentious behaviour and should thus be banned, whereas music which was restrained and dignified would promote noble and orderly conduct.[11]

Like Mozi, Xunzi was concerned with maximizing benefit to society, and his social and political philosophy is underpinned by his theory of human nature. If there were no social distinctions, the evil in human nature would flourish, disorder and chaos would result, and there would be no material progress. There should thus be a rigid social hierarchy, with each person's social position being determined by ability and skill. Everyone should have their own specific duties or tasks, and should not try to interfere with the responsibilities of others. The perfect society would be unchanging; its social strata would be set up and maintained by obedience to *li*, or the Confucian rituals of propriety. Maximum social order and benefit is to be achieved under the control of just one wise ruler, a recommendation that could obviously lead to political authoritarianism, however benevolent. There is also an anti-historical strain to Xunzi's work. Behind particular historical and social events lies an unchanging, all-embracing order and unity, the Way or Dao, which encompasses all individual things and processes.

There are many similarities between Xunzi's perfect society and that of Plato in *The Republic*. Both achieve order or harmony through their hierarchical structure, and the social stratum to which people belong is decided by their levels of training and ability. Plato's philosopher-rulers have attained wisdom by their insight into an ultimate reality which lies behind history and change, as has Xunzi's sage-king.

Mozi, Zhuangzi, the legalists and the logicians are comprehensively criticized by Xunzi for not having found and followed the Dao. All were obsessed by only one aspect of the Way. Mozi was exclusively concerned with material benefit, the legalists with strong government and state policy, the logicians with language and Zhuangzi with metaphysical speculation, particularly about Heaven, which Xunzi regarded primarily as the source of natural laws and regularities such as the order of the seasons. According to Xunzi, the Way resolves all particulars, paradoxes and distinctions by transcending them; it is unchanging, all-encompassing and all-enfolding. To discover and follow the Way is to attain enlightenment. Everyone is theoretically capable of its discovery, but only the few who achieve wisdom actually find it. The mind is compared to a container of water; if it is still, it will become clear, but if it is disturbed, the sediment in the water will be stirred up. Similarly, Xunzi says,

> If you guide [the mind] with reason, nourish it with clarity, and do not allow external objects to unbalance it, then it will be capable of determining right and wrong and of resolving doubts. But if you allow petty external objects to pull it about, so that its proper form becomes altered and its inner balance is upset, then it will not be capable of making even gross distinctions.[12]

The mind or intellect must become still, clear, emptied and unified in order to open itself to an understanding of and obedience to the Way. It must resist all distractions, such as a longing for the past or anxiety about the future, as such factors will cloud the understanding. A lack of understanding will cause moral and social disorder and even confusion in our sensory judgements. We should not empty our minds by ignoring particular facts or sense-impressions, but should cut through or go beyond them to discern the pattern or structure beneath. We should resolve the apparent distinction between ourselves and the rest of existence, as all things ultimately form a unity. In following the Way, *wuwei* is achieved. There is action through inaction, and effortlessness through effort; we and the processes of nature are one. Sage-kings and wise teachers have found the Way and should leave markers, in the form of Confucian rituals, as a guide for the unenlightened.

Xunzi's belief that what is real is ultimately one and unified is similar to that of the Dutch philosopher Benedict Spinoza (1632–77). Spinoza denied that what exists is merely an aggregate of discrete and isolated elements. Instead, he maintained that all things are modes or aspects of an infinite whole, which is God or nature.[13]

The interest that Xunzi displayed in the reform of language, or the 'rectification of names',[14] was partly on social and partly on logical grounds. Language is a social phenomenon which functions primarily as a means of communication, and is at its most useful when it is fixed and clear, not shifting and ephemeral. Words are conventional: to use a modern example, the English 'knee' and the French 'genou' both refer to the same part of the body. Clarity in language is a pointer to the Way. It helps the understanding, particularly of laws and ritual, and thus reinforces the social order. By contrast, confusion in language tends to promote social disorder and is detrimental to our search for the Way. The sorry state of language in his time was, according to Xunzi, caused partly by the indiscriminate introduction of strange and obscure new terminology, particularly by philosophers and logicians. Only the sage-kings should create new words as and when needed, thus ensuring the political control of language. The focus of Xunzi's involvement with the logical aspects of language was on classification. One common name or noun was to be used for all things of one class, and a different noun for things of another class. Classes are distinguished by their similarities and differences. All horses, for example, have similar forms or shapes, and all human beings have different forms from horses, but similar forms to each other. The similarities and differences are real qualities, belonging to extra-mental things, and are open to discrimination by the senses working in conjunction with the intellect. If a thing undergoes natural development, the same name is used to refer to it at all stages; for example, a youth who becomes an old man is regarded as one and the same person throughout. Some classes and their corresponding nouns are more general than, and incorporate, other classes and their names: for example, 'horse' is a more general term than, and includes, 'white horse'. A reliance on the different degrees of generality enabled Xunzi to resolve the logical confusion of the thinker Gongsun Long [Kung-sun Lung] (born c.380 BCE), who stated that a white horse is not a horse. According to Gongsun Long, the term 'horse' does not exclusively refer to white horses, as it can be used of black and yellow horses as well. Thus, 'white horse' is the name of a different and distinct class from 'horse', and a white horse is not a horse.[15] For Xunzi, 'white horse' refers to a class of things which is more restricted than, but included in, the class of things to which the name 'horse' refers. In modern terminology, being a horse is a necessary, but not a sufficient, condition of being a white horse.

Western philosophy throughout its history has been concerned with issues of logic and language. Many linguists, such as Ferdinand de Saussure (1857–1913), have pointed out that the form of words is conventional, and Xunzi's view that only the sage-kings should be in control of language is similar to the contemporary position that power groups such as the media have an influence over the language used in society. In the twentieth century, there has been much discussion about the relationship of language to reality. Linguistic relativists take the view that language creates or constructs what we take to be reality, but Xunzi would be in agreement with their opponents who maintain that there is an extra-linguistic reality, which language can describe.

Notes

1 For a discussion on a form of legalism, see the essay on Hanfeizi, pp. 254–8 in this book.
2 See the essays on Confucius and Laozi, pp. 217–26 and pp. 240–8 in this book.
3 See the essay on Mencius, pp. 233–40 in this book.
4 Burton Watson, *Basic Writings of Mo Tzu, Hsun Tzu and Han Fei Tzu*, New York and London: Columbia University Press, 1967, p. 157.
5 See the essay on Confucius, pp. 217–26 in this book.
6 See the essay on Mencius, pp. 233–40 in this book.
7 Watson, op. cit., Part II, pp. 168–9.
8 Watson, op. cit., Part II, p. 171.
9 See the essay on Mozi, pp. 226–33 in this book.
10 Watson, op. cit., Part II, p. 113.
11 See Plato, *The Republic*, many editions, Book Two.
12 Watson, op. cit., Part II, pp. 131–2.
13 See Spinoza, *Ethics*, trans. R. Elwes, New York: Dover, 1955, Part I.
14 See the essay on Confucius, pp. 217–26 in this book.
15 Chan Wing-tsit, *A Source Book in Chinese Philosophy*, Princeton: Princeton University Press, 1963, p. 126.

Xunzi's writings

There are extensive selections from Xunzi's writings in the following publications:

Chan Wing-tsit, *A Source Book of Chinese Philosophy*, Princeton: Princeton University Press, 1963, ch. 6.

Fung Yu-lan, *A History of Chinese Philosophy*, 2 vols., trans. D. Bodde, Princeton: Princeton University Press, 1983, vol. I, ch. XII.

Watson, Burton, *The Basic Writings of Mo Tzu, Hsun Tzu and Han Fei Tzu*, New York and London: Columbia University Press, 1967.

See also in this book

Confucius, Mozi, Mencius, Laozi, Zhuangzi, Hanfeizi, Kang Youwei

Sources and further reading

Chan Wing-tsit, *A Source Book in Chinese Philosophy*, Princeton: Princeton University Press, 1963.

Cua, A.S., *Ethical Argumentation: A Study in Hsun Tzu's Moral Epistemology*, Honolulu: University of Hawaii Press, 1985.

Fung Yu-lan, *A History of Chinese Philosophy*, trans. D. Bodde, 2 vols, vol. I, Princeton: Princeton University Press, 1983.

Fung Yu-lan, *The Spirit of Chinese Philosophy*, trans. E.R. Hughes, London: Kegan Paul, Trench, Trubner, 1947.

Hansen, C., *A Daoist Theory of Chinese Thought*, New York: Oxford University Press, 1992, ch. 9.

Watson, Burton, *Basic Writings of Mo Tzu, Hsun Tzu and Han Fei Tzu*, New York and London: Columbia University Press, 1967.

HUINENG (HUI-NENG) 638–713 CE

Huineng, known as the Sixth Patriarch, is generally acclaimed as the most influential exponent of Chan Buddhism in China. Chan is widely known in the West by its Japanese name, Zen. The term derives from the Sanskrit *dhyana*, meaning 'meditation'.[1]

Zen Buddhism is generally held to have its foundations in the teachings of Bodhidharma, a southern Indian Buddhist who travelled to China early in the sixth century. His teaching was at first transmitted and developed in a linear way by five successive patriarchs, but then a split ensued that divided his followers into a northern and a southern branch of Chinese Buddhism. In the north, a monk called Shenxiu [Shen-hsiu] led a vigorous school in which emphasis was placed on the achievement of enlightenment by a gradual process of meditation, quietude and a purification of the baser parts of the mind. It was this movement and its leader that were at first deemed to be the inheritors of the patriarchal wisdom, but it was the southern school, led by Huineng, that eventually became the recognized authority for the transmission and interpretation of Zen teaching.

The doctrines ascribed to Huineng were radical and transforming. They included the rejection of traditional rituals of reciting and reading the scriptures and of the making of offerings to the Buddha as means to salvation. In place of such practices Huineng taught that a person could experience an immediate intuitive insight that might occur at any time and in any circumstances. For him, the aim of Zen is a direct, unconceptualized enlightenment that is sudden and totally illuminating. The differences between the approaches of the northern and southern schools are pithily characterized in the epigram '*nan dun, bei jian*', meaning 'suddenness of the south, gradualness of the north'.[2] The southern movement, it has been remarked, was one in which 'the Chinese mind completely asserted itself, in a sense, in opposition to the Indian mind'.[3]

The accounts of Huineng's life are largely legendary. They describe him as having been an uneducated youth from southern China, a woodseller and a pounder of rice in a monastery granary who nevertheless was capable of the clearest philosophical insight and understanding. In an autobiographical passage in *The Platform Sutra of the Sixth Patriarch*, a work that has become the basic classic of Zen Buddhism, Huineng recounts that during his time as a rice-pounder in the monastery of Hongren [Hung-jen], he competed with other monks, among them Shenxiu who was to become leader of the northern school, to compose a verse that would qualify the writer to become the Sixth Patriarch. He first describes how, at midnight, the monk, Shenxiu, holding a candle, wrote his verse on the wall of the south corridor of the monastery. It ran:

> This body is the Bohdi tree;
> This mind is a bright mirror's stand,
> Polish it unceasingly,
> And do not let the dust fall on it.[4]

Huineng then offers us his own verse, which was written at his dictation on the west wall of the monastery and which was to qualify him to receive the patriarchal inheritance. The verse embodies a point of view that is quite different from Shenxiu's and reveals that even then, in the early days of his monkhood, Huineng had found the idea that was to inform all his later teaching, namely, that reality is a kind of 'emptiness' or void. His verse ran as follows:

In enlightenment there is no tree;
The bright mirror is not a stand,
Since there is really nothing at all,
Where could dust alight?

When the verses had been considered, Huineng was secretly summoned at night into the presence of the Fifth Patriarch who read the *Diamond Sutra* of Nagarjuna to him'.[5] Upon hearing the *Sutra*, Huineng experienced immediate enlightenment. Thereupon the robe that signified inheritance of the patriarchy was bestowed on him. Already, in this first spiritual accession, he had begun to act in a characteristically innovative way: in achieving a sudden rather than a gradual enlightenment and also in exemplifying and affirming the authority of the *Diamond Sutra* rather than that of the traditionally acclaimed *Lankavatara Sutra*.[6]

The emergence of the southern doctrine as a distinct school and as powerfully formative in the development of Zen was a more curious and intricate matter than has so far been implied. Historical sources have shown that it depended on the actions of Huineng's discipline, Shenhui, rather than on anything done by Huineng himself, and that it took place in 732 CE, nineteen years after Huineng's death, when Shenhui attended the Great Dharma Ceremony in the monastery of Dayunsi [Ta-yun-ssu] in Honan province. There Shenhui ceremonially delivered an address in which he reviewed the development of the two schools of thought, inveighing against the practices of the north where Shenhui was taken to be the patriarchal inheritor and arguing that the possession by the southern school of the Dharma seal and robe of the Fifth Patriarch clearly signified that Huineng was rightfully the Sixth Patriarch and, accordingly, the source of authentic doctrine. This public declaration marked the beginning of a series of heated debates that continued for several years and that culminated in the drawing up by Shenhui of a definitive list of patriarchs, the sixth of which was Huineng. The details of this prolonged and bitter conflict reveal a huge chasm between the avowed philosophy of life and the actual conduct and passions of many of its protagonists.[7]

Huineng's teaching contrasts with Shenxiu's in almost every respect. Shenxiu's essential doctrine for his followers is contained in a manuscript entitled 'The teaching of the Five Means by the northern school'.[8] In summary, these 'means' or practices consisted of a sustained, concentrated meditation on one thought, leading to a state of receptivity to supreme knowledge, an emancipation from illusory attachments and from the sense of dualism of body and mind, and the discovery of the path of Oneness on which enlightenment and Suchness are experienced. In contrast, as already mentioned, Huineng eschewed the practices of carefully disciplined meditation and correction of the mind as advocated by Shenxiu. His profoundly different, spontaneous kind of approach allows the mind to take its own course and find its own way. In this it reveals the influence of **Daoism**, with which it has several strong affinities. The two movements share the belief that reality is fundamentally monistic and also ultimately ineffable and indescribable. They are also alike in their attitudes of detachment from worldly matters.[9]

The most radical and transforming element in Huineng's thought is embodied in a momentous declaration of his: 'From the first not a thing is.' That declaration is implicit in the words of his verse on the monastery wall and it not only established the basis of his approach but also reveals him as heir to Nagarjuna's philosophy of *sunyata*, or emptiness, a doctrine deriving from the *Prajnaparamita Sutras* and which holds that all things are to be understood as ultimately 'empty'; that is, as without substance, essence or permanence of any kind.

Sunyata, emptiness or the Void, is not a simple concept.[10] It is not a mere denial of substantiality, qualities, differences, and so on; nor is it meant to be descriptive of a certain type of experience. Rather, it indicates that the way things are is ineffable and unconceptualizeable; that nothing exists in separateness, permanence or independence. It describes a standpoint from which all everyday conceptions and attachments, even while they are being employed in the business of daily living, are to be understood in the light of the knowledge of their ultimate illusoriness and unreality. To be able to see them thus is to be free from bondage to them; one's thought is then not attached to illusions but is able to be aware of the emptiness of True Thusness, or ultimate reality. In Huineng's teaching, to come to this awareness is to return to the original, free-floating purity of one's self-nature, which, he maintained, always remains unspoilt, even though its natural wisdom, or *prajna*, may become obscured by illusions. In the *Platform Sutra* Huineng wrote:

> Self-nature is always pure, just as the sun and moon are always shining. It is only when they are obscured by clouds that there is brightness above but darkness below, and the sun, moon and the stars cannot be seen . . . It is only because externally people are attached to spheres of objects that erroneous thoughts, like floating clouds, cover the self-nature so that it is not clear.[11]

Huineng regarded the pure self-nature as identical with Buddha-nature: it is the nature of the enlightened being. But to see into one's pure self-nature is not to uncover some enduring or fundamental element of one's being, nor is it to achieve some end or purpose. It is more like a return to what has always been, to a groundless condition of being that is ultimate and unquestionable. The consciousness of the enlightened being realizes the emptiness and unity of the real and is also aware of the teeming phenomena, or *dharma*,[12] of the world, but it does not create a dualism of entities and nothingness. Distinctions are lost in such enlightenment in that it involves a merging between the knower and the known. All ordinary, desirous attachments to things have slipped away. In Zen this is often described as 'the bottom of a tub falling out'.[13] When it takes place, lightness, clarity, emptiness, supervene. There is a sense in which everything is known and yet, at the same time, an awareness that there is nothing to be known. This condition has been spoken of as No-Mind or No-Thought, or 'the unconscious made conscious'.[14] In Huineng's teaching, emphasis is always on this experience of wisdom (*prajna*) through sudden enlightenment (*satori*) rather than on a gradual and disciplined accession to a state of higher knowledge. He did not think of enlightenment as something to work towards and then achieve; rather, it is the abrupt cessation of all process or continuity. It has at once the feeling of the transcendence of time and space, and the feeling of a full participation in the totality of things.

In the form in which it is known today, *The Platform Sutra of the Sixth Patriarch*, the work that embodies Huineng's central ideas, is thought to have been compiled by several of his followers using a range of sources. Its title of '*sutra*', a term applied only to those writings held to contain direct transmissions of the Buddha's words, indicates something of its importance and influence, and it has been pointed out that its doctrines are richly informed not just by Huineng's thought but by the broader teaching of the whole tradition of the Six Patriarchs.[15] It has come to represent the essence and the culmination of a remarkable and generative development in Chinese Buddhism.

After Huineng's death the doctrines he represented became known as the Zen of the Patriarchs and as such became distinct from, though not in any harsh conflict with, the Zen of the Perfected One, the latter title referring to the practices and teaching associated with Bodhidharma. Zen continued to flourish, manifesting itself in a variety of forms, until it became diminished, first, in the mid-ninth century, by persecution and later, in the eleventh and twelfth centuries, by the challenge of a powerful revival of Confucianism. In Japan it took strong root and has always played an important role in Japanese culture. In the twentieth century a significant proportion of the western world has developed an intense interest in Zen Buddhism, turning to it not simply as an antidote to the busy materialism and transactions of the market-place, but also as part of a movement towards a philosophy that accords value to those intimations of transcendence that haunt the inner lives of many human beings.

Notes

1 *Dhyana* (meditation) is discussed and related to *prajna* (wisdom) in D.T. Suzuki, *The Zen Doctrine of No Mind*, ed. Christmas Humphreys, London: Rider, 1991, pp. 31–9.

2 Heinrich Dumoulin, *Zen Buddhism: A History*, vol. I, *India and China*, trans. James W. Heisig and Paul Knitter, New York: Macmillan, 1988, p.107.

3 Wing-tsit Chan, *A Source Book in Chinese Philosophy*, Princeton: Princeton University Press, 1969, p. 425.

4 There are numerous translations of this verse and Huineng's competing verse. The translations used here are the ones given in R.C. Zaehner (ed.), *Encyclopaedia of Living Faiths*, 4th edn, London: Hutchinson, 1988, p. 332.

5 For a fuller exposition of Nagarjuna's thought see the essay on him in this volume, pp. 95–103

6 The *Lankavatara Sutra* was generally thought to have been commended by Bodhidharma to his disciples. Although it was influential in the development of all the Zen schools it was particularly important in the teaching of Shenxiu's northern school

7 A more detailed account of the development of this struggle is in Dumoulin, op. cit., vol. I, ch. 7.

8 Shenxiu derived much of this from predecessors and from Mahayana *sutras* and *sastras*.

9 Daoism is discussed more fully in the essay on Laozi, pp. 240–8 in this volume.

10 For more on *sunyata* see the essay on Nagarjuna, pp. 95–103 in this book.

11 Quoted in Chan, op. cit., pp. 437–8.

12 The word *dharma* has acquired many meanings. In the present context it refers to the natural order of constituents of the world. But it can also mean, in a general way, religious practices, laws or customs, the Buddha's doctrine and teaching, knowledge of the true functioning of things, and many other things besides.

13 See Fung Yu-lan, *A History of Chinese Philosophy*, trans. D. Bodde, 2 vols, vol. 2, Princeton: Princeton University Press, 1963, p. 399.

14 For example, in Suzuki, op. cit., p. 31ff.

15 See Dumoulin, op. cit., p. 128.

See also in this book

Nagarjuna, Laozi, Chinul, Dogen, Bankei, Nishida, Suzuki

Huineng's writings

A text that is thought to be the earliest extant version of *The Platform Sutra* (*Liuzi tan jing*) [*Liu-tsu t'an-ching*] was found at Dun Huang [Tun-huang] in 1907. It was probably written between 830 and 860 CE. Numerous other versions of this *sutra* exist in many reprints, some of them greatly expanded, and the Dun Huang manuscript is held by scholars to be a defective copy of an earlier text. *The Platform Sutra* divides roughly into two sections: autobiographical and instructional, and doctrinal. There is a translation in paperback in:

A.F. Price and Wong-Mou-lam (trans.), *The Diamond Sutra and the Sutra of Hui-neng*, Boston: Shambala, 1990.

Sources and further reading

Chan Wing-tsit, *A Source Book in Chinese Philosophy*, Princeton: Princeton University Press, 1963

Dumoulin, Heinrich, *Zen Buddhism: A History*, vol. I, *India and China*, trans. James W. Heisig and Paul Knitter, New York: Macmillan, and London: Collier Macmillan, 1988

Fung Yu-lan, *A History of Chinese Philosophy*, trans. D. Bodde, 2 vols, vol. 2, Princeton: Princeton University Press, 1983

Suzuki, D.T., *The Zen Doctrine of No Mind*, ed. Christmas Humphreys, London: Rider, 1991

FAZANG [FA TSANG] 643-712 CE

Fazang, also known by his title Xianshou, is the leading Chinese representative of a subdivision of **Mahayana** Buddhism called the **Huayan [Hua-yen:** 'flower-garland', 'flowery splendour' or 'wreath'] school, which came to China in the sixth century CE. Mahayana Buddhism added a metaphysical dimension to the original teachings of the Buddha[1] and the Huayan regarded as pre-eminent, and based its teachings on, the lengthy *Avatamsaka Sutra*.[2] This set of aphorisms is concerned with the nature of reality, the relationship between the Absolute and its many *dharmas* or manifestations in the physical realm, and the Buddha nature or buddhahood of all sentient beings. Huayan has been highly influential ever since its introduction into China, and is regarded as one of the most philosophically sophisticated forms of Buddhism. It spread to Korea, and under the name of the Kegon school, it has also been of great importance in Japan.

Fazang attempted to synthesize many of the strands of Chinese Buddhist thought current in his time. However, he was opposed to the Weishi, the Consciousness-only or Mere Ideation school, partly based on the work of Vasubandhu.[3] The major figure of this movement in China was the scholar Xuanzang [Hsuan-Tsang: 596–664 CE], who travelled extensively in northern India and translated many Buddhist texts, including those of Vasubandhu, from Sanskrit into Chinese. Xuanzang asserted that the division between what we take as particular, persisting external things or *dharmas*, and the apparently permanent self, is illusory. The *dharmas* are merely transitory mental representations of an evolving consciousness. By contrast, Fazang, whose doctrines are characterized by Wing-Tsit Chan as the 'one-and-all' philosophy[4] maintained that the realm of particular things has a degree of relative, independent reality. It both interpenetrates and is interpenetrated by the underlying, undifferentiated, qualityless **sunyata**, the Void or Emptiness.[5]

According to the *Songgaosengzhuan* [*Sung Kao Seng Chuan:* the *Sung Compilation of Biographies of Eminent Buddhist Monks*, a tenth-century work] Fazang was born in Zhangan, the modern Sian in the Shanshi province of central China. He came from a non-Chinese family; his grandfather had emigrated to China from a town near Samarkand in Uzbekistan. Fazang is said to have assisted Xuanzang for a time in the task of translating Buddhist writings into Chinese, 'but differences in viewpoint caused him to leave the translation-hall'.[6] After Fazang became a Buddhist monk at the age of 28, his main interest lay in developing the teachings of the monks Dushun [Tu-shun: 557–640] and Chihyan [Chih-yen: 602–668], the founders of the Huayan school. In 704, he lectured to the Empress (self-styled Emperor) Wu, a keen supporter of Buddhism against Confucianism, on the principles of the *Avatamsaka Sutra*, using the golden lion placed in the entrance-hall to the palace as an illustration of its main tenets.

Fazang was a prolific writer, producing more than sixty works in his lifetime. The text based on the lecture to the Empress Wu, the *Essay on the Golden Lion*, is the most famous. Two other treatises of importance in Fazang's thought are the *Hundred Theories in the Sea of Ideas of the Avatamsaka Sutra* and *The Contemplation of the Mysterious Meaning of the Avatamsaka Sutra*.

As Paul Williams comments, 'Hua-yen [Huayan] thought is complex . . . and the *Golden Lion*, perhaps because of its brevity, nevertheless remains . . . an obscure document'.[7] However, commentators are agreed on its main tenets. According to Fazang, there are two levels of reality. In the *Essay on the Golden Lion*, the gold from which the lion is made is used as the metaphor for the more fundamental of the two levels, that of the noumenal world or *li fa jie*, the realm of principle. The noumenal is immutable and timeless, formless and characterless, beyond existence and non-existence; it is 'the substance which by its own nature is clear, pure, all-perfect and brilliant'.[8] The second level of reality, symbolized by the form or shape of the lion, is the *shi fa jie*, or realm of things, containing particular, perceptible phenomena or *dharmas* which are in constant flux and transformation. The two levels are interdependent and interpenetrative: the lion could not exist without the gold from which it is made, and gold has to have some form or shape.

Noumenon and phenomena are also linked by universal causation; the former is the origin or primary cause of the latter. The secondary cause lies in the phenomenal realm, and is the activity of the craftsperson. Because it is caused, the lion has no intrinsic nature. Instead, it is empty or void, as it partakes only of the underlying nature of the gold from which it is made. As Fazang puts it, 'The character of the lion is unreal; there is only real gold . . . apart from the gold there is no character of the lion to be found'.[9] As the *dharmas* (the golden lion) participate in the nature of the noumenon (the gold), the noumenon also has no intrinsic nature; it is *sunyata*, a non-nihilistic, predicateless emptiness or voidness. From a purely empirical perspective, the *dharmas* are real, because they are the objects of the senses. From a higher and more adequate perspective which incorporates the understanding, the *dharmas* only appear to be real, as they have dependent and thus relative existence, and point beyond themselves to their origin, the noumenon.

According to Michael Brannigan,[10] Fazang synthesizes the apparent opposites *wu* and *you*. Particular phenomena have *you*, a term which conveys the dynamism of existence or being, their capacity for change or transformation. The *you* of the *dharmas* cannot be absolute, because they are caused; their existence must thus be penetrated by the *wu* from which they originate. The noumenal realm has *wu*, which in the context of the Huayan is not absolute non-being, but is infiltrated by the being of the *dharmas*.

Fazang maintains that all things are linked not only by mutual interdependence and interpenetration, but also by mutual implication. Neither the eye of the lion nor, to use a western example, the grin of the Cheshire cat in Lewis Carroll's *Alice in Wonderland*, can exist alone, but have to exist together with the other parts of the lion or cat, such as their ears, whiskers and fur. Similarly, a particular *dharma* cannot exist in isolation, but must exist in the context of all other *dharmas*.

Each phenomenon also implies the noumenon; neither the eye nor the grin can exist without the whole of the lion or cat. Two other metaphors are used by Fazang to illustrate this point. In the first, a statue of the Buddha is placed at the centre of a circular hall of mirrors. Each mirror reflects not only the statue, but the reflections, and an infinity of reflections of the reflections, of the statue in all the other mirrors. The second metaphor is the net of Lord Indra, the ruler of heaven in Hindu mythology. The net has a jewel at each intersection of its web. Each jewel reflects the whole of the net, including all the other jewels and their infinite reflections. Mutual interdependence and implication mean that each and every *dharma* reflects each and every other, and the whole of ultimate reality itself. Reality can thus be known through any one particular phenomenon. As causation is equivalent to implication, it reduces to a logical relationship.

The German philosopher Leibniz (1646–1716) held a doctrine similar to that expressed in Fazang's metaphors of the hall of mirrors and Indra's net. Each individual substance or soul, or in Leibnizian terminology each monad, of which there is an infinite number, 'is a perpetual living mirror of the universe';[11] all finite monads reflect or express not only each other, but also the whole of reality.

In common with other Buddhist philosophers, Fazang in *The Contemplation of the Mysterious Meaning of the Avatamsaka Sutra* asserted that the belief that reality is governed by temporal conditions is false. The division of time into past, present and future is arbitrary and entirely dependent on our own narrow, blinkered perspective which results in **avidya**, or ignorance of the true nature of reality. Our view of time is transformed when we consider that each of the divisions of time has its own past, present and future. The future of the past and the past of the future is the present. Thus the compartmentalization of time breaks down and we realize that, from a true perspective, there is only simultaneity. This has consequences for causation and language. There is no sequence of causes and effects; instead, everything exists in an eternal present. Fazang expresses the point as follows: 'The gold and the lion exist simultaneously, all-perfect and complete . . . this is called . . . simultaneous completion and mutual correspondence'.[12] Equally, there is a mismatch between tensed language and reality; the former cannot truly correspond to the latter, but covers only what we erroneously take to be the time-sequence.

The goal of the adherents of Huayan is to become a **Bodhisattva**, a person who partakes of the Buddha nature but delays entry to **nirvana** in order to help others to escape the cycle of rebirth, or **samsara**.

According to *The Contemplation of the Mysterious Meaning of the Avatamsaka Sutra*, the *bodhisattva* is both wise and compassionate, and understands that the two qualities are mutually interdependent and interpenetrative. Wisdom is achieved through the knowledge that neither the phenomenal nor the noumenal realm have intrinsic natures, and thus are empty. Compassion for all sentient beings can be reached through the knowledge that the noumenal and the phenomenal realms are interdependent. If we achieve wisdom, we are freed from *samsara* and if we attain compassion we avoid extinction in *nirvana*. The compassion of the *bodhisattva* is dispassionate, impartial and all-embracing. It 'considers all as one body with [it]self and [resolves] to teach and transform all living beings'.[13] *Bodhisattvas* do not undertake any action to manifest their compassion but, by their presence, serenity and lack of attachment to the things of this world, they are living exemplars of release from *samsara* to those who have not yet reached enlightenment.

Fazang clearly states that compassion is dependent on metaphysical knowledge. To put it in more formal terms, knowledge of certain metaphysical truths is the necessary and sufficient condition of compassion. There is currently great controversy about whether moral qualities depend on intellectual expertise.[14] Any connection between the two is certainly not self-evident. Impartial, all-embracing feelings are not the exclusive province of the metaphysical specialist, but can be a characteristic of people whatever their level of intellectual achievement. The separation of moral qualities from action can also be questioned. Compassionate beings must behave with compassion on at least some occasions for that characteristic to be assignable to them.

In keeping with his syncretist approach, Fazang maintained that the various Buddhist schools can be arranged in a hierarchy. Each school incorporates the teachings of those lower than itself in the hierarchy, but comes closer to an appreciation of ultimate reality. The doctrine of the **Theravada** has the least insight; it would assert only that the Golden Lion, being caused, has no intrinsic nature. The Consciousness-Only school teaches that *dharmas* not only have no true nature, but they have no true existence either. The **Tiantai** [T'ien-T'ai; J: Tendai] school takes up the theme of the *dharmas* and states that they have relative existence. **Chan** [J: Zen] Buddhism maintains that ultimate reality is nameless and beyond existence and non-existence. Finally, the Huayan, with its doctrines of interdependence and interpenetrability, offers an all-encompassing theory of reality.

Huayan has built upon the original teachings of the Buddha to produce an integrated and elaborate metaphysical system. Even if we do not regard it as providing definitive answers to deep metaphysical questions, its doctrines have been of enduring interest to those who believe that reality is something more than what is presented to us by the senses alone.

Notes

1 See the essays on Nagarjuna and Vasubandhu, pp. 95–103 and pp. 103–14 in this book.
2 There have been three translations of the *Avatamsaka Sutra* from Sanskrit into Chinese.
3 See the essay on Vasubandhu, pp. 103–14 in this book.
4 Chan Wing-Tsit, *A Source Book in Chinese Philosophy*, Princeton: Princeton University Press, 1963, pp. 406–8.
5 See the essay on Nagarjuna, pp. 95–103 in this book.
6 Quoted in Fung Yu-lan, *A History of Chinese Philosophy*, 2 vols, vol. II, trans. D. Bodde, Princeton: Princeton University Press, 1983, p. 340.
7 P. Williams, *Mahayana Buddhism: Its Doctrinal Foundations*, London: Routledge, 1989, p. 130.
8 Fung Yu-lan, op. cit., p. 341.
9 Chan Wing-tsit, op. cit., p. 409.
10 Michael Brannigan, *The Pulse of Wisdom*, Belmont, Calif.: Wadsworth, 1995, pp. 72, 81.
11 Leibniz, *Philosophical Writings*, ed. G.H.R. Parkinson, London: Dent, 1973, p. 19.
12 Chan Wing-tsit, op. cit., p. 411.
13 Ibid., op. cit., p. 418.
14 See Arthur Danto, *Mysticism and Morality*, Harmondsworth: Penguin Books, 1976, ch. 4.

Fazang's writings

Extensive selections from the writings of Fazang are to be found in the following publications:

Chan Wing-tsit, *A Source Book in Chinese Philosophy*, Princeton: Princeton University Press, 1963, ch. 25.
Fung Yu-lan, *A History of Chinese Philosophy*, trans. D. Bodde, 2 vols, vol. II, Princeton: Princeton University Press, 1983, ch. XII.

See also in this book

Nagarjuna, Vasubandhu, Buddhagosa, the Buddha, Chinul, Dogen

Sources and further reading

Brannigan, Michael, *The Pulse of Wisdom*, Belmont, Calif.: Wadsworth, 1995

Chan Wing-tsit, *A Source Book in Chinese Philosophy*, Princeton: Princeton University Press, 1963

Danto, Arthur, *Mysticism and Morality*, Harmondsworth: Penguin Books, 1976

Fung Yu-lan, *A History of Chinese Philosophy*, trans. D. Bodde, Princeton: Princeton University Press, 1983

Williams, Paul, *Mahayana Buddhism: Its Doctrinal Foundations*, London: Routledge, 1989

ZHUXI [CHU HSI] 1130–1200 CE

Zhuxi [Chu Hsi] is the major representative of a group of neo-Confucian philosophers who flourished in China in the eleventh and twelfth centuries CE.[1] His ideas exerted a powerful influence on Chinese life and culture from the thirteenth to the twentieth century. He worked in the rationalist tradition, seeking to understand the principles of things and their relationships within a metaphysical unity. His philosophy is remarkable for its comprehensive synthesis of traditional doctrines: he drew together into one system Confucius' teaching on benevolence, Mencius' on humanity and righteousness, the *yinyang* doctrine of cosmic forces, the doctrine of the Five Agents of water, fire, wood, metal and earth, and a number of important elements of **Daoist** and Buddhist teaching. It was he who arranged and wrote commentaries on the Four Books, strengthening their Confucian components and presenting them in the form in which they became the basis of the Chinese civil service exams. His writings are contained in sixty-two volumes.

Zhuxi was born in Fujian [Fukien] province in south-eastern China. For several years he studied with his father, who was an important civic official, and from 1154 to 1157 he held the post of a district keeper of records. Although dedicated to scholarship he had a keen political consciousness. He frequently petitioned the emperor concerning the inefficiency of administrators and officials and he opposed the acceptance of what he regarded as the humiliating terms of a peace agreement made with invaders from the north. After 1163 he refused all offers of public office for some years, preferring to undertake the work of a temple guardian so that he could study in peace and at the same time benefit from conversation with other scholars. When he did return to public life, as a prefect, as a minister in the army department and as a junior expositor, his denunciations of incompetence and corruption provoked repercussions from the officials whose mismanagement he exposed. He was accused of numerous crimes and a petition was made for his execution. The result was that all his posts were taken from him. In spite of much disfavour from officialdom, when he died almost a thousand people attended his funeral.

Zhuxi's chief philosophical concern is to give an account of the ultimate nature of things in relation to which everything else about the world and humankind might be understood. The account derives from two major concepts: those of Principle (*li*) and material force *qi* [*ch'i*]. Zhuxi describes ultimate reality as Principle. It is eternal, unchanging and wholly good. In itself it is an undifferentiated unity but it is also actualized in each individual entity by means of material force, which is the fundamental physicality, or energy-matter, of the cosmos. Each individual entity, although temporal and incomplete in its material aspect, embodies Principle in its entirety. Zhuxi writes:

> There is principle before there can be material force. But it is only when there is material force that principle finds a place to settle. This is the process by which all things are produced, whether large as heaven and earth or small as ants ... Fundamentally, principle cannot be interpreted in the senses of existence or non-existence. Before heaven and earth came into being, it already was as it is.[2]

Zhuxi also refers to Principle as the Great Ultimate, remarking that 'the Great Ultimate is nothing other than principle' and that it is 'the principle of heaven and earth and the myriad things.'[3]

The distinction between Principle and material force should not be thought of as exactly resembling the distinction, prevalent in much western philosophy, between mind and matter. What has to be remembered is that neo-Confucianism sees the individuation of both mental and physical entities as being brought about by means of material force and that the emphasis in Zhuxi's philosophy is not so much on a dualism of Principle and matter as on an organic unity in which an individual mind is as much dependent on material force as an individual body is. Thus he writes:

> That which integrates to produce life and disintegrates to produce death is only material force. What we called the spirit, the heavenly, and earthly aspects of the soul *hun po* [*hun-p'o*] and consciousness, are all effects of material force.

Therefore when material force is integrated, there are these effects. When it is disintegrated there are no more . . . as this material force integrates into a particular instance, its principle is also endowed in that instance.[4]

Zhuxi accounts for motion and change in the cosmos by reference to the doctrine of *yinyang*. The doctrine is an extremely ancient one that was formulated in writing as early as the third century BCE. It is usually expounded in conjunction with that of the Five Agents already mentioned. The term *yin* refers to passive, weak, negative processes or forces and *yang* to active, strong, constructive ones. Their alternations between activity and tranquillity produce the Five Agents of wood, metal, water, fire and earth. In his account of change Zhuxi says: 'There is no other event in the universe except *yin* and *yang* succeeding each other in an unceasing cycle. This is called change. However . . . there must be the principles that make them possible. This is the great Ultimate.'[5] He maintains that through the *yinyang* motion of material force, sediment from water formed the earth; that waves, over long periods of time, gradually solidified into mountains; that 'the most turbid water formed the earth and the purest fire became wind, thunder, lightning, the stars and the like.'[6] Principle, he maintains, becomes visible through *yin* and *yang*. It 'attaches itself to *yin* and *yang* as a man sits astride a horse.'[7] Once *yin* and *yang* have produced the Five Agents the Agents are fixed in their physical natures and become differentiated in individual things.

Zhuxi's moral theory is extrapolated from his metaphysics. An individual human nature is a manifestation of Principle in the individual and since Principle is fundamentally good it follows that human nature is fundamentally good. But, as Zhuxi observes, 'there are those who are good from their birth and those who are evil from their birth'.[8] How then does evil enter into human beings? Zhuxi's answer is that the goodness of an individual's nature may be constrained by the kind of material force in which it is embodied. He says:

If the sun and moon are clear and bright, and the climate temperate and reasonable, the man born at such a time and endowed with such material force . . . should be a good man. But if the sun and moon are darkened and gloomy, and the temperature abnormal, all this is evidence of violent material force. There is no doubt that if a man is endowed with such material force, he will be a bad man.[9]

In saying this, Zhuxi does not want to posit a dichotomy of good and evil or the existence of a positive power of evil. Material force, he says, is differentiated into good and evil in accordance with its purity and impurity; there are not two distinct things in nature opposing each other. He quotes some words of Cheng Yi [Ch'eng I]: 'What is called evil is not original evil. It becomes evil only because of deviation from the mean'.[10]

Moral goodness, then, consists for Zhuxi in balance, harmony and appropriateness in relationships between the elements of things. It depends on an organic and ultimately monistic integration of the cosmos. In contrast, evil is an imbalance brought about by a turbidity or density of material being. Proper moral activity, Zhuxi maintains, aims at achieving an understanding and realization of **ren** [*jen*], or humanity, the Confucian virtue, variously translated as benevolence, human-heartedness, altruism, sympathy and community with others, and described by Zhuxi as the character of man's mind and the principle of love. When the natural goodness of principle is able to operate unimpeded in an individual the result is *ren*. Benevolence, self-mastery, righteousness and wisdom will flow from the person who has achieved it. Impartiality is the condition of *ren*, though it is not identical with it.

Evil, according to Zhuxi may be overcome by the acquisition of true knowledge. The ethical dimension of human nature is fostered by what he calls 'the investigation of things'. Knowledge of things and of their principles enables the individual's capacity for self-mastery to develop. Knowledge is the means to the attainment of an increased understanding of the role of feelings in human life and of the ways in which a person who has *ren* will respond to the multiplicity and complexity of the world. The fundamental natural goodness of a person needs to be preserved, and knowledge of what that goodness consists of enables the person to function well, thereby bringing material force into harmony with the principle it embodies and allowing the individual's true destiny to be realized. He urges the cultivation of a discipline of mind which he describes as 'seriousness': a steadfast dedication to right thinking and truth.

Zhuxi's ethical theory is extremely well balanced. It is agnostic concerning the existence of a God as the source of all things and as architect of a design and purpose for the universe. Thus it does not place humankind in thrall to a cosmic plan or end. Its claims concerning the fundamental goodness of Principle and its presence in human beings do not create a burden of original sin, while the account of material force offers an understanding of human moral variety. At the same time, Principle and material force, taken together, provide the possibility for change and self-improvement in that knowledge of Principle is necessarily knowledge of good; and since Principle is always embodied in material force, this knowledge is also knowledge of how particular goods are manifested in the realm of human experience and human action.

Zhuxi's synthesis of traditional ideas and his grounding of them in a comprehensive metaphysical scheme gained an enthusiastic following and provided material for much philosophical debate in the centuries succeeding his death. His whole philosophical system became the structure that supported the Chinese cultural edifice until the early years of the twentieth century and expressed something that is present in almost every manifestation of Chinese philosophy, namely, the aspiration to become harmoniously integrated with the natural processes of the cosmos. It has been pointed out that Zhuxi's thought, and neo-Confucianism in general, represent the synthesis of a dialectical movement in which the classical period of the sixth to third centuries BCE was the thesis and the succeeding neo-Daoist and Buddhist era the antithesis. His organic conception of the cosmos has been compared with that of Alfred North Whitehead, and numerous similarities have been noted between his ideas and those of the seventeenth-century German philosopher Gottfried Leibniz.[11] In the 1930s Zhuxi's philosophy became the basis of the new rational thought of Feng Yulan [Fung Yu-lan], one of China's most eminent modern philosophers.

Notes

1 The other major members of this group were the Ch'eng brothers, Ch'eng Hao (1032–85) and Ch'eng I (1033–1107).
2 Translated from the *Complete Works of Chu Hsi* (1714 edition) in Chan Wing-tsit, *A Source Book in Chinese Philosophy*, Princeton: Princeton University Press, 1963, p. 529.
3 Chan Wing-tsit, op. cit., p. 638.
4 Ibid., pp. 637, 638.
5 Ibid., p. 641.
6 Ibid., p. 642.
7 Ibid., p. 641.
8 Ibid., p. 624.
9 Ibid., pp. 624, 625.
10 Ibid., p. 598.
11 The impact of neo-Confucianism on Leibniz may be seen in the works he wrote about China, now collected in: Julia Ching and Willard Oxtoby, *Moral Enlightenment: Leibniz and Wolff on China*, Monumenta Serica Monograph series no. XXVI, Nettetal: Steyler Verlag, 1992, and D.J. Cook

and H. Rosemont, *Gottfried Wilhelm Leibniz: Writings on China*, Chicago and La Salle, Ill.: Open Court, 1994.

Zhuxi's writings

Zhuxi arranged the *Analects* of Confucius, the *Great Learning*, the *Doctrine of the Mean* and the *Mencius* to form the Four Books that became, in 1313, the basis of the Chinese civil service examinations. Many of his writings are published in a collection of his literary works, available in Chinese only. Translations of selected passages are in Chan Wing-tsit, *A Source Book in Chinese Philosophy*, Princeton: Princeton University Press, 1963. See also:

Wittenborn, Allen (trans.) *Further Reflections on Things at Hand: A Reader* [Zhuxi's *Hsu chin-ssu lu*] Lanham: University Press of America, 1991.

For a fuller picture of the breadth of Zhuxi's competence see Carsun Chang's *The Development of neo-Confucian Thought*, Westport, Conn.: Greenwood Press, 1957, pp. 243–8.

See also in this book

Confucius, Mencius, Laozi, Dai Zhen, Kang Youwei, Yi Yulgok, Mao Zedong

Sources and further reading

Chan Wing-tsit, *A Source Book in Chinese Philosophy*, Princeton: Princeton University Press, 1963
Chang, Carsun, *The Development of neo-Confucian Thought*, Westport, Conn.: Greenwood Press, 1957
Fung Yu-lan, *The Spirit of Chinese Philosophy*, trans. E.R. Hughes, London: Kegan Paul, Trench, Trubner, 1947
——, *A History of Chinese Philosophy*, trans. D. Bodde, 2 vols, vol. 2, Princeton: Princeton University Press, 1983

WANG YANGMING (WANG SHOU-JEN)[1]
1472–1529 CE

Wang Yangming was an idealist, the leading figure in the philosophy known as the School of Mind that developed during the Ming dynasty (1368–1644 CE). Although he is now honoured chiefly as a philosopher and scholar, in his time he was also an eminent statesman and general, a brilliant strategist who notably defeated the rebellion of Prince Chen Hao and organized an effective suppression of banditry. His philosophy of Mind, although in the mainstream of neo-Confucianism, stands as a contrast to the ideas of his great neo-Confucian predecessor, Zhuxi (Chu Hsi).[2] Both men had a typically Confucian concern with morality, but Zhuxi's teaching is dominated by what is often known as 'the investigation of things', Wang Yangming's by the exploration of mind. By the end of the fifteenth century Zhuxi's philosophy, till then regarded as the official doctrine in China, was showing signs of trivialization and disintegration, and there was a climate of receptivity that welcomed the new ideas being generated by Wang Yangming.

Wang Yangming was born in Yuyao in the province of Chekiang. He travelled widely during his youth and then made himself a room in a cave, using it as a study to prepare himself for the civil service examinations. Subsequently he entered government service, enjoying respect and esteem until he incurred displeasure through an incident in which he was judged to have shown discourtesy to a favoured eunuch. As a result he was banished to live with barbarians and convicts in the remote town of Lungchang in the province of Kueichow. Once settled there with a few of his followers he began his philosophical studies, pursuing his already widely eclectic interests. While still in his teens he had been attracted to both Daoism and Buddhism, and he now turned his attention to a critical study of Zhuxi's doctrine of the investigation of things. By 1508 he had formulated a theory of his own and in 1510 he was readmitted to royal service. He soon displayed wisdom and resourcefulness in many capacities and became strongly influential in matters of government.

Wang Yangming was something of a polymath: his learning was formidably broad and deep, and he was a poet as well as a philosopher. Somewhat late in life, at the age of 55, he was persuaded by his students to write down his teachings. His ideas quickly attracted widespread interest and although he did not live long enough to develop them fully, his reputation grew in the years beyond his death. In 1567 he was posthumously awarded the honorific title of Wen Cheng (Wen-ch'eng) and in 1584 was accorded the supreme honour of being offered sacrifice in the Confucian temple.

A story is told of the way in which Wang Yangming, having striven for some years to follow Zhuxi's teaching, reached the point of repudiating and supplanting some of the fundamental ideas of his predecessor. Zhuxi's central idea was that *li*, or Principle, was in every thing in the universe and that in order to attain knowledge of *li* and thereby of goodness, each thing should be investigated. In pursuit of such an investigation and of the knowledge of *li*, or Principle, which according to Zhuxi would lead to moral perfection, Wang Yangming and some friends decided to make an intensive study of a bamboo plant. Several days of sustained concentration yielded no increase in their understanding; indeed, they declared themselves unwell as a result of it, and this led them to conclude that they were not worthy of enlightenment and sagehood. But Wang Yangming did not cease to ponder the matter and in 1508, during his exile in remote Keichow and at a time of crisis when he was having to tend his sick retainers rather than they him, he experienced a revelation. What came to him at that time was the thought that it was a mistake to try to become a sage by seeking *li* in the things of the world; instead, he should be looking into his own mind to find all the principles of the universe. The mind, he decided, once cleared of confusion and muddle, would yield what he called an 'intuitive knowledge' of *li* and moral goodness. From these realizations he derived his fundamental tenet, namely, that Principle and Mind are one, and from that he concluded that all things and events, as well as principles, belong in the mind.

Wang Yangming's elaboration of his doctrine has some puzzling aspects that have provoked a good deal of controversy. To be clear about his claims, if that is possible, we have to bear in mind that he saw knowledge and action as in a certain sense inseparable, and he maintained that in what he called 'the original state' there is no such thing as knowledge without practice. Knowing, he said, is the origin of doing and doing the 'realization' of knowledge, and from that he concluded that both knowledge and doing are of the mind. His conception of what counts as knowledge is crucial for an understanding of exactly what he is saying here. He saw knowledge as a direct, intuitive apprehension that is untainted by any intrusion of selfish desires concerning what is known. And in knowing something in this way, he held, one also knows and performs the action that follows from it. In the *Record of Instructions* he wrote: 'If now we concentrate our thoughts upon extending the intuitive knowledge, so as to sweep away all the barriers [caused by selfish desire], the original state will then again be restored, and we will again become part of the profundity of heaven.'[3] Wang Yangming's asserted unity of knowledge and action was challenged not only by his critics but by his followers as well. It was put to him that knowledge and action were not inseparable in the way he said they were because very often people know what they ought to do but do not in fact do it, as when, for example, a son does not accord the filial piety he knows is due to his father. Wang's response to this objection was that in such cases there is always a failure of knowledge, a lack of real understanding; there is, perhaps, a clouding of the intuitive apprehension by selfish considerations, and so the alleged knowledge is inadequate and does not generate the action. He pointed out that we do not first see something beautiful and then subsequently decide to love it: the knowledge of its beauty and the love of it are unitary, just as smelling a bad smell and disliking the smell are unitary.[4] In the same way, intuitive knowledge of something embodies knowledge of how to act in respect to that something.

Of course, there is nothing in the above account that constitutes any convincing proof of Wang Yangming's claims about the priority of Mind. However, it does provide an explanation of what he means when he speaks of knowledge and of the unity of knowledge and action, and it does enable us to see the chain of connections he is positing in the following perplexing but frequently-quoted remarks:

> The controlling power of the body is the mind. The mind originates the idea, and the nature of the idea is knowledge. Wherever the idea is, we have a thing. For instance, when the idea rests on serving one's parents, then serving one's parents is a 'thing' . . . I say there are no principles but those of the mind, and nothing exists apart from the mind.[5]

Wang Yangming likened intuitive knowledge to the sun: in itself it is perfect, but it may easily become obscured by the clouds of desire. He held that the mind in its original state is not clouded by desire and that it manifests the unity of knowledge and action that is required for human virtue. He also maintained that when the mind achieves a return to this 'illustrious virtue' it enters into a condition of oneness with heaven and earth. When this stage is reached it is as if the person participates in the being of all things. We become, he says, part of 'the illustrious virtue'.[6] His prescription for gaining this state is to persevere in banishing the clouds that veil our innate moral knowledge so that it may be fully realized in action. In this connection he speaks of the Unity of Activity and Quiescence (*dong* and *jing*), a condition in which the mind remains inactive, poised, ready, perceptive, and reliant on its own understanding, while externally the person performs whatever action is determined by intuitive knowledge. Some commentators have suggested that in describing this kind of mental detachment Wang Yangming is espousing a Buddhist-like renunciation of the world of affairs and favouring purely meditative practices, but it is scarcely likely that a man so seriously involved in the business of government and politics would advocate that sort of renunciation and Wang Yangming certainly did not adopt such a course himself. He asks,

If one wishes to extend one's intuitive knowledge, does this mean that one should stupefy oneself with shadows and echoes, and suspend oneself in empty unreality? It is necessary to accept the reality of (external) affairs. Hence the 'extension' of knowledge necessarily consists in 'the investigation of things'.[7]

Like most Confucian philosophers, Wang's prime concern was the achievement of virtue for himself and all humankind. Knowledge of good is his supreme practical aim and because, for him, to know is to act, knowledge of the good and knowledge of moral conduct are one.

Numerous commentaries on and varying translations of the terms used in the writings of Wang Yang Ming and Zhuxi have added to the complexities of the interpretation of their ideas. What is unequivocally clear is that Zhuxi held that each human mind contains within itself the Supreme Ultimate and, accordingly, all the Principles of things, though not the actual things, or physical objects, governed by those Principles. In contrast, Wang Yangming maintained that Heaven and Earth and all things and objects are actually in our minds. Thus, as Fung Yu-lan has succinctly remarked of him: 'his philosophy represents an idealism with which Zhuxi could never agree'.[8]

Notes

1 Wang Yangming was also known as Wen-ch'eng in *Ming-Ju Hsiuh-An*, Huang Tung-hsi's biographical sketches of Ming dynasty Confucianists.
2 See the essay on Zhuxi (Chu Hsi) in this book, pp. 278–83.
3 Quoted in Fung Yu-lan, *A History of Chinese Philosophy*, 2 vols, vol. 2, trans. D. Bodde, Princeton: Princeton University Press, 1983, p. 602.
4 In Liu Wu-Chi, *A Short History of Confucian Philosophy*, Harmondsworth: Penguin Books, 1955, p. 172.
5 Quoted in Wade Baskin, *Classics in Chinese Philosophy*, Towota, NJ: Rowman & Allanheld, 1974, p. 575.
6 Fung Yu-lan, op. cit., p. 602.
7 Ibid.
8 Fung Yu-lan, op. cit. p. 610.

Wang Yangming's writings

Instructions For Practical Living and Other neo-Confucian Writings of Wang Yangming, trans. Wingtsit Chan, New York: Paragon Books Reproduction Corporation, 1964

The Philosophy of Wang Yangming, trans. Frederick Goodrich Henke, Chicago: Open Court, 1916

See also in this book

Confucius, Zhuxi, Xiong Shili

Sources and further reading

Chang, Carsun, *The Development of neo-Confucian Thought*, Newhaven: College and University Press, 1963

Ching, Julia, *To Acquire Wisdom: The Way of Wang Yangming*, New York: Columbia University Press, 1976

Creel, H.G., *Chinese Thought: From Confucius to Mao Tsetung*, Chicago: University of Chicago Press, 1953

De Bary, Theodore, *Self and Society in Ming Thought*, New York: Columbia University Press, 1970

—— *Neo-Confucian Orthodoxy and the Learning of Mind-and-Heart*, New York: Columbia University Press, 1981

Fung Yu-lan, *A History of Chinese Philosophy*, trans. D. Bodde, 2 vols, vol. 2, Princeton: Princeton University Press, 1953

Ivanhoe, P.J., *A Concordance to Wang Yangming's 'Ch'uang hsi ou'*, San Francisco: Chinese Materials Center, 1979

Liu Wu-chi, *A Short History of Confucian Philosophy*, Harmondsworth: Penguin Books, 1953

DAI ZHEN (TAI CHEN) 1724–1777 CE

After the introduction of **Zen** (or *Chan*) Buddhism into China in the first century CE,[1] enthusiasm for its ideas spread rapidly. As it gained hold, the new Zen movement became a threat to the stability of traditional Chinese Confucianism, which began to appear lifeless and degenerate by contrast. At the same time the increasing popularity of Zen functioned as a spur to the reaffirmation and reform of Confucianism. The ensuing revival of the latter was named the School of Nature and Principle. In the West it became known as neo-Confucianism.

As neo-Confucianism, over several centuries, acquired philosophical vigour and sophistication, it developed and elaborated idealist, rationalist and, eventually, empiricist forms, and encompassed a broad range of interests including education, politics, linguistics, the study of texts, ethics, science and engineering. By the seventeenth century, its expression in the entrenched, rationalistic philosophy originally propounded by the twelfth-century neo-Confucianist, Zhuxi was undergoing close critical scrutiny from scholars and philosophers embarked on an empiricist programme of enquiry, and in the eighteenth century this long-gathering critical reaction came to a head in the work of Dai Zhen, a philosopher who represents the culmination of the empiricist movement in neo-Confucian thought. Dai Zhen replaced the broadly dualistic, abstract and speculative approaches of Zhuxi [Chu Hsi] and other neo-Confucianists with a philosophy of material monism and a mode of investigation based on facts, evidence and inductive method. The movement of which he is such an eminent representative is often known as the Han Learning because it took the classics of the Han dynasty (206 BCE–AD 220)[2] for its basic texts and the Han interpretation of the concept of Principle (*li*)[3] as the order immanent in things for its central idea. Under Dai Zhen's influence neo-Confucianism shed many of the Daoist and Buddhist ideas with which it had become imbued.[4] His development and consolidation of the burgeoning empiricism of the time earned him the title of Great Master of Investigation Based on Evidence.

The unassuming family of cloth merchants into which Dai Zhen was born lived quietly in Siuning at the southern border of Anhwei province. His scholarly and critical abilities became apparent when he was still quite young. It is reported that at the age of 10 he questioned his schoolmaster about the reliability of the Confucian text *The Great Learning*,[5] pointing out that during the many centuries that had elapsed since Confucius lived the numerous interpreters and transmitters of his work might have wrought considerable change in the Master's ideas. 'How', asked Dai Zhen 'do we know that this is what Confucius said?'[6] The anecdote certainly exhibits the boy's critical acuity, but what is more significant is that it reveals the intellectual temper characteristic not only of Dai Zhen's own mind but of the whole approach and methodology of the Qing movement, the school of learning of which he was to become such an important member.

In his late teens Dai Zhen was sent to study with Jiang Yong [Chiang Yung], a learned and prosperous man who taught his pupil across a broad curriculum that included the doctrines of Sung neo-Confucianism,[7] the school of thought Dai Zhen was later to oppose. His polymath ability soon began to manifest itself in the writing of books and treatises that covered many topics[8] and for most of his lifetime he was known chiefly for his work in mathematics, waterworks, engineering, phonetics and the analysis and criticism of texts. In 1773 he was appointed to the Board of Compilers of the Imperial Manuscript Library, Siku Quanshu [Ssu-k'u Ch'uan-shu].[9] It was not until a century after his death that his philosophical writings, which had been largely ignored by his contemporaries, began to command the respect they merit.

Dai Zhen's critical assault on the neo-Confucianism of his predecessors is substantially contained in his book *Elucidation of the Meaning of Words in Mencius*. His critique takes its impetus from three things: his dedicated study of early Confucian texts: his adherence to empiricist methods of investigation; and his passion to discover the exact words and truths of the early Confucian sages. He was always ready to challenge any pronouncement that was merely authoritarian, and worked always to verify for himself anything that was offered as evidence for an assertion or belief. He wrote: 'To aspire to get at the truth, a man must purge himself completely of all his dependence'; and, 'A scholar should be deluded neither by others nor by himself.'[10]

Dai Zhen's fundamental objection to the received neo-Confucianism of his time was that it erred from the truth in that it offered a dualistic rather than a monistic account of the ultimate nature of things. His own view, derived in part from his study of ancient texts, in part from empiricist methodology, was that the universe is an organized physical unity whose coherence and orderliness are embedded or immanent in its physicality rather than imposed by a principle external to it. Central to the neo-Confucian debate on this topic was the elucidation and understanding of the meaning of the concept of Principle, or *li*, and its relationship to another major Confucian concept, Ether, or *qi* [*ch'i*], the stuff or matter from which evolved the particular things of the world.

Li is not a simple concept. Even at is most primitive level, and before it had acquired its full philosophical weight, it was of large importance in Confucianism and carried a range of meanings. In the teaching of Confucius *li* was the word for the religious rites and the rules governing familial respect and social relations: those structures of life which, in Chinese culture, were held to render all things well wrought, clearly defined and harmonious. Broadly speaking, the *li* were understood to be imposed from without on to natural human propensities in order to regulate them and achieve a mean in conduct. They were not seen as unchanging and so could vary according to circumstances. Nevertheless, they were not merely superficial rules of conduct expedient for the smooth running of society, but had profounder implications relating to the moral integrity of individuals and their relationships with the cosmos. For the committed practitioner, the external enactments of the *li* were the concomitants of a genuine inward disposition to exercise the virtues they formalized and to realize a harmony between heaven and earth.

After Confucius' own time, the term *li* gradually acquired more complex meanings and a metaphysical dimension. Instead of broadly referring to the formulated rules and customs of human conduct in society, it came to be used to signify some kind of ruling principle of the physical universe, the order or organization of Nature as a 'dynamic pattern . . . embodied in all living things . . . in human relationships and in the highest human values'.[11] This use of *li* has a close metaphorical affinity with its original literal meaning of 'veins or markings in a block of jade' and it is not difficult to see how, from such thinking, questions about the philosophical status of Principle can arise. Is it, for example, to be conceived of as immanent, like the veins in jade or the grain in wood; or as something transcendent, bestowed by heaven to impart form to *qi* and existing, rather in the manner of a Platonic form, independently of the stuff it rules?

It was, as already noted, this latter, rationalistic conception of the universe that Dai Zhen opposed, primarily on philosophical grounds but also in an awareness of the unsavoury political uses to which the notion of a transcendent and unchallengeable ordering Principle could be, and had been, put.[12] Moreover, he saw the heresy of dualism as well as the speculations of idealist and rationalist neo-Confucianism as the consequences of the tainting influences of **Daoism** [*Taoism*] and Buddhism. In *The Meaning of Mencius* he wrote:

> According to the Taoists and Buddhists, as far as the individual self is concerned, it may be divided into a physical body and a spiritual intelligence, the latter being primary. Extending this idea upward, they regard this spiritual intelligence as the primary factor in Heaven and Earth, from which they go on to seek for whatever lacks shape and form, regarding it as genuine existence, whereas whatever possesses shape and form they look upon as illusory.[13]

Dai Zhen's countering of the dualist thesis of the separation of Nature and Principle deploys all the major categories of neo-Confucianism: **Dao**, **yin** and **yang**, *li* and *qi*, **ren**, and the Five Elements. He characterizes *Dao*, or the Way, as a continual and compensating motion that includes not only the alternating movements of *yin* and *yang* but also the Five Elements, since each of the Five Elements possesses *yin* and *yang*. The Five Elements are water, fire, wood, metal and earth; *yin* and *yang* are two forces. *Yin* is negative, passive and weak; *yang* is positive, active and constructive. In placing the Five elements and *yin* and *yang* within the *Dao*, Dai Zhen is associating the *Dao* with Nature (Ether, or *qi*) rather than with a transcendent realm, as in Zhuxi's teaching. Zhuxi had claimed that 'Within the universe there are *li* and *qi*. *Li* constitutes the *Dao* that is "above shapes"; it is the source from which things are produced. *Qi* constitutes the instruments that are "within shapes"; it is the [material] means whereby things are produced.'[14] Dai Zhen makes no such sharp division between Principle and Ether (Nature), but he does draw a distinction *within* Ether concerning what is 'above shapes' and what is 'within shapes'. He says that 'shape' designates the individual object that is produced when Ether (qi) condenses and evolves, but qi itself is 'above shapes' in that it is logically prior to them. Similarly *yin* and *yang*, when thought of as forces, are 'above shapes', as are the Five Elements insofar as they are not manifest as particular entities consisting of wood, fire, water, metal and earth. These latter, particular entities are 'within shapes', as are individual human beings.

The question arises whether Dai Zhen, in locating what is 'above shapes' as well as what is 'within shapes' within the evolutionary processes of Ether, has abolished all need for the concept of Principle. But in fact, he has no thought of abolishing it; it has an essential place in his account and the part it plays there is consonant with the original meaning of *li* as veins in jade. Principle, he maintains, is *ren*, or love, that orderly and harmonious pattern of production and reproduction that manifests propriety and righteousness and that allows for the flourishing of the distinct essences of things. Principle, conceived of in this way, does not rule from a position of transcendence but is contained in material things as the necessary forms of their respective species.

Ren is a concept that is not easily translated in a way that imparts its full or exact meaning. It is variously paraphrased as 'benevolence', 'goodness', 'perfect virtue', 'humanity', 'human-heartedness' and 'love'. It signifies what is highest and most noble in human sentiment and conduct: the disposition to a comprehensive virtue that engenders a harmonious communion between all human beings and between humanity and heaven. In characterizing *Li* as *ren*, or love, Dai Zhen effectively consolidates his doctrine of monism, developing his materialist thesis to encompass the moral as well as the material aspects of existence. He maintains that the moral life is the full and proper expression of human physicality. Human beings are part of the motion of the universe, that 'unceasing production and reproduction brought about by the evolutionary operations of the Ether'.[15] They naturally possess capacities for feeling *qing*, [*ch'ing*], desires (*yu*) and knowledge, *zhi* [*chih*], and when desires and feelings are supplemented by knowledge, then they achieve a full and virtuous expression. 'The ancient sages', he wrote, 'did not seek benevolence, righteousness, propriety, and wisdom outside the realm of [human] desires, and did not consider these in isolation from blood, breath, mind and spirit.'[16] He maintained that 'all activities in the world should consist of nothing more than encouraging this fulfilment of [human] desires, and expression of [human] feelings'[17] and he believed that through careful, scientific observation of the orderliness and the distinctions that operate in nature, human beings might acquire the sagacity to live in harmony with *Li*, in awareness of the grain and veins of things. Dai Zhen did not advocate the total sacrifice of personal interests and self-fulfilment any more that he advocated the kind of desireless life of contemplation associated with the Buddhist and Daoist traditions that he believed had damaged the purity of Confucian thought. For, he argued, 'When a man is void of all desire, he would take a wholly apathetical attitude toward the miserable and hardpressed life of the people throughout the world. To let others live but not to live oneself is against nature.'[18]

It is no surprise that Dai Zhen's philosophy was neglected during his lifetime. Although he was an inheritor rather than a founder of the empirical and investigative method, he was radical and innovative in developing it. To many of his contemporaries his views were alien and unacceptable once they were seen to extend beyond the borders of orthodox scientific investigation. What was so daunting to others was that he was *comprehensively* scientific in his outlook, much as was the seventeenth-century English philosopher Thomas Hobbes. He believed, much like Hobbes, that a scientific model of enquiry could be transposed from the study of objects to the study of the moral and social life of humankind, and yield a similar, indeed, a total understanding. It could not have been easy for his contemporaries to welcome a philosophy the starting point of which was the tenet that everything, including the moral life of human beings, is fundamentally matter in motion. Perhaps more difficult still, even for those who recognized the significance of his ideas, was to align themselves with his repudiation of the established and revered doctrines of Zhuxi. Two of his contemporaries, Hong Bong [Hung Pang] and Zhangxue Cheng [Chang Hsueh-che'ng], made some efforts to disseminate his thought but with little success.[19] It was not until the early years of the twentieth century, when articles on Dai Zhen's ideas began to appear in journals of philosophy and sinology, that he was accorded what is surely his rightful stature: that of a philosopher of remarkable modernity in his own time, and one whose ideas would continue to enrich the intellectual investigation of the nature of things. Jospeh Needham has remarked that 'Tai Chen, though a contemporary of

Rousseau and almost of Blake, would have found himself at home in a post-Freudian world'.[20]

Notes

1 For a fuller account of the introduction of Zen (Chan) Buddhism into China, see the essay on Huineng, pp. 266–72 in this book.

2 The Han dynasty marks the full flourishing and maturity of early Confucianism and the wide propagation of its central texts, subsequently organized as the Four Classics or Four Books: the *Doctrine of the Mean*, *The Great Learning*, the *Analects*, and the *Book of Mencius*.

3 The meaning of '*li*' as 'Principle', rather than the 'rites' of early Confucianism, is indicated in this essay by the use of the capital letter (*Li*).

4 The interrelationships of Daoism, Buddhism and Confucianism are not easily summarized. Some commentators have maintained that Zhuxi had synthesized the three in his philosophy, others that he had stripped Confucianism of the influences of the other two. What is certain is that Dai Zhen would have been critical of any elements of Daoism and Buddhism that Zhuxi had retained or incorporated in his doctrine. For more on Daoism see the essay on Laozi in this book, pp. 240–8

5 *The Great Learning* is one of the Four Classics of Confucianism. See note 2 above.

6 There is a version of this story in Mansfield Freeman, 'The philosophy of Tai Tung Yuan', *Journal of the North China Branch of the Royal Asiatic Society*, no. 65, 1933, pp. 50–71.

7 The Song dynasty (960–1279 CE) encompassed many brilliant cultural achievements including the philosophy of Zhuxi, whose ideas largely dominated Confucianism until the eighteenth century.

8 Dai Zhen's first book was completed in 1744 when he was only 20. It was a short treatise on the use of Napier's rods (John Napier [1550–1617] was a Scottish mathematician, the inventor of logarithms, who devised a calculating machine using a set of rods called 'Napier's Bones'). Thereafter he rapidly became known for his annotations of works dealing with a wide range of technological and scientific subjects.

9 Dai Zhen's academic career was remarkably full and varied. He held a number of posts as tutor, researcher and editor of ancient texts. During this busy time he took and failed the Chinese civil service exams six times. After the sixth failure he was allowed by special decree to be deemed to have passed and was appointed a graduate in the Hanlin Academy where he worked until his death two years later.

10 Quoted in Liang Ch'i-ch'ao, *Intellectual Trends of the Ch'ing Period*, trans. Immanual C.Y. Hsiu, Cambridge, Mass.: Harvard University Press, 1959, p. 56.

11 Fung Yu-lan, *A History of Chinese Philosophy*, trans. D. Bodde, 2 vols, vol. 2, Princeton: Princeton University Press, 1982, p. 444, footnote.

12 It has been pointed out that there had developed a tendency 'to justify the activities of the government of the day by viewing them as natural corollaries of the universal "laws of Nature" '. (See Joseph Needham, *Science and Civilization in China*, 2 vols, vol. II, Cambridge: Cambridge University Press, p. 514.)

13 Fung Yu-lan, op. cit., vol. 2, p. 652.
14 Ibid., p. 542.
15 Tai Chen, *Elucidation of the Meanings of Words in Mencius*, Peking: Ancient Texts Press, 1956, 3.105.
16 Liang Ch'i-ch'ao, op. cit., p. 61.
17 Tai Chen, op. cit., 3.105.
18 Liang Ch'i-ch'ao, op. cit., p. 60.
19 Hung Pang died young and so his attempts to spread Dai Zhen's philosophical thought were cut short. Chang Hsueh-che'ng could not fully accept Dai Zhen's castigation of Zhuxi's doctrine and his enthusiasm for Dai Zhen was tempered by that reservation.
20 Needham, op. cit., p. 515.

Dai Zhen's major writings

Yüan Shan (1763), trans. Cheng Chung-ying as *Tai Chen's Inquiry into Goodness*, Honolulu, East-West Center Press, 1971

Meng zi zi yi shu zheng, Tai Chen on Mencius, a translation by Ann-ping Chin and Mansfield Freeman, New Haven: Yale University Press.

See also in this book

Confucius, Mencius, Laozi, Huineng, Zhuxi, Chinul, Yi Yulgok

Sources and further reading

Chan Wing-tsit, *A Source Book in Chinese Philosophy*, Princeton: Princeton University Press, 1963

Chang, Carsun, *The Development of neo-Confucian Thought*, Westport, Conn.: Greenwood Press, 1957

Fang Chao-ying, 'Tai Chen', in Arthur W. Hummel (ed.), *Eminent Chinese of the Ch'ing Period, 1644–1912*, vol. I, Washington DC, USA Government Printing Office, 1944, pp. 695–700.

Fung Yu-lan, *A History of Chinese Philosophy*, trans. D. Bodde, 2 vols, Princeton: Princeton University Press, 1982

Needham, Joseph, *Science and Civilization in China*, 6 vols, vol. II, Cambridge: Cambridge University Press, 1969

KANG YOUWEI (K'ANG YU-WEI) 1858–1927 CE

Nineteenth-century China was characterized by a great influx of ideas from the West which began to permeate the whole of Chinese cultural life, and by the slow disintegration of the power and authority of the Ching (Manchu) dynasty which had ruled China since 1644. The royal Court had become locked into elaborate but meaningless ceremonial which did nothing to address the needs of the vast majority of the Chinese population. The defeat of China by Britain in the Opium War (1840–2), which led to major trade concessions to western countries, and the victory of Japan in the Sino-Japanese war of 1894–5 convinced many political thinkers, foremost amongst whom was Kang Youwei, that the need for political reform was urgent. In 1898, Kang Youwei presented to the young Emperor a series of reforms based on a limited constitutional monarchy. The Emperor tried to institute the changes suggested, but was out-manoeuvred by the conservative court elements, led by the Empress Dowager. Kang Youwei avoided execution by escaping to Japan, and for the next sixteen years he travelled to Hong Kong, Canada and the United States, where he was asked to undertake various lecture tours. He was invited to return to China after the declaration of the Chinese Republic in 1912.

Kang Youwei was born in the Nanhai district of Kwangdong (Kwangtung), near Canton. While a student he became strongly influenced by the social and moral, rather than the speculative, aspects of neo-Confucian thought, and because of his adherence to Confucianism he was given the title of Sage Kang. Before his period of exile, he taught in various universities including that of Canton, and whilst in Beijing in 1895 he established the Society for National Strength and New Learning. After his return to China, he began to advocate that Confucianism should become the state religion, and he was involved in two failed attempts to restore the Emperor to the throne. For the last decade of his life, he was regarded, not as a radical reformer, but as an arch-reactionary.

In his programmes for political and religious reform, Kang Youwei claimed to have been inspired by Chinese rather than western sources. He revived the controversy between the Old and the New Text or Script Schools, dating back to the Han dynasty (206 BCE–220 CE). The names of the schools refer to the dispute over which of the two versions of the Classics[1] was the more authentic: that written in the New Script introduced under the Han rulers, or that allegedly recorded in the Old Script of the earlier Zhou dynasty (1122 BCE?–256 BCE), but not achieving a position of importance until the second century CE.[2] Kang Youwei was a firm supporter of the New Text school, and denounced the Old Text writings as being forgeries composed by Liuxin (Liu Hsin) (46 BCE–23 CE)[3].

As Derek Bodde points out,

> The controversy between the two schools, however, was
> much more than one of textual criticism, for it embraced wide

ideological differences as well . . . Ideologically speaking . . .
the New Text school tended towards various superstitious
excesses (such as the belief that Confucius was a supernatural
being) which were shunned by the more rationalistic and
sober minded Old Text school.[4]

Kang Youwei was not immune from such extravagances. He
promoted the view that Confucius was primarily a social and religious
reformer, whose views could be derived from a careful reading of the
Modern Script versions of the Classics to determine their esoteric
doctrines. Although Kang Youwei advocated a thoroughgoing reform
of the Chinese political system, he was sufficiently traditionalist to
endorse his recommendations with the name of Confucius. Accordingly, the comprehensiveness of Confucius' thought is said by Kang
Youwei to be of a 'surpassing god-like sageness', which showed that
Confucius was a 'divine being' whom all later thinkers should have
taken as a model, but whose insights were 'damaged' and 'corrupted
by the bigoted meanness'[5] of the later rationalist neo-Confucians
Xunzi [Hsun Tzu] and Zhuxi [Chu Hsi].[6]

Kang Youwei advocated a theory of gradual social evolution which
was based on the Three Ages, those respectively of Chaos or Disorder,
of Small Tranquillity or Rising Peace, and of Great Peace and Great
Unity. Each of the Ages is characterized by social progress; in the
first of the three, humankind originally lived in clans, then tribes, and
lastly identified itself with the region which it inhabited. Confucius
was born in the Age of Disorder, when the inhabitants of his native
state of Lu regarded as foreigners the citizens of all other regions
which were later to compose China. The second Age is that in which
we live, and is marked by the division into nation-states. The Age of
Great Peace and Great Unity will come about with the elimination
of nations and of racial distinctions. Within each of the Ages, there
are progressive or reactionary elements; thus, in the Age of Chaos,
Confucius provided an insight into the two future phases of society,
and in the present Age, 'there are barbarian Red Indians in progressive
America and primitive Miao, Yao, Tong [T'ung] and Li tribes in
civilised China'.[7] A different political system was suited to each of
the Ages. The present era is one of the wish for self-determination
and independence, which can best be achieved by a constitutional
monarchy and parliamentary representation. Harm is caused to the
people if an era does not have the political institutions appropriate to
it. Each historical period is also characterized by certain personal
relationships. The individualism of the Age of Disorder is replaced by

the relationships of husband and wife, and father and son, of the Age of Rising Peace.

Although the present era is an improvement on the previous one, it is still marked by suffering. We, as beings who cannot bear to see the sufferings of others, an idea derived ultimately from Mencius,[8] wish to remove the causes of our distress, and this will bring about our entry into the Age of Great Unity. Our sufferings are manifold; Kang Youwei asserts that they 'are so innumerable as to be unimaginable, changing from place to place and from time to time'.[9] He groups the more common ones into six types: those caused by being alive, including that of rebirth; those from natural disasters; those which are the result of our personal condition, such as being an orphan or being childless; those brought about by human institutions, such as oppressive taxation, or punishment and imprisonment; those caused by our own feelings, such as sexual desire; and those from being held in honour, such as being a sage or a monarch. Kang Youwei's emphasis on suffering is a Buddhist, not a Confucian, doctrine and some of the sufferings which he lists, such as rebirth, are entirely Buddhist. However, as Wing-tsit Chan comments, 'the Buddhist outlook leads to compassion, and compassion is none other than the mind that cannot bear to see the suffering of others. K'ang was [thus] syncretic'.[10]

Kang Youwei identifies the ultimate cause of our suffering as that of division or distinction, and in the Age of Great Unity, all such differentiations will be eliminated. There will be no nation-states, but instead the whole world will constitute one state. There will be no private ownership, but instead public works in agriculture, industry, navigation and the construction of roads will be initiated by the world government, which will also provide public housing for everyone. There will be no titles or social ranks, but everyone will be equal in society, thus removing the causes of envy and the feeling of superiority. There will be only one language and local customs will die out. Racial distinctions will disappear through voluntary interracial interbreeding, and the social institutions of marriage and the family will no longer obtain. Our feelings of compassion for our loved ones will be extended to include the whole of humanity, and even all sentient beings. There will be no disease, and vast material benefits will accrue to everyone; as Kang Youwei puts it, 'New inventions appear every day . . . happiness will reach its limit'.[11] Each human being will attain a perfect existence, not in some transcendent sphere, but here on earth. Kang Youwei can thus be regarded as one of the most ardent of utopian political philosophers.

The concern expressed by Kang Youwei about the universality of compassion and the desire for improvement in the material conditions of the whole of humanity is reminiscent of the views of Mozi [Mo Tzu]. Both Kang Youwei and Mozi advocated that the love and respect which is now limited to only certain people, such as our parents, should be extended to everyone. Mozi's interest in the material conditions of life and the wish to see them improved is reflected in Kang Youwei's enthusiastic description of future life in the Age of Great Unity.

Utopian and progressive systems of political philosophy are also strongly represented in the western tradition. Marxists also believe that history can be divided into stages, from feudalism to capitalism to communism, and that human beings will only come into their own, or be truly fulfilled, in the final phase of communism.

Kang Youwei's philosophy can be criticized because it lacks detail on the motivation for the transition from the Age of Small Peace to the Age of Great Unity. He simply asserts that human nature is fundamentally good, and social progress will ensure that our goodness will be given the opportunity to manifest itself, but we are then left with the problem of why we now have what he regards as limiting or repressive political and social institutions and personal relationships. His view that human beings will all eventually use only one language would be seen by many linguists and philosophers of language as naive. Language develops by its own internal momentum, and many separate languages can evolve from just one origin.

Several Confucian concepts were identified by Kang Youwei with natural phenomena. In keeping with the teachings of Mencius, he maintained that human beings were a part of nature, and that both could be explained in the same way. Both are infused with *qi* [ch'i], the life-force or energy which animates all things, and which is derived from the infinite, undifferentiated, primal source or Great Origin, the *taiyuan* [t'ai yuan][12] from which everything emerges. He states:

> Heaven is a single spiritual substance, and man too is a single spiritual substance. Though different in size, they both share the vast energy derived from the Great Origin . . . This spiritual thing is electricity, possessed of consciousness. As electric light, it can be transmitted everywhere. As spiritual energy, it can activate everything . . . in its entirety, it is the Origin; divided, it is man.[13]

Kang Youwei also endows the *qi* manifested in human beings with a moral dimension. It is none other than the human reluctance to see the sufferings of others, which Kang equates with ***ren*** [jen], the crucial Confucian concept of benevolence or humanity.[14] This is the altruism and fellow-feeling which will characterize the relationships and behaviour of all human beings towards each other in the Age of Great Peace. Kang thus endows electricity with metaphysical and moral, as well as natural, aspects. His attempt to fuse philosophy with what was then the recent technological innovation of electricity may seem quaint, but many philosophers in the western tradition have also engaged in similar endeavours, the latest of which is to assimilate minds to computers.

Kang Youwei is an important figure in Chinese political philosophy. His utopianism, whilst in some respects crude and lacking in detail, inspired his pragmatic recommendations for change in pre-revolutionary Chinese politics. His thought is but one example of the syncretism prevalent in twentieth-century Chinese intellectual life. There are both Buddhist and western elements in his political system, but Kang above all recognized the need to appeal to the revered authority of Confucius, whose ideas still permeate post-revolutionary China.

Notes

1 The Classics comprise the following: *Shijing* [*Shi Ching*] or the Book of Odes, from the early Zhou period; *Shujing* [*Shu Ching*], or the Book of History, records from 7000 to 2000 BCE; *Yijing* [*I Ching*], or the Book of Changes, concerning divination; *Lijing* [*Li Ching*], or the Book of Rites, on rules of social conduct; and *Chunqin* [*Ch'un Ch'in*], the Spring and Autumn Annals, records from 722 to 464 BCE. Many of the teachings of the Classics were developed in the Four Books, which are: *Lunyu*, or the Analects of Confucius; *Daxue* [*Ta Hsueh*], or the Great Learning, on politics; *Zhongyong* [*Chung Yung*], or Doctrine of the Mean, on moral precepts; and *Mengzi* [*Meng Tzu*], the Book of Mencius. See the essay on Confucius in this book, pp. 217–26, and for the details of the controversy between the Old and the New Text schools, see Fung Yu-lan, *A History of Chinese Philosophy*, 2 vols, trans. D. Bodde, Princeton: Princeton University Press, 1983, vol. II, chs II–IV, ch. XVI.

2 See Fung Yu-lan, op. cit., p. 7, translator's note.

3 See Ibid., p. 677, p. 676n

4 Ibid., p. 7, translator's note.

5 Ibid., pp. 678, 679.

6 See the essays on Xunzi and Zhuxi, pp. 259–66 and pp. 278–83 in this book.

7 Chan Wing-tsit, *A Source Book in Chinese Philosophy*, Princeton: Princeton University Press, 1963, p. 727.

8 See the essay on Mencius, pp. 233–40 in this book.
9 Chan Wing-tsit, op. cit., p. 731.
10 Ibid., p. 732.
11 Ibid., p. 734.
12 The concept of *yuan* was first introduced by Dong Zhongshu [Tung Chung Shu] (2nd century BCE) of the New Text school, and was closely related to the concepts of *yin* and *yang*, cosmic inertia and dynamism respectively. See Fung Yu-lan, op. cit., pp. 19-20, 685.
13 Ibid., p. 685.
14 See the essay on Confucius, pp. 217–26 in this book.

Kang Youwei's major writings

Study of the Classics forged during the Hsin [Xin] Period, 1891
Study of Confucius as a Reformer, 1896
Commentary on the Evolutions of Rights, probably 1898
Commentary on the Doctrine of the Mean, 1900
Commentary on the Analects, 1902
Book of the Great Unity, probably 1902

Extensive extracts from Kang Youwei's works are to be found in:
Wing-tsit Chan, *A Source Book in Chinese Philosophy*, Princeton: Princeton University Press, 1963, ch. 39
Fung Yu-lan, *A History of Chinese Philosophy*, 2 vols, trans. D. Bodde, vol. 2, Princeton: Princeton University Press, 1983, ch. XVI

See also in this book

Confucius, Mozi, Mencius, Xunzi, Zhuxi, Mao Zedong

Sources and further reading

Chan Wing-tsit, *A Source Book in Chinese Philosophy*, Princeton: Princeton University Press, 1963
Fung Yu-lan, *A History of Chinese Philosophy*, 2 vols, trans. D. Bodde, vol. 2, Princeton: Princeton University Press, 1983
Lo Jung-pang (ed.), *K'ang Yu-wei, 1858–1927, A Symposium*, Seattle: University of Washington Press, 1964
Thompson, L.G. (trans.), *Ta T'ung shu, The One-World Philosophy of K'ang Yu-wei*, London, Allen & Unwin, 1958

XIONG SHILI (HSIUNG SHI-LI) 1883–1968 CE

Xiong Shili is regarded as one of the most original and influential of China's twentieth-century philosophers. As a young intellectual he was witness to and participator in the turmoil that followed the

Hundred Days Reform of 1898 and that culminated in the overthrow of the Ching dynasty and the founding, in 1911, of the Republic. He grew up in a society that was in cultural ferment, in which Confucianism was waning and people were rapidly absorbing and exploring western influence while at the same experiencing the profound loss of traditions and values so long established that they had seemed part of the natural structure of the Chinese world. His philosophy has roots in the neo-Confucianism of Wang Yangming,[1] in the Consciousness-Only Buddhism[2] he studied as a young man, and in the *Book of Changes* (*I Ching*).[3] It also takes nourishment from the philosophy of Henri Bergson (1859–1941), the French philosopher who posited the idea of a vital force, *élan vital*, as the fundamental reality. Xiong, too, posited an original, immaterial substance which, like Bergson's *élan vital*, is in a constant flux of evolution.

Xiong Shili was born in Huanggang in Hubie Province, the third of six boys in a poor family. His early years were very hard. It is believed that his mother died when he was an infant and his father when he was only 11 years old. In his teens he worked in the fields with his brothers. When just a young boy he had studied Confucius with his father and as he grew up he was able to borrow books and read widely. From the age of 18 he became involved with revolutionary politics. He joined the army and at the same time engaged in anti-Manchu activities. Politics absorbed him until, in 1918, he resolved to become an academic. He first turned attention to traditional studies, to Consciousness-Only Buddhism, which he studied with Ouyang Jianwu at the Institute of Buddhism at Nanjing, and then to the idealist and humanist neo-Confucian philosophy of Wang Yangming. In the latter he found a system of thought that emphasized the fundamental unity of existing things. By combining this with the notion of perpetual transformation he was able to formulate a system of his own; one that was idealist, dynamic, visionary, and politically conscious. He held the post of teacher of New Consciousness-Only at the University of Beijing, and posts at Fuxing Academy in Loshan, at the National Zhejiang University and eventually at Beijing again, where he held a professorship from 1925 until his death.

When Xiong came to formulate his own philosophy he rejected the notion, central to the Consciousness-Only school, that consciousness is the basic philosophical concept. In its place he posited the idea of an 'original substance' that is in constant flux. He maintained that substance and motion are mutually necessary: that there can be no movement without substance and no substance without movement. Accordingly, the fundamental character of his 'original substance' is that it changes unceasingly in a constant movement of production and reproduction: it is simply the perpetual coming into and going out of existence. He writes: 'We must realize that original substance has neither physical form nor character, is not physically obstructed by anything, is absolute, whole, pure, strong and vigorous.'[4]

Xiong ascribes the impetus for the continual transformation that takes place in the original substance to its intrinsic pattern of what he calls 'closing' and 'opening'. He carefully describes these two kinds of movement as 'tendencies' of the original substance. 'Closing' is the tendency of the substance to unite and integrate, and in so doing 'to become physical forms and concrete stuff'.[5] In contrast, 'opening' is the tendency of the substance to maintain and perpetuate itself. But we are not to conceive of these two tendencies as alternating in their activities. Xiong says that the tendency to 'opening' arises simultaneously with that of 'closing'. 'Opening' is 'its own master . . . strong and vigorous',[6] and just as, for the sake of understanding, we may speak of 'closing' as matter, so may we speak of 'opening' as mind. What he also wishes to make clear is that 'closing' and 'opening' are not forces that operate on the original substance, or that are in any way separate from it; they are simply its essential nature: the ways in which it is what it is. In 'closing', it is as if the integrative, consolidating movement of the original substance achieves the density we describe as matter. And at the same time as 'closing' is taking place, though independently of it, there occurs the movement of 'opening', the activity of mind. Xiong also emphasizes the shifting and continual ephemerality of these movements. As soon as a closing or an opening takes place it disappears, 'without preserving its former tendency in the slightest degree'.[7] In all this, it is mind that is primary. It pervades concreteness, although it is not itself concrete, and although it is present as manifestation in all the myriad things it does not thereby lose its own nature. It can be understood as will since it always has a definite direction, namely its tendency to fulfil its own nature. It is also describable as consciousness, which Xiong equates with function. In its original condition mind is **ren** [*jen*], or humanity, the substance common to all things in heaven and earth, 'the source of all transformations and the foundation of all things'.[8]

As already mentioned, for Xiong the original substance is fundamentally immaterial. It is eternal, it is goodness and reason, and it is the basis of all existence. As such it is unknowable and indescribable, although it is revealed by motion and evolution. Its activities are both matter and spirit but they are nevertheless simply aspects of the same single and immaterial unity. Xiong emphasized that substance and function are one, even though they are different. He described substance as what is originally there and function as its operation. He wrote:

> we say that the universal operation of the original substance is its great functioning. By functioning is meant putting substance into functioning, and by substance is meant the true character of function. Therefore substance and function are basically one . . . yet in the final analysis they cannot but be different, for in universal operation there are physical forms which are fathomable, whereas the original substance of the universal operation has no physical form, is most hidden and subtle, and is difficult to know.[9]

In his writings on Confucianism Xiong confronts an objection to his doctrine of the unity of substance and function. The objection, raised by a supposed interlocutor, is that if, as Xiong maintains, the 'ten thousand things' are part of the unceasing and dynamic functioning of the original substance, then the distinctness of the things one from the other is lost and they are really all the same. The interlocutor says, 'they will lose their own selves . . . if the ten thousand things are merely traces of transformations, how can they possess evidently independent selves?[10] In reply Xiong uses a vivid analogy. The waves of the sea, he points out, are also traces and forms, but the water is not something outside the waves, just as the white drops of a violently bursting torrent, which are also traces and forms, are not outside the torrent. He says, 'The ten thousand things manifest themselves and seem to be individual objects, but really their self-nature consists in the great functioning operating without ceasing.'[11]

A good deal of the story of the development of neo-Confucianism recounts the progress of a debate about the relationship between *qi* [*chi*] (material force) and *Li* (Principle).[12] Xiong identifies *qi* with the perpetual tendency of original substance to produce and reproduce; that is, with function. And he regards the myriad of things of the world ('the ten thousand things') as the trace or manifestation of function, or material force. In reasserting the ultimate unity of original substance he urges us not to suppose that material force could be present in the manifestations apart from the intrinsic tendencies. He firmly rejects the idea, present in Song (900–1279) and Ming (1368–1644) thinking, that *Li* (Principle) may be regarded as 'order within material force' on the grounds that it leads to the dualistic view that *qi* is what is real and *Li* merely 'an empty form'. His own view is that there is never a sharp bifurcation of the two. He says: 'the word "principle" is a general term for both substance and function, whereas the word 'material force' refers only to function'.[13] The term '*Li*' may be used to cover both substance and function because although substance is 'absolutely quiet' in its original state, all its principles are 'brilliantly present' in the countless manifestations produced by function through 'openings' and 'closings'. *Li* is at once substance *and* function and as such it is one and not two.

Xiong's espousal of a metaphysic of the unity of the whole of reality took considerable strength not only from its Confucian and Buddhist roots but from the needs of a civilization in upheaval and a cultural psyche long nurtured on doctrines of harmony and equilibrium. Much of political and social significance is derivable from a basic presupposition of cosmic unity. If the original substance is eternal and is goodness and reason, perpetually transforming and evolving into better states, then there is a framework for a political, social and personal morality that includes equality, co-operation, and human benevolence as well as progress and development. It is clear from much of his writing that these are values that Xiong Shili passionately sought to realize. It was remarked of him in the mid-twentieth century that 'he has influenced more young Chinese philosophers than any other contemporary Chinese philosopher'.[14]

Notes

1 See pp. 283–8 in this book.
2 Consciousness-Only doctrine derives from Theravada Buddhism. It holds that everything is Mind and that perception is always perception of mental entities. See the essay on Vasubandhu, pp. 103–14 in this book.
3 The Book of Changes (*I Ching*) is one of the Five Classics. The older sections of it are believed to have reached their present form in the century before Confucius. It is a book of oracles, using sixty-four hexagrams to generate interpretations of chance concatenations of things and events.
4 Chan Wing-tsit, *A Source Book in Chinese Philosophy*, Princeton: Princeton University Press, 1963, p. 766.
5 Ibid.
6 Ibid.
7 Ibid., p. 765.
8 Ibid., p. 769.
9 Ibid.
10 Ibid., p. 771.
11 Ibid., p. 772.
12 Throughout this book *Li*, meaning 'Principle', is capitalized in order to distinguish it from *li*, the formal rites of good conduct in early Confucianism.

13 Chan Wing-tsit, op. cit., p. 767.
14 Ibid., p. 765.

Xiong Shili's writings

Between 1935 and 1947 Xiong Shili's pupils collected and published many of his writings under the title *Shi-li yu-yao* (The Essence of Hsiung Shili). A supplementary volume was added in 1949.

The New Theory of Consciousness-Only, classical Chinese edition and vernacular Chinese edition, 3 vols, Shanghai: Commercial Press, 1932, 1940–4

The Essence of Shili, 4 vols, Peking University, 1935–1947 (Supplementary volume, 1949)

Comprehensive Explication of the Buddhist Theory of Philosophy, Beijing: Peking University, 1937

Essentials of Studying the Classics, Shanghai: Zhengzhong Publishing House, 1944

The Original Confucianism, Shanghai: Longmen United Bookstore, 1944

An Essay Illuminating the Mind, Shanghai: Longmen United Bookstore, 1959

Development of the Philosophy of Change, Beijing, Chinese Academy of Science (printed unofficially), 1961

'On the principles of things and principles of heaven', *Xuiyan*, vol. 12, April 1948

See also in this book

Vasubandhu, Confucius, Zhuxi, Wang Yangming

Sources and further reading

Boorman, H. (ed.) *Biographical Dictionary of Republican China*, New York and London: Columbia University Press, 1970

Briere, O., *Fifty Years of Chinese Philosophy 1898–1950*, London: Allan & Unwin, 1963

Brown, Stuart, Collinson, Diané and Wilkinson, Robert, *Biographical Dictionary of Twentieth-century Philosophers*, London: Routledge, 1996

Chan Wing-tsit, *A Source Book in Chinese Philosophy*, Princeton: Princeton University Press, 1963

Keli Fang (ed.), *A Collection of Modern Neo-Confucianism*, Beijing: Chinese Social Sciences Publishing House, 1983

Shaughnessy, Edward L. (ed.), *I Ching: The Classic of Changes*, New York: Ballantyne Books, 1997

Xiong Shili, 1948, 'On the principles of things and principles of heaven', *Xuiyuan*, vol. 12, April

—— 1961, *Elaborating the Principle of Heaven and Earth*, Hong Kong

—— 1961, *Development of the Philosophy of Change*, Beijing, Chinese Academy of Science (printed unofficially).

MAO ZEDONG (MAO TSE-TUNG) 1893–1976 CE

A persistent feature of Chinese philosophical thought is its non-divorce from the rest of life. This belief is itself a manifestation of a bedrock assumption in the Chinese outlook, that the universe is a whole before it is its parts, and that its ideal state is harmony. Thus philosophers in China have always been expected to live their philosophy, and the subject has not, at least until very recently, been divorced from religion or academized as it has largely been in the West. Daoists, Confucians and Buddhists all put their philosophy into practice. With this in mind it is to that extent understandable that Marxism, as filtered through the experience of Russian revolutionaries, should have been found acceptable in China. Of course, it provides a justification for political revolution and a programme for modernization, but Marxism does more than that. It is a philosophy involving a set of ethical and political goals which can be striven for, and so touches almost every area of existence. It supplies its adherents with a vision of the future and a mission to fulfil. Were it not for its denial of the reality of mind or spirit, it would invite classification as an atheistic religion. Mao Zedong became convinced of its truth as a young man, and lived by its light throughout his entire political career. He did not simply accept Marxism with Leninist additions, however, but added emphases and interpreted key concepts in such a way that it is legitimate to speak of Maoism as a special variant of Marxism.

Mao was born, eldest of four children, into a peasant family in the village of Shaoshan (Hunan province) on 26 December 1893. During his childhood, Mao's father, who had hitherto been poor, managed to become a reasonably affluent farmer, and so his childhood was spent in comparatively comfortable surroundings. However, his early experience of the lives of the peasantry and the hardships they suffered never left him. At the age of 7, he went to his local primary school and was set to work on the Confucian classics. By the time he was 13, Mao had begun to rebel against his father's authority. The latter had intended that Mao should be educated only enough to be useful as a book-keeper, but the boy had other ideas. He was determined to pursue his education, and in 1913 entered a teacher training school in Zhangsha [Changsha], from which he graduated five years later. Here he became politically aware, and read not only Chinese but some western works.

From Zhangsha, Mao went in 1918 to Beijing [Peking] to work in the University Library. While there, he fell under the influence of two leading intellectuals who were to be central to the founding of the

Chinese Communist Party (CCP), Li Dazhao [Li Ta-chao] and Zhen Duxiu [Ch'en Tu-hsiu]. He also read the few available Chinese translations of Marxist texts. When in the summer of 1921 the first meeting of the CCP took place in Shanghai, Mao was present, thus becoming one of its founder-members. Between 1921 and his assumption of its leadership in 1935 Mao worked constantly for the party. He survived the massacres, notably that of 1927, of CCP members organized by the Kuomindang [Kuomintang] under Jiang Gaishek [Chiang Kai-shek]. The leaders of the CCP, following training in Russian Marxism, had concentrated their efforts in the cities, thus making it easy for the Kuomindang forces to round them up. Mao, by contrast, saw the source of a Chinese revolution in the peasantry, and transferred his major effort to organizing 'soviet' areas in the countryside in Kiangsi and Hunan. This did not escape the notice of Jiang, who began a series of five campaigns aimed at the destruction of the CCP (1930–5). It was in response to the fifth campaign that Mao set out on the Long March, abandoning Kiangsi for northern Shensi via a circuitous route almost 6,000 miles long. During this march, especially at the Zunji [Tsunji] conference in January 1935, Mao was acknowledged as leader of the CCP.

The period 1936–49 was one of almost constant warfare, first, in a very fragile alliance with the Kuomindang, against the Japanese (1937–45), and then against the Kuomindang in the civil war of 1947–9. Jiang was forced to withdraw to Taiwan in 1949, and on 1 October in that year Mao proclaimed the People's Republic of China. Between 1949 and his death in September 1976, Mao's energies were devoted to the modernization of China on communist lines. The main features of this period – the Great Leap Forward, the Cultural Revolution, relations with the USSR and the USA, and the Lin Biao [Lin Piao] affair – are all the subject of extensive literature. Whatever the final verdict on these events, Mao's place in history is manifestly secure.[1]

Mao's philosophy is his own variation on Marxism-Leninism, and it is necessary to have a brief outline of this world-view in mind in order to understand Mao's version of it. Marxism-Leninism is epitomized in histories of thought as dialectical materialism. It is called materialism because of one of its basic metaphysical assertions, namely that all that exists is material in nature and none of it mental. Mind or spirit is not a second type of substance, discrete from matter, but can only be a mode or property of matter. It is called dialectical because it is held that the unfolding of the changes in matter, which is another way of referring to history, follows an inevitable, discernible and repeated pattern which is called dialectical.[2] The dialectical progression of history unfolds as follows: at no time is reality stable. It always consists of elements which are in tension with one another, and these tensions are referred to as contradictions. The set of contradictions obtaining at a given time, T^1, is called the thesis in the dialectical progression. Because there is internal tension, there will be change, resulting in the formation of some new contradictions at time T^2, and this is called the antithesis. The second state will inevitably mutate into a third state at T^3 which will embody elements of the conditions obtaining in both T^1 and T^2, and is called the synthesis. This synthesis is also the thesis in the next triadic movement of the dialectical progression. This dialectical progression of change is held to be a law of history, in the same sense of 'law' as that term is used in science, i.e. as a basis for verifiable prediction.

Further, Marx divides all the elements of a given society into two classes, the base (in German *Unterbau*) and the superstructure (*Oberbau*). The base comprises the economic conditions at the time: what counts as wealth and how it is distributed, the 'relations of production' in Marxist terms. The superstructure contains all other important social institutions: the system of government; the legal and educational systems; philosophy and the arts, and religion. Marx contends that the base always determines the superstructure, that is, that when changes occur in government, the law, etc., no matter what justifications are given for them in terms of the 'progress of justice' and the like, the real cause is always an economic one. In capitalist society, he argues, the main function of the superstructure is to disguise from the proletariat that they are being exploited, or to make them accept this situation. In classical Marxism, only one important institution stands outside the dialectic, and that is science, which is held to be objectively true. This move is needed in order to avoid Marxism's being self-refuting: were Marxism to be classed as a philosophy it would merely be part of the superstructure. Instead, Marx classes his views as science and therefore objectively true, and in this he is followed by Mao.[3]

This set of ideas is used by Marx as the basis for an analysis of society and its future. He holds that capitalism will inevitably collapse because of its own internal contradictions, and that after revolutionary change the classless society of communism will emerge, in which each will produce according to his or her ability and give to others according to their need. The future is one in which a perfect human society will inevitably come about. There will be 'an association, in which the free development of each is the condition for the free development of all'.[4]

None will be oppressed, alienated or exploited. Marxism-Leninism is, like Maoism, profoundly optimistic in its vision of the future.

Mao Zedong accepted all the foregoing, though occasionally (as will be seen) with certain modifications. His main philosophical interests were first in the concept at the centre of the dialectical thought of both Hegel and Marx, that of contradiction, and second in epistemology, where he elaborates on the ideas of Lenin.

The concept of contradiction (C: *maodun* [*mao-tun*]) is to be understood in an extended sense in Mao's thought. It is not used in the restricted logical sense of the term in which two incompatible propositions, *p* and not-*p*, are said to contradict one another. Rather, contradiction in Mao's sense is a tension between the components of any thing or situation, and is an omnipresent, fundamental property of reality, from the realm of the laws of physics to complex social phenomena:

> mechanical motion under external force occurs through the internal contradictoriness of things. Simple growth in plants and animals, their quantitative development, is likewise chiefly the result of their internal contradictions. Similarly, social development is due chiefly not to external but to internal causes.[5]

It follows that the only way to understand any aspect of reality is to grasp its internal contradictions, for they constitute its nature:

> materialist dialectics holds that in order to understand the development of a thing we should study it internally and in its relations to other things; in other words, the development of things should be seen as their internal and necessary self-movement, while each thing in its movement is interrelated with and interacts on the things around it.[6]

It is to be stressed that for Mao contradiction is ubiquitous and ceaseless: 'without contradiction nothing would exist.'[7]

This basic notion Mao elaborates at some length, and his elaboration is itself dialectical in form. He asserts next that looked at from one point of view, contradiction is universal and looked at from another, is characterized by particularity. To say that contradiction is universal is to stress that it is present in all things at all times: 'contradiction exists in the process of development of all things, and . . . in the process of development of each thing a movement of opposites exists from beginning to end',[8] and this applies in equal measure both to the inner process of human thought and to external social interactions. It is not enough, however, to know that contradiction is omnipresent. If one is to be successful in politics and in other areas of life, it is necessary to have the sharpest possible grip on the particular instance of contradiction with which one is confronted, for 'This particular contradiction constitutes the particular essence which distinguishes one thing from another'.[9]

This is a point to which Mao returns repeatedly in his writings, and for good reason. There is a danger involved in the study of comprehensive world-views like Marxism that its adherents can be as much blinded by it as alerted through it to the nature of reality. The theory can supply ready-made, as it were, an analysis of any kind of situation, e.g. that it is a complex of mutable contradictions whose progressive change is inevitable, and so on. Successful political action, or indeed successful action of any kind, does not come from resting content with generalities of this kind. Success in politics, Mao argues, comes from precise knowledge of the particular circumstances of the here and now. He warned consistently of the danger of assuming that courses of political action that had worked in Russia would work without change in China. Many CCP officials had been trained in Moscow, and Mao saw in their subsequent behaviour evidence of what he called 'dogmatism', i.e. a tendency to apply pure Marxist dogma without any regard to political reality. This he saw as a path to certain failure, and his main reason for writing his chief philosophical essays was to combat precisely this tendency:

> Our dogmatists are lazy-bones. They refuse to undertake any painstaking study of concrete things, they regard general truths as emerging out of the void, they turn them into purely abstract unfathomable formulas . . . They understand nothing of the Marxist theory of knowledge.[10]

Much of the further analysis Mao devotes to contradiction is aimed precisely to reinforce the need for exact scrutiny of existing conditions. He next introduces the concepts of principal contradiction and the principal aspect of a contradiction. Contradictions very rarely occur singly in the real world: the situations requiring our attention are almost invariably a complex of two or more contradictions, and one of these will always be more important than the rest. This principal contradiction we must seek to identify, since it is this which is the chief determinant of the nature of the situation as a whole.[11]

Further, within any individual contradiction, of the two elements in tension, one will be more important than the other, and this is the principal aspect of the contradiction. It is important to identify this, because 'The nature of a thing is determined mainly by the principal aspect of a contradiction, the aspect which has gained the dominant position'.[12] Because the nature of reality is one of constant change, the role of principal and subordinate aspects in a single contradiction is not fixed: these positions can and do change, and when this happens, the nature of the thing constituted by the contradiction changes also. Mao's elaboration of this point leads him to diverge from Marx in an important respect. Marx had held that, in the case of the base to superstructure relationship, the roles of each component never change, in that the base always determines the superstructure. This Mao rejects, consistently with his view that reversal of the role of aspects is possible in *any* contradiction:

> it must also be admitted that in certain conditions, such aspects as the relations of production, theory and the super-structure in turn manifest themselves in the principal and decisive role. When the superstructure (politics, culture, etc.) obstructs the development of the economic base, political and cultural changes become principal and decisive.[13]

Mao continues with the assertion that, although in one sense a contradiction consists of two aspects which are in tension, in another these aspects are identical. This at first sight puzzling assertion becomes far less so in the light of Mao's spacious definition of the concept of identity: it does not mean either numerical identity or identity of sets of properties. Instead: 'identity, unity, coincidence, interpenetration, interdependence (or mutual dependence for exis-tence), interconnection or mutual co-operation – all these different names mean the same thing.'[14] Granted this very broad sense of identity, Mao can assert that 'in given conditions, each of the contra-dictory aspects within a thing transforms itself into its opposite, changes its position to that of its opposite'.[15] The change of position of the aspects of a contradiction from subordinate to principal or vice versa Mao calls an example of conspicuous change, a type of change he contrasts to what he terms relative rest. This distinction is needed to answer an obvious objection to the basic metaphysical thesis that contradictory change is omnipresent, and that is that some institutions or phenomena exist for so long that to say that they exemplify change and tension is far-fetched. Mao replies that what appears to be stasis is merely relative, an even balance of opposing forces. Such conditions always degenerate, and conspicuous change results.[16]

Finally, in his attempt to combat dogmatism in Marxist thinking on contradiction, Mao argues that not all contradictions are antagonistic. Consistently with his thesis of omnipresent change, Mao argues that non-antagonistic contradictions may come to be antagonistic, and vice versa. For example, contradiction between the exploiting and exploited classes exists in all forms of society – slavery-based, feudal, or capitalist – but for most of the time this contradiction is not antagonistic. However, it follows from the principle of the constancy of change that states of relative rest do not continue indefinitely, and when 'the contradiction between the two classes develops to a certain stage . . . it assumes the form of open antagonism and develops into revolution'.[17] This distinction is needed because Mao accepts that contradiction will not cease under socialism, and nor was it absent between different groupings within the CCP. However, to fail to see that these two classes of contradiction are non-antagonistic is likely to lead to inappropriate modes of action to resolve them: different classes of contradiction must be treated differently.

The theme of the need to pay the closest attention to the real facts of any situation recurs in Mao's epistemology, his second main philosophical interest. He begins from the assertion that knowledge arises not from the disinterested desire to know the truth, but as a result of our need to understand the world in order to produce what we need to survive:

> Man's knowledge depends mainly on his activity in material production, through which he comes gradually to understand the phenomena, the properties and the laws of nature, and the relations between himself and nature . . . None of this knowledge can be acquired apart from activity in production.[18]

The truth of any assertion is to be measured not in terms of logical consistency or theoretical cogency but by successful application to the world: 'Only social practice can be the criterion of truth. The standpoint of practice is the primary and basic standpoint in the dialectical-materialist theory of knowledge.'[19] Further, it follows from the metaphysical assertions that change is constant and progress inevitable, that human knowledge, if always complete, is always progressing step by step to higher levels.[20]

The process whereby knowledge arises from practice is said by Mao to have two major stages of which the first is 'the stage of sense-perceptions and impressions'.[21] In this stage, objects in the world impinge on the sense organs and evoke sense-perceptions of these objects together with a rough impression of their relations. The first stage of knowledge does not penetrate to the heart of reality; this occurs only at the second, rational or conceptual stage. As social practice continues,

> a sudden change (leap) takes place in the brain in the process of cognition, and concepts are formed. Concepts are no longer the phenomena, the separate aspects and the relations of things; they grasp the essence, the totality and the internal relations of things.[22]

Though these stages are separable in analysis, in life they are unified in the experience of practice. Neither sensation alone nor reason alone is an adequate foundation for knowledge: each complements the other, and the findings of their joint product must be tested against reality in action. Consistently with his metaphysics of change, Mao is insistent that theory must be constantly measured against a mutable world. He identifies two common groups of thinkers in communist circles who fail to do this and who in consequence make mistakes: the first is the group who become set in their convictions and whose ideas lag behind the changing facts ('die-hards'), and the second are those who fantasize ahead of the possible ('leftists'), whose ideas ignore the pace at which change can realistically be made to occur.[23]

Mao shows a willingness to follow his own line of thought against Marxist authorities not only on the question of the base-superstructure relationship but also in respect of his attitude to those features of the superstructure normally referred to as the culture of the period. In the thought of Lenin, all aspects of culture are to be controlled to serve political ends, and one result of this was the set of aesthetic prescriptions for artists called Soviet Realism. Mao's theoretical position is different. In the fields of art and science, differences are to be settled

> through free discussion in artistic and scientific circles and through practical work in these fields . . . We think that it is harmful to the growth of art and science if administrative measures are used to impose one particular style of art or school of thought and to ban another.[24]

and this policy is that of 'Letting a hundred flowers blossom and a hundred schools of thought contend'.[25]

This philosophy involves a number of difficulties. Some are those inherent in all forms of Marxism, e.g. whether its claim to be a science can be sustained; whether its 'laws' of history can produce testable predictions; whether the concept of class can be defined in such a way as to do all the work required of it, and the like. Other difficulties are peculiar to Maoism, e.g. whether the concept of contradiction (in the Maoist sense) can usefully be applied to natural as opposed to social phenomena; or whether the distinction between Mao's two stages of knowledge is defensible (since both are conceptual). In certain respects, by contrast, Maoism is refreshing, especially in its consistent stress on the need to avoid falling into dogmatic habits of thought. Mao was certainly no blind follower of Marx, Engels, Lenin and Stalin. He had the firmest grip on the fact that, in politics, to ignore the hard facts is to court disaster, and this realism marks him out from many lesser Marxist thinkers.

Notes

References to the four-volume *Selected Works of Mao Tse-tung*, Peking, Foreign Languages Press, 1967, are given as SW + vol. number + page.

1 For more detail on Mao's life, cf. S. Schram, *Mao Tse-tung*, Harmondsworth: Penguin Books, 1966.
2 The concept of dialectic, like so much else, Marx took over from the philosophy of Hegel (1770–1831). In Hegel's philosophy, however, ultimate reality is spiritual in nature, and so his philosophy is epitomized as dialectical idealism; cf. the articles on Hegel and Marx in D. Collinson, *Fifty Major Philosophers*, London: Routledge, 1988.
3 Whether the claim of Marxism to be a science is sustainable is another matter, cf. the classic critique in H.B. Acton, *The Illusion of the Epoch*, London: Cohen & West, 1955.
4 K. Marx and F. Engels, *Manifesto of the Communist Party* (1848), Moscow: Progress Publishers, 1965, p. 75.
5 *On Contradiction* (1937), SW, I, p. 313. In extending the application of the concept of contradiction from society to natural processes, Mao is following a line of thought initiated by Engels, cf. his *Anti-Dühring* (1878), 2nd edn, Moscow: Foreign Languages Publishing House, 1959, Pt I, ch. xii, pp. 164ff.
6 *On Contradiction*, SW, I, p. 313.
7 Ibid., p. 316.
8 Ibid.
9 Ibid., p. 320.
10 Ibid., p. 321.
11 Ibid., p. 331.
12 Ibid., p. 333.
13 Ibid., p. 336.
14 Ibid., p. 337.
15 Ibid., p. 338.

16 Ibid., p. 342.
17 Ibid., p. 343.
18 *On Practice* (1937), SW, I, p. 295.
19 Ibid., p. 297: though he does not say so explicity, Mao accepts Lenin's copy theory of knowledge, according to which true knowledge is a mirror-like reflection in the mind of reality. This theory denies the Kantian assertion that the structure of knowledge reflects the structure of the mind. cf. V.I. Lenin, *Materialism and Empirio-Criticism*, Moscow: Foreign Languages Publishing House, 1947.
20 *On Practice*, SW, I, p. 296.
21 Ibid., p. 297.
22 Ibid., SW, I, p. 298; reiterated in *Where Do Correct Ideas Come From?* (1963) in *Four Essays on Philosophy*, Beijing: Foreign Languages Press, 1968, pp. 134–6.
23 *On Practice*, SW, I, pp. 305–6.
24 *On the Correct Handling of Contradictions Among the People* (1957), in *Four Essays on Philosophy*, op. cit., p. 114.
25 Ibid., p. 113.

Mao Zedong's writings

Though the collected writings of Mao run to many volumes, his philosophical thought is concentrated in four essays:

On Practice, 1937
On Contradiction, 1937
On the Correct Handling of Contradictions Among the People, 1957
Where Do Correct Ideas Come From?, 1963

These essays are printed in the various selected and collected editions of Mao's works, but are conveniently available printed together as *Four Essays on Philosophy*, Beijing: Foreign Languages Press, 1968.

See also in this book

Kang Youwei

Sources and further reading

Mao Zedong

Selected Works of Mao Tse-tung, 4 vols, Peking: Foreign Languages Press, 1967
Four Essays on Philosophy, Peking: Foreign Languages Press, 1968
'On dialectical materialism – a fragment', trans. C.S. Chao in *Studies in Soviet Thought*, vol. III, no. 4, December 1963, pp. 270–7.

About Mao Zedong

The Philosophical Thought of the Mao Zedong: Studies from China 1981–1989, Armonk, NY: M.E. Sharpe, 1992

Schram, S., *Mao Tse-tung*, Harmondsworth: Penguin Books, 1966

Soo, F.Y.R., *Mao Tse-tung's Theory of Dialectic*, Dordrecht: Reidel, 1981 (Sovietica series, vol. 44)

Other works referred to

Acton, H.B., *The Illusion of the Epoch*, London: Cohen & West, 1955

Engels, F., *Anti-Dühring* (1878), Eng. trans., 2nd edn, Moscow: Foreign Languages Publishing House, 1959

Lenin, V.I., *Materialism and Empirio-Criticism*, (1909), Eng. trans., Moscow: Foreign Languages Publishing House, 1947

Marx, K. and Engels, F., *Manifesto of the Communist Party* (1848), Eng. trans., Moscow: Progress Publishers, 1965

Part 6

KOREAN PHILOSOPHY

INTRODUCTION

Intellectual thought and development in Korea have always been influenced, though never dominated, by its geographical proximity to China. As in China, the three major traditions of Daoism, Confucianism and Buddhism were early to be found in the Korean peninsula. During the Three Kingdoms period (57 BCE–668 CE), before Korea was unified, adherents of each tradition were to be found amongst the members of each society. Daoism never achieved a position of pre-eminence, and thus the history of Korean thought for the past twenty centuries has been dominated by Buddhism and Confucianism, which throughout most of that time have coexisted without conflict.

From the time of the Three Kingdoms onwards, there was a continuous exchange of scholars between China and Korea. Some Koreans penetrated as far as India in search of Buddhist writings and sources. **Mahayana** Buddhism came to the peninsula during the Three Kingdoms period, in the forms of the **Pure Land** and the **Tiantai** [T'ien-t'ai] schools. Pure Land Buddhism is characterized by its emphasis on devotional practice and its promise to the faithful of rebirth in the Paradise of the West. Tiantai Buddhism has attempted to synthesize the important insights achieved by other doctrinal schools of Mahayana Buddhism, and has been of great influence in Korea. The first major Korean Buddhist thinker, Wonhyo (617-686 CE), contributed to the development of both Pure Land and Tiantai thought, and influenced later Korean scholars. He wrote a commentary on the *Avatamsaka Sutra*, the chief source of the **Huayan** [Hua-yen] school of Chinese Buddhism, which in turn helped to shape the thought of the Chinese philosopher Fazang (643–712 CE), the leading exponent and developer of Huayan. Like the major thinkers of Tibet, Wonhyo distinguished between public or exoteric Buddhist doctrines, and concealed or esoteric teachings, a trend continued by later Korean Buddhists.

In 668 CE, the kingdom of Silla embarked upon a programme of expansion to unify the whole of the Korean peninsula, a project which was finally achieved in 676. During the United Silla period (668–935 CE), Buddhism maintained its position of pre-eminence in the intellectual and cultural life of Korea, even fostering the study of Confucianism in its monasteries. Two further schools of Buddhism, Huayan [K: Hwaom] and **Zen** [C: Chan; K: Son] were introduced from China at about the time of unification, and have continued to be influential up to the present day. Huayan doctrine has a high metaphysical content, with its theories that there is mutual interpenetration and interdependence both between ultimate reality and the phenomena which it generates, and between the phenomena themselves. Zen Buddhism has often been considered primarily as a school of meditation, with its emphasis on paradox, ellipsis and sudden enlightenment as a release from *samsara*, the cycle of rebirth. During the period of the Koryo dynasty (937–1392), two attempts were made to synthesize the teachings of Zen and other Buddhist movements, including Huayan. The first, by the Tiantai monk Uichon (1055–1101) was a failure, and merely resulted in the Zen movement becoming more hostile to the doctrinal schools. The second, by the Zen monk Chinul (1158–1210), was inspired by the earlier attempt and met with considerable success, although from that time onwards Zen has been the dominant force in Korean Buddhism.

During the late Koryo dynasty, Confucianism steadily gained ascendancy. To parallel the examination system in Buddhism, both state and private Confucian academies were set up, to train students for civil service examinations which the children of Buddhist monks were not allowed to take. There was a steady introduction into Korea of Confucian texts, particularly those of the Chinese scholar Zhuxi [Chu Hsi] (1130–1200 CE). For the first time, there was hostility between Buddhists and Confucians. Buddhism was blamed for the increasing instability of the Koryo dynasty; many of its monasteries held large tracts of land which were not under State control, and many of the most able young Koreans became Buddhist monks, so their services were lost to the state. Confucians maintained that Buddhists should be eligible for, not exempt from, military service despite their pacifist beliefs. Buddhism was accused of not taking account of familial and social relationships, and of pessimism because it ignored the concerns of this world in favour of exclusive emphasis on personal salvation and escape from *samsara*. With the disintegration of central state control, Confucians hoped to 'creat[e] a new moral and socio-political order out of the old society dominated by the Buddhist tradition'.[1] The struggle between Buddhism and Confucianism in Korea was finally resolved in favour of the latter in the early years of the Choson dynasty (1392–1910) , and the official state ideology remained Confucian until the fall of Choson. Confucianism provided the ethical and political theories that underpinned the new dynasty, and contributed to its remarkable stability and longevity. As Edward Chung puts it, 'Korea [was] the most thoroughly Confucianised state [in East Asia] during the five centuries of the Choson dynasty'.[2]

Precise historical details of the transmission of neo-Confucianism from China to Korea are a matter of dispute, but Confucianism has always had both metaphysical and ethico-social dimensions, owing to its overarching belief that there is a continuation between non-human and human nature. Korean neo-Confucians pursued the exploration, refinement and interrelationship of such crucial concepts as *li*, the principle or regulator of all particular things and of the universe as a whole, and *qi* [*ch'i*], the energy, dynamism or material force which pervades all things.

On the ethical and social levels, Korean neo-Confucianism promoted self-discipline, moral cultivation, and the crucial importance of familial and social relationships, as the basis of political order and stability. As in China, prominence was given to the status of education. The issues with which the neo-Confucian thinkers of Korea were concerned had a practical impact on the everyday lives of the people, with their steady production of texts on economics, education and politics. In keeping with the teachings of the Chinese philosopher Mencius, one area of absorbing interest to many Koreans, including Yi T'oegye (1501–1570) and Yi Yulgok (1536–1584) was that of human goodness and the relationship between the emotions and the 'four beginnings' of benevolence, righteousness, propriety and wisdom, which became known as the 'four-seven' debate. Neo-Confucian theories on this issue had implications for the problem of the source of evil.

Later neo-Confucian thought in Korea displayed a tendency to degenerate into abstruse factional disputes, some of which were based on developments in the 'four-seven' debate and continued until the fall of the Choson dynasty. From China and Korea, neo-Confucianism penetrated into Japan, where it was never a pervasive force, but retained a high degree of pragmatism and cohesion.

Owing to its geographical position, Korea has always been vulnerable to the expansionist ambitions of its more powerful neighbours, China, Japan and Russia. After the defeat of China in the Sino-Japanese war of 1894–5, Japan formally annexed Korea in 1910, thus bringing to an end the Choson dynasty with its Confucian-inspired ideals. In the aftermath of the Second World War, Korea was divided, and the partition was officially recognized at the end of the Korean war in 1953. North Korea has, since then, adopted Communism as its official ideology.

Until relatively recently, Korea was simply regarded as the passive recipient of Chinese Buddhist schools of thought, and as a staging-post in their transmission from China to Japan. Edward Conze, the eminent Buddhist scholar, made the following comment: 'Korean Buddhism was chiefly significant by acting as an intermediary between China and Japan . . . It was noteworthy for the fervour with which it was practised'.[3] The revival of Korean Buddhist scholarship in South Korea over the last three decades of the twentieth century proved this not to be the case, and further contributions will no doubt be forthcoming. Similarly, the historical and philosophical survey of Korean neo-Confucianism undertaken by scholars in both South Korea and the United States has shown it to be a rich tradition with particular concerns of its own. Korea is thus beginning to be recognized as a source of intellectual ideas of great interest and importance.

Notes

1 E.Y.J. Chung, *The Korean neo-Confucianism of Yi T'oegye and Yi Yulgok*, New York: State University of New York Press, 1995, p. 9.
2 Chung, op. cit., p. 15.
3 E. Conze, *A Short History of Buddhism*, London: Allen & Unwin, p. 94.

CHINUL 1158–1210 CE

Korean Buddhism flourished from the time of the inception of the Unified Silla dynasty (668–935 CE) until the middle years of the Koryo period (937–1392 CE). There was mutual support between Buddhism and the successive royal houses, to the extent that the founder of the Koryo dynasty, Wang Kon (also known as T'aejo) declared, 'All the great enterprises of our kingdom depend upon the protective power of all the Buddhas'.[1] From the ninth century onwards, there was tension between the **Zen** (C: Chan; K: Son) movement, with its emphasis on sudden insight into ultimate reality, and other Buddhist schools, with their insistence that the true nature of reality could only be arrived at after years of intensive study of the *sutras* and the commentaries on them produced by earlier Buddhist thinkers of distinction. Two attempts were made to reconcile these different approaches. The second of these was undertaken by Chinul, a Zen monk who had also studied the central *sutras* of other Buddhist schools. Chinul's solution to the problem was to combine the 'sudden awakening' of Zen with the 'gradual cultivation' of the mind advocated by most other Buddhist sects. It gained many supporters throughout the centuries, and is still favoured by many Korean Zen adherents today.

There are several sources for details of Chinul's life. Besides the autobiographical references scattered throughout his writings, there is the memorial inscription set up with royal permission a year after Chinul's death, and a record of his establishment of what is now the monastery of Songgwang, composed towards the end of his life. Chinul was born in 1158, in the Korean province of Hwanghae. According to the inscription, his father was an administrative official at the National Academy and, becoming concerned about Chinul's poor health as a child, vowed to dedicate his son to Buddhism if he were cured. After this event, Chinul was restored to full health, and was duly initiated into a Buddhist order of monks at the age of 8. Reservations about this account have been expressed by the modern commentator Hee-Sung Keel,[2] who maintains that it may be one of the pious and legendary accretions attached to the biographies of eminent monks. Whatever the truth about Chinul's initiation, he had been received into a Zen monastic order by his early twenties, and shortly afterwards made a pact with other young monks to retreat to the countryside to set up a society dedicated to the promotion of *samadhi*, or meditation, and *prajna*, or wisdom. The motivation for this intention was probably the condition of Korean society and of the Buddhist monasteries at the time. Centralized political control in twelfth-century Korea was gradually breaking down, and Korean Buddhism was no longer distinguished by intellectual vigour. Its monasteries had become important centres of agriculture and trade, and its monks had become desirous of power and material benefits. Chinul's vow to become one of the founders of an alternative way of life was not realized for several years, but he left the capital of the Koryo kingdom and travelled to the south of the country, in order to pursue religious enlightenment and self-cultivation. Unusually for a Zen monk, Chinul did not attach himself to a recognized Zen master, but pursued the study of the *sutras* of the various Buddhist schools in order to reach religious maturity. In 1188, he renewed his vow to set up a new Buddhist community, and sent out an invitation to like-minded people of other Buddhist sects and also to those whose background was in Confucian or Daoist learning to join him in this enterprise. A home for the community was found on Kong mountain, and the establishment immediately began to attract many new adherents. An offshoot of the settlement was set up under the auspices of another society, that for the cultivation of Son (Zen), initiated by Chinul and one of his disciples. The result was the foundation of the Songgwang monastery, which is today one of the leading centres in Korea for the study of Buddhism. From 1190 onwards, Chinul interspersed his teaching at and administration of the monastery with periods of religious retreat. In 1210, after a short period of illness, Chinul died. His importance to Korean Buddhism was recognized by the conferral of the posthumous title, 'The Buddha Sun Shining Universally'.

In Chinul's ontology, ultimate reality is referred to as the True Mind; it is what other Buddhist thinkers call **sunyata**, the predicateless Void or Emptiness. It is not to be understood in nihilistic terms, but it is ungenerated, all-inclusive and all-encompassing, without substance or essence. It cannot be conceptualized, but only gestured towards in language. In keeping with his syncretist leanings, Chinul maintained that there are many symbols of the True Mind, each to be found in a different *sutra*. He states:

> The *Avatamsaka Sutra* names it the *dharmadhatu* . . . In the *Prajnaparamita Sutras* it is referred to as 'nirvana', because it is the sanctuary of all the saints. In the *Golden Light Sutra* it is said to be 'suchness' because it is true, permanent and immutable . . . In the definitive sutras [the *Complete Enlightenment Sutra*] it is named 'complete enlightenment' because it destroys darkness and shines solitarily of itself.[3]

For Chinul, the True Mind is to be distinguished from what we regard as our discrete, empirical, limited minds that endow us with our individuality and separateness. According to Chinul, True Mind is uncaused and has no effects. It transcends time, having no beginning or end. It is all-pervasive, being beyond both existence and non-existence, and is unmoving and tranquil. All particular phenomena are manifestations or appearances of True Mind, the noumenon that can be ascertained in and through them. Chinul takes over from the **Huayan** (Hua-yen) school the theory that all phenomena are mutually interdependent, interpenetrative and reflective, as is each and every phenomenon with True Mind itself.[4] In Chinul's words, 'There is . . . in the mirror of one's mind a perception of the inexhaustible *dharmadhatu* . . . The unimpeded interpenetration of all phenomena . . . [is] never separate from the pure enlightened nature [the *dharmadhatu*]'.[5]

Chinul's theory as taken over from the Huayan, that one phenomenon mirrors all other particulars and ultimate reality itself, is similar to the views of the German philosopher Leibniz (1646–1716). According to Leibniz, an individual substance, or what he calls a monad, of which there is an infinite number, is a mirror or reflection of all other monads, and of the whole of reality. Each monad is thus a microcosm for all others, and for the entire universe.

One general problem arising from most interpretations of Buddhism, including that of Chinul, is why ultimate reality should manifest itself in a multiplicity of phenomena. Chinul does not provide an account of the impetus behind or reason for such particularization, nor why *sunyata* or True Mind does not simply remain at the level of undifferentiated, ungenerated, predicateless Suchness.

Despite Chinul's wish to incorporate the approaches of the doctrinal Buddhist schools into his own philosophy, he reserves particular scorn for those members of the **Pure Land** sect whose devotional practices had been reduced to the recitation of the name of the Buddha Amitabha in the expectation that this would ensure their rebirth in the remote Paradise of the West. As Chinul puts it,

> Whereas the expedient *sutras* talk about this world as an impure land, a separate world as the Pure Land . . . the meaning of seeking rebirth in the Pure Land, as expounded by the Buddha and the patriarchs . . . is in every case not separate from one's own mind. I do not know from where, if not from the source of one's own mind, one is to enter [the Pure Land].[6]

As previously mentioned, Chinul advocated a 'sudden awakening' to ultimate reality. Such an immediate insight into the true nature of things is not the result of intellectual understanding, but of some form of direct intuition. It could be provided by the words or teachings of a Zen master or, as in Chinul's own case, by reading a passage or passages from the *sutras*. The words, teachings or passages 'come alive' in moments of illumination; they do not obscure or stand in the way of ultimate reality, but are an indicator of it. Chinul himself had several experiences crucial to his religious development, gained from reading various sections of the *Huayan Sutra* and the *Platform Sutra* of the Sixth Patriarch of Zen, the Chinese philosopher Huineng.[7] His insights from these experiences were that *sunyata*, or the true nature of ultimate reality, is to be discerned from its manifold phenomena or appearances; that all human beings have the capacity for gaining wisdom, or an insight into the real nature of things; and that many do not do so because they are distracted by appearances. Chinul recommends that Buddhists should not restrict themselves to the study of the central *sutras* of their own order or school, but should be open to illumination from any source. The danger of limited study is the descent into linguistic or terminological dispute, which can become yet one more barrier to insight. As Chinul puts it, 'How can it be right that people do not penetrate to the very root but squander their time in futile arguments and disputes, each feeling comfortable in what he is accustomed to'.[8] Language thus has to be treated with caution. It can function as an analytical tool in which we could become enmeshed to the detriment of our spiritual progress, or it can act as a guide to true illumination.

The 'gradual cultivation' advocated by Chinul complements the 'sudden awakening'. Even if we have had the experience of direct intuition into ultimate truth, this still does not eliminate the encrustations that dim the light of our minds, nor prevent us from falling more deeply into the distractions provided by everyday life. Gradual cultivation enables us to be open to the possibility of the enhancement of our spiritual lives: to borrow a metaphor from Chinul, it polishes our minds to make them more receptive to future illumination. We are not subject only to the confusions and diversions that beset us in this life, but we have to contend with those from previous existences as well. Chinul thus advocates intensive study and reflection to rid ourselves of this huge burden which has accrued from our being entangled in **samsara**, the cycle of death and rebirth. The True Mind is the ground of our empirical mind, and Chinul advocates looking inwards in our search for ultimate reality.

The 'sudden awakening and gradual cultivation' method does not give us a full appreciation of ultimate reality. In his works, Chinul also gives the characteristics of *hwadu*, an advanced meditative technique limited to the most able, though not exclusively to those initiated into the Son order. *Hwadu* leaves behind discursive thought, understanding, knowledge and language. As Chinul says, 'Those of vast potential . . . leave behind words and cut off thought . . . the noumenal nature of suchness is separate from words and severed from thinking'.[9] The *hwadu* method of meditation requires us to empty our minds of their contents, and thus to allow their complete merging and annihilation in the voidness of Suchness or *sunyata*. Ultimate reality is undifferentiated and admits of no distinctions and no resolution into particulars. Both language and conceptualization are ways of articulating or expressing our experiences, and they simply assume that there is a distinction between separate entities and classes of entity. Without such differentiation, neither language nor conceptualization is possible. Similarly, cognitive knowledge relies on the discrimination between the knower and the known. Without particularization, reality is ineffable and inexpressible.

Chinul's writings show a comprehensive grasp of the major texts of most schools of Buddhism. In the West, Zen Buddhism has often been regarded as bibliophobic, paradoxical and puzzling. The recent and growing study of Chinul and the Korean Son school is to be welcomed as providing a more balanced picture of a rich and fascinating tradition.

Notes

1 Quoted in R.E. Buswell (trans. and ed.), *The Korean Approach to Zen: The Collected Works of Chinul*, Honolulu: University of Hawaii Press, 1983, p. 17.
2 Hee-Sung Keel, *Chinul: The Founder of the Korean Son Tradition*, Berkeley, Calif.: University of California Press, 1984, pp. 12–13.
3 Buswell, op. cit., pp. 163–4.
4 See the essay on Fazang in this book, pp. 272–8.
5 Buswell, op. cit., pp. 213, 217.
6 Chinul, *Discourses on the Dharma by Pojo*, Wolchong Monastery, Kangwondo, 1937, trans. and quoted by Keel, op. cit., p. 138, 139.
7 See the essay on Huineng in this book, pp. 266–72.
8 Chinul, *Condensation of the Treatise on Hua-Yen*, trans. and quoted by Keel, op. cit., p. 31.
9 Buswell, op. cit., p. 242, 243.

Chinul's writings

Chinul's major works have been translated into English and are to be found in R.E. Buswell (trans. and ed.), *The Korean Approach to Zen: The Collected Works of Chinul*, Honolulu, University of Hawaii Press, 1983.

See also in this book

Patanjali, Huineng, Fazang, Dai Zhen, Dogen, Bankei, Hakuin, Nishida, Suzuki, Nishitani

Sources and further reading

Buswell, R.E., *The Korean Approach to Zen: The Collected Works of Chinul*, Honolulu: University of Hawaii Press, 1983
Dumoulin, H., *Zen Buddhism: A History*, trans. J.W. Heisig and Paul Knitter, London: Macmillan, 1988
Hee-Sung Keel, *Chinul: The Founder of the Korean Son Tradition*, Berkeley, Calif.: University of California Press, 1984
Lee, P.H., *Lives of Eminent Korean Monks*, Cambridge, Mass.: Harvard University Press, 1969

YI YULGOK 1536–1584 CE

Yi Yulgok was one of a number of eminent thinkers who contributed to the renaissance of Confucianism in Korea in the fifteenth and sixteenth centuries CE. His work was influenced by Chinese neo-Confucians, notably the philosopher Zhuxi [Chu Hsi].[1] In common with other members of the school, Yi Yulgok believed that human nature and the nature of ultimate reality can both be explained by an elucidation of a set of Confucian concepts supplemented by the doctrine of *yinyang*, the belief in cosmic dynamism. He saw his task as one of producing a comprehensive philosophical system which would avoid any charge of dualism. Of particular concern in Korean philosophy was what came to be known as the 'four-seven' debate, to which Yi Yulgok made a major contribution. This was the issue of the precise interrelationship between the 'seven feelings' of joy, anger, sorrow, fear, love, hatred and desire, and the innate human capacity for goodness (or, more specifically, the 'four beginnings', of humanity or *ren* [jen], righteousness, propriety and wisdom), a key teaching of Mencius.[2]

Details of Yi Yulgok's life and career are to be found in the autobiographical references in his works. The descendant of a long line of state officials, his early education was in the Confucian classics.

The study of these texts was a requirement for entry into the Korean civil service under the Choson dynasty, which ruled Korea from 1392 to 1910. When Yi Yulgok was 16, his mother died, and he entered a Buddhist monastery in the remote Diamond mountains, where he spent several years learning the principles of the **Huayan** [Hua-yen] and **Zen** [C: Chan] schools of Buddhism. As he puts it, 'When I lost my mother, I studied Buddhist scriptures seriously to erase my sorrow';[3] more particularly, he attempted to find answers to the issues of life and death not yielded by his previous intellectual interests. After leaving the monastery, he returned once again to the study of Confucianism, though he never displayed the hostility to Buddhist teachings common to many of his contemporaries. At the age of 23, he met the distinguished scholar Yi T'oegye (1501–70), many of whose views, especially those on the 'four-seven' issue as disseminated by T'oegye's disciple Song Hon Ugye, were later challenged by Yi Yulgok. In 1565, he took up the first of a number of government posts and thereafter alternated between public service and the pursuit of his scholarly and philosophical interests. He was a prolific writer, producing both philosophical works and practical recommendations on education, economics and defence. His writings subsequently served as the basis for the later *sirhak*, practical learning or pragmatic, movement in Korea. His diary of events at the Choson court is still considered to be a valuable historical document.

The metaphysical foundation of Yi Yulgok's neo-Confucianism begins with the concept of *taiji* [T'ai chi], the primordial state of the universe, often rendered as the 'Great Ultimate'. *Taiji* is present in everything; it is uncreated and indestructible. Further, it is infinite and all-encompassing, undifferentiated and predicateless. It is the resolution of all opposites, being neither empty nor full.

Taiji is the source of, and inseparable from, *yin* and *yang*. *Yin* is to be regarded as inertia and passivity, darkness and tranquillity. It is not to be considered as the absence of cosmic force, but as possessing equal force to *yang* which, in turn, is activity and dynamism. *Yin* and *yang* are uncreated and indestructible; their interplay and relative dominance account for change in and the production and destruction of particular things. If *yang* is predominant over *yin*, a universe of distinct phenomena is created and maintained in existence. If, however, *yin* is in the ascendancy, the realm of particular things is destroyed and sinks back into non-existence. Thus Yi Yulgok allows for the creation and destruction of successive universes. The waxing and waning of *yin* and *yang* is governed by *taiji*. As Yi Yulgok states, 'When there was fullness of *yin*, *t'ai chi* was there. When the next world was about to be created, and when there was fullness of *yang*, *t'ai chi* was also there'.[4] As *yin* and *yang* are logically and ontologically correlative, all particular things contain the potential for their own destruction, and when there are no phenomena, there is still creative potential.

Taiji is similar to the *apeiron* of the pre-Socratic Greek philosopher Anaximander (610–546 BCE). *Apeiron*, too, is the primordial condition of the universe. It is uncreated, infinite and without qualities, but is that from which all particular things and their attributes arise.

Yin and *yang* are the two aspects or manifestations of **qi** [ch'i], or material force, which is the cause of and displayed in both particular cosmic phenomena and human thoughts and actions. When *qi* becomes active, it is *yang*, but when it falls back into passivity and inertia, it is *yin*. *Qi* itself is thus subject to endless change, but such transformations are not random nor chaotic. Instead, the mutations of *qi* are governed by **Li**, or the principle or regulation of change. *Li* in turn is an aspect or manifestation of *taiji*. Thus Yi Yulgok succeeds in providing an account applicable to both the universe and human nature, in terms of the interrelationship of several concepts. Both the cosmos and human beings have the same essential components of *qi*, *yin* and *yang*, and thus human nature is continuous with nature as a whole. The 'way of heaven' and the 'way of humankind' are ultimately one and the same.

According to Yi Yulgok, human beings are organic unities. Both thinking and bodily movement are physical activities, and each is dependent on *qi*. When the *qi* of individual human beings is in imbalance, it affects not only themselves but the whole of society. Yi Yulgok thus advocates moral self-cultivation, or the development of the virtues, to ensure that one's *qi* is kept under control. The *qi* of the ruler, or sage-king, is of the utmost importance because he has the most influence on society. It may be the case that virtuous ministers do not change the moral character of their ruler, but what the king does will affect his ministers and, through them, the common people. Yi Yulgok said, 'I have heard that the ruler, by correcting his mind, corrects the court, and by correcting the court, corrects all directions'.[5] *Qi* can thus influence both moral and cosmic phenomena.[6]

As previously mentioned, one area of concern to Korean neo-Confucians was the 'four-seven' debate, which was based on the teachings of Mencius about innate human goodness. The issues which they tried to settle included that of the source of evil; whether some feelings were good and others evil; and whether the 'four beginnings', like the 'seven feelings',[7] were emotions and if so, why the two groups were to be distinguished.

Yi Yulgok considered human beings to have both a physical and a moral aspect. The former consists of instinctive and spontaneous desires; if we are hungry, we wish to eat, if thirsty, to drink, and if cold, to warm ourselves. Even the sages have these desires, and should not try to eliminate them, but to control them. If they are out of control, there cannot be development of the moral aspect of a person's character. The 'four beginnings' and the 'seven feelings' are all to be found in the moral aspect of human nature. They are not separate: as Yi Yulgok states, 'Since the "seven feelings" include the "four beginnings" in themselves, it is not possible to say that the "four beginnings" are not the "seven feelings" and the "seven feelings" are not the "four beginnings". How can they be divided?'.[8] The feelings, if properly directed, are a manifestation of the beginnings; for example, the desire to seek the truth and to take the sages as our role-models manifests the 'beginning' of humanity. Similarly, hating someone who does wrong is a particular manifestation of the 'beginning' of righteousness. The 'beginnings' are the reason for, or necessary conditions of, the 'feelings'. None of the 'seven feelings' is inherently evil. If they are directed to their proper objects, then they are good, but if focused on inappropriate objects, then they are evil. The origin of both good and evil is to be found in human nature, and Yulgok thus avoids the charge of assigning them to separate sources. As the 'four beginnings' are innate in human nature, they are governed by *Li*. The 'seven feelings', if properly focused, are a combination of both *Li* and *qi*, and if not directed to their appropriate objects, consist of *qi* alone.

For Yi Yulgok, the will is that aspect of human nature which 'compares and measures', or deliberates. It has the power to control *qi*, and thus the appropriateness of feelings, or their direction to their proper objects. As he puts it, 'The will is the commander of *ch'i* [*qi*]; when the will is established there is no way *ch'i* can avoid being moved'.[9] Any one of three factors can prevent the will from being properly used: lack of faith in the teachings of the wise, lack of wisdom, and lack of courage. In the words of Yi Yulgok,

> Those who do not believe in the sages . . . only enjoy [their] words, but do not themselves put them into practice. They speak of the sages . . . but walk in the mundane world . . . Those who lack in wisdom think that their talents are not good enough, and are thus satisfied in going backwards, not forwards even a single step . . . Some people may know that the sages . . . do not deceive us . . . but still they remain neglectful and do not try to improve themselves; they have

great difficulty tearing themselves away from today's pleasures to tomorrow's [moral] transformation . . . this is because of lack of courage.[10]

According to Yi Yulgok, the will can be properly directed only if there is a correct understanding of reality, which involves the recognition of how the various Confucian concepts are related to each other. For such an understanding, there must be clarity in thought and an appropriate use of language. He states:

> Learners who wish to practise the Confucian learning must be careful regarding language. Many human faults come from [the misuse of] language; so words must be careful, truthful, spoken at the proper time, and given in a serious manner.[11]

This concern about language links Yi Yulgok with Chinese philosophers such as Xunzi [Hsun Tzu], and Confucius himself, who were concerned with the correct use of language, or what is often known as the 'rectification of names'.

The ethical theory of Yi Yulgok is reminiscent of that of Aristotle. Although Aristotle did not say that moral qualities are feelings, he stipulated that they are virtues only if used in the right conditions and on their proper objects. Otherwise, they are vices. For example, the person who gives to those in need displays the virtue of generosity, but if he gives to those more fortunate than himself, he indulges in the corresponding vice of prodigality. Moral qualities are, for Aristotle, directed by the will, which is the faculty of deliberation, and the way to moral self-cultivation and improvement is gradual and requires experience.

In Yi Yulgok's philosophical system, there appears to be a duplication of function of the will and of Li in respect to properly directed feelings. The will directs the feelings to their appropriate objects, and Li is responsible for their governance and regulation, which seems to amount to the same thing. The reason why Yi Yulgok wished to include Li as well as qi in correctly focused feelings is understandable: he wanted to find a place for both concepts in his account of the feelings and thus to avoid any trace of dualism in his philosophy. However, in averting such charges, he has fallen into the criticism that there are two elements, Li and the will, which discharge the same function.

Until relatively recently, Korean thought was little known in the West and used to be regarded as a mere appendage to Chinese philosophy. This view is now changing, and Korea is rightly regarded as having fertile original thinkers of its own, including Yi Yulgok, who have contributed to its rich intellectual traditions.

Notes

1 See the essay on Zhuxi [Chu Hsi] in this book, pp. 278–83
2 See the essay on Mencius in this book, pp. 233–40
3 *Yulgok Chonso*, Seoul, Songgyun'gwan University Press, 1985, vol. I, p. 56; quoted in E.Y.J. Chung, *The Korean neo-Confucianism of Yi T'oegye and Yi Yulgok*, New York: State University of New York Press, 1995, p. 27.
4 *Yulgok Chonso*, op. cit., vol. I., p. 183; quoted in Young-Chan, *The Korean neo-Confucianism of Yi Yulgok*, New York: State University of New York Press, 1989, p. 28.
5 *Yulgok Chonso*, op. cit., vol. I, p. 310; quoted in Ro, op. cit., p. 34.
6 Yi Yulgok thought that the ruler, by moral self-discipline, could avert natural disasters.
7 As E.Y.J. Chung points out (op. cit., p. 39), there is no evidence that Mencius was aware of the doctrine of the seven emotions.
8 *Yulgok Chonso*, op. cit., p. 199; quoted in Ro, op. cit., p. 61.
9 *Yulgok Chonso*, op. cit., p. 428; quoted in Ro, op. cit., p. 104.
10 *Yulgok Chonso*, op. cit., p. 431; quoted in Ro, op. cit., pp. 104–5.
11 *Yulgok Chonso*, op. cit., p. 330; quoted in Ro, op. cit., p. 106.

Major works

The major writings of Yi Yulgok are to be found in *Yulgok Chonso* [*The Complete Works of Yulgok*], 3 vols., Seoul: Songgyun'gwan University Press, 1985. Some works can also be found in *Yulgokjip* [*The Collected Writings of Yulgok*], Seoul: Minjok Munhwa Ch'ujinhoe Press, 1969.

See also in this book

Confucius, Mencius, Zhuxi, Dai Zhen

Sources and further reading

de Bary, W.T., and Kim Haboush, JaHyun (eds), *The Rise of neo-Confucianism in Korea*, New York: Columbia University Press, 1985

Chung, E.Y.J., *The Korean neo-Confucianism of Yi T'oegye and Yi Yulgok*, New York: State University of New York Press, 1995

Ro Young-Chan, *The Korean neo-Confucianism of Yi Yulgok*, New York: State University of New York Press, 1989

Part 7

JAPANESE PHILOSOPHY

INTRODUCTION

On three occasions the direction of Japanese history has been modified significantly by external influences: the first was the arrival of Buddhism, initially from Korea and then from China; the second was the first influx of western ideas in the sixteenth century; and the third, still going on, is the period of cultural exchange with the West which followed the Meiji restoration in 1868. The first and third of these are reflected in the ideas of the thinkers considered in this section.

Historians of Japan generally cite 552 CE as the date at which Buddhism can be said to have arrived from the Asian mainland, as it is recorded in ancient chronicles that, in that year, the first image of the Buddha was transported from Korea. As was also the case in Tibet, Buddhism supplanted the native religion – in the case of Japan, Shinto – as the major force shaping the spiritual life of the nation, and has continued to be so ever since. Gradually, the major forms of **Mahayana** Buddhism which had evolved in China established themselves in Japan, acquiring new emphases to suit the Japanese temperament as they did so. It is often assumed in the West that much the dominant form of Japanese Buddhism is **Zen**, the best known outside Japan, but the truth of the matter is somewhat more complex. Zen did of course come to flourish in Japan, but historically it was not the first form of Buddhism to do so. Nor has it been, in terms of the number of adherents, the most popular: other sects, notably **Shingon** (i.e. **Tantric**), Jodo or **Pure Land** and Tendai (C: **Tiantai** [T'ien-t'ai] have always been as influential in these respects as Zen.

Tendai Buddhism, which has its roots in Chinese thought of the fifth century CE, was introduced to Japan early in the ninth century by Saicho (767–822 CE; he is also referred to by means of his title Dengyo Daishi or Great Teacher Dengyo). Saicho established a Tendai monastery on Mount Hiei, an institution which was to become extremely powerful, and which exercised great influence over many subsequent developments in the evolution of Japanese Buddhism. The Tendai tradition is here represented by its late variant Nichirenism. Though this school of thought now has the status of a separate sect with its own sub-sects, and has a presence in the West, the philosophical debt to the parent tradition is extensive, and the basis of Nichiren's practice is a set of beliefs which would have been acceptable both to Saicho and his Chinese mentors, notably the acceptance of the *Lotus Sutra* as the key text of Buddhism.

One of the major areas of contrast between Zen on the one hand and other Buddhist sects, Tendai included, is its insistence that no **sutras** are of central importance on the path to enlightenment: Zen locates its religious authority in a direct line of unwritten transmission of the **dharma** from the Buddha to all Zen masters. In view of its later extensive impact on Japanese life, it is interesting to reflect that Zen took longer to establish itself in Japan than either Tendai or Shingon. Influences of Chinese Zen can be traced in Japan from the seventh century, and the first Chinese master to visit the islands, Daoxuan [Tao-hsuan], did so in the Tempyo period (729–749 CE), yet no major school of Japanese Zen came into being throughout the entire Heian period (794–1185 CE). The title of the founder of Japanese Zen goes to Eisai (1141–1215 CE; also called Zenko Kokushi). He was an adherent of a form of **Rinzai** (C: Linji [Lin-chi]) Zen, which he took back to Japan from China, establishing the first Rinzai temple there, the Shofukuji (on Kyushu) in 1191. For a complex series of historical, political and religious reasons, some discussed in the essays which follow, Rinzai Zen has become the form of Buddhism most familiar to the West. Not least among the reasons for this is the inspiration it was to furnish to certain Japanese customs and art forms, notably the tea ceremony, *noh* drama, *haiku* verse, flower arrangement and various martial arts. The Rinzai Zen sect is here represented by its reviver and greatest systematizer, Hakuin.

Until recently, far less well known in the West is the second major Zen sect, **Soto** (C: Caodong [Ts'ao-tung]), represented here by its founder, and a major figure in Japanese philosophical history, Dogen. Dogen took the ideas of his Chinese masters and developed them into a comprehensive and powerful philosophy. The area of major contrast between Soto and Rinzai thinkers concerns Zen method: the Rinzai sect lays special stress in meditation on the problems called **koans**, while the Soto sect places greater emphasis on the practice of seated meditation or **zazen**: Dogen goes so far as to identify this practice with **nirvana**. It is in respect of method that Bankei, the third Zen master considered here, differs from both Dogen and Hakuin. For Bankei, any set method, *koan* practice, *zazen* or any of the other techniques listed in the records of the Zen masters, is likely to prove a hindrance on the path to enlightenment. A key feature of his Zen is spontaneity, which he equates with the working of the Buddha-mind or reality, and adherence to any fixed set of rules, he argues, is more likely to hinder spontaneity than promote it. Taken together, the ideas of Dogen, Bankei and Hakuin typify the three most significant Japanese approaches to Zen.

This section ends with a consideration of three twentieth-century Japanese thinkers, each in his way exemplifying a response to the opening of Japan to western cultural influences, which began in 1868. It is largely as a result of the work of D.T. Suzuki that Zen is as well known in the West as it is. A **Rinzai** scholar able to write excellent English, Suzuki made it his mission in life to make the west aware of Zen. This he did via a lifetime of intensive publication, especially the three major books of *Essays in Zen Buddhism* published in the 1920s and 1930s. Nishida and his younger contemporary Nishitani were founder and member respectively of what has come to be known as the Kyoto school of philosophy, which may turn out to be Japan's most significant contribution to the philosophy of the twentieth century. These philosophers have certain basic beliefs in common, notably a bedrock religious intuition which is never questioned. This conviction is that reality itself is **sunyata** or void, a predicateless unity. Further, they would both accept that we have a true 'self' (if one may so put it) which is identical with this void, the identity being revealed when the phenomenal or everyday ego is dissipated by the appropriate disciplines. What is so distinctive and original about the members of the Kyoto school is their study and use of western philosophical ideas in an attempt to articulate this profoundly eastern basic position. With great intellectual daring, they set out to see if western philosophical methods and conceptual frameworks could be used to articulate their outlook, and the results of their investigations are among the most illuminating discussions of east–west similarities and differences to date.

Nishida, Suzuki and Nishitani are encouraging examples with which to end this book. It is quite clear that, as with other modern thinkers from the eastern traditions, e.g. Radhakrishnan, they understood western thought very well, and there is no reason to suppose that their traditions must remain not fully comprehensible to the West. Hard work and sympathetic imagination will take us a long way on the path to mutual understanding.

DOGEN KIGEN 1200–1253 CE

Dogen is the founder of the **Soto** (C: [Caodong *Ts'ao-tung*]) school of Zen Buddhism in Japan, and is by common consent one of the finest philosophers his country has produced. His many writings cover all aspects of Zen, from its metaphysical bases to practical regulations for the organization of monastic communities, together with suggestions for the correct practice of *zazen* (seated meditation) which he regarded as essential to Zen. His major work, the *Shobogenzo* (Treasury of the Eye of the True Dharma), consisting of ninety-three fascicles or essays in its standard edition, is regarded as one of the greatest of Japanese philosophical texts. In it, he takes the ideas of the Chinese Zen masters and develops them with rigour and originality.

The facts of Dogen's life have been overlaid by generations of Soto hagiography, and the historicity of some of the stories concerning him is disputed. A number of basic items, however, are generally agreed on. He was born in 1200 into a branch of the wealthy Minamoto family. He lost both his parents during childhood, and this is said to have awakened in him, very early in life, a sense of what he would later call the 'dew-like' impermanence of human existence.[1] He is said to have run away from home at the age of 12 to a Tendai[2] monastery near Mount Hiei where his uncle Ryokan Hogen was in charge. Dogen became dissatisfied with the teaching at this monastery, and for six years or so he moved between teachers, finally settling down in 1217 with Myozen (1184–1225).

Dogen's dissatisfaction with his early teachers was caused by what he called his 'great doubt', a problem these masters could not resolve: if all sentient beings everywhere possess the Buddha-nature (this term is explained below), and in consequence are capable of enlightenment, why then are special ascetic practices held to be necessary to pursue buddhahood? The need to resolve this difficulty was one of the chief motives for Dogen's visit to China, to which he travelled with Myozen in 1223, and where he stayed for four years. What he did for most of the first two years is not clear: what is clear is that his life was changed by the accession to the abbacy of the monastery on Mount Tiantong [T'ien-t'ung] of the Zen master Caotong Rujing [Ts'ao-t'ung Ju-ching] (J: Tendo Nyojo, 1163–1228), whom Dogen met in 1225, and with whom he studied for two years. One of the works attributed to Dogen, the *Hokyo-ki* (C: *Baoqingji* [*Pao-ch'ing chi*]) or Record of the Pao-ch'ing Era, is a diary of this meeting and of Rujing's teaching, though how much of this text is historically reliable is very difficult to say.

Rujing's views on Zen method made a great impact on Dogen, and through him on the whole history of Soto Zen in Japan. Though he used some **koans**, Rujing was in general critical of the practices of the Linji [Lin-chi J: **Rinzai**] school of Zen, in which the *koan* exercise is central. By contrast, he insisted that the essential Zen practice is seated meditation (J: *zazen*), and that nothing else is needed.[3] Proper meditation is 'single-minded intense sitting without burning incense, worshipping, reciting [Amithaba's name], practising repentance, nor reading **sutras**'[4] This insight resolved Dogen's great doubt and it was during a **zazen** session in the summer of 1225 that Dogen achieved enlightenment, and was agreed by Rujing to have done so.

Dogen stayed with Rujing until 1227, when he decided to return to Japan. Rujing gave him a written seal of approval, i.e. a document stating that Dogen was the recipient of direct transmission of the **dharma** in the line unbroken from the Buddha to himself.[5] This seal was all Dogen took back with him to Japan: he took neither *sutras* nor holy relics, since such things are irrelevant to Zen. He devoted the rest of his life to establishing Soto Zen in his native country, setting up the first independent Soto Zen temple in Japan, Koshohorinji, in 1236. There he stayed until the envy of the Buddhist community on Mount Hiei became a threat, and he removed to the province of Echizen in 1243. Two years later, his last monastery, Eiheiji (Eternal Peace), was completed, and here Dogen spent the remaining years of his life. Throughout this post-Chinese phase of his life, he wrote prolifically, his output ranging from formal treatises in *kanbun* (i.e. Chinese) to Japanese verse. At its best, his work ranks with the finest of Buddhist literature.

However abstract his thought may appear, Dogen's root purpose in all his writings is the same, to assist the aspirant on the road to enlightenment, and the enlightenment is direct apprehension of being-as-is. He follows the parent **Mahayana** tradition in adopting as his bedrock metaphysical position the assertion that being-as-is or reality is nondual. That is, being-as-is is not the ordinary world of individuals in space and time, but an undifferentiated oneness to which no concepts apply, since concepts imply divisibility or duality. Dogen has many ways of putting this point. Thus, for example, he quotes with approval the saying of the ninth-century master Gensha (C: Xuansha [Hsuan-sha], 831–908) that the universe (i.e. what there is) is 'one bright jewel':

> The essential message is that the whole universe is not vast, not small, round or square, not balanced and correct, not

lively and active, not standing way out. Because furthermore it is not birth and death, coming and going, it is birth and death, coming and going. Being thus, having in the past gone from here, it now comes from here.[6]

That is, since reality is nondual, none of the above concepts, which presuppose division, can apply to it.

The consequences of this metaphysics are profound and far-reaching, and Dogen draws them out with great thoroughness. The major epistemological consequence is that all conceptual thinking, and all perception which involves awareness under conceptual descriptions, are false to the nature of being-as-is, and hinder apprehension of it. The world as it is experienced via conceptual thought is a world of individual things in time and space, standing in causal relations to one another. This entire structure is illusory, or as Dogen puts it, using a classic Buddhist image, 'flowers in the sky'.[7] This belief also shapes Dogen's style, which as can be seen from the foregoing typical quotation concerning the one bright jewel, is paradoxical and deliberately made difficult to follow (even more so in the original text of the *Shobogenzo* where Chinese and Japanese alternate within single sentences). Dogen's aim in writing in this way is to disrupt the flow of conceptual thought, which must be halted before being-as-is can be experienced directly. Again, since being-as-is is nondual, it follows that our ordinary consciousness of time, one of the most fundamental elements of our experience, involving awareness of discrete moments and events, must be delusory. Being-as-is and time must be identical, since what there is is a oneness and if time is anything, it is therefore being: 'So-called time of being means time is already being; all being is time.'[8]

Further, since all awareness of division is delusory, it follows that our assumption that there is a valid distinction to be drawn between the self and the rest of the universe is false, and we must seek to break free of this distinction. Dogen quotes with approval a saying of the Third Patriarch of Zen, Sengcan [Seng-ts'an] (J: So-san, d. 606 CE):

'To achieve the Way is not difficult; just reject discrimination.' If you cast aside the mind that discriminates, then at once you gain awakening. To abandon the discriminating mind means to break free from the Self.[9]

Our ordinary conception of the self is entirely false:

> To seek to know the self is invariably the wish of living beings. However, those who see the true self are rare. Only buddhas know the true self. People outside the way regard what is not the self as the self. But what buddhas call the self is the entire universe.[10]

This at first sight startling conclusion follows from Zen metaphysics, and is paralleled in other mystical traditions, Islamic, Hindu and Christian. There is a distinction to be drawn between the surface ego or phenomenal self and the true self, in Zen terms the 'original face'. The former is a delusion, one of the false conceptual constructs which hides reality from us. When by suitable practices conceptual thinking is halted, reality is revealed. The true self, original face or Buddha-nature, is this reality. Since reality is unitary, it is all there is and so, as Dogen puts it, the true self is the entire universe.

Moreover, since the Buddha-nature or being-as-is is one and indivisible, it is present everywhere, and so present in everyone. From this it follows that everyone can become a Buddha, i.e. can attain enlightenment. What is needed is a way of freeing us from the delusions of conceptual thought, thereby allowing us to realize the Buddha-nature within us. Dogen has much to say about Zen technique and its relation to enlightenment.

The essential Zen Buddhist practice, in Dogen's view, is *zazen* (seated meditation) and it is with *zazen* that his name, and that of the Soto school, is always linked. Throughout his ministry, Dogen insisted on the need for rigorous practice of *zazen*:

> reverse the intellectual practice of investigating words and chasing after talk; take the backward step of turning the light and shining it back. Of themselves body and mind will drop away, and your original face will appear. If you want such [a state], urgently work at *zazen*.[11]

Conceptual thought is delusory: hence we must cease to 'chase after talk', since language embodies conceptual structures. The path to reality is a journey inward, and so it is necessary to 'shine the light back' or 'to turn the light around', a Zen expression meaning to attempt to shift attention ('the light') away from ordinary experience of objects in the phenomenal world and turn it inward, to the original, innate essence of the mind itself, i.e. its inherent Buddha-nature.[12] If this is achieved, 'body and mind drop away', i.e. all divisions and attachments are transcended, including attachment to the illusory self of mundane experience, and the 'original face' or Buddha-nature will appear.

A number of comments on this passage are appropriate. First, it is difficult to find in Dogen's writings – which were, of course, only one aspect of his teaching – a precise statement as to how one is to 'turn the light around', i.e. what meditational techniques can be used in order to free us from the grip of conceptual thought. Thus Dogen gives instructions on how to sit properly for *zazen*, how to breathe and how to arrange one's clothing, and then comments: 'Whenever a thought occurs, be aware of it; as soon as you are aware of it, it will vanish. If you remain for a long period forgetful of objects, you will naturally become unified.'[13] If this practice is followed properly, we arrive eventually at the state of 'nonthinking', by which Dogen means the state other Zen masters term 'no-mind', the state in which conceptual thinking is suspended. Yet this appears to be hardly more than a restatement of the view that 'nonthinking', or non-conceptual awareness of being-as-is, is enlightenment. No doubt in his monastic practice, Dogen would have used a number of meditational techniques, including **koan** study. (The denigration of *koan* study by later members of the Soto sect is not shared by Dogen, who uses them in his writings when he sees fit.)

Second, the direct awareness of reality in which enlightenment consists is strictly speaking indescribable, since no concepts can apply to it: 'The realm of all buddhas is inconceivable. It cannot be reached by consciousness' (i.e. by conceptual thought).[14] Again, it cannot be conceived of in advance, since it cannot be conceived of at all: 'Realization is not like your conception of it. Accordingly, realization cannot take place as previously conceived . . . Realization does not depend on thoughts, but comes forth far beyond them.'[15] Moreover, since direct awareness of being-as-is is unconnected with any skill in conceptual thinking, all forms of intelligence or cleverness which manifest themselves in conceptual thinking are irrelevant to the pursuit of the true *dharma* and indeed are generally a hindrance to this end, since we are proud of and attached to our intellectual attainments: 'Because study [of the Way] has no use for wide learning and high intelligence, even those with inferior capacities can participate.'[16] More important are a true wish to follow the Buddha way, and obedience to a good Master.

Third, it must be stressed that for Dogen the practice of *zazen* and enlightenment are not related as means and end, but are identical, a point on which he insists repeatedly. Thus when a questioner asks: 'What of those who have already understood the Buddha's correct teaching? What do they expect from *zazen*?', Dogen replies:

> To suppose that practice and realization are not one is nothing but a heretical view; in *buddha-dharma* they are inseparable . . . Therefore, when we give instructions for practising, we say you should not have any expectation of realization outside of practice, since this is the immediate original realization.[17]

It is important to be clear how strong a claim this is: for Dogen, *zazen* is not merely a meditational technique for the practice of **dhyana**, however powerful. It is itself complete realization: it is itself *nirvana*: '*Zazen* is not the practice of *dhyana*: it is just the *dharma* gate of ease and joy. It is the practice and verification of ultimate **bodhi**.'[18] It would be difficult to find a more thoroughgoing expression of the value of *zazen* than this.

What is the state of mind of those who have attained enlightenment? Dogen gives a hint as to what it is like to have arrived at this pitch of development in the *Shobogenzo* essay 'Ocean seal concentration' (J: *Kai-in zammai*). The title is taken from a work originating in the *Kegon* (C: **Huayan** [Hua-yen]: 'Flower Garland') school of Buddhism, *Return to the Source Contemplation*. Here the enlightened mind is compared, in an ancient Buddhist image, to a calm ocean: 'if the wind stops (i.e. delusion ceases) the ocean water is calm and clear, and all images can reflect in it . . . The "ocean seal" is the awareness of true thusness.'[19] Reflecting on this passage, Dogen comments: 'Prior moment, succeeding moment – each successive moment does not wait for the next: prior element, succeeding element – the 'elements do not await each other. This is called the ocean seal concentration.'[20] That is: the enlightened consciousness is aware of the nondual nature of being-as-is; however, the sage or enlightened person must continue to function in the world, and so conceptual discriminations must continue to be made. What is different is the attitude of the sage to the latter: after enlightenment, there is awareness of division and succession but entirely without the desire to cling to or arrest anything or any time. Since the surface ego is seen to be an illusion, so there are no further wants or desires, only the boundless compassion of the enlightened for those still caught in the *samsara*. The flow of events is simply reflected in the consciousness of the sage, with absolute clarity and impartiality, just as it is. This is release or eternal life, which is neither a future state nor another place, but is experienced here and now by the enlightened.

It is interesting to reflect that this powerful and well-articulated philosophy was unknown outside the Soto school for centuries after

Dogen's lifetime: the *Shobogenzo* was not published in any form by the Soto school until 1816, and only in this century has Dogen's stature come to be widely recognized. In the intervening period, Soto Zen had little official recognition or cultural influence. Thus from the Kamakura (1185–1333) to the Muromachi periods of Japanese history (1393–1573 CE), the ascendancy was gained by the rival Rinzai sect of Zen, which exercised a major influence on the forms of Japanese culture best known in the West: *noh* drama, the tea ceremony, etc. Later generations of Soto and Rinzai adherents sharpened the doctrinal differences between the sects in ways with which their founders would not always have sympathized. For example, under the fourth Soto patriarch, Keizan Jokin (1268–1325 CE), the *koan* was officially completely discarded as an aid to enlightenment in favour of silent sitting.[21] (In practice, *koans* have continued in use in Soto training, if without the emphasis given to them by the Rinzai sect.) By contrast, Dogen preferred to stress that Buddhism is unified. A classic Zen image pictures the five schools of Zen as five petals of a flower. Dogen changes the emphasis, stressing that all the petals belong to the same plant: 'the opening of five petals is one flower.'[22] That is, the divisions within Buddhism are less important than the *dharma* or truth which is common to them all.

Dogen's philosophy involves all the classic difficulties of nondualism, notably why the one should have manifested itself at all as the many, and why this manifestation (i.e. the universe we live in) should involve so much suffering and evil. Dogen's reply would be that to be concerned with such issues is to be trapped in the web of conceptual thought: if we practise *zazen* and turn the light around, these problems evaporate, together with all the painful illusions of the *samsara*.

Notes

References to the *Shobogenzo* are given in the form: S + name of fascicle.

1 cf. *Shobogenzo zuimonki* (Things Overheard at the Treasury of the Eye of the True Dharma); see R. Masunaga, *A Primer of Soto Zen*, London: Routledge, 1972, pp. 66–7. Note: despite the similarity of their titles, this work, a very basic introduction to Zen discipline, is distinct from Dogen's masterpiece, the *Shobogenzo*.

2 For an outline of the beliefs of the Tendai school of Buddhism, see the essay on Nichiren in this book, pp. 347–58. Mount Hiei was the centre of the Buddhist 'establishment' in Japan.

3 For more detail, cf. I. Miura and R.F. Sasaki, *Zen Dust*, New York: Harcourt, Brace, 1966, pp. 18–19; on Rinzai Zen, see the essays on Hakuin and Suzuki in this book, pp. 368–77 and 388–96.

4 *Hokyo-ki*, section 16 in T.J. Kodera, *Dogen's Formative Years in China*, London: Routledge, 1980, p. 124. 'Reciting Amitabha's name' is a reference to the use of the **Nembutsu** in the Pure Land school of Buddhism (see the essay on Suzuki).

5 cf, S, fascicles *Busso* (Buddha Ancestors) and *Shisho* (Document of Heritage).

6 S, fascicle *Ikka myoju* (One Bright Jewel), T. Cleary (ed. and trans.), *Shobogenzo: Zen Essays by Dogen*, Honolulu: University of Hawaii Press, 1988, p. 59.

7 S, fascicle *Kuge* (Flowers in the Sky), *passim*.

8 S, fascicle *Uji* (Being Time), Cleary, op. cit., p. 104. This doctrine of the identity of being and time has been regarded as one of Dogen's most original contributions to Zen thought.

9 *Shobogenzo zuimonki*, in Masunaga, op. cit., p. 92.

10 S, fascicle *Yuibusu yobutsu* (Only Buddha and Buddha), in K. Tanahashi (ed. and trans.), *Moon in a Dewdrop*, Shaftesbury, Dorset: Element Books, 1988, p. 164.

11 *Fukan zazen gi* (Principles of Seated Meditation), Tenpuku manuscript, in C. Bielefeldt, *Dogen's Manuals of Zen Meditation*, Berkeley and Los Angeles; University of California Press, 1988, p. 176.

12 The idea of 'turning the light around' is not peculiar to Zen, nor to oriental thought, but is common to all forms of mysticism which hold that God or reality is within us. Thus the German mystic Jakob Boehme (1575–1624 CE) states that we see God with a 'reversed eye' (*ungewandtes Auge*), a point noted by K. Nishida, *Inquiry into the Good*, New Haven, Conn. and London: Yale University Press, 1990, p. 81.

13 *Fukan zazen gi*, Tenpuku manuscript, in Bielefeldt, op. cit., p. 181.

14 S, fascicle *Bendo-wa* (On the Endeavour of the Way), in Tanahashi, op. cit., p. 148.

15 S, fascicle *Yuibutsu yobutsu*, in Tanahashi, op. cit., p. 161.

16 *Shobogenzo zuimonki*, in Masunaga, op. cit., p. 38. cf. Padmasambhava's insistence that illiterates can gain enlightenment.

17 S, fascicle *Bendo-wa*, in Tanahashi, op. cit., p. 151.

18 *Fukan zazen gi*, Koroku version, in Bielefeldt, op. cit., p. 181.

19 In Cleary, op. cit., p. 76.

20 S, fascicle *Kai-in zammai*, in Cleary, op. cit., p. 78.

21 cf. Miura and Sasaki, op. cit., p. 19.

22 S, fascicle *Kuge*, in Cleary, op. cit., p. 66.

Dogen's major writings

Shobogenzo (Treasury of the Eye of the True Dharma)
Shobogenzo zuimonki (Things Overheard at the Treasury of the Eye of the True Dharma)
Hokyo-ki (Record of the Baoqing Era)
Fukan zazen-gi (Principles of Seated Meditation)
Of these the first is much the most important.

See also in this book

the Buddha, Huineng, Fazang, Chinul, Nichiren, Bankei, Hakuin, Nishida, Suzuki, Nishitani

Sources and further reading

Abe, M., *A Study of Dogen: His Philosophy and Tradition*, Albany, NY: State University of New York Press, 1992

Bielefeldt, C., *Dogen's Manuals of Zen Meditation*, Berkeley and Los Angeles: University of California Press, 1988 (includes translations of the various versions of the *Fukan zazen gi* and related documents)

Cleary, T. (ed. and trans.), *Shobogenzo: Zen Essays by Dogen*, Honolulu: University of Hawaii Press, 1988 (thirteen essays from the *Shobogenzo*)

Heine, S., *Existential and Ontological Dimensions of Time in Heidegger and Dogen*, Albany, NY: State University of New York Press, 1985

Heine, S., *Dogen and the Koan Tradition: A Tale of Two Shobogenzo Texts*, Albany, NY: State University of New York Press, 1994

Kim, Hee-Jin, *Dogen Kigen, Mystical Realist*, rev. edn, Tucson: University of Arizona Press, 1987

Kodera, T.J., *Dogen's Formative Years in China*, London: Routledge 1980 (contains a translation of the *Hokyo-ki*, with extensive annotation and commentary)

La Fleur, W.R. (ed.), *Dogen Studies*, Honolulu: University of Hawaii Press, 1985

Masunaga, R., *A Primer of Soto Zen*, London: Routledge, 1972 (a complete translation of the *Shobogenzo zuimonki*)

Miura, I. and Sasaki, R.F., *Zen Dust*, New York: Harcourt, Brace, 1966

Nishiyama, K. and Stevens, S., *Dogen Zenji's Shobogenzo (The Eye and Treasury of the True Law)*, 4 vols, Sendai: Japan: 1975–1983

Tanahashi, K. (ed. and trans.), *Moon in a Dewdrop*, Shaftesbury, Dorset: Element Books, 1988

NICHIREN 1222–1282 CE

The Buddha prophesied that after his death human history would be divided into three periods, usually referred to as the Former, Middle and Latter Days of the Law, the Law being the Buddhist **dharma** or Truth. In the *shobo*, or Former period, the True Law would be dominant; in the Middle, *zoho* (or *zobo*) period, a simulated Law would be propagated, whilst the Latter or *mappo* period would be an age of degeneracy in which the *dharma* would be under real threat. Most Japanese of the thirteenth century, including Nichiren, believed that the *mappo* period had begun around the middle of the eleventh century CE, and that they were therefore living in an age of confusion and decline. For this belief they found confirmation in a number of natural disasters which afflicted Japan, chiefly between 1256 and

1260: in these few years the country was devastated by a succession of crop failures consequent on dire climatic conditions, epidemics, earthquakes, floods and fires, to be followed by repeated threats of invasion by the Mongols. It was during this period that the young monk Nichiren was forming his outlook. Almost a perfect exemplar of the religious enthusiast, Nichiren believed he knew exactly why Japan should be so afflicted, and further how to rescue his country from its peril. He promulgated his views fearlessly and repeatedly, never repudiating them even in the face of persecution, exile, and the threat of an execution from which he had the narrowest of escapes. Though in his lifetime the sect he founded cannot be said to have prospered, it has endured to this day, and one of its sub-sects, Nichiren Shoshu ('The Genuine Nichiren Sect') has in this century considerably advanced its international standing.

Nichiren ('Sun Lotus') is the religious name taken later in life by Zennichi Maru, by tradition humbly born in the second month of 1222 in the fishing village of Kominato (present-day Chiba prefecture).[1] His life falls into three well-defined phases. The first, 1222–1253, comprises his childhood and his extensive studies of the Buddhist sects of his day. At the age of 12, Nichiren entered the temple of Seicho-ji (in Kominato), where his master Dozen-bo (d.1276) instructed him in the doctrines of the **Tendai** sect of Buddhism. ('Tendai', and other sectarian terms, are explained in what follows.) His ambition was no less than to become the wisest man in Japan, and to this end he steeped himself in Chinese and Indian classics. After some three or so years, he became dissatisfied with Dozen-bo's instruction, and set out to visit other centres of Buddhist learning, including some of the temples in the Nara area and the centre of the Tendai sect on Mount Hiei. He returned to Seicho-ji in 1253, utterly convinced of the truth of the insights arrived at in the course of his study. In the fourth month, he preached a sermon to his teacher and other priests, announcing his new views. They enraged the authorities in the area, and Nichiren was thrown out of the temple, narrowly escaping arrest. With this begins the second phase of his life, from 1253 to 1274, the period of his mission and exile.

During this period, Nichiren undertook a number of missionary journeys, and on several occasions petitioned the government to heed his religious warnings, return to the path of true Buddhism and so save the country from ruin. One of these petitions is his first major work, the *Rissho Ankoku Ron* (Establishment of the Legitimate Teaching for the Protection for the Country, 1260). As was to happen more than once, this essay caused only annoyance, and not only was its content ignored but it drew upon Nichiren the wrath both of certain officials and of some elements in the Buddhist establishment (it should be noted, however, that Nichiren for his part was never sparing in his criticism of other sects). In the twenty-one years of his missionary activity, Nichiren underwent exile and had a number of narrow escapes: on one occasion his cottage was burned down; on another, two of his followers were killed in an ambush and he himself narrowly escaped death when a sword-stroke cut his forehead. He was also sentenced to death, only to be reprieved almost at the last moment.[2]

This period of his life came to an end in 1274 when, released from his last period of exile, Nichiren withdrew to a remote hermitage, Minobu, at the foot of Mount Fuji. Here he spent the third period of his life, 1274–1282, in retreat and in the greatest poverty. It was no doubt the harsh physical conditions of his life, combined with the effects of similar deprivations whilst in exile, which brought on his final illness. On his way to try to recover at a more hospitable place, Nichiren died at Ikegami (near present-day Tokyo) in the tenth month of 1282. Never once did he waver in the conviction that he had discovered the final, ultimate truth revealed by the Buddha.

To understand fully what that truth was, in Nichiren's view, it is necessary to grasp the main tenets of the Tendai sect of Buddhism in which he was initially trained, and of which his own thought is a development. Tendai is the Japanese form of **Tiantai** [T'ien-t'ai] ('Celestial Platform'), the religious name given to the Chinese thinker Zhihgai [Chih-kai] (538–597 CE) who was its third patriarch and main systematizer.[3] As a recent scholar has pointed out, it is a charac-teristic of Chinese schools of Buddhism (as opposed to Indian and Tibetan schools) to base their beliefs on one or a small number of selected *sutras* from the vast canon of Buddhist literature, and to derive their religious understanding from the work or works thus selected. This is done on the basis of a schema for the ranking of *sutras* (C: *panjiao* [*p'an chiao*]), from which the chosen *sutra* of the school in question emerges as the ultimate or highest teaching of the Buddha. Thus for example the **Huayan** (flower garland; J: *Kegon*) sect base their views on the very lengthy *Avatamsaka Sutra*. In the case of the Tiantai sect, the chosen text, held to be the repository of the ultimate religious truth, is the *Saddharma pundarika sutra* (literally: The Sutra of the Perfect Law of the Lotus), in Chinese *Miaofa lianhua jing*. [*Miao-fa Lien-hua Ching*], this in turn rendered into Japanese as *Myoho renge kyo* (literally: The Mystic Law of the Lotus Sutra).[4] It is generally referred to as the *Lotus Sutra* and all Tendai Buddhists, Nichiren included, regard this work as the Christian world regards the Bible. It consists of twenty-eight chapters, and is agreed by scholars to have been composed over somewhat more than two centuries, probably completed by the end of the second century CE. Members of the Tiantai sect argue that the ultimate revelation of Buddhism is contained in chs 15–28 of the *sutra*, which they discriminate from chs 1–14 in ways which will become clear.

In the works of Tiantai and his fellow patriarchs are developed a number of beliefs, derived from their reading of the *Lotus Sutra*, which form the basis of Nichiren's philosophical outlook and which he was finally to extend. The key passage, on which the whole Tendai philosophy is based, occurs in the sixteenth (J: *juryo*) chapter of the *Lotus Sutra*, which concerns the Life-Span of the Tathagata, i.e. the Buddha. Nichiren translates the passage and comments on it as follows:

> The *Juryo* chapter reads 'the time is limitless and boundless – a hundred, thousand, two thousand, hundred thousand *nayuta* **kalpas** – since I in fact attained buddhahood'. Present within our lives is the Lord Shakyamuni who obtained the three bodies before *gohyaku-jintengo* [i.e. the inconceivably remote past], the original Buddha since time without beginning.[5]

The exact meaning of all the technical terms in this passage does not matter: what is of the utmost significance is the construction which Nichiren, following a venerable Tendai tradition, puts on the words of the Buddha. It is held in the **Theravadin** tradition that once the Buddha entered *nirvana* he passed beyond the reach of humankind. Here, by contrast, it is held that the Buddha has existed since 'time without beginning'. This was taken by Tiantai (and after him Nichiren) to be equivalent to saying that the Buddha exists outside time altogether, i.e. that his mode of being is eternal. This is, in effect, to move from the view of the Buddha as a historical figure to the Buddha as God or absolute. Buddha is ultimate reality or being-as-is, and as such can be present in our lives, as Nichiren stresses. Now the Buddha is not physically present in our lives, and is to be found (as will become clearer) within our minds. Therefore, the Tendai tradition goes, reality is mental, and is one mind. This is stated plainly in a Chinese work in this tradition, the *Dacheng zhiguan famen* [*Ta-ch'eng Chih-kuan Fa-men*] (Mahayana Method of Cessation and Contemplation):

> That in all things which for all time has been independent of speech, terms, and mental causation, and which in the final

analysis is everywhere the same, undergoes no change, and cannot be broken or destroyed: such is the one mind.[6]

Reality is one and mental, beyond all conceptual distinctions and indescribable in language.

This generates at once the philosophical difficulty of giving an account of the relation of the one mind or Buddha-nature and the phenomenal world of spatio-temporal individuals. In the Tiantai tradition, this is done by reference to the metaphor of a storehouse:

> The Tathagata-Storehouse [another standard Tiantai way of referring to the one mind or reality] embraces the natures of all sentient beings, each of which differs from the others, thus constituting differences within what is without difference. Thus the natures of each and every one of these sentient beings, for all time, contain qualities that are immeasurable and boundless. This statement has reference to all the impure things of the mundane world [i.e. the phenomenal world of ordinary experience] . . . But because [the one mind] also contains the pure nature, it is capable of manifesting the attributes of all the Buddhas.[7]

Thus the one mind has 'stored' in it all possible natures, pure and impure. It follows further that stored within in are what we discriminate as good and evil, and this is the Tiantai account of how evil is possible. It is to be stressed, however, that such distinctions are relative only and from the point of view of the absolute or one mind correspond to nothing: 'The storehouse in its substance is everywhere the same and in actual fact undifferentiated.'[8]

Further important consequences flow from this metaphysics. First, if no conceptual distinctions are ultimately real, that between the **samsara** and *nirvana* must be included. Put another way, this is the Mahayanist doctrine that *samsara* and *nirvana* are one and the same. Nichiren finds this doctrine symbolically expressed in a passage in the *Hoto* (eleventh) chapter of the *Lotus Sutra*, in which a treasure tower appears from beneath the earth, occupied by the Taho Buddha, said ordinarily to inhabit an eastern part of the universe. The Buddha Shakyamuni joins the Taho Buddha, and they sit side by side in the tower. In a letter to a samurai disciple, Nichiren comments as follows:

> Taho represents all phenomena and Shakyamuni, the true aspect . . . Although these are two, they are fused into one

351

in the Buddha's enlightenment. These teachings are of prime importance. They mean that earthly desires are enlightenment and that the suffering of birth and death are *nirvana*.[9]

Nirvana is not a future condition or another place. *Nirvana* is correct understanding or enlightenment, and can be experienced here and now (cf. the Hindu concept of **moksa**).

Second, the thesis that reality is one mind entails two further central Tiantai doctrines, those of the integration (or interpenetration) of all things, and the view that one moment of thought can encompass the whole of reality (J: *ichinen sanzen*: literally: one moment – the three thousand realms, i.e. all there is). The first of these doctrines is approached in the Tiantai tradition by a further reference to the unreality of all conceptual distinctions:

The fact that all things, whether mutually opposed or not, such as purity and pollution, good and bad, height and lowness, this and that, brightness and darkness, sameness and diversity, tranquillity and disorder, being and non-being, etc., can all be integrated, is because, being manifestations, they have no reality in themselves, but must depend upon mind to arise. Because in the substance of mind there is an integration, therefore in its manifestations there is also no barrier.[10]

Since there are no divisions in reality, everything there is is the One Mind in its totality. As Nichiren puts it, 'since there is mutual possession of the Ten Worlds [i.e. all there is], then any one world contains all the other worlds'.[11]

This has a direct consequence in terms of the way in which successful meditation (J: *kanjin*) is to be described, and this is the doctrine of *ichinen sanzen*. *Kanjin* means to see into one's own mind, using a correct technique. When this is done successfully, what is experienced is our real nature, which is the Buddha-nature. The Buddha-nature is the one mind or reality, all there is. Tiantai states this doctrine in the vocabulary of the Buddhist analysis of reality in terms of Ten Realms. Nichiren quotes from a Japanese version of one of the Chinese master's most important works, the *Maka shikan* (Great Concentration and Insight: C: *Mohe zhiguan* [*Mo-ho chih-kuan*]):

The mind at each moment is endowed with the Ten Worlds. At the same time, each of the Ten Worlds is endowed with all the others [i.e. because of their mutual interpenetration], so that one mind actually possesses one hundred worlds. Each of these worlds in turn possesses thirty realms, which means that in one hundred worlds there are three thousand realms. The three thousand realms of existence are possessed by the mind in a single moment.[12]

The exact and complex details of the analysis of the phenomenal world into Ten Worlds and Thirty Realms are not of present importance. Tiantai's main point is that by correct meditation, the whole of reality is accessible to experience.

The doctrine of the one mind has a further consequence to which Nichiren draws attention repeatedly, because he expects most people to find it hard to understand or accept. This is the doctrine that everything there is, every sentient being (including *icchantikas* or non-believers in Buddhism) and every inanimate object, possesses the Buddha-nature. As has been noted above, it follows from the **monistic** metaphysics of the Tendai school that all conceptual distinctions have reference to the phenomenal world only, not to reality, and this applies to the distinction between sentient and non-sentient beings as it does to every other distinction. Whatever there is has the Buddha-nature. This startling but logically legitimate consequence of Tendai thought was worked out in detail by the ninth Tiantai patriarch, Zhanran [Chan-jan] (711–782 CE), who delighted in expressing it in the most dramatic way: 'Therefore we may know that the single mind of a single particle of dust comprises the mind nature of all sentient beings and Buddhas.'[13]

All these beliefs, the core of the Tendai tradition and derived from the *Lotus Sutra*, were accepted by Nichiren. His own original contribution to Buddhist thought was to extend and adapt these views to suit the circumstances in which he found himself, i.e. the period of *mappo* or decline. In a degenerate age, the human spirit needed a simple but powerful and sure restorative to lead it back to the truth of Buddhism, and this Nichiren believed he had found in what he calls the Three Great Secret Laws (J: *sandai hiho*).[14] These are: the title (J: *daimoku*); the true or fundamental object of worship (J: *honzon* or *gohonzon*); and the Seat of Ordination or place of worship (J: *kaidan*).

The *daimoku* or title is the Japanese translation of the title of the *Lotus Sutra*, preceded by the word *namu* (pronounced 'nam') meaning 'adoration to' or 'devotion to'. Thus the complete title is *Nam' Myoho renge kyo* (Adoration to the Mystic Law of the Lotus Sutra). This is to be chanted rhythmically as a **mantra**, often to the accompaniment of a drum. Each of the words of the *daimoku* is invested by Nichiren with a number of profound significances, such that the title as a whole epitomizes the teaching of the *Lotus Sutra*, and therefore the truth of Buddhism. For example, *myoho* is made up of the syllables *myo* and *ho*, which can be take to denote reality and appearance, and a view of the relation between these two is at the core of Tendai philosophy. Again, *renge* means 'lotus flower', a central symbol in Buddhism. The lotus produces its flower and seed-pod simultaneously, and so can symbolize the doctrine of the simultaneity of cause and effect. *Kyo* means a *sutra* or a teaching of the Buddha. Nichiren argues that, once we realize that our own lives are the Mystic Law, we realize that so too are the lives of all others: 'our lives – both our bodies and our minds, ourselves and our surroundings, are the entity of *ichinen sanzen* and the Buddha of absolute freedom.'[15]

The *daimoku* is to be chanted whilst contemplating the *honzon* or true object of worship. In one sense, the *honzon* is Shakyamuni conceived as the cosmic Buddha or one mind, but the term is also used by Nichiren to refer to a **mandala** which he designed in 1279 as a representation of the cosmos and aid to worship.[16] By comparison with other Buddhist *mandalas*, it is spartan in appearance, consisting only of names written in black ink. At the centre are the five characters for *Myoho renge kyo*, and around it the names of the Ten Worlds. The recitation of the *daimoku* while contemplating the *honzon* is Nichiren's method for meditation: though the goal is the same, the method is much simpler than had been advocated by Tiantai. Nichiren had no difficulty in finding a sanction for such a change in the *Lotus Sutra*, one of whose principal doctrines is that the means chosen to bring the world to see the truth of Buddhism must be varied as appropriate to the standing conditions of the day, notably the spiritual capacity of those alive at the time.

The third element in Nichiren's teaching is that of the *kaidan* or Seat of Ordination. Whilst this term has its original sense of the (physical) place where those wishing to join the *sangha* or Buddhist community come to be ordained (i.e. to receive the Buddhist precepts and to vow to keep them), it is also invested by Nichiren with a much wider and profounder significance:

> As for the Seat of Ordination, when the Law of the Sovereign and the Law of the Buddha are united and become one, and sovereign and subjects become one in their faith in the

doctrine of the Three Great Mysteries . . . At that time an
imperial edict and a decree from the shogun will be granted;
a most exalted place – similar to Vulture Peak [the location of
one of the most celebrated of all the gatherings held by the
Buddha and so a sacred place] – will be found, and there the
Seat of Ordination will be erected.[17]

Not only does Nichiren here suggest a union of church and state in
the service of true religion, but also, consistently with his view that
the *Lotus Sutra* is the ultimate religious truth, so the place where vows
are made to live by it becomes no less than the religious centre of the
whole world:

To this Seat of Ordination will come not only all the people
of the three countries – India, China and Japan – to repent
their sins and be saved, but even Brahma and Indra and the
other gods will come and gather round it.[18]

Nichiren believed with unshakeable firmness that these doctrines
constituted the ultimate truth of Buddhism, the final religious truth,
adherence to which was the only possible way to salvation. It follows
that those who advocated other doctrines were leading humankind
astray and must be stopped, and it is no surprise to find that the fervour
with which Nichiren preached his own views is matched by an equal
fervour in his lengthy and repeated condemnations of those with other
convictions. The chief target of his attack, no doubt because it was the
most popular Japanese Buddhist sect of the day and so the most
dangerous form of heresy (in his view), was the Jodo or **Pure Land**
sect. This sect has a history reaching back to China in the fourth
century CE, but had been extremely successful in Japan as a result of
the work of Honen (1133–1212) and his disciple Shinran (1173–1262).
The chief doctrine of Jodo is that salvation can be attained only
by calling on the name of Amida Buddha by the use of the mantra
Namu Amida Butsu (Reverence to Amida Buddha), referred to as the
Nembutsu. Those who do this will be reborn in Amida's Pure Land.[19]
In the growth of Jodo Nichiren saw the cause of the calamitous times
in which he lived. The Jodo sect do not acknowledge the authority of
the *Lotus Sutra*, and anyone who does this is lost: 'There can be no
doubt that the *Nembutsu* leads to the hell of incessant suffering.'[20]

Equally dangerous in Nichiren's view was Zen, which recognizes
no *sutras* but contends that the Buddha's true doctrine was transmitted
directly to the mind of his disciple Mahakasyapa and then in an

unbroken line of Zen masters. Again, Zen does not involve preaching, and thus disregards the practice of Shakyamuni. Zen, too, (Nichiren contends) had played its part in bringing Japan to the edge of ruin, appealing to the unfilial, lazy and immoral,

> to young priests who are too lazy to apply themselves to their studies, and to the disreputable nature of prostitutes . . . [Zen followers] are not more than swarming locusts feeding upon the people of the nation. That is why Heaven glares down and the gods of the earth shudder.[21]

These are the words of a man utterly convinced of the truth of his beliefs and of his mission to propagate them, as Nichiren undoubtedly was. Besides his passionate moral conviction, the purely philosophical difficulties of the relation of one and many in Tendai thought, with its implications for the problem of evil, were of little concern to him. Nichiren is best regarded as a prophet. His goal was to save Japan and, indeed, all humankind from ruin by means of the Three Great Secret Laws. In comparison with this, his own comfort, even his own life, he held to be of little account. Nichiren suffered greatly, and was prepared to die for the sake of what he believed.

Notes

P. Yampolsky (ed.), *Selected Writings of Nichiren*, New York: Columbia University Press, 1990, is cited as Y.

1 The Nichiren Shoshu sect always refer to him as Nichiren Daishonin (Great Sage Nichiren); other sub-sects generally use the title Shonin (sage).

2 Much of this is known to us from Nichiren's autobiographical work, *Shuju Onfurumai Gosho* (On Various Actions of the Priest Nichiren, 1276), Y, pp. 319–42.

3 Zhihgai lived and taught in the Tiantai mountains; hence the later title. Nichiren had the greatest respect for him, and always refers to him as Tendai Daishi (Great Teacher Tiantai). Tendai Buddhism was introduced into Japan by Saicho (767–822 CE), a Japanese monk who travelled to China. Saicho is often referred to by a title conferred later, Dengyo Daishi (Great Teacher Dengyo). Saicho established the Tendai centre on Mount Hiei.

4 On the main tendencies of Chinese Buddhism, cf. Paul Williams, *Mahayana Buddhism: The Doctrinal Foundations*, London: Routledge, 1989, pp. 116–66. The most widely used Japanese version of the *Lotus Sutra* is translated from the Chinese translations completed by the great scholar Kumarajiva in 406 CE.

5 *Kanjin no Honzon Sho* (The True Object of Worship, 1273), Y, p. 165.

6 Quoted in Fung Yu-lan, *A History of Chinese Philosophy*, 2 vols, vol. 2, Princeton: Princeton University Press, 1953, pp. 361–2. This work is usually

attributed to Tiantai's predecessor Huisi (515–555), though Dr Fung doubts if it is his work.

7 *Ta-ch'eng Chih-kuan Fa-men*, in Fung, op. cit., p. 362. The metaphor of the storehouse is one instance of the influence on the Tiantai school of the Yogacarin analysis of the eight consciousnesses. See the essay on Vasubandhu in this book, pp. 103–14.

8 Fung, op. cit., p. 364.

9 *Shijo Kingo-dono Gohenji* (Earthly Desires are Enlightenment, 1272). (Shijo Kingo is the name of the addressee.)

10 *Ta-ch'eng Chih-kuan Fa-men*, in Fung, op. cit., p. 374.

11 *Kaimoku Sho* (The Opening of the Eyes, 1272 – the eyes to be opened are those of humanity as a whole, and they are to be opened to the truths of Buddhism), Y, p. 95.

12 Quoted by Nichiren in *Kanjin no Honzon Sho*, Y, p. 150. Nichiren claims that the doctrine of *ichinen sanzen* is found only in one place in all the literature of Buddhism, namely, the *juryo* chapter of the *Lotus Sutra*, cf. *Kaimoku Sho*, Y, p. 57.

13 Chan-jan, *Chin-kang pi* (Diamond Stick), in Fung, op. cit., p. 385. A further consequence of the same view is that women can attain buddhahood (cf. *Kaimoku Sho*, Y, p. 121). This was denied in many versions of Buddhism, where it was claimed that reincarnation as a man was a necessary precondition for enlightenment.

14 First referred to in this way by Nichiren in the essay 'Hoon Sho' (Repaying Debts of Gratitude, 1276), and developed in later works, cf. Y, p. 315.

15 Letter to Jakunichi-bo Nikke, 1279, Y, p. 358. For a detailed interpretation of the *daimoku* from the standpoint of the Nichiren Shoshu sub-sect, cf. R. Causton, *Nichiren Shoshu Buddhism: An Introduction*, London: Rider, 1988, pp. 96–222.

16 cf. e.g. *Kanjin no Honzon sho*, Y, pp. 166–7; *Hoon sho*, Y, p. 315; for the cosmic Buddha as *Honzon*, cf. *Sandaihiho Sho*, tr. P.P. del Campana, *Monumenta Nipponica*, vol. 26, nos 1–2, 1971, p. 218.

17 *Sandaihiho Sho*, p. 220.

18 Ibid.

19 These views Honen set out in his *Senchaku Hongan Nembutsu Sho* (Selection of the Nembutsu of the Original Vow, 1198). Pure Land Buddhism takes as basic three *sutras*: the Larger and Smaller *Sukhavativyuha*, and the *Amitayurdhyana Sutra*. For a brief outline of Amidism, cf. Williams, op. cit., pp. 251ff.

20 *Senji Sho* (The Selection of the Time, 1275), Y, p. 241. The attack on Jodo begins with Nichiren's first major essay, the *Rissho Ankoku Ron*, 1260, cf. Y, pp. 24ff, and is a constant theme of his work.

21 *Senji Sho*, Y, p. 218.

Nichiren's Writings

By common consent, the most important of Nichiren's many works are:

Rissho Ankoku Ron (Treatise on the Establishment of the Legitimate Teaching for the Protection of the Country), 1260
Kaimoku Sho (Essay on the Opening of the Eyes), 1272

Kanjin no Honzon Sho (Essay on the True Object of Worship), 1273
Senji Sho (Essay on the Selection of the Time), 1275
Hoon Sho (Essay on Repaying Debts of Gratitude), 1276
Shuju Onforumai Gosho (literally: The Letter on Various Actions; usually called:
   On Various Actions of the Priest Nichiren), 1276
Sandaihiho Sho (Essay on the Three Great Secret Laws), 1281

See also in this book

the Buddha

Sources and further reading

NSIC = Nichiren Shoshu International Center, Tokyo

Letters of Nichiren, trans. B. Watson and P.B. Yampolsky (Columbia Asian Studies
   series), New York: Columbia University Press, 1996
Major Writings of Nichiren Daishonin, 4 vols, Tokyo, NSIC, 1979; 1981; 1985;
   1986
Causton, R., *Nichiren Shoshu Buddhism: An Introduction*, London: Rider, 1988
Del Campana, Pier P., 'Sandaihiho Sho by Nichiren', *Monumenta Nipponica*,
   vol. 26 nos 1–2, 1971, pp. 205–24
Kirimura, Y., *Buddhism and the Nichiren Shoshu Tradition*, Tokyo: Nichiren
   Shoshu International Center, 1986
Petzold, B., *The Buddhist Prophet Nichiren – A Lotus in the Sun*, 1977, Tokyo:
   Hokke Janaru, 1978
Williams, P., *Mahayana Buddhism: The Doctrinal Foundations*, London: Routledge,
   1989
Yampolsky, P. (ed.), *Selected Writings of Nichiren*, New York: Columbia
   University Press, 1990 (contains the first six of the works listed above, with
   some letters)

On the Tendai/Tiantai background, cf.

Fung Yu-lan, *A History of Chinese Philosophy*, trans. D. Bodde, 2 vols, vol. 2,
   Princeton: Princeton University Press, 1953, pp. 360ff.
Swanson, P.L., *The Foundations of Tien-t'ai Philosophy*, Berkeley, Calif.: Asian
   Humanities Press, 1989

There are a number of English versions of the *Lotus Sutra*, notably:

Soothill, W.E., *The Lotus of the Wonderful Law or the Lotus Gospel*, Oxford:
   Clarendon Press, 1930 and subsequent editions.

BANKEI YOTAKU 1622–1693 CE

In the writings or stories of many of its masters, **Zen** appears as an
austere discipline requiring years of asceticism in order to bring about
satori or enlightenment. The enlightenment experience is usually said

to occur, if at all, only after prolonged physical and mental training of shattering rigour. Bankei's Zen is by contrast approachable and unfrightening, in many ways reminiscent of the gentler spontaneities of **Daoism** (cf. Laozi). Whilst he attained his own *satori* only after ascetic practices which brought him close to death, Bankei came to believe that this method was mistaken and unnecessary, and in his own ministry advocated a much simpler way to the goal of Zen. He had a genuine concern not only for monks but for lay people of all ranks, and he took care to speak to them directly and with reference to their own concerns. Whilst his thought rests on the philosophy of the **Mahayana**, he keeps technicalities out of his discourse as far as possible, focusing instead on how to lead a daily life in the light of Zen teaching. Absent from his sermons or *dharma* talks are references to the *sutras* or *koans* or the lives of past masters; instead there is a sharp focus on the concerns of our daily lives, especially the ego, its attachments and emotions. Human nature has not changed since Bankei wrote, with the result that he addresses us as directly as his audience at the time.

Bankei was born in 1622 in Hamada, a village on the shore of the Inland Sea (present-day eastern Hyogo prefecture). His father, Sugawara Dosetsu, who died when Bankei was 10, was a physician of samurai rank. Bankei is reputed to have been sensitive but strong-willed to the point of waywardness as a child. As with Dogen and Hakuin, he showed religious sensibility early, not only in a profound aversion to death (and so a sense of ephemerality), but also in his reaction to his schooling. As was normal, at the age of 11 Bankei was set to learn by rote the Confucian classic *The Great Learning* (C: *Daxue* [*Ta-hsueh*]; J: *Daigaku*). He was puzzled by the statement in that work that 'The way of great learning lies in clarifying Bright Virtue' (C: *mingde* [*ming-te*], and was unable to obtain from his teachers a satisfactory statement of what Bright Virtue might be. He later interpreted this incident as the start of his religious quest, which was to occupy him for fourteen years.

Bankei's dissatisfaction with his school manifested itself as repeated truancy, and in consequence his elder brother (head of the family after their father's death) evicted him from the house. For some years Bankei lived in a hut erected for him by a relative, relentlessly searching after the nature of Bright Virtue. In 1638, his quest took him to the city of Ako and the Zen master Umpo Zenjo (1568–1653 CE). Here Bankei was ordained a monk and given the religious name Yotaku (Long Polishing [of the Mind Gem]) – the name Bankei he acquired later, in his early thirties. He stayed with Umpo for three years, pursuing a Zen programme based on **zazen**. Thereafter he spent many years in wandering (J: *angya*), a traditional part of Zen training, relentlessly practising seated meditation in conjunction with an ascetic way of life. This could not continue without detrimental physical effect, and he contracted tuberculosis. Bankei was almost at the point of death when after fourteen years of struggle he had a *satori*. He coughed up a mass of black phlegm which rolled down the wall of his hut:

> Suddenly, just at that moment, it came to me. I realized what it was that had escaped me until now: *All things are perfectly resolved in the Unborn*. I realized too that what I had been doing all this time had been mistaken.[1]

His health improved at once, and he set out to find a teacher who could confirm his enlightenment.

This confirmation he finally received in 1651 from a Chinese Rinzai Zen master, Dosha Chogen (1600?–1661? CE, C: Daozhe Chaoyuan [Tao-che Ch'ao yuan]), who had lately arrived in Nagasaki. Dosha maintained that, although he had achieved *satori*, Bankei's enlightenment was not complete. At first incredulous, Bankei submitted to further training and achieved a further *satori* in 1652. At this point Dosha accepted that his pupil's training was complete. Between 1652 and 1657, Bankei moved between various retreats, with a handful of disciples of his own. This came to an end when he was officially made spiritual heir to his former master Umpo, and Bankei began the period of thirty-six years of ministry which occupied the rest of his life, becoming a famous and much sought-after teacher. He died in 1693 at the Ryumon-ji. He was asked shortly before death if, in traditional Zen manner, he would compose a death verse. He said

> I've lived for seventy-two years. I've been teaching people for forty-five. What I've been telling you and others every day during that time is all my death verse. I'm not going to make another one now, before I die, just because everyone else does it.[2]

Having said this Bankei died, showing to the last the same spirit of independence in which he had lived.

At the centre of Bankei's thought is the concept of the Unborn (J: *fusho*) or Buddha-mind (J: *busshin*). The Unborn is being-as-is or reality, a predicateless unity which is in a sense at the source of all things: 'The Unborn is the origin of all and the beginning of all. There is no source apart from the Unborn and no beginning that is before the Unborn.'[3] This is Bankei's preferred way of stating the Zen doctrine that all sentient beings possess the Buddha-nature or Buddha-mind, the eternal, divisionless unity behind the appearance of the ordinary world of spatio-temporal individuals or *samsara*. Since the Unborn is an eternal unity, no concepts properly apply to it, since concepts are devices whereby we articulate experience by making divisions in it. Since reality is a unity, all conceptual thought and all appearance of division are unreal:

> Thoughts arise temporarily in response to what you see and hear; they don't have any real existence of their own. You must have faith that the original mind [i.e. Buddha-mind] that is realized and that which *realizes* the original mind are not different.[4]

i.e. because the Unborn is entirely undifferentiated.

Bankei had become aware of the Unborn in *satori* but he did not expect those who came to hear him and had not attained this rare experience to take what he had to say purely on trust. The Unborn, since it is the source of all, is constantly at work, and Bankei tries to give an insight into its nature by means of an analysis of perception. In ordinary perception, there is one element in the field of consciousness to which we pay special attention, and the rest of the field becomes peripheral. Thus, when Bankei's audience was assembled before him, its members focused their attention on him; but this did not prevent them from discriminating unrelated sounds occurring outside the lecture hall, though without any effort of attention whatsoever. If a dog barked or a crow cawed, these discriminations would be registered effortlessly in consciousness. Now since the attention of the ego is concentrated on the speaker, whatever registers these peripheral perceptions, Bankei argues, is not the ego. The only other possibility is that this peripheral perception, effortless and accurate, is the working of the Buddha-mind: 'You are able to hear and distinguish sounds when they do occur without consciously intending to hear them because you're listening by means of Unborn Buddha-mind.'[5] This example gives a hint of what it is like to be enlightened or, as Bankei prefers to say, 'to live in the Unborn'.

The question of what method it is appropriate to use to free ourselves of the illusions of the surface ego and attain the life of the Unborn is one on which Bankei's views are startling and original. He

dismisses as mistaken the central recommendations of both the **Soto**
and **Rinzai** schools of Zen. The Soto school, founded in Japan by
Dogen, gives absolute primacy to single-minded intense sitting or
zazen, which Dogen goes so far as to *identify* with enlightenment. This
Bankei dismisses as a misunderstanding of *zazen*:

> For hundreds of years now the Zen teaching in both China
> and Japan has been mistaken. People have thought, and still
> do, that enlightenment is obtained by doing *zazen* . . . They're
> dead wrong. *Zazen* is another name for the primary mind.
> It signifies peaceful sitting. A peaceful mind. When sitting, it
> just sits. When doing *kinhin* [walking to relieve drowsiness],
> it just walks.[6]

Bankei is equally dismissive of the *koan* Zen practice of the Rinzai
sect. The *koans* Bankei refers to as 'old tools', and dismisses those who
practise 'tool Zen' as 'eyeless bonzes' who are 'unable to teach directly
. . . if they don't have their implements to help them, they aren't up to
handling people'.[7] The goal of the *koan* method is to paralyse rational
thought by means of the insoluble *koan*, and this is referred to as
'raising a great ball of doubt' in the mind of the aspirant. This Bankei
regards as a harmful form of training:

> Instead of teaching [the aspirants] to live by the Unborn
> Buddha-mind, they start by forcing them to raise this ball of
> doubt any way they can. People who don't have a doubt are
> now saddled with one. They've turned their Buddha-minds
> into 'balls of doubt'. It's absolutely wrong.[8]

There is a common error behind both these approaches, in
Bankei's view, and indeed behind any approach which claims to have
possession of *the* method for Zen. The great masters of the past
used many different methods to attain the Unborn in themselves
and others: Bodhidharma gazed at a wall; Tokusan (782–865) used a
staff, and Rinzai (d.867) used shouting and so on. These were all
spontaneous, appropriate responses to the circumstances in which they
found themselves at the time. To sanctify these as the only practices to
be used in Zen is an understandable human tendency, but a mistaken
one:

> Each [technique] was different, and yet all were measures
> used in response to an occasion present at a certain time.

> They were the expedient means of good and able masters.
> Intrinsically, there is no fixed **Dharma**. If you try to give the
> *Dharma* a fixed interpretation, you merely blind your own
> eye.[9]

You 'blind your own eye' because by codifying past practice or seeking
the answer in the *sutras* or the records of the masters you become more
and not less wedded to fixed patterns of conceptual thought, thereby
reinforcing the strength of the surface ego. This is exactly contrary
to the goal of Zen. The role of the Zen master is not to take refuge in
set rules or practices, but to confront each aspirant directly now, and
so deal with each individual as to bring about life in the Unborn.
Consistently with this view, Bankei refused to write down his own
teachings, and forbade his attendants to do so: once written down, his
views (he feared) would simply become another bogus 'authority',
getting in the way of enlightenment.

While he abjures any special method, Bankei does have some
suggestions as to how to approach enlightenment, closely linked with
his descriptions of what it is like to be enlightened or 'live in the
Unborn'. The obstacle to enlightenment is the surface ego with its
desires and its attachment to conceptual thought. This surface ego is
constructed after birth, largely on the basis of the observation and
imitation of others, and obscures the true Buddha-mind which
(Bankei asserts) is our only innate characteristic. The Buddha-mind
is not something we have to seek: we have it already (we are all
Buddhas, as Bankei puts it). What we need to do is to allow it to
operate naturally, and to do that we must neutralize the ego. This
is not easy, and does require great effort. However, rather than direct
the effort into asceticism, Bankei recommends that we try instead to
rid ourselves of our attachment to the thoughts of the surface ego. The
first step on this path is not to seek to direct one's thoughts, to dwell
on some and try to shun others by the use of the will. Instead, 'let
them arise when they arise. Don't have any thought to stop them. If
they stop, let them stop. Don't pay any attention to them. Leave them
alone. Then illusions won't appear.'[10]

The homeliness of Bankei's language belies the profundity and
radicality of the change in consciousness which this practice brings
about. To live in the Unborn or to be enlightened is to live in such a
way that the surface ego is dissipated or neutralized. Such a condition
brings absolute peace and harmony: 'In the Unborn, all things
are perfectly resolved.'[11] Consciousness becomes a mirror, merely
reflecting what comes before it, without attachment and with the

effortless, intuitive immediacy of which the peripheral perception (described above) gives a faint hint. Because there is no ego there is no attachment, and since there is no attachment there is no fear, even fear of death: 'When the time comes for [an enlightened person's] physical elements to disperse in death, he will give himself completely to the dispersal and die without regret or attachment.'[12] Again those who live in the Unborn are aware of the futility of conceptual discrimination, unrelated as it is to the nature of being-as-is. It is this, Bankei points out, which lies behind the usually misunderstood Buddhist statement that *samsara* and *nirvana* are one and the same: they are the same because this distinction, like all distinctions, fails to correspond to any feature of reality.[13] In reality there is only the Unborn, and neither *samsara* nor *nirvana*.

Equally unreal to the enlightened are any of the moral distinctions between good and evil over which human beings contend so fiercely: become wedded to those distinctions and, as Bankei often puts it, the Buddha-mind is transformed into a fighting spirit. Loving good and hating evil may seem to be the core of moral insight: Bankei comments that to adopt these attitudes reinforces the ego and so prevents enlightenment:

> You think that good
>   Means hating what is bad
> What's bad is
>   The hating mind itself
>
> Good, you say,
>   Means doing good
> Bad indeed
>   The mind that says so![14]

This does not mean that Bankei considered himself 'above morality', in the sense in which that phrase is sometimes used. Rather, to Bankei as to all mystics, moral rules or codes are necessary only for those who live in the world of the ego or *samsara*, and who need to check their impulses to selfishness. The enlightened are free of ego and so of selfish desires: in such a condition moral rules are simply otiose. Those living in the Unborn have what Kant termed a 'holy will': their spontaneous action is the 'action' of the One, or, in western vocabulary, is the will of God.

To live in the Unborn transforms every aspect of life and informs every type of human activity. To live in the Unborn or to be enlightened is by definition to be free of illusion, and to be free of illusion is to be always in possession of the truth:

> Once you come to know without any doubt that the marvellous illuminative wisdom of the Unborn is the Buddha-mind and that the Buddha-mind puts all things in perfect order by means of the Unborn, then you can no longer be deluded or led astray by others.[15]

One important special case of this wisdom is insight into other people: 'I never err in my judgement of people, nor does anyone else who has the eye of the Unborn. Our school has been called the "Clear-eyed" section for that reason': when the eye to see others opens, 'you can see straight into their hearts'.[16] This is no mere claim to telepathy, but a strict consequence of Bankei's metaphysics and epistemology: those who live in the Unborn are (as it were) in touch with the mind of God. To those in such a condition ignorance is impossible.

Not surprisingly, in view of this, the mode of action of the enlightened is also quite other than that of those who have not transcended the ego, whatever their profession. Bankei explained this to a devotee of the martial arts named Gesso, a master of the *yari* or Japanese lance. Those who live in the Unborn have no attachment to the ego and its discriminations and so exist in the state Zen writers refer to as 'no-mind'. Whoever is in such a state does not, properly speaking, *act* at all, since action involves the intention of an individual ego. 'In performing a movement, if you act with no-mind, the action will spring forth of itself.'[17] If in combat it is necessary to deliberate over a course of action, you are already at some distance from the Unborn. For the Zen adept, combat, like any other form of action, is pure spontaneity: the arrow shoots itself, since there is no 'I' or ego left to shoot it. Such a condition is at the limits of describability in our ordinary language, designed to embody conceptual distinctions, as Bankei's description of combat shows:

> When, without thinking and without acting deliberately, you manifest the Unborn, you won't have any fixed form. When you are without fixed form, no opponent will exist for you in the whole land. Not holding on to anything, not relying one-sidedly on anything, there is no 'you' and no 'enemy'. Whatever comes you just respond, with no traces left behind.[18]

It is to be stressed that, although Bankei gives this description of enlightened action in a martial context, it is generalizable to all areas of behaviour.

Bankei's thought fell into obscurity not long after his death, no doubt in part because it contradicts, in terms of recommendations over Zen method, the subsequently dominant '*koan* Zen' of Hakuin. It has emerged again only in this century, thanks to the work of D.T. Suzuki (see pp. 388–96), who re-edited the relevant texts (see Bibliography) and made a powerful case for regarding Bankei as one of the most original figures in the history of Japanese Zen. This philosophy is not without its difficulties, notably over whether any evidence for the Unborn is furnished by peripheral perception, though one should not lose sight of the fact that the *dharma* talks in which this argument is used repeatedly were designed to be heard by a lay audience. Elsewhere, Bankei's works leave no room to doubt that they are the work of a true Zen master. His greatest strength is to give a clearer indication than most of what it is like to live in the state of enlightenment: fearless, entirely without confusion of mind, without attachment and – to end with the point Bankei returns to most often – with pure spontaneity. Eternal life belongs to those who live in a timeless present.

Notes

References to P. Haskel, *Bankei Zen: Translations from the Record of Bankei*, New York: Grove Weidenfeld, 1984, are given as H, and to N. Waddell, *The Unborn: The Life and Teaching of Zen Master Bankei 1622–1693*, San Francisco: North Point Press, 1984, as W.

1 *Ryumon-ji Sermons*, W, p. 45 (the Ryumon-ji ['Dragon Gate Temple'] was one of Bankei's major temples during the latter part of his life). For reasons which will become clear, Bankei refused to write down any of his teachings, and equally refused to allow his disciples to do so either: fortunately, he was disobeyed, and the chief part of what is now called the *Record of Bankei* consists of verbatim notes of two sets of *dharma* talks or sermons delivered in 1690 at the Ryumon-ji and the Hoshin-ji (another of his temples). The only written items by Bankei himself are a few letters and a small number of poems in Chinese and Japanese.

2 W, p. 23. On Bankei's life, cf. W pp. 1–23; H, Introduction and pp. 140–64.

3 *Ryumon-ji Sermons*, W, p. 36.

4 Letter to his [female] disciple Rintei (1630–1702), probably written in the early 1660s. H, p. 136.

5 *Ryumon-ji Sermons*, W, p. 36.

6 *Butchi kosai zenji hogo* (The Dharma Words of Zen Master Butchi Kosai [i.e. Bankei]), W, p. 122. This work, probably compiled around 1730, is a series of reminiscences by Bankei's attendant Itsuzan Sonin, 1655–1734. *Butchi*

kosai zenji (Zen Master of Beneficent Enlightened Wisdom) was a title bestowed on Bankei by the emperor, *c.*1690.

7   *Ryumon-ji Sermons*, W., p. 57.
8   Ibid.: not surprisingly, Bankei's Zen was anathema to Hakuin, who systematized and revitalized the *koan* method.
9   *Butchi kosai zenji hogo*, W, pp. 126–7.
10 *Ryumon-ji Sermons*, W, p. 49. Bankei's assertion that the Buddha-mind is our *only* innate characteristic involves him in a libertarian interpretation of the doctrine of **karma** with stern implications for our moral responsibility for our own characters. Some try to blame their bad traits on *karma*, but Bankei objects: 'You don't steal because of *karma*. Stealing itself is the *karma*' (*Ryumon-ji Sermons*, W, p. 68). Our actions are the result of our decisions, and any decision can be changed. A very similar anti-innatism is present in Sartre's existentialism, and leads logically to a similar view. In Sartre's philosophy, we create our own nature ('existence precedes essence') and to try to shuffle off responsibility to ambient circumstance or inherited traits is what he calls 'bad faith'. The logical patterns in these two philosophies are in this respect the same. On Sartre, cf. D. Collinson, *Fifty Major Philosophers*, London: Routledge, 1988, pp. 157ff.
11 *Ryumon-ji Sermons*, W, p. 34.
12 op. cit., W, p. 56: it will be clear that 'life in the Unborn' is the same state as is described in the Hindu tradition as **moksa** or release. It is eternal life here and now.
13 Ibid.
14 *Honshin no uta* (Song of the Original Mind, 1653), H, p. 128.
15 *Ryumon-ji Sermons*, W, p. 48.
16 Ibid., pp. 47–8.
17 *Instructions to Layman Gesso*, H, p. 138.
18 Ibid., H, pp. 138–9.

Major work

Bankei wrote very little himself. The text which contains his words, *The Record of Bankei*, is made up chiefly of *dharma* talks or sermons recorded by his disciples.

See also in this book

the Buddha, Huineng, Chinul, Dogen, Hakuin, Nishida, Suzuki

Sources and further reading

The key passages of *The Record of Bankei* are available in two English translations:

Haskel, P., *Bankei Zen: Translations from the Record of Bankei*, New York: Grove Weidenfeld, 1984; reissued 1989
Waddell, N., *The Unborn: The Life and Teaching of Zen Master Bankei 1622–1693*, San Francisco: North Point Press, 1984

D.T. Suzuki issued a series of works by and about Bankei in Japanese from 1940 onwards, and it is to these works that Bankei owes his present growing stature in the history of Zen thought. Most important of these is *Zen shiso-shi kenkyu*, I (*Studies in the History of Zen Thought*, first series), Tokyo, 1943, translated by Norman Waddell as 'Dogen, Hakuin, Bankei: three types of thought in Japanese Zen', in *The Eastern Buddhist*, vol. IX (n.s.), no. 1, 1976, pp. 1–17; no. 2, 1976, pp. 1–20.

HAKUIN EKAKU 1685–1769 CE

The history of almost all religious movements includes periods of vitality, periods of consolidation and periods of decline: during these last, the great truths are no longer the objects of earnest belief, no longer felt on the pulse. This pattern is evident in the history of the **Rinzai** (C: Linji [Lin-chi]) school of **Zen**. The Japanese school traces its lineage ultimately back to Nampo Jomyo (1235–1309) and his successors Daito Kokushi (1282–1338) and Kanzan Egen (1277–1377). This school flourished and became dominant over the rival **Soto** school (cf. the essay on Dogen) during the Kamakura period (1185–1333). As time passed, however, this dominance led to complacency and complacency to stagnation. Rinzai Zen came to be associated more with artistic and literary life than with the urgent, dedicated pursuit of religious truth, and this was the state of affairs at the beginning of the Tokugawa period (1603–1867). Hakuin earned his place in history by reversing this decline. He revived Rinzai Zen both by his own example and by means of his many written works. He and his heirs[1] codified *koan* practice, and devised a monastic rule or system which has lasted until the present day. Nor was his concern restricted to the life of the monks in his charge: he wrote at length to advise eminent lay-believers, and had in addition a genuine regard for the simple and unlettered labourers, whose lot was hard to endure. He often went to the fields near his monastery to talk to them, giving such consolation as it was in his power to give.

Hakuin was born on 19 January 1685 in the village of Hara near the foot of Mount Fuji.[2] The chief influence in the childhood of the gifted and sensitive boy was his mother, a member of the Nichiren sect. Early evidence of his unusual openness to religious matters was shown in his reaction to a sermon he heard in a local temple at the age of 7 or 8. The priest described the hot hells of the Buddhist system, and this frightened the boy deeply. Shortly afterwards, in the course of a hot bath, the heat of the water reminded him of the description of the hells, and he records that he 'let out a cry of terror that resounded through the neighbourhood'.[3] He resolved to become a monk, a course of which his parents did not approve, and left home at the age of 15 in order to begin his training. He received his primary ordination at the Shoinji (temple) in March 1699. After some years, during which he experienced a crisis of faith later restored by intense meditation, he achieved a number of minor enlightenment experiences, and then what he believed to be a major one.

Hakuin's travels between teachers took him next to Iiyama (present-day Nagano prefecture), where he met the Zen Master Dokyo Etan (1642–1721)[4] and presented the Master with a written statement of his understanding of Zen. To Hakuin's astonishment and mortification, Etan roared with laughter and shouted at him that he was a 'poor hole-dwelling devil'.[5] Rather than being put off by Etan's harsh treatment, which was unremitting, Hakuin redoubled his efforts to achieve enlightenment. He finally did so, seemingly to Etan's satisfaction, some eight months later. As so often in Zen, the trigger for awakening was a trivial incident. Hakuin had gone to a nearby village, and encountered a man who tried to beat him with a broom. At that moment, all the *koans* were solved, and Hakuin grasped the Great Matter, i.e. became enlightened. Thereafter, Etan no longer abused him.[6]

The austerities Hakuin practised before achieving enlightenment were by now beginning to take their toll, and he fell ill. The experience of 'meditation sickness' and its cure impressed him deeply, and Hakuin left a detailed account of it in one of his best-known works, *Yasen kanna* (A Chat on a Boat in the Evening, 1757). Besides trying physical symptoms, mentally he was 'distressed and weary, and whether sleeping or waking . . . always became lost in wild fancies',[7] and so was unable to practise Zen. After fruitless consultations with a number of doctors, Hakuin was recommended to visit a hermit living in the mountains of Shirakawa, Master Hakuyu (1646–1709). Hakuyu, basing his treatment on the ideas of the *I Jing* [*I Ching*] and Daoism, instructed Hakuin in a special type of introspection (J: *naikan*). This Hakuin faithfully adopted, with the result that within three years his health was fully restored. For the rest of his long life, Hakuin was to caution against too much asceticism in the practice of Zen.[8]

In 1716, Hakuin received a message that his father was dying, and he returned to the temple near his home, the Shoinji. There he was to remain for the rest of his life. He restored the ruinous building, and made it the centre of the Rinzai school in his time. His fame gradually spread throughout Japan, and he never lacked for disciples. He left the Shoinji only to give lectures by means of which to raise funds for both its maintenance and that of its monks. Not only did he continue to write, but achieved distinction as a painter and calligrapher; almost a thousand surviving paintings are attributed to him. Hakuin died peacefully in his sleep, aged 83, on 18 January 1769.

Underlying all Hakuin's thought are the metaphysical beliefs which Zen took over from the parent **Mahayana** school of Buddhism. In this school, the fundamental belief is that the world of ordinary experience, of discrete individual entities causally interacting in space and time, is a delusion, the world of the *samsara*. Being-as-is or reality is a divisionless unity, a oneness. The ultimate metaphysical truth, the '*dharma* principle' in Hakuin's terms, is that 'all things are a nondual unity representing the true appearance of all things. This is the fundamental principle of Buddhism.'[9] This oneness is such that no conceptual descriptions apply to it: concepts are our way of articulating divisions within experience, and reality exhibits no divisions:

> If you say it is in existence it will not be there; if you say it is in non-existence it will not be there either. This place, where words and speech are cut off, this free and untrammelled place, is provisionally called the Wondrous Law.[10]

Since it has no divisions, reality is changeless, it 'has not changed one iota since before the last *kalpa* began, nor will it change after it has ended'.[11] Further, it follows that if all divisions are unreal, the division between the self and the not-self, normally regarded as a logically indispensable precondition for human experience as such, is itself unreal. Moreover, as the Buddha taught, it is this erroneous belief in the reality of the self which brings about all our suffering: 'Because of this view that the self exists, we have birth and death, Nirvana, the passions, enlightenment.'[12]

The goal of Zen is to free us from these false beliefs in the reality of the *samsara* and to give us direct experience of being-as-is. This project presupposes that reality is experienceable by us. It is experienceable by us because we are all manifestations of reality: our belief in our own self and so our personal separateness is an illusion, and we have a real nature which is utterly different. In the vocabulary of Zen, this is the view that all entities possess the Buddha-nature (= reality). Hakuin states this often; for example, at the opening of his poem *Zazen wasan* (The Song of Zazen):

All beings are primarily Buddhas.
Like water and ice,
There is no ice apart from water;
There are no Buddhas apart from beings.[13]

The Buddha-nature, our real nature or 'original face', is ordinarily hidden from us by the web of delusion inherent in conceptual thought, and Zen training is designed to free us from the immensely powerful grip in which we are held by such thought. Hence the goal of Zen is often described as attainment of the state of 'no mind' or 'no thought': this means, not extinction, but non-conceptual awareness, free of delusion, including the delusion of selfhood.

Since we all have the Buddha-nature, it follows that the path to awareness of it is inwards. Reality is not to be found by exploration of the *samsaric* universe, but at the base of consciousness. Awareness of reality is wisdom (S: **prajna**), and so Hakuin says that *prajna* is not far off:[14]

Not knowing how close Truth is to them,
Beings seek for it afar – what a pity! . . .
But if you turn your eyes within yourselves
And testify to the truth of Self-nature –
The Self-nature that is no nature,
You will have gone beyond the ken of sophistry.[15]

The method recommended by Hakuin by which we can be freed from the delusions of conceptual thought is that of carefully sequenced work, under a master, on the special problems called *koans*. '*Koan*' is the Japanese form of the Chinese *gongan* ['*kung an*'], which means a public record or announcement, e.g. the public records of cases and judgments in law courts.[16] The *koans* are in effect the recorded sayings of the Zen masters: they both facilitate the path of others on the way to enlightenment (the early masters had no such aids) and provide a standard by which enlightenment claims can be tested, thus preventing the importation of private eccentricities into Zen. A number of *koan* collections, chiefly originating from China in the Sung period, were in use for Zen training in Hakuin's day, and have continued to be so.[17] Hakuin's contribution was to organize their use into a system, and to enrich the *koan* literature with a number of his own.

The nature of the *koan* can be illustrated with one of the best-known examples, a *koan* formulated by Hakuin himself:

What is the Sound of the Single Hand? When you clap together both hands a sharp sound is heard; when you raise one hand there is neither sound nor smell . . . This is something that can by no means be heard with the ear.[18]

So long as conceptual thought is employed, the *koan* has no solution, and the aspirant is brought into a mental condition for which the physical equivalent is being faced with a blank wall. The aim of the *koan* is to baffle the rational mind, to cause it to exhaust itself, and so bring it to breaking point: only in this way, Hakuin contends, can the powerful grip of conceptual thought be broken. Hakuin's descriptions of the state of mind induced by *koan* practice are unusually full and detailed. Here he describes his own state of mind when, in his early twenties, he had been set Joshu's *koan* '*mu*':[19]

Suddenly a great doubt manifested itself before me. It was as though I were frozen solid in the midst of an ice sheet extending tens of thousands of miles. A purity filled my breast and I could neither go forward nor retreat. To all intents and purposes I was out of my mind and '*Mu*' alone remained.[20]

By means of intense concentration on the *koan*, Hakuin had reached the point at which ordinary self-consciousness disintegrates: there ceases to be an 'I' and all there is is the *koan*.

This state of mind may continue for some time – in Hakuin's case it was for several days. If the aspirant is fully prepared, the next stage is a timeless moment of awakening or enlightenment: **satori** or its near synonym *kensho* in Japanese. Often, this breakthrough follows a trivial incident; in the present instance, Hakuin by chance heard the temple bell,

and I was suddenly transformed. It was as if a sheet of ice had been smashed or a jade tower had fallen with a crash . . . In a loud voice I called 'Wonderful, wonderful.' There is no cycle of birth and death through which one must pass. There is no enlightenment one must seek. The seventeen hundred *koans* handed down from the past have not the slightest value whatsoever.[21]

It is asserted in Mahayanist metaphysics that all things are one, and this is the insight gained in the nondual awareness which constitutes enlightenment. Since all things are one, **samsara** and **nirvana** are found to be identical. *Nirvana* is not a future state or a different place: to the enlightened, it is here now:

> When one reaches this state of the realization of True Reality in one's own body, the mountains, rivers, the great earth, all phenomena, grass, trees, lands, the sentient and the non-sentient all appear at the same time as the complete body of the unchanging True Reality. This is the appearance of Nirvana, the time of awakening to one's own nature.[22]

Reality is revealed to have no defects or limitations and to be subject to none of the conditions which pertain to entities we class as existent. Echoing the thought of Nagarjuna, Hakuin prefers to describe reality as a void: 'All is vast perfection, all is vast emptiness.'[23]

Zen masters have often warned against not differentiating between major and minor awakenings, and against becoming complacent after a first *satori*. Hakuin, after his experience with Etan described above, was well aware of this problem, and in his writings develops the theme of degrees or grades of enlightenment to a pitch of great sophistication. The Chinese master Dongshan Liangjie [Tung-shan Liang-chieh; Tozan Ryokai, 807–869] had much earlier put forward a view of five degrees of insight, termed the Five Ranks (C: *Dongshan wuwei* [*Tung-shan wu-wei*]; J: *Tozan goi*), and on this view Hakuin commented at length.[24] Thus for example, whilst in common with many other Zen thinkers Hakuin accepts the Yogacarin doctrine of the eight consciousnesses (cf. Vasubandhu), he warns against holding that insight into the eighth or store-consciousness (*alaya-vijnana*) is ultimate: rather, it is a 'dark cave' to be smashed open.[25] Again, the nondual insight described above in Hakuin's own words should not be thought to be the final goal: it is only the first of the Five Ranks, and the aspirant must take care not to cling to it, since clinging is evidence of desire, and desire is an attribute of a self not completely eliminated.[26] The initial *satori* is to be refined by unremitting further practice on graded *koans* until the Fifth Rank, Unity Attained, is achieved.[27] One who attains this Rank is ready once again to lead what is termed an ordinary life, though transfigured by Zen insight. The way of Zen does not end with a single *satori*: Hakuin himself had many, and he and his successors made provision for their cultivation in a highly advanced scheme of training.

It might be assumed that the extensive programme of *koan* practice implied in the above would leave hardly any time for any activity other than meditation, and in a sense this is so. However, it is important to stress that for Hakuin, meditation is not synonymous with *zazen* (seated meditation), though *zazen* is an important aspect of his programme. Instead, Hakuin insists that every activity, if informed by Zen, is a form of meditation. It is necessary to develop the capacity to meditate during all forms of action:

> What is true meditation? It is to make everything: coughing, swallowing, waving the arms, motion, stillness, words, action, the evil and the good, prosperity and shame, gain and loss, right and wrong, into one single *koan* . . . Make your saddle your sitting cushion; make the mountains, rivers and the great earth the sitting platform; make the whole universe your own personal meditation cave.[28]

Not surprisingly, Hakuin had little patience with those Zen adherents, chiefly the Soto school of his time, who equated meditation exclusively with *zazen*, and who did not insist on the use of *koans*:

> They practise silent, dead sitting as though they were incense burners in some old mausoleum . . . If you examine these people you will find they are illiterate, stinking, blind, shaven-headed commoners with no power whatsoever to guard the fortress of the **Dharma**.[29]

In Hakuin's view, such people do not even approach the levels of insight available to those who follow his practice of *koan* meditation in action.

Hakuin nowhere disguises the difficulty of the programme he advocates. He stresses that the Zen aspirant needs not only faith in the master and the attainability of the goal, but also perseverance and courage. Awakening is unlikely to come before the student has gone through an extensive programme of *koan* practice, probably lasting some years, and unwavering perseverance is needed to prevent failure during this time. Courage is needed because the unseating of the grip of ordinary thinking processes by *koan* practice, 'raising the great ball of doubt', is not always pleasant. As has been indicated, the aim is to bring the reasoning mind to breaking point, the 'Great Death': that Hakuin should describe the state in this way indicates the profundity of the mental upheaval involved in Zen. What justifies the effort – it takes every ounce of strength – is the experience of enlightenment:

At this moment what is there that you lack?
Nirvana presents itself before you,
Where you stand is the Land of Purity.
Your person, the body of Buddha.[30]

The insight of enlightenment brings absolute peace, absolute fear-lessness and absolute joy. Small wonder that despite the rigour of the training so many should have followed the path.

Notes

References to P.B. Yampolsky (ed. and trans.), *The Zen Master Hakuin: Selected Writings*, New York and London: Columbia University Press, 1971, are given as Yampolsky.

1 His direct heir Gasan Jito (1727–1797), and then Inzan Ien (1751–1814) and Takuju Kosen (1760–1833).
2 Hakuin Ekaku, the name by which he is always known, is a combination of two religious names he took later in life. He was born Sugiyama Iwajiro.
3 *Orategama Supplement*, Yampolsky, p. 116 (the word 'Orategama', the title of one of Hakuin's best-known works, has traditionally been said to be the proper name he gave to his favourite tea-kettle).
4 Also known as Shoju Rojin.
5 *Orategama Supplement*, Yampolsky, p. 119.
6 Ibid., p. 120.
7 *Yasen Kanna*, trans. R.D.M. Shaw and W. Schiffer, in *Monumenta Nipponica*, vol. 13, nos 1–2, 1956, p. 113.
8 Before leaving the figure of Hakuyu, it is of interest to note that, according to Hakuin, he had carried his yogic practice (Daoist in his case) to such a point that like Milarepa, he needed only a cotton shirt in the bitterest cold. (cf. *Yasen Kanna*, p. 125). Hakuin was to continue to recommend '*naikan*' for the rest of his life, cf. e.g. the opening of *Orategama* I, Yampolsky, pp. 29ff., written almost forty years after the meeting with Hakuyu.
9 *Orategama* III, Yampolsky, p. 87.
10 Ibid., p. 89.
11 Ibid., p. 90. A **kalpa** is an immense stretch of time: 'eon' gives something of the same meaning in English.
12 *Orategama zokushu*, Yampolsky, p. 134.
13 *Zazen wasan*, 11, 1–4, trans. Sumiko Kudo in Zekei Shibayama, *On Zazen Wasan: Hakuin's Song of Zazen*, Kyoto, 1967, p. 1. There is another translation of the poem in I. Miura and R.F. Sasaki, *Zen Dust*, New York: Harcourt Brace, 1966, pp. 251–3.
14 *Orategama* II, Yampolsky, p. 76.
15 *Zazen wasan*, 11.5–6 and 28–31, trans. Sumiko Kudo in Zekei Shibayama, op. cit., pp. 1–2.
16 This explains why, in the great *koan* collections, it is customary to refer to each entry as a 'case'.
17 The best-known *koan* collections, referred to with some frequency in later Zen literature, are:

- (a) *The Record of Lin-chi*/C: *Linji lu* [*Lin-chi lu*]/J: *Rinzai roku*. Lin-chi died in 866 CE. The initial date of compilation and printing is disputed. A second edition appeared *c.*1120 CE.
- (b) *The Blue Cliff Record*/C: *Biyan lu* [*Pi-yen lu*]/J: *Hekigan roku*, published 1128 CE.
- (c) *The Gateless Gate* (or: *Pass Without a Gate*)/C: *Wumen guan* [*Wu-men kuan*]/J: *Mumonkan*, published 1229 CE.

18 *Yabukoji* (1753), Yampolsky, p. 164. Hakuin had a taste for naming his works after bushes and shrubs. 'Yabukoji' is *Aridisia japonica*. The same work is sometimes referred to by an alternative title, *Sekishu no onjo* = Sound of the Single Hand.

19 *The Gateless Gate*, case 1: 'A monk asked Joshu, a Chinese Zen master: "Has a dog Buddha-nature or not?" Joshu answered *"Mu"* [= no-thing].' (In Paul Reps (comp.), *Zen Flesh, Zen Bones*, Harmondsworth: Penguin Books, 1971, p. 95.) This is a *koan* very often set for beginning Zen students. Joshu Jushin is Zhaozhou Congshen [Chao'chou Ts'ung-shen] (778–897 CE), a great Zen master of the late Dang [Tang].

20 *Orategama Supplement*, Yampolsky, p. 118. Such a state as Hakuin here describes has close parallels in the experience of western mystics, cf. e.g. St John of the Cross, *The Dark Night of the Soul*, Bk II, ch. xvii or St Teresa of Avila, *The Interior Castle*, Fifth Abode, ch. I.

21 Yampolsky, p. 118.

22 *Orategama zokushu*, Yampolsky, p. 139.

23 *Yabukoji*, Yampolsky, p. 166.

24 In his *Tojo goi hensho kuketsu* (Treatise on the Five Ranks), Pt 3 of his *Keiso dokuzui* (Poison Blossoms from Thorn Thickets), 1758.

25 *Tojo goi hensho kuketsu*, trans. R. Sasaki in *Zen Dust*, p. 66.

26 Ibid., pp. 27–8.

27 The graded *koans* are described in detail by a modern *roshi* (Zen Master), Miura Isshu, in *Zen Dust*, pp. 35–76.

28 *Orategama* I, Yampolsky, p. 58.

29 *Yabukoji*, Yampolsky, p. 170.

30 *Zazen wasan*, 11.41–44, trans. Sumiko Kudo in Zekei Shibayana, op. cit., p. 3.

Hakuin's major writings

(N.B. Hakuin often named his works after plants, or chose otherwise eccentric titles for his essays and letters. The literal equivalents are given below.)

Hebiichigo (lit. the snake-strawberry)
Keiso dokuzui (Poison Blossoms from Thorn Thickets)
Orategama; Orategama Supplement ('Orategama' is said to have been the proper name of Hakuin's tea-kettle. The work is sometimes called The Embossed Tea-Kettle.)
Yabukoji (the shrub *Aridisia japonica*)
Yasen kanna (A Chat on a Boat in the Evening)
Zazen wasan (The Song of Zazen)

See also in this book

Vasubandhu, the Buddha, Chinul, Dogen, Bankei, Nishida, Suzuki, Nishitani

Sources and further reading

Hakuin's works

Only a fraction of Hakuin's literary output is available in English. The two most extensive selections are:

Yampolsky, P.B., *The Zen Master Hakuin: Selected Writings*, New York and London: Columbia University Press, 1971 (which also contains a complete list of Hakuin's writings)

Shaw, R.D.M., *The Embossed Tea-Kettle: Orategama and Other Works of Hakuin Zenji*, London: Allen & Unwin, 1963

Waddell, N., *The Essential Teachings of Zen Master Hakuin*, Boston: Shambala, 1994

Hakuin's *Yasen kanna* (A Chat on a Boat in the Evening), trans. R.D.M. Shaw and W. Schiffer, SJ, also appeared in *Monumenta Nipponica*, vol. 13, nos. 1–2, 1956, pp. 101–27

Hakuin's poem *Zazen wasan* (The Song of Zazen), with a lengthy commentary, is available in Zenkei Shibayama, *On Zazen Wasan: Hakuin's Song of Zazen*, trans. Sumiko Kudo, Kyoto, 1967

Miura, I. and Sasaki, R.F., *Zen Dust*, New York: Harcourt, Brace, 1966, a richly annotated study of the history of the *koan* in Rinzai Zen. Together with much else it contains a further translation of the *Zazen wasan* and an almost complete version of Pt 3 of Hakuin's *Keiso dokuzui* (Poison Blossoms from Thorn Thickets).

About Hakuin

Stevens, J., *Three Zen Masters: Ikkyu, Hakuin, and Ryokan*, Tokyo and New York: Kodansha International, 1993

Other works

The major *koan* collections referred to in note 17 have been translated into English, see:

Schloegl, I., *The Zen Teaching of Rinzai: A Translation from the Chinese of the Lin-chi lu*, Berkeley, Calif., Shambhala, 1976

Reps, Paul (comp.) *Zen Flesh, Zen Bones,* Harmondsworth: Penguin Books, 1971 (contains a version of the *Mumonkan*)

Sekida, Katsuki, *Two Zen Classics*, New York and Tokyo: Weatherhill, 1977 (contains the *Mumonkan* and the *Hekigan roku*)

NISHIDA KITARO 1870–1945 CE

Japan emerged from a long period of *sakoku* or isolation in the middle of the nineteenth century CE, beginning a period of cultural exchange and exploration which is still going on. The Japanese began not only to make their achievements known in the West (Suzuki was a leading figure in this area), but also to absorb and evaluate the achievements of western culture, including philosophy. The achievement of Nishida Kitaro was to be the first Japanese to use the methods and findings of western philosophy as a means to articulate a philosophical outlook profoundly coloured by **Zen**. This is itself an intellectual project of exceptional boldness. Many writers in the Zen tradition contend that the crowning nondual experience of Zen is in principle inarticulable in conceptual terms (cf. Dogen and Hakuin), but this Nishida declined to accept. Impressed by the powerful metaphysical systems of the West, he set out to investigate whether the central experience of Zen, and the world-picture asso-ciated with it, could be given a conceptual articulation. It is to be stressed that Nishida is not a follower of any one western school, even less merely an eclectic. He explores the great systems of the West, even that of Hegel to which he owed the most extensive debt, from a single, consistent point of view, i.e. their adequacy as frameworks for the articulation of Zen experience. What emerges in the end is a unique world-picture which is his own, in which the points of convergence and divergence betwen the two intellectual traditions appear with peculiar sharpness.

Nishida was born on 19 April 1870 near Kanazawa (Ishikawa prefecture), his father for a time a teacher, his mother a devotee of Jodo (**Pure Land** Buddhism). During his schooling, Nishida was instructed in the Chinese classics, and a Confucian strain entered his outlook, to remain there permanently. It was during his schooldays at Kanazawa that he met D.T. Suzuki, and the two were to remain firm friends for the rest of their lives. After studying philosophy at Tokyo University, Nishida was employed as a teacher at several schools (1895–1909), teaching principally psychology, logic, ethics and German. During this period, as well as reading extensively amongst the classics of western philosophy, Nishida engaged deeply in Zen meditation, and this experience set the basic direction his thought was to follow throughout his life. His diary at the time reveals the depth of this influence. 'I shall be an investigator of life. Zen is music, Zen is art. Zen is movement; apart from this there is nothing wherein one must seek consolation of the heart.'[1] It was during this period that he developed the ideas set out in his first work, *Zen no kenkyu* (An Inquiry into the Good, 1911).

Nishida left school-teaching in 1909, spending one year on the staff of Gakushuin University, Tokyo, before moving to Kyoto University in 1910. He was promoted to the chair of philosophy there in 1914, and retained this post until his retirement in 1928. Both during his professorship and afterwards, Nishida continued to think and to write, issuing substantial works refining and developing his own philosophy. Attacked by Japanese nationalists before the Second World War for being too receptive to foreign influences, Nishida was unrepentant (as was his friend Suzuki). In his last days, he watched the cities of Japan burning after Allied air raids. He died on 7 June 1945, at Kamakura.

As so often with those who live the life of the mind, Nishida's biography is outwardly dull, somewhat like that of Kant, for example, whose works he greatly admired. He himself summed up his life like this:

> My whole life has been extremely simple. For the first half I sat facing a blackboard and for the second half I stood back to a blackboard. With regard to a blackboard I have made only one complete turn – with this my biography is exhausted.[2]

Inwardly, by contrast, Nishida lived with great intensity, occupied unceasingly in the attempt to resolve some profound philosophical problems. The major changes in Nishida's philosophy, of which there are a number, are not the results of shifts in his basic position. Rather, his fundamental starting point and deepest conviction remain constant. The changes he made to his system are each an attempt to improve his answer to the central problem which is his unchanging theme. This problem is posed by Zen experience, in the following way.

At the heart of Buddhism in all its forms, and so of Zen, is the experience of enlightenment, and this experience is mystical in character. Insofar as it can be conveyed in conceptual terms, it is direct apprehension of reality, and reality is found to be not the ordinary world of discrete individuals, causally interacting in time and space, but a predicateless unity. This insight generates philosophical problems of the greatest profundity, of which the most basic is that referred to in the West as the problem of the one and the many: if reality is a predicateless unity, how and why does it (the one) give rise to the universe as we ordinarily experience it, a universe of spatio-temporal individuals standing in complex mutual interrelations (the many)? No less urgent is the question whether the enlightenment experience can be given a coherent conceptual framework, since concepts are by definition the means by which we articulate our experience, i.e. introduce divisions into it. Nearly all mystics claim that no conceptual framework for this experience is possible. Nishida's originality and daring consist in his combined acceptance of the nondual nature of reality together with his refusal to admit that it cannot be conceptualized. The aim of Nishida's thought, constant at all points in his career, is to provide a conceptual framework of the kind typical in western metaphysics for an intuition concerning the nature of reality which is profoundly Japanese. He set out to produce nothing less than a metaphysics for mysticism.

Nishida's first attempt to formulate such a conceptual framework is set out in *An Inquiry into the Good* (1911).[3] Though this work, like the *Ethics* of Spinoza which impressed Nishida profoundly, has a title which suggests a work of moral philosophy, the moral recommendations put forward in it are grounded on a complete metaphysics, with which the book opens. Nishida begins by outlining his view of being-as-is or reality, and this he calls pure experience.[4] This term is used by Nishida in a special, technical sense. Pure experience is prior to the distinction between subject and object, knower and known. It is not the experience of any individual, but just experience:

> by pure I am referring to the state of experience just as it is without the least addition of deliberative discrimination ... In this regard, pure experience is identical with direct experience. When one directly experiences one's own state of consciousness, there is not yet a subject or an object, and knowing and its object are completely unified.[5]

Pure or direct experience is of reality itself: 'Just like when we become enraptured by exquisite music, forget ourselves and everything around us, and experience the universe as one melodious sound, true reality presents itself in the moment of direct experience.'[6] The distinctions between subject and object, mind and matter, 'derive from two different ways of looking at a single fact ... But these dichotomies are not inherent in the fact itself.'[7]

Being thus prior to all discriminations whatsoever, pure experience is prior to time:

> Because time is nothing more than a form which orders the content of our experience, the content of consciousness must

first be able to be joined, be united, and become one in order for the idea of time to arise. Otherwise we would not be able to link things sequentially and thereby think in terms of time. The unifying activity of consciousness is not controlled by time; on the contrary, time is established by the unifying activity. At the base of consciousness is a transcendent, unchanging reality apart from time.[8]

All our ordinary mental events are individuated by reference to time. It follows that, in Nishida's view, self-consciousness is possible only because there is pure experience, and not vice versa.

Facing the next question, how the many arise from the one, Nishida's answer is reminiscent of the ideas of the western philosopher to whom he owed his most extensive and constant debt, Hegel. The sole reality, he contends, is inherently self-contradictory, and it is the working out of contradictions which generates change:

The fundamental mode of reality is such that reality is one while it is many and many while it is one . . . Since these two dimensions cannot be separated, we can say that reality is the self-development of a single entity. A reality that is both one and many must be self-moved and unceasing. A state of quiescence is a state of independent existence free from conflict with others; it is a state of oneness that rejects plurality. In such a situation, reality cannot come into being.[9]

On the basis of this metaphysics, Nishida grounds his early theology and ethics. The universe is a sole reality, both infinite unity and infinite opposition; an independent, self-fulfilled infinite activity: 'We call the base of this infinite activity God. God is not something that transcends reality, God is the base of reality. God is that which dissolves the distinction between subjectivity and objectivity and unites spirit and nature.'[10] The ethics based on this metaphysics and theology are transparently Buddhist in inspiration. Nishida adopts the Buddhist distinction between the true self (the 'original face' or Buddha-nature present in us all) and the ordinary self. The goal of ethics, the one true good, is to realize the true self. To do this is to dissolve the illusory consciousness of the ordinary self and to unite with God.

Our true self is the ultimate reality of the universe, and if we know the true self we not only unite with the good of humankind in general but also fuse with the essence of the universe and unite with the will of God – and in this religion and morality are culminated. The method through which we can know the true self and fuse with God is our self-attainment of the power of union of subject and object.[11]

This is pure Zen, in modern language.

As Nishida came to recognize, there are a number of difficulties in this philosophy, chiefly with the concept of pure experience itself. At times, as can be seen from the quotations above, Nishida speaks of it much as Suzuki, for instance, speaks of *satori*. At others, his descriptions of it are far more reminiscent of psychological descriptions of pre-conceptual experience or the 'sense-data' of some western philosophies.[12] The attempt to characterize the nature of reality in terms inescapably endowed with overtones of individual psychology will not work, as Nishida himself realized and admitted. To refine his philosophy, he needed to improve this basic metaphysical concept, his way of characterizing reality itself, and the subsequent changes in his philosophy are attempts to do precisely that.

The first major shift is made in a work published in 1917, *Jikaku ni okeru chokkan to hansei* (*Intuition and Reflection in Selfconsciousness*). In this work, the fundamental metaphysical concept, the term used to designate ultimate reality, is no longer pure experience, but absolute free will. The book, as Nishida himself states, is a meditation on the philosophy of Johann Gottlieb Fichte (1762–1814). It is not surprising that Nishida should have felt attracted to Fichte's ideas. Fichte's philosophy is an uncompromising idealistic **monism**: he holds that reality is unitary and mental, an absolute which he regards as a primal self, logically prior to the common-sense distinction between the self and the not-self. The absolute self gives rise to all there is by means of its non-temporal activity. Further, in order to characterize the activity of the absolute, Fichte introduces the concept of an Act (German: *Tathandlung*). In ordinary speech, an act can only be predicated of a limited, self-conscious individual, whereas in Fichte's technical sense of the term, an Act 'does not and cannot appear among the empirical states of our consciousness, but rather lies at the basis of our consciousness and alone makes it possible'.[13]

It is not necessary to master all the details of Fichte's thought in order to see why it should have appealed to Nishida. To repeat, the latter's central problem is how to give a conceptual framework to a world-view based on Zen insight, which posits a nondual reality which in some way has given rise to the phenomenal world. In Fichte,

Nishida found a western philosopher engaged on a recognizably similar task, though arrived at in the development of an independent philosophical tradition. In his middle-period works, Nishida takes the Fichtean notion of Act and uses it in his conceptualization of the mode of being of the true self or reality. What Nishida in this work calls *jikaku* or self-consciousness is the nondual mode of awareness, prior to the distinction between the ordinary self and not-self.[14] The essential property of self-consciousness is absolute free will, and he attempts to explain all phenomena as developments of free acts of self-consciousness in this sense. The same conceptual scheme is used in two other major works, *Ishiki no mondai* (*The Problem of Consciousness*, 1920) and *Geijutsu to dotoku* (*Art and Morality*, 1923).

The conceptual scheme elaborated in these three works is more adequate to its task than the concept of pure experience used in *An Inquiry into the Good*, yet it still remains open to a version of the same objection of psychologism, i.e. Nishida has not managed entirely to eliminate inappropriate elements borrowed from human psychology from his description of the mode of being of the one to which they cannot apply. In the case of Fichte's philosophy, it is very hard to see how primordial reality can be called a self in any understandable sense, nor how an Act can be other than predicable of limited individuals (who are by definition non-primordial), and Nishida's use of the latter term, as he came to see, is open to comparable objections. Once again, Nishida was his own best critic. Not content with two attempts, he replaced the conceptual scheme of act and self-consciousness with his final metaphysical category, the concept of the place of nothingness (*mu no basho*), a notion from which all psychological connotations have been eliminated.[15] This idea was first used by Nishida in his work *Hataraku mono miru mono e* (From the Actor to the Seer, 1927), and was developed by him, in the elaboration of an increasingly complex system, in all his major works thereafter.

The place of nothingness is the concept by means of which Nishida designates reality or the one in the final phase of his thought. All other concepts are related to it or defined by reference to it.[16] With characteristic boldness, Nishida defines the mode of being of reality in such a way as at once to deny the adequacy of Aristotelian logic (on which western philosophy is almost exclusively based) and to give an answer to the question of how one and many are related. His answer is that they are the same or, as he puts it, they have absolutely contradictory identity (*zettai mujunteki jikodoitsu*): 'The world of reality is essentially the one as well as the many . . . This is why I call the world "absolute contradictory self-identity"',[17] a conclusion consonant with a long tradition in Buddhist thought, according to which *samsara* and *nirvana* are ultimately identical.

However, if the underlying idea is not new, Nishida's formulation of it certainly is. Western logic embodies a number of basic principles or 'laws of thought'. Among these are the law of identity (a thing is itself and not another thing: *a* is *a*) and the law of contradiction (the statements *p* and not-*p* cannot both be true). Nishida's logic of place denies both: the real is both one and many, and contradictory descriptions of it can both be true. Faced with the conclusion that Zen experience cannot be accommodated within Aristotelian logic, Nishida asserts that this latter logic is inadequate and replaces it with his own. In the logic of place, or field logic, subjects are determined by their place. The logical place of a concept is the enveloping universal in terms of which it is defined. If the definition of an object is found to embody contradictions, a deeper, more encompassing universal must be found in terms of which it can be defined. The more general the enveloping universal, the more concrete it is. The ultimate and most concrete of universals Nishida calls nothingness. It is that which is only place and has no place in anything else. This cannot be called being and so must be called nothingness.

Using his logic of the place of nothingness, Nishida goes on to assert that he can account for a major feature of the universe, namely that it is not static but subject to constant change. Reality is self-contradictory; self-contradictions involve tensions, and tensions produce change. As a result, reality is essentially creative: 'At the base of the world, there are neither the many nor the one; it is a world of absolute unity of opposites, where the many and the one deny each other.'[18] This mutual negation of one and many is creative: 'Such a world, as unity of opposites, from the formed towards the forming, is essentially a world of "poiesis".'[19] Using this basic framework, Nishida redescribes all the facets of existence, all generated by mutual contradiction ultimately grounded on nothingness.

Nishida devoted his last work, *Bashoteki ronri to shukyoteki sekaikan* (The Logic of the Place of Nothingness and the Religious World-view, 1945),[20] to an analysis of religion within the conceptual framework just outlined. The key to understanding religion is to grasp the true nature of the self and its relation to being-as-is or reality. It follows from Nishida's logic that the mode of being of the self is self-contradictory:

the self and the absolute are always related in the paradoxical form of simultaneous presence and absence . . . This logic conceives of the religious form of life as constituted in the contradictory identity of the self and the absolute.[21]

From this two important consequences flow, of which the first is that religion is not merely one aspect of life among many which can be ignored or attended to according to taste. Rather, religion is part of the very fabric of reality:

> The question of religion lies not in what the self should be as a consciously active being, but in the question of what the self is: not in how the self should act, but in the self's very is and is not.[22]

Second, it follows that religious consciousness is not a special gift vouchsafed to only a few:

> The religious mind is present in everyone. One who does not notice this cannot be a philosopher.[23]

This is because the true self and the one (God) are identical: in the language of Mahayana Buddhism, the Buddha-nature is present in us all. The way to God is inward. In Nishida's vocabulary, we approach God by investigating the contradictions inherent in the self: 'religion can be grasped only by a logic of absolute affirmation through absolute negation.'[24] The vocabulary is that of Hegelian dialectic; but the thought comes from Zen.

Whether this philosophy is acceptable depends on the answer to the deep philosophical question of whether dialectical logic is ultimately coherent, and it is a tribute to the power of Nishida's philosophy that it turns on issues of this degree of profundity. His special achievement is to have highlighted very sharply the essential point of divergence of the two philosophical cultures he combined. The direct experience of the one, whatever it is called in the varying eastern traditions, appears to be unformulable in terms of western logic. If it is to be formulable at all, and so included in philosophy (in the western sense of the term), a new logic is needed, and this Nishida, who appreciated the problem with perfect clarity, attempted to formulate. The Kyoto school of philosophy which he founded has developed his ideas since his death; but his example is one which any philosopher approaching this area of investigation must address, and that is a considerable achievement.

Notes

1 Quoted in Shimomura Torataro, *Nishida Kitaro and Some Aspects of his Philosophical Thought*, printed as afterword to V.H. Viglielmo's translation of *Zen no kenkyu* as *A Study of Good*, Tokyo: Government Printing Bureau, 1960, p. 198.

2 Quoted in Shimomura Torataro, op. cit., in Viglielmo, op. cit, p. 197.

3 As the Sources and Further Reading section makes clear, this work has been translated twice into English. *An Inquiry into the Good* is the title of the second version by M. Abe and C. Ives (used here); the earlier Viglielmo translation has the title *A Study of Good*.

4 The term 'pure experience' is borrowed from William James and the psychologist Wilhelm Wundt (1832–1920), but it will be clear that it is only the term that Nishida has borrowed, it being used in a sense entirely his own. This is generally true of Nishida's other terminological borrowings. At various times he uses terms from Plato, Aristotle, Spinoza, Leibniz, Kant, Hegel, James, Bergson and Husserl. For an outline of the ideas of each of these thinkers, see the relevant sections of D. Collinson, *Fifty Major Philosophers*, London: Routledge, 1991.

5 *An Inquiry into the Good*, pp. 3–4.

6 Ibid., p. 48.

7 Ibid., p. 49.

8 Ibid., pp. 60–1.

9 Ibid., p. 57.

10 Ibid., p. 79.

11 Ibid., p. 145.

12 cf. e.g. Ibid., p. 8.

13 J.G. Fichte, *Wissenschaftslehre*, 1794: trans. P. Heath and J. Lachs, as *The Science of Knowledge*, Cambridge: Cambridge University Press, 1982, p. 93.

14 Abe points out that what is meant by *jikaku* in Japanese is somewhat different from 'self-consciousness' in English. Its connotations in Japanese are religious rather than epistemological. It indicates a state in which reality awakens to itself: 'self-awakening' is a better way of translating it. *Inquiry into the Good*, p. xxi.

15 The term 'place' (but not its meaning in Nishida's thought) is borrowed from Plato, who uses the concept of *topos* in his dialogue *Timaeus*.

16 This nothingness is not mere absence, as it would be in ordinary western philosophical usage. Though the term is western, its sense in Nishida's thought is oriental. Its connotations are those of *mu* in Zen, and stretch back ultimately to the *Prajnaparamita Sutras* and the Void (*sunyata*) of Nagarjuna. This nothingness is the ground of all being, not its absence.

17 Nishida, *The Unity of Opposites* from *Philosophical Essays: Third Series*, trans. R. Schinzinger in *Intelligibility and the Philosophy of Nothingness*, Westport, Conn.: Greenwood Press, p. 163. As Schinzinger indicates, Nishida's Japanese *zettai mujunteki jikodoitsu* (absolutely contradictory identity) can also be rendered as 'the unity of opposites', preferred by some translators.

18 Nishida, op. cit., p. 168.

19 Ibid., p. 167.

20 The words 'of Nothingness' do not appear in the Japanese. The translator has very reasonably added them to the title of the English version of this work.

21 *The Logic of the Place of Nothingness and the Religious World-view*, p. 83.
22 Ibid., p. 76.
23 Ibid., p. 85.
24 Ibid., p. 91.

Nishida's major writings

An Inquiry into the Good, 1911
Thought and Experience, 1915
Intuition and Reflection in Self-consciousness, 1917
The Problem of Consciousness, 1920
Art and Morality, 1923
From the Actor to the Seer, 1927
The Self-consciousness of the Universal, 1930
The Self-determination of Nothingness, 1932
Thought and Experience. Continuation, 1937
Fundamental Problems of Philosophy (2 vols), 1933–1934
Philosophical Essays (3 vols), 1933–1945
The Logic of the Place of Nothingness and the Religious World-view, 1945

See also in this book

the Buddha, Huineng, Chinul, Dogen, Bankei, Hakuin, Suzuki, Nishitani

Sources and further reading

Works by Nishida

Art and Morality, trans. D.A. Dilworth and V.H. Viglielmo, Honolulu: University
of Hawaii Press, 1973
Fundamental Problems of Philosophy: The World of Action and the Dialectical World,
trans. D.A. Dilworth, Tokyo: Sophia University, 1970
Intelligibility and the Philosophy of Nothingness, trans. R. Schinzinger, Westport,
Conn.: Greenwood Press, 1973 (three of Nishida's essays, from different
periods of his development)
Intuition and Reflection in Self-consciousness, trans. V.H. Viglielmo, with Y.
Takeuchi and J.S. O'Leary, Albany, NY: State University of New York
Press, 1987
Last Writings: Nothingness and the Religious World-view, trans. D.A. Dilworth,
Honolulu: University of Hawaii Press, 1987
A Study of Good, trans. V.H. Viglielmo, Tokyo: Government Printing Bureau,
1960; *An Inquiry into the Good*, trans. M. Abe and C. Ives, New Haven,
Conn. and London: Yale University Press, 1990

About Nishida

Abe, M., 'Nishida's philosophy of "place"', *International Philosophical Quarterly*,
vol. 28, no. 4, 1988, pp. 355–71

Carter, R.E., *The Nothingness Beyond God: An Introduction to the Philosophy of Nishida Kitaro*, New York, Paragon House, 1989; 2nd edn 1997

Dilworth, D.A., 'The initial formulation of "pure experience" in Nishida Kitaro and William James', *Monumenta Nipponica*, vol. 24, nos 1–2, 1969, pp. 93–111

Viglielmo, V.H., 'Nishida Kitaro – the early years', in D. Shively (ed.), *Tradition and Modernism in Japanese Culture*, Princeton: Princeton University Press, 1971, pp. 507–62

Nishitani, K., *Nishida Kitaro*, trans. Yamamoto Seisaku and J.W. Heisig, Berkeley: University of California Press, 1991

SUZUKI DAISETZ TEITARO 1870–1966 CE

The word 'Zen' is in common usage in the West, and **Zen** itself is pursued as a way of life at various centres both in Europe and America. Before the turn of the present century, both the word and the practice were effectively unknown outside the Far East, and the change is due to a considerable extent to the work of one man, Dr D.T. Suzuki, a Rinzai Zen scholar of great distinction. It was via Suzuki's works, chiefly the three volumes of *Essays in Zen Buddhism* published in the 1920s and 1930s, that the western world gained its first understanding of Zen. Suzuki buttressed this achievement by means of many further works, numbering some thirty books in English and over ninety in Japanese (still mostly untranslated) together with many articles in journals. He complemented the *Essays* by a range of more introductory works, translations of important *sutras* from the Sanskrit, works comparing elements of eastern and western thought, and to an increasing degree toward the end of his life, detailed studies of the Shin sect of **Pure Land** Buddhism. His English works owe their success not only to their authority and erudition, but also the high quality of his English style. Suzuki is one of those non-native writers of English, like Conrad or Santayana, whose command of the language shames many of its native users. The lucidity of Suzuki's English works makes their difficult subject-matter as accessible as it can be. Many have followed the pathway Suzuki opened, and western literature on Zen has proliferated since his time, but Suzuki will always have the distinction of having been the initiator of this process, and his place in the history of twentieth-century thought is secure.

D.T. Suzuki was born in 1870 in Kanazawa, in the Ishikawa prefecture of Japan, the youngest of five children. Though the family profession was medicine, his parents were deeply involved with Buddhism, and he grew up in an ambience permeated by Zen and to some extent by Shin Pure Land practices. He went to university in Tokyo in 1890, but spent most of his time studying Zen at Engakuji (Kamakura) with the Masters Imagita Kosen and Shaku Soen. During this period, he was invited by the American scholar of Buddhism Dr Paul Carus to assist him in the editing and translation of Buddhist works for the West (Carus was closely associated with the Open Court Publishing House in Chicago). One effect of the invitation was to cause Suzuki to throw all his strength into trying to achieve enlighten-ment by means of the Zen techniques he was later to describe so brilliantly, and this he did. In one of his rare autobiographical pieces, Suzuki describes his state of mind immediately after enlightenment: 'I remember as I walked back from the monastery to my quarters in the Kigen'in temple, seeing the trees in moonlight. They looked transparent and I was transparent too.'[1] When Suzuki came to write about Zen, therefore, he did so from the vantage point not merely of scholarship but of profound personal experience.

Suzuki went to America in 1897, and stayed abroad for eleven years, working for ten of them as an editor at the Open Court Company, detained (as he put it) by poverty. This period not only laid the foundations of his scholarship – a number of translations date from these years – but also refined his already considerable command of English. He left America in 1908 and spent almost a year touring Europe (and translating Swedenborg's *Heaven and Hell* into Japanese). By the time he returned to Japan in April 1909 he had decided on what was to be his life's work and mission: to make the West aware of the spiritual attainments of Zen. Uniquely placed to understand the achievements of East and West, Suzuki believed that each has much to offer the other. Despite its excellence in technology and in various other areas involving intellection, the West was regarded by Suzuki as having failed to penetrate, other than spasmodically, to certain areas of spiritual development long cultivated in the East, and these he determined to try to communicate. As he put it:

> Technology and science are quite splendid, but they tend to create an attitude of indifference toward the value of the individual. Individuality is much talked of in the West, but it is in legal or political terms that it is prized. In terms of religion or faith, however, concern among Westerners with regard to individuality is extremely weak. Furthermore, with industrialization or mechanization, man comes to be used as a thing, and, as a result, the unbounded creativity of mankind is destroyed. Therefore, in order to emphasize the importance

of true individuality and human creativity, I consider it necessary to write about Zen more and more.[2]

This is precisely what he went on to do. Back in Japan he secured a post teaching English that he held for twelve years or so (1909–21), and during this time he continued to write, translate and publish indefatigably. He obtained his first major academic post when in 1921, at the age of 51, he was appointed Professor of Buddhist Philosophy at Otani University. This year also saw the foundation of the influential journal *The Eastern Buddhist* which he coedited with his wife, Beatrice Lane Suzuki. Thereafter his long life is a record of unbroken and prolific scholarship, involving many visits abroad and resulting in worldwide acclaim as an authority on Zen and other aspects of Buddhism. This mode of life was punctuated only by the Second World War. He wrote that he regarded the war in the Pacific as a ridiculous conflict for his people to have initiated, and spent the war years at his home in Kamakura, writing. Suzuki was no friend to militarism, whatever its origin.

The round of publishing and of public appearances and meetings resumed after the war. Among many others, he met and impressed the psychologist Carl Gustav Jung in 1953: Jung thereafter contributed prefaces and commentaries to eastern texts, including some by Suzuki himself. Suzuki was still writing at the end of his life. He died aged 95 in Tokyo in July 1966, greatly honoured by academic and religious communities throughout the world.

Suzuki's central achievement is to have made the West aware of the goal and methods of the **Rinzai** school of Zen, derived very largely from the codification by Hakuin. As in all Zen, the goal is enlightenment, and the experience of enlightenment is called in Japanese *satori* (C: *wu*). The method advocated as the surest means to *satori* is the mental discipline of *koan* meditation: although Suzuki refers occasionally to *zazen* (the central practice in Dogen's Zen), it was manifestly far less important to him than the *koan* exercise. Indeed, sometimes he writes of *zazen* as if it were in danger of leading merely to quietism or mental calm, and this is in many ways the antithesis of Zen.

Suzuki accepts as his fundamental metaphysical belief the thesis that being-as-is or reality is nondual: it is an undifferentiated oneness. From this it follows that all the divisions imposed on experience by the intellect are false, down to the most basic metaphysical categories of space, time and identity. Being-as-is is neither temporal nor spatial and contains (so to speak) absolutely no divisions, not even that between self and not-self. Apprehension of reality is possible, and this apprehension is *satori*. It follows further that *satori* cannot be achieved merely by thinking about it, nor learned from books or a master, though a master can help us achieve it: *satori* is incommunicable, and can only be directly experienced.

Satori, in Suzuki's analysis, has eight important properties:[3]

(1) *irrationality*: *satori* cannot be achieved by reasoning. It is ineffable and invariably mutilated whenever an attempt is made to explain it by word or gesture. This follows from the metaphysical assertion that reality is nondual, and that no concepts apply to it. Concepts are precisely the means by which we register divisions within experience, and so in principle cannot apply to reality, which manifests no divisions of any kind. Since reasoning is the paradigm of conceptual intellection, reasoning is useless as a means to *satori*, indeed is a hindrance to it.

(2) *noetic quality*: that is, *satori* is not vacancy or voidness but is an experience with a content. It is knowledge of the most complete and adequate kind, but is ineffable. This noetic quality, Suzuki argues, sharply differentiates *satori* from **dhyana** or meditation: the latter he regards as a mental condition in which the mind is utterly void of thought and entirely quiet. It has no positive content, which *satori* does.

(3) *authoritativeness*: no amount of logic can refute *satori*. It is an experience which takes place in the innermost recesses of consciousness. Nothing concerning such an experience is open to question: hence its absolute finality.

(4) *affirmation*: that which is authoritative but negative can never be final, since negation is of no value to us, providing no resting place. *Satori* involves an affirmative attitude to everything there is.

(5) *sense of the beyond*: reality is nondual, and from this it follows that, in common with all other distinctions, that between the self and the not-self is illusory. In *satori*, the normal sense of the self explodes:

The feeling that follows is that of complete release or a complete rest – the feeling that one has arrived finally at the destination. As far as the psychology of *satori* is concerned, a sense of the Beyond is all we can say about it; to call this the Beyond, the Absolute, or God, or a Person is to go further than the experience itself and to plunge into a theology or a metaphysics.[4]

(6) *impersonal tone*: Christian mystics, when describing their experience, often use vocabulary which apparently indicates a personal, even a sensual aspect to their experiences, e.g. spiritual matrimony; the fire of love; the bride of Christ. There is nothing in *satori* which is equivalent to this. It is entirely impersonal in tone.

(7) *feeling of exaltation*: the general feeling which accompanies all the activities of our ordinary consciousness, i.e. when thinking conceptually, is one of restriction and dependence. In *satori*, these shackles, often so deep in our consciousness as to go unnoticed, break apart, and a feeling of exaltation results.

(8) *momentariness*: *satori* comes upon us abruptly and is momentary. If an experience is not momentary, it is not *satori*.

This last feature is especially important, and is a strict consequence of Zen metaphysics. Since reality is a divisionless oneness, it must be immutable: were it changeable, it would be describable in concepts and so not nondual. Since no events or changes are ascribable to being-as-is, reality is not in time: without events there is no time, and therefore reality is eternal. (Eternity is the mode of being in which no temporal predicates apply, not everlasting being in time.) Since it is the direct apprehension of reality, *satori* cannot be an event in time. It is, as mystics are forced to say in a vocabulary designed to deal with temporal existence, a timeless moment. Zennists put the point as follows: *satori* occurs when consciousness realizes a state of 'one thought' (J: *ichinen*). *Ichinen* is an absolute point without duration. Thus Suzuki writes: '*Satori* obtains when eternity cuts into time or impinges upon time, or, which is the same thing after all, when time emerges into eternity.'[5] Those who achieve *satori* are freed from the tyranny of ordinary time consciousness, in which we crave the eternal amid relentless mutability.

Finally, it follows that, properly speaking, *satori* is not an intuition, since an intuition is a mental event in a consciousness operating at ordinary conceptual levels. There is no self/not-self distinction in being-as-is nor any distinction between mental and non-mental. Therefore *satori* cannot be the mental event of an individual. Instead, 'When [reality] perceives itself as it is in itself there is a *satori*.'[6] *Satori* is reality, so to speak, conscious of itself.

The attainment of *satori* is the goal of Rinzai Zen, and the method which has been evolved for its attainment is the *koan* exercise. The major obstacle to *satori* is the conventional operation of the mind engaged in conceptual, discriminatory thought, and *koans* are designed to bring this type of mental activity to a halt. The *koan* exercise forces the dissolution of our mundane mental activity, breaking it up at its foundations and permitting the efflorescence of our true being, 'the original face' or Buddha-nature. A *koan* is a puzzle which cannot be solved by any amount of conceptual thought: the more ratiocinative effort is put into solving it, the more impenetrable it becomes. The best known is perhaps Hakuin's 'one hand': we all know the sound of two hands clapping. What is the sound of one hand?[7] So long as this problem is approached by means of the pathways of conceptual thought and conventional logic, it is insoluble, a blank wall facing the mind. It can only be solved by those who have attained *satori*: from the perspective of nondual insight, it is solved with ease, as are the rest of the 1,700 *koans* it is said to be necessary to resolve before one can claim to be a Zen Master or *roshi*. To solve the *koan* is not to *understand* anything; rather it is to experience the presence of reality (the divisionless oneness) as much in one hand as in two.

The *koan* exercise was adopted by Zennists in the tenth and eleventh centuries (CE), chiefly to prevent Zen from falling into either of two degenerate states, a subject of mere logical debate on the one hand, or simply quietism on the other. The Masters decided that it was necessary to use the insight gained from nondual apprehension as a means to help aspirants to *satori*. The Master gauges the state of readiness of the aspirant, and sets a *koan* of the appropriate degree of difficulty. The aspirant is instructed to bring all his or her powers to bear on solving it. The impenetrability of the *koan* to rational analysis brings the mind to the highest possible tension, leaving it with two options only: 'either to break down and possibly go out of mind, or to go beyond the limits and open up an entirely new vista, which is *satori*.'[8] By means of question and answer sessions or **mondo** the Zen Master can estimate how far the aspirant has progressed along this road, and can tell when *satori* is imminent. At this point, the Master will use whatever means is needed to bring about *satori* and this means can be a word, a gesture or, not infrequently, a blow; and *satori* follows.

While the bulk of Suzuki's scholarship is devoted to Zen, it is not by any means confined to it, and to see him solely as a Zen scholar is to underestimate the range of his achievement. Thus he wrote a book comparing the mysticism of Meister Eckhart with that of the Japanese (*Mysticism, Christian and Buddhist*, 1957). The subject other than Zen to which he devoted most effort, however, is Pure Land Buddhism, notably in its Shin version. (Pure Land is the most popular form of Buddhism in Japan, with more adherents than Zen.) He wrote of this at many points in his career, and it came to bulk larger in his thought as he grew older. The goal of Pure Land adherents is rebirth in the Pure Land of Buddha Amitabha (another way of describing enlightenment), and the chief means which has been evolved to secure this end is the *mantra* or repeated incantation of Buddha's name called the Nembutsu, *Namu Amida Butsu* in Japanese (C: *o-mi-duo-fo* [*o-mi-to-fo*]: 'Reverence to Amida Buddha').[9] This practice is more complex than might at first appear, having certain analogies with the *koan* exercise in respect of the suppression of ordinary conceptual thought and the bringing about of enlightenment. When, late in life, Suzuki wrote a book attempting to pick out the essence of the religious consciousness of the Japanese, it was on Shin that he focused principally, rather than Zen (though Zen, of course, is far from ignored):

> Shinshu experience is really nothing else than the experience of Japanese spirituality. That it emerged within a Buddhist context was a matter of historical chance – it does not prevent in the least the essential quality of the Shin Sect from being identified with Japanese spirituality.[10]

Suzuki's thought is open to the objections inherent in nondualism: chiefly, how to give an account of why an eternal, perfect unity should manifest itself as a temporal, mutable and divided universe, and why this universe should involve so much suffering and evil. Again, some of his own formulations are open to question, e.g. whether the assertion that *satori* has a noetic content is consistent with the thesis that no conceptual articulations apply to reality. Such difficulties, however, should not lead us to underestimate the extent of Suzuki's achievement. Behind his entire output lies an optimistic and cheering belief: different cultures can be brought to understand one another. Bridges can be built, and we are not condemned to live in the windowless boxes to which relativistic theories of culture would seek to consign us. Suzuki set out to build such a bridge, and he succeeded.

Notes

References to D.T. Suzuki's *Essays in Zen Buddhism*, London: Luzac, 1st, 2nd, 3rd series, 1927/1933/1934 are given as EZB; to his *An Introduction to Zen Buddhism*, London: Rider, 1983, as IZB; and to his *Living by Zen*, London: Rider, 1982, as LBZ.

1 *Early Memories* in M. Abe (ed.), *A Zen Life: D.T. Suzuki Remembered*, New York and Tokyo: Weatherhill, 1986, p. 11.

2 *An Autobiographical Account*, in Abe, op. cit., p. 25.
3 cf. EZB, 1st series, pp. 213–50; 2nd series, pp. 16ff.; LBZ, ch. III; IZB, ch. VIII, and in many other places.
4 EZB, 2nd series, pp. 18–19.
5 LBZ, p. 53. cf. Nichiren's **Tendai** doctrine of *ichinen sanzen*.
6 LBZ, p. 50.
7 cf. the essay on Hakuin in this book, pp. 368–77.
8 LBZ, p. 165.
9 On *mantras*, cf. *Tibetan philosophy: Introduction* in this book, pp. 179–83 and see also the essay on Nichiren, pp.347–58.
10 D.T. Suzuki, *Japanese Spirituality (Nihon-teki reisei* [1944]), trans. N. Waddell, Japan Society for the Promotion of Science, 1972, pp. 20–1.

Suzuki's writings

(Restricted to works that Suzuki wrote originally in English)

Essays in Zen Buddhism, 1st series, 1927; 2nd series, 1933; 3rd series, 1934
Introduction to Zen Buddhism, 1949
The Zen Doctrine of No-mind, 1949
Living by Zen, 1950
Mysticism, Christian and Buddhist, 1957

See also in this book

the Buddha, Chinul, Dogen, Bankei, Hakuin, Nishida, Nishitani

Sources and further reading

Abe, M. (ed.), *A Zen Life: D.T. Suzuki Remembered*, New York and Tokyo: Weatherhill, 1986
Suzuki, D.T., *Essays in Zen Buddhism*, London: Luzac: 1st series 1927, 2nd series 1933; 3rd series, 1934
Suzuki, D.T., *The Field of Zen*, New York: Harper & Row, 1970 (1st edn London: the Buddhist Society, 1969)
Suzuki, D.T., *An Introduction to Zen Buddhism*, London: Rider, 1983 (1st edn 1949, revised 1969)
Suzuki, D.T., *Japanese Spirituality*, trans. N. Waddell, Japan Society for the Promotion of Science, 1972; repr. New York: Greenwood Books, 1989; first published as *Nihon-teki reisei*, Tokyo: Daitoshuppansha 1944
Suzuki, D.T., *Living by Zen*, London: Rider, 1982 (1st edn 1950)
Suzuki, D.T., *Mysticism, Christian and Buddhist*, London: Allen & Unwin, 1988 (1st edn 1957)
Suzuki, D.T., *The Training of the Zen Buddhist Monk*, Berkeley: Wingbow Press, 1974 (1st edn Kyoto: Eastern Buddhist Society, 1934)
Suzuki, D.T., *The Zen Doctrine of No-mind*, London: Rider, 1991 (1st edn 1949; 2nd edn 1969)

There exists also in the public domain a cassette of a conversation between

Suzuki and Professor Huston Smith (of MIT): 'Encounter with Daisetz Suzuki' (Learning Plans, 1969, cassette no. 010 3152L), a discussion of Zen.

NISHITANI KEIJI 1900–1991 CE

Nishitani Keiji was one of the leading figures to emerge from the ongoing interchange of philosophical and religious thought between Japan and the West which began with the Meiji restoration in 1868. He, together with his mentor Nishida Kitaro, was a member of the Kyoto school, a group of thinkers who adapted some of the concepts of western philosophy, particularly those of German idealism and existentialism, to the expression of the unmediated experience of **Zen** Buddhism. Of particular interest to Nishitani were the similarities between Zen and existentialist ontology. He was not uncritical of western concepts, maintaining that the many dualisms to be found within western thought, such as those of subjectivity and objectivity, time and eternity, being and nothingness, creator and created, the personal and the impersonal, could and should be superseded by *sunyata*, the Void or emptiness. *Sunyata* is not to be understood in nihilistic terms, but instead is the all-encompassing predicateless unity which underlies all phenomena.

Nishitani was born on 27 February 1900 in Ishikawa Prefecture, the same rural district of central Japan as Nishida. At the age of 7, he moved with his family to Tokyo, where he completed his education. In his career, he held various academic appointments at Kyoto Imperial University, later renamed Kyoto State University, and at the Buddhist Otani centre for higher education. From 1936 to 1939 he was a student of Martin Heidegger at Freiburg, where he attended lectures on Nietzsche and nihilism. These interests reflected his earliest philosophical concerns: as he records in his autobiography *The Days of my Youth*, 'My life as a young man can be described in a single phrase: it was a period absolutely without hope . . . my life at the time lay entirely in the grips of nihility and despair . . . my decision, then, to study philosophy was in fact . . . a matter of life and death'.[1] The development of Nishitani's thought can thus be seen not merely as a matter of intellectual concern, but as having fundamental existentialist implications.

For Nishitani, moments of personal crisis such as 'death, nihility or sin' open up the issues of the nature of religion and the meaning of life. Such experiences 'undermine the roothold of our existence' and we are brought to confront the 'gaping abyss . . . at the very ground on which [we] stand'.[2] However, they allow us to break through everyday reality which is compartmentalized into various activities and disciplines such as the economic, the scientific, the technological and the philosophical. All of these are characterized by their utility and are but manifold presentations of *sunyata*. The all-enfolding unity or Void of *sunyata* dissolves or supersedes, yet is manifest in every particular, such as a leaf at daybreak or the cry of a child. The self which is conscious of itself and set against all other things is real, but not ultimately so. To break through to ultimate reality, we have to go beyond the 'shattered fragments' constituted by particulars, to the standpoint of *sunyata* wherein every distinction is resolved into the ground of unity.

In pursuing this theme Nishitani is especially critical of Descartes, who set up an unbridgeable mechanistic dualism between physical things, the essence of which is extension, and our own minds or egos, which are unextended and conscious of themselves. In Nishitani's memorable words, Descartes propounded a scheme of things 'whereby each individual ego became like a lonely but well-fortified island floating in a sea of dead matter'.[3]

The reference to 'dead matter' reveals Nishitani's concern with becoming rather than being. Particular things, including ourselves, have no fixed nature or essence, as Descartes thought was the case with both matter and the self. Instead, everything is in an everlasting process of flux, in that things perpetually come into existence, change and fall back into extinction. Both *sunyata* and our recognition of it are processes; our perception of the true condition of reality is our authentic mode of being and when we become aware of it, it realizes itself or becomes actual in that awareness.

According to Nishitani, there are two levels of doubt. The first, of which the chief example in western philosophy is Cartesian doubt, is the ego's scepticism of the existence of other particular things. The second, the elemental or Great Doubt, leads to the Great Death and the Great Enlightenment. The Great Doubt is 'existentially serious', and 'mak[es] itself present to the self out of the ground of the self and of all things . . . the self becomes Doubt itself'.[4] The isolated, self-centred ego discovers that it, too, has no fixed essence, but is in reality empty. The ego dies to itself in the Great Death, but through **samadhi**, the self-transcending process of meditation or contemplation, it bursts through its own solitude and is reunited in the Great Enlightenment with *sunyata*, the ground of everything including itself.

Nishitani acknowledges that the philosophy of Sartre, whilst it stops short of the Great Death, is a major advance on that of Descartes.

Whilst the ego in Sartre is still isolated, it has no essence, but is empty and perpetually becomes what it wants to be.

In Nishitani's view, the dualism between creator and created found in the Christian tradition can be resolved by *sunyata*. The whole of creation has come from nothing and contains its origins within itself, or is encompassed by nothingness. The Christian God has personal characteristics, but there is a distinction between him and his ground of being, the godhead, which is impersonal and has absolute emptiness. From the perspective of human beings who think of themselves as his creatures, God is considered to be the creator. However, once we break through our creatureliness, we recognize God as he truly is, in the voidness of his godhead. The godhead becomes one with everything else in the unity of *sunyata*. The ultimate oneness of creator and created can be reached through the process of what is known by the Greek term *kenosis*, whereby God has emptied himself of himself to take on the form of humankind in Jesus Christ. In the Incarnation, Christ's divine, non-differentiated, impartial love acts as the exemplar for human, partial love. In such a transformation we too lose our individuality to become divine.

For Nishitani, the most accurate Christian teaching about the Godhead is not to be found in traditional Christian doctrine and dogma, but in the 'negative theology' of such mystics as Meister Eckhart. Nishitani summarizes Eckhart's thinking in the following words:

> First, he locates . . . God at a point beyond the personal God who stands over against created beings. Second, this . . . godhead is seen as an absolute nothingness . . . Third, only in the godhead can man truly be himself, and only in the openness of absolute nothingness can the consummation of the freedom and independence of man in subjectivity be effected.[5]

Nietzsche's philosophy is given qualified praise for its recognition that the God of traditional Christianity has been found inadequate. However, instead of breaking through the 'death of God' to the godhead, Nietzsche takes the path of self-affirmation to the Superman.

In Buddhism, Nishitani considers **samsara**, the cycle of reincarnation, to be a starting-point for the achievement of *sunyata*. He recognizes that the doctrine of *samsara* has a mythical content, but contains an existential truth. *Samsara* is ignorance of our true being and leads to the suffering of the ego. We begin to break through our isolated selves when we realize that our own personal suffering is but a small part of the suffering of all other existing things. When we confront death, we realize that it is the end of our selves, but death also means the end of death. The recognition of this truth allows us to break free of *samsara* and its attendant suffering, both personal and universal, and to enter *sunyata*.

Nishitani contrasts various western conceptions of history and time with those of Buddhism. All western theories of history rely on the Judaeo-Christian presupposition that time is linear, and religious theories consider time to be ruled over or created by a personal God. Human individuality is, according to Nishitani, a permanent feature of all Judaeo-Christian approaches to history, but this assumption leads to existence in *avidya*, the ignorance of the true nature of reality. In Christianity, the end of history lies outside itself, in eschatology. The Incarnation and death of Jesus Christ open up history to God's *agape*, or impartial love, which transforms history into timelessness and endows it with meaning.

Various secular and anthropocentric views of history are also considered by Nishitani. The Enlightenment enthroned reason and refused to accept supernatural interventions into history. Enlighten-ment thinkers thus refused to accept a timeless eschatology, but in its place they set up progress to give meaning to history. Progress is also a theme of Marxism: impersonal historical forces will culminate in a future communist society. Finally, there is the nihilist approach, which rejects all attempts to impose a meaning on history, but instead asserts that history is simply a 'blind' succession of events.

The Buddhist conceptions of time and history are more elaborate than the western, as Buddhism considers time to be both cyclical and linear. The cycles, or **kalpas**, of time are endless, and suggest recurrence. The linearity of time is explicable by the succession of *kalpas*. Each *kalpa* is composed of a series of discrete moments, or individual 'nows', and each 'now' is new and transitory. Time, which is impermanent, is at all times on the point of vanishing, or nihility. Through nihility is revealed *sunyata*, which encompasses all time and impermanence by its absolute emptiness. The present, or the succession of fleeting 'nows', is transhistorical, and opens up a way into *sunyata*, which gives meaning to history. From the perspective of **karma**, the doctrine of a universal cosmic force or causation whereby the consequences of our actions in this life come to fruition in the next one, all human actions are caught up in the realm of history. Within *karma* and history, we are concerned with our selves or egos, and our actions are manifestations of our wills. Once we recognize, through the practice of a will-less *samadhi*, that egos are enmeshed in a causal nexus, we see through *karma* to nihility, and through nihility to *sunyata*. We realize that our true selves are not-selves, and that not-selves are united with the whole of existence in absolute emptiness.

Nishitani asserts that, whilst philosophical concepts enable us to make some progress in grasping the true nature of reality, they are by themselves inadequate. *Sunyata* is beyond representation and conceptualization, and thus discursive language that relies on conceptualization is an unsuitable medium for its expression. The best way of indicating the immediate experience of *sunyata* is by the subtleties and metaphors of poetry. Reason comprehends its objects from the perspective of itself as a subject, and thus is dependent on a dualist ontological structure. It cannot consequently come into contact with the nature of ultimate reality, which can only be expressed by paradox and ellipsis. Cognitive knowledge, similarly, assumes a distinction between a subject and its objects. The only true knowing capable of grasping *sunyata* is a non-cognitive knowing which is non-knowing of the non-objective reality as it is in itself.

Nishitani's metaphysical system leaves us with several problems. He simply assumes that ultimate reality is nondualistic, and that becoming takes precedence over being. Another difficulty is to be found in his foray beyond reason into paradox. In traditional western philosophy, logical consistency has usually been invoked as a restraint against falling into obscurantism or meaninglessness. Such expressions as 'a non-cognitive . . . knowing of non-knowing', or 'selfness . . . is not this thing or that, therefore it is this thing or that'[6] place a great strain on credibility. No doubt the reply to such objections would be that they are trivial and show a non-comprehension of *sunyata* and the immediate experience of it.

Despite the problems outlined in the paragraph above, Nishitani has performed a great service to philosophy by incorporating elements of both western and eastern tradition. In the words of one of his commentators,

> Nishitani's philosophical mission is undoubtedly rendered all the more difficult because of his standing both within and without his tradition, and yet precisely because he attempts to 'question his own through the eye of the foreign' . . . the European foreigner obtains an extraordinary 'eye into his own'.[7]

Notes

1 Nishitani Keiji, *The Days of my Youth*, Tokyo: Shinchosha, 1980, pp. 195, 198.
2 Nishitani Keiji, *Religion and Nothingness*, trans. J. van Bragt, London: California University Press, 1982, p. 3.
3 Ibid., p. 11.
4 Ibid., p. 18.
5 Ibid., p. 63.
6 Ibid., pp. 139, 124.
7 Nicholas Davey, 'Nishitani Keiji', in *Biographical Dictionary of Twentieth-century Philosophers*, ed. S. Brown, D. Collinson and R. Wilkinson, London and New York: Routledge, 1996, pp. 574–6.

Nishitani's major writings

The Philosophy of Fundamental Subjectivity, 1940
Nihilism, 1946
Studies in Aristotle, 1948
God and Absolute Nothingness, 1949
What is Religion? 1961
My Philosophical Development, 1961
The Days of my Youth, 1980

See also in this book

Nagarjuna, the Buddha, Chinul, Dogen, Hakuin, Nishida, Suzuki

Sources and further reading

Nishitani's works in English

The Self-overcoming of Nihilism, trans. G. Parkes and Setsuko Aiharo, Albany, NY: State University of New York Press, 1990
Religion and Nothingness, trans. Jan van Bragt, London: California University Press, 1982
The Buddha Eye: An Anthology of the Kyoto School, ed. Frederick Franck, New York: Cross Road, 1992 (contains three essays by Nishitani, 'The awakening of self in Buddhism', 'The I–thou relation in Zen Buddhism' and 'Science and Zen')

About Nishitani

Parkes, G. (ed.), *Nietzsche and Asian Thought*, Chicago: University of Chicago Press, 1991
Van Bragt, J., Introduction to *Religion and Nothingness*, London: California University Press, 1982
Waldenfels, H., *Absolute Nothingness: Foundations for a Buddhist–Christian Dialogue*, New York: Paulist Press, 1980

GLOSSARY

acarya **(S):** the word for a Hindu or Buddhist teacher or spiritual mentor.

Advaita (S): 'nondual'. The doctrine of the Vedanta school of Hindu thought that teaches that reality is fundamentally nondual and that each individual self, or *atman*, is ultimately identical with Brahman.

ahimsa **(S):** lit. non-violence, from S: *himsa*, violence. In Gandhi's thought, love of all things.

ahura **(Pahlavi):** in Zoroastrianism, a 'lord' or god.

ajiva **(S):** see *jiva*.

akasa **(S):** space, or the ether.

Allah (A): the Supreme Being, God, worshipped by Muslims. Islamic doctrine permits no images of Allah.

ananda **(S):** bliss. Together with *sat* and *chit*, *ananda* is ascribed to Brahman, the Hindu divine principle.

ansar **(A):** 'helper'. The word for the followers of Muhammad who supported him in Medina.

arhat **(S):** means 'the worthy one'. This is the person who has attained personal liberation. In Theravada Buddhism this is the highest stage of achievement. It contrasts with the Mahayana ideal of the *bodhisattva*, the person who attains buddhahood but also strives altruistically for the salvation of others.

atman **(S):** in the classical Hindu philosophies, the true soul or self, as distinct from the *jiva* or phenomenal ego. In discussions of the relation of *atman* to ultimate reality, some thinkers, notably Sankara, distinguish the individual soul or self from the one Soul or Self that is actually Brahman.

Avesta **(Pahlavi):** the Zoroastrian scriptures.

avidya **(S); in P:** *avijja***):** literally, 'not knowledge'; often translated as 'ignorance' in the Vedantic teaching of Hinduism. In Buddhism *avidya* usually refers to the state of spiritual blindness in which a person is ignorant of the true nature of reality; c.f. *vidya*.

bardo (T; in S: *antarabhava*): literally, 'between two': the name given to any intermediate state of being, especially that in which the soul is dissociated from a body between incarnations.

Bhagavad Gita (S): 'The Song of the Lord', the best-known of the Hindu scriptures and thought to have been written in the fourth and third centuries BCE. It is a treatise on spiritual development in the Karma Yoga tradition, the Way of Right Action.

bhakti (S): the intense love and surrender of humankind to God, arising out of a full knowledge of God. Its consequence is unselfish conduct. The Buddhist Bhakti schools include the Shingon and Shin of Japan.

bhikshu (S; in P: *bhikkhu*): a Buddhist mendicant monk of the Theravada school.

bodhi (S): the spiritual condition of Buddhist enlightenment, brought about by wisdom (*prajna*) and compassion (*karuna*).

bodhicitta (S): literally, 'the mind for enlightenment'; i.e. the desire to become enlightened; the resolve to follow the path of the Buddha.

bodhisattva (S; in P: *bodhidsatta*): the person who is dedicated to achieving enlightenment for the sake of others as well as for the self and who delays accession to *nirvana* in order to help others in their search. The term is used chiefly in Mahayana Buddhism, which teaches that everyone who strives for buddhahood is a *bodhidsattva*; cf. *arhat*.

Brahma Sutra (S): a collection of aphorisms about Brahman, the ultimate reality and divine power; probably composed by Badarayana and an important text in Vedantic philosophy.

Brahman (S): the term, in Hinduism, for the ultimate reality and divine power.

Brahmin (S): the name for a member of the Hindu priestly class. [Note: this word is sometimes transliterated as 'Brahman', but in order to distinguish it in a simple way from Brahman meaning 'divine power' (see the preceding entry), the alternative 'i' spelling has been used.]

Chan [Ch'an] (C; in J: Zen; in S: *dhyana*, in P: *jhana*): meditation; the realization of truth and reality. The name of an influential school of Chinese Buddhism.

chit (S): the Hindu word for 'consciousness' or 'mind'; one of the three attributes of Brahman, the others being *ananda* (bliss) and *sat* (existence).

daeva **(Pahlavi):** in Zoroastrianism, the name for an evil spirit.

Dao [Tao] (C): Way, Principle, or cosmic order. In Confucianism *dao* usually refers to the ethical way of life. In Daoism it is the word for the metaphysical first principle of the universe.

darsana **(S):** philosophy. The word's literal meaning is 'sight' or 'vision'. In Indian philosophy each school of thought is a *darsana*, an insight into the nature of things as well as a reasoned and critical exposition of a set of ideas.

de [*te*] **(C):** spiritual power, or virtue.

dharma **(S; in P: *dhamma*):** a word with a number of important meanings. The Sanskrit form is from the Aryan root '*dhr*', meaning to sustain or uphold. According to the context of its use it may mean doctrine, law, virtue, moral rightness, standard, norm, entity, cosmic order, or the existents of the natural realm. In Buddhism, it often refers to the Buddha's teaching; in Hinduism, righteousness, the right way of life, virtue or law.

dhyana **(S; in P: *jhana*; in C: Chan; in J: Zen):** the generic term for meditation, the various types of which are named and graded differently in the different traditions.

dualism: the metaphysical theory which posits that reality consists fundamentally of two distinct substances.

duhkha **(S; in *dukkha*):** pain, misery, the condition of unenlightenment; a central concept in Hinduism.

dvaita **(S):** the Hindu Vedantic doctrine of dualism. It upholds a distinction between Brahman and the world, and also between individual selves and the physical universe.

gatha **(Pahlavi):** a hymn or song. In Zoroastrianism the *gathas* are the hymns of the *Yasna*, the liturgy, and are the only direct source of Zoroaster's own doctrine. Commentators have drawn attention to the similarity of the *gathas* to the hymns of the Vedic scriptures and also to affinities between the thoughts expressed in them and the concepts of Neo-Platonism.

guru **(S; in T: *bla ma*):** a holy man or teacher, prominent in Tantric forms of Hinduism and Buddhism and the most important figure in the life of a Tantric aspirant who owes him absolute obedience.

hadith **(A):** the collection of Traditions derived from accounts of the life of Muhammad and from which the customs and practices of Islam have been formulated.

hijrah **(A):** 'migration'. The migration of Muhammad from Mecca to Medina in 622 CE marks the beginning of the Muslim calendar whose year is calculated according to the revolutions of the moon around the earth, resulting in one that is eleven days shorter than the solar year which forms the basis of the Christian calendar.

Hinayana (S): the 'Lesser Vehicle'; a term used by Mahayana Buddhists to refer to the doctrines of Theravada Buddhism. The term 'Hinayana' is offensive to Theravadins, and 'Theravada' is greatly to be preferred.

Huayan [Hua-yen] (C; in J: Kegon; in S: Avatamsaka): lit. 'flower garland'; a school of Chinese Buddhism also influential in Japan. Founded by Dashun [Ta-shun] (557–640 CE) and Zhiyan [Chih-yen] (602–668 CE).

hunpo [hun-p'o] **(C):** the soul.

i [yi] **(C):** the habit or practice of making the appropriate moral response to all situations.

Islam: the doctrine and religious community founded by Muhammad the prophet. The word is from the root 'slm' (A) meaning 'to be in peace as an integral whole'. 'Islam' means to surrender to God's law and thus to be an integral whole. The Muslim is 'the person who surrenders'.

Jainism: an ancient Indian religion founded on the belief that corruption and evil can be overcome by asceticism. It teaches the scrupulous avoidance of harm to all living creatures.

jiva or *jivatman* **(S):** the surface ego or phenomenological self, as opposed to the *atman*, in Hindu thought. In Jainism it is the sentient being, as distinct from the *ajiva*, the non-sentient.

jivanmukta **(S):** in orthodox Indian thought, one who is free while living, i.e. who has attained *moksa*, q.v.

kalpa **(S):** an immense stretch of time, somewhat as 'eon' is in English.

karma **(S):** a cosmic law and force which is instantiated in actions and which guarantees that we reap as we have sown. In Hinduism *karma* is believed to determine all that takes place in the universe and is inseparable from the doctrine of reincarnation in that it determines a future incarnation by reference to a present one; not by transmigration of soul but by transmigration of character.

khudi **(A):** selfhood; a concept that has special significance in the Islamic philosophy of Muhammad Iqbal (1877–1938 CE).

koan **(J; in C: *gongan [kung-an]*):** a special kind of problem, question or riddle used in Zen, especially but not exclusively in the Rinzai school. It is expressed in a brief phrase and is not susceptible to rational solution. The *koan* 'What is the sound of one hand clapping?' is unanswerable so long as rational, conceptual thought is concentrated on it. The purpose of all *koans* is to stultify reason and so permit a direct realization of reality.

li and *Li* **(C):** in early Confucianism the *li* are the formal rites of good conduct. In later Confucianism, *Li* is the Principle that governs all things.

lila **(S):** play or sport; a term used in the Vedanta school of Hindu philosophy to describe the activity of the World-Soul in creating the Cosmos.

Madhyamika (S): the Middle Way; a school of Mahayana Buddhism that advocates a path midway between pairs of opposites. The term is often used to refer to Nagarjuna's philosophy.

Mahamudra (S; in T: Phyag-chen): 'great symbol': (1) a system of yoga associated especially with the Tibetan Whispered Transmission school (*bKa'brygud pa*) of Buddhism; (2) a stage in *mahasandi yoga*, q.v.

mahasandi **(S; in T: rDzogs chen):** 'great perfection': a system of yoga associated especially with the *rNying ma pa* (the Old Ones) school of Tibetan Buddhism.

Mahayana (S): the 'Greater Vehicle' of the Buddhist tradition; a developed and modified form of Buddhism, to be contrasted with Theravada Buddhism (Hinayana or 'the Lesser Vehicle') which preserves the Buddha's original doctrines.

mandala **(S):** a visual representation of the universe, usually circular in shape, used as an aid to meditation, especially but not exclusively Tantric.

mantra **(S):** a word widely used to name a kind of sacred, repetitive chant to which is ascribed a special efficacy helpful to prayer and meditation. It is used especially in Tantric yogas to aid the visualization of deities.

maya **(S):** usually but not always aptly translated as 'illusion'. *Maya* is best thought of in conjunction with *avidya*. When in the state of *avidya*, the object of thought and perception is *maya*, that is, the everyday world taken, in the state of spiritual blindness which is *avidya*, to be the ultimate reality.

Middle Way: see Madhyamika.

ming **(C):** Fate, Destiny; the Decree of heaven.

moksa **(or *moksha*) (S):** in Hinduism, 'release'; the spiritual condition that is the goal of religious endeavour; a state of freedom from all desire and the result of insight into the true nature of reality.

mondo **(J):** in Zen, a technique of question and answer used by the Zen master in a *sanzen* interview and designed to break down the habit of conceptual reasoning in disciples.

monism: the view that reality is fundamentally one substance.

monotheism: the view that there is only one God, as in the teaching of Judaism, Islam and Christianity.

mu: see *sunyata*.

muhajirun **(A):** the 'believers' who emigrated with Muhammad from Mecca to Medina.

Muslim: 'a person who surrenders'; from the root 'slm' (A), meaning 'to be in peace as an integral whole'. 'Islam' is from the same root and means 'to surrender to God's law and thus to be an integral whole'. Muslims believe that the creed of Islam is God's eternal religion.

nama–rupa **(S):** name and form: the ordinary conceptual framework of human experience. To take this for ultimate truth is to be in the state of *avidya*, q.v.

nembutsu **(J):** the repeated phrase or mantra central to the practices of Pure Land Buddhism: in J, *Namu Amida butsu* (Reverence to Amida Buddha).

nirvana **(S; in P: *nibbana*):** the 'blowing out' or extinction of desire and ignorance.

nirvikalpa **(S):** the highest form of meditation; that without content.

noesis **(Greek):** a Platonic term for the highest kind of knowledge; a direct, intuitive comprehension of universals unsullied by the particularities of sense-experience.

nominalism: the view that general words such as tree, dog, house, etc., are not the names of actual entities but are words applied to groups of similar things.

Pali: 'the text language', Magadhi, which, from around the first century CE, was developed for the writing of the scriptures of Theravada Buddhism. The Pali Text Society was founded in 1881 by T.W. Rhys Davids and has published most of the Pali canon in the Roman alphabet.

Parsi (pl. Parsis): a term deriving from the ancient word for Persia (*pars*). Parsi is the name for a descendant of the Zoroastrians who fled from Persia to take refuge in India in the seventh and eighth centuries CE.

prajna **(S):** the ultimate wisdom which, in Mahayana Buddhism, is a state of total identity with the Buddha essence.

prajnaparamita **(S):** perfection of wisdom.

prakrti **(S):** Nature, in Hinduism, the primordial and eternal material of the universe.

pramana **(S):** in Indian thought, a source or standard of knowledge.

Pure Land (in J: Jodo; in C: Jingtu [Ching-T'u]): an important school of Buddhist thought, founded in the fourth century CE, which taught that after death the faithful would be led to Paradise, or the Pure Land.

purusha **(S):** our real nature, or True Mind, as opposed to our empirical minds. That of which we have knowledge through contemplation or meditation.

qadi **(A):** an Islamic judge.

qi [*ch'i*] **(C):** the Confucian term for life-force or 'matter-energy'; the active cause of all material entities.

qing [*ch'ing*] **(C):** feeling.

Qur'an [Koran]: the holy book of Islam, the words of which, according to Muhammad, were imparted to him by the angel Gabriel.

Ramadan (A): the ninth month of the Muslim calendar, during which food and drink must be abstained from in daylight hours. Ramadan marks the belief that this is the time when the words of the Koran were sent down to humankind.

ren [*jen*] **(C):** the virtue of love or benevolence, a fundamental concept in Confucianism.

Rig Veda: means 'verse knowledge' or 'word knowledge'. It is the oldest of the Hindu scriptures.

Rinzai Zen (J; in C: Linji [Lin-chi]): a leading Zen school, founded in China by Lin-chi (ninth century CE) and revivified in Japan by Hakuin. Rinzai Zen lays great stress on the use of *koans*.

ru [*ju*] **(C):** the literati, or scholarly class, of which Confucius was a member.

samadhi **(S):** an advanced form of *dhyana*, or profound meditation, sometimes rendered as contemplation, sometimes as self-realization. The exact sense varies with tradition and context but common in all its uses is the notion that *samadhi* is either the ultimate goal of spiritual progress or very close to it.

samsara **(S; in P:** *sangara*, **and in some romanizations,** *sangsara*)**:** in Buddhism and Hinduism, the cycle of rebirths, often referred to as 'the wheel of life', through which the individual passes in accordance with *karma*, the law of action that ensures that we reap as we have sown.

Sanskrit: the language of ancient Aryan India and of the early brahmanic scriptures.

sanzen **(J):** in Zen, an interview between an aspirant and a Zen master, or *roshi*, for the purpose of assessing the aspirant's progress.

sat **(S):** the Hindu name for being or existence; one of the three attributes of Brahman, the others being *chit* (consciousness) and *ananda* (bliss).

satori **(J; in C: wu):** the Zen term for the experience of direct insight into the nature of reality; sometimes translated as 'awakening'.

Satya **(S):** truth; in Gandhi's thought, the name for ultimate reality.

satyagraha **(S):** the political strategy of non-violent resistance.

Shingon (J): lit. 'true word': the Japanese esoteric or Tantric school of Buddhism, founded by Kukai (774–835 CE; also called Kobo Daishi).

siddha **(S):** one who has achieved advanced yogic accomplishments, especially in the context of Tantrism.

siddhi **(S):** accomplishment on the path to and including enlightenment achieved by means of yoga.

skandha **(S; in P: *khandha*):** The five groups of elements (c.f. *dharma*) used in early Buddhism to classify all existents. They are: *rupa* (matter), *vedana* (feeling), *samjna* (mental conceptions), *samskara* (forces, desires, drives) and *vinjana* (pure consciousness or sensation).

smrti **(S):** knowledge based on memory, tradition, inference or a combination of these. To be contrasted with *sruti*, q.v.

Soto Zen (J; in C: Caodong [Ts'ao-Tung]): an influential Zen sect whose doctrine, which emphasizes the importance of the practice of *zazen* as a means to enlightenment, was introduced into Japan by Dogen (1200–1253 CE).

sruti **(S):** sacred knowledge, self-evident insight that is independent of concepts; cf. *smrti*.

Sufi (A): a Muslim mystic. 'Sufi' means 'coarse wool' and refers to the white woollen clothing worn by these mystics.

Sunnah (A): 'the path of Tradition' followed by orthodox Muslims. The term derives from an Arabic word meaning 'custom'.

Sunni (A): the majority and orthodox group within Islam. Its members place reliance on the *sunnah*, the traditions and practices of the prophet Muhammad.

sunyata **(S; in J: *mu*; in T: *stong-pa-nyid*):** 'emptiness' or the Void. In the Middle way philosophy of Nagarjuna *sunyata* describes the true condition of all things; that is, without essence and so without differentiation. On this understanding of reality even *samsara* and *nirvana* are recognized as being ultimately without differences.

sura **(A):** the name given to each of the 114 sections of the Qur'an.

sutra **(S; in P: *sutta*):** a work attributed to an enlightened being. A work that is a commentary on a *sutra* is called a *sastra*. In some uses, '*sutra*' can also mean each individual proposition in the whole work. In Buddhism, a *sutra* generally contains words attributed to the Buddha. '*Sutra*' means literally 'a thread'.

suttapitaka **(P)**: the dialogues of the Buddha, collected in the second of the three 'baskets' of the Buddhist scriptural canon.

taiji **[*t'ai chi*] (C)**: The primordial, uncreated and indestructible state of the universe, often rendered as the 'Great Ultimate'.

taiyuan **[*t'ai yuan*] (C)**: The uncreated and eternal origin of all things; that which permeates the whole of existence; the source of universal energy. *Taiyuan* is particularly associated with the *yinyang* theory.

Tantrism: the name given to the esoteric forms of Hinduism and especially of Buddhism. The revealed scriptures of these schools are referred to as *tantras* (rather than *sutras*) and the schools make extensive use of *mantras* and *mandalas*. Tantric Buddhism is often referred to as the Vajrayana (S) or Diamond Vehicle. Whether the Vajrayana is to be counted as a third major form of Buddhism, on a par with the Theravada and the Mahayana, or is more properly a branch of the latter, is disputed.

tat tvam asi **(S)**: 'That art thou'. '*Tat*' refers to Brahman and '*tvam*' to the individual self or soul. The phrase occurs in the *Chandogya Upanisad* and is used in Hinduism as a *mantra* that teaches that each individual soul, or *atman*, is one with the *Atman* of Brahman, the divine power.

Theravada (S): 'the teaching of the elders'; the name of the more conservative branch of Buddhism, sometimes known as Hinayana, 'the Lesser Vehicle'. See: Hinayana.

Tiantai [T'ien-tai] (C; in J: Tendai): lit. 'celestial platform': influential school of Chinese and Japanese Buddhism. Also called the Lotus school as a result of the centrality it accords to the *Lotus Sutra*. Its main systematizer was Zhiyi [Chih-i] (538–597 CE).

Tripitaka **(S; in P: *Tipitaka*)**: lit. three baskets: the scriptures of the Theravada School of Buddhism, divided into the *Vinayapitaka*, *Suttapitaka* and *Abhidhammapitaka*.

Upanisads **(S)**: the concluding portion of the Vedas, which are the four major scriptures of Hinduism.

Vajrayana (S): Diamond vehicle: see Tantrism.

Veda (S): 'knowledge'. The *Vedas* are the first part of the Hindu scriptures and consist of hymns, rituals and religious writings. The term is sometimes used to refer to the whole of the sacred canon of Hindu scriptures which culminates in the *Upanisads*, q.v.

Vedanta (S): one of the six major philosophical systems of India that developed from about 200 CE onwards. The word derives from the Sanskrit *veda* (knowledge) and *anta* (end). Its best-known exponent is Sankara (788–820 CE).

vidya (S): knowledge; often occurring in Hindu texts in the compound form *Brahmavidya*, knowledge of Brahman, the ultimate goal of spiritual endeavour, c.f. *avidya*.

visesa (S): 'particularity'; the ultimate unit of real existence; a particular soul or atom.

Visistadvaita Vedanta (S): the Hindu school of qualified nondualism propounded by Ramanuja, who maintained that individual selves, although parts of the body of Brahman, are not identical with the self of Brahman.

wu: see *satori*.

wuwei [wu–wei] (C): non-action, in the sense of refraining from manipulating a situation or set of circumstances but living in accordance with natural laws. In Buddhism it refers to deeds performed without thought of self and therefore having no implications for the *karma* of the doer.

yana (S): vehicle, path: a practical method for the attainment of enlightenment.

Yasna (Pahlavi): sacrifice; the name of the Zoroastrian liturgy recited by priests during the sacrificial ceremonies. The *Yasna* has seventy-two chapters.

yinyang (C): the theory of the interaction of the passive (*yin*) and active (*yang*) principles of the universe understood as the cause of all things.

yoga (S): literally, a means of union, that is, between the individual and the divine. *Yoga* is any set of practices designed to bring about this union but is used especially of the practices set out in the *Yoga Sutras* of Patanjali. A male practitioner of *yoga* is a *yogi* or *yogin*; a female practitioner is a *yogini*.

Yogacara (S): the Mind Only school of Indian Buddhism, founded in the fourth century CE by the brothers Vasubandhu and Asanga; sometimes known as Consciousness-Only or Vijnanavada.

you [yu] (C): desire.

zakat (A): a poll tax paid by followers of Islam for the benefit of the needy.

Zarathustra: the Persian and so the true name of Zoroaster. (The latter is a Greek formulation.)

zazen (J): the Zen discipline of seated meditation, used by all schools but of special significance in Soto Zen.

Zen (J): see Chan.

zhi [chih] (C): wisdom.

GENERAL BIBLIOGRAPHY

Baskin, W., *Classics in Chinese Philosophy*, Totowa, NJ: Rowan & Allenheld, 1972

Carr, B. and Mahalingam, I., *Companion Encyclopedia of Asian Philosophy*, London and New York: Routledge, 1997

Chan, Wing-tsit, *A Source Book in Chinese Philosophy*, Princeton: Princeton University Press, 1963.

Cleary, J.C., *Zen Dawn*, Boulder, Colo.: Shambhala, 1991

Conze, E., *Buddhism*, 3rd edn, Oxford: Bruno Cassirer, 1957

Dasgupta, Surandranath, *A History of Indian Philosophy*, 5 vols, Cambridge: Cambridge University Press, 1922–55

Dumoulin, H., *A History of Zen Buddhism*, trans. P. Peachey, London: Faber & Faber, 1963

Fahkry, M., *A History of Islamic Philosophy*, New York: Columbia University Press, 1970; London: Longman, 1983

Fung Yu-lan, *A Short History of Chinese Philosophy*, ed. D. Bodde, New York, Free Press, 1948

Fung Yu-lan, *A History of Chinese Philosophy*, trans. D. Bodde, 2 vols, Princeton: Princeton University Press, vol. 1, 2nd edn, 1952; vol. 2, 1952

Hughes, E.R., *Chinese Philosophy in Classical Times*, London: Dent, 1942

McGreal, P., *Great Thinkers of the Eastern World*, New York: Harper Collins, 1995

Nakamura, H., *Ways of Thinking of Eastern Peoples*, ed. P.P. Weiner, Honolulu: University of Hawaii Press, 1964

Nasr, S.H. and Leaman, O. (eds) *History of Islamic Philosophy*, Cambridge: Cambridge University Press, 1985; Routledge, 1996

Needham, J., *Science and Civilization in China*, Cambridge: Cambridge University Press, publication began in 1969, and is ongoing.

Radhakrishnan, S., *Indian Philosophy*, 2 vols, London: Allen & Unwin, 1940 edn

Radhakrishnan, S. and Moore, C.A. (eds), *A Source Book in Indian Philosophy*, Princeton: Princeton University Press, 1957

Sharif, M.M., *A History of Muslim Philosophy*, 2 vols, Wiesbaden: Harrassowitz, 1963–6

Note

In extracts quoted from translated texts, material given in parentheses was added by the original translator; material given in square brackets has been added by the authors of this book.

INDEX